Advance Praise for *Father Ed*...

"A long-awaited and much-needed biography of one of the most influential, yet most unknown, spiritual figures of modern times. Anyone who has benefited from the insights of Alcoholics Anonymous, a program that led to millions of freer lives, owes a debt of gratitude to Dawn Eden Goldstein for her carefully researched and lovingly told story of Father Ed. Highly recommended."

—**James Martin, SJ, author, *Learning to Pray***

"An important and long overdue work that fills a gap in the history of the twelve-step movement, Dawn Eden Goldstein's study of Father Ed Dowling's life and work is a delight to read and very moving.... Her insightful biography brings to life the personality of Fr. Dowling, of whom Bill W. wrote, 'He was the greatest and most gentle soul to walk this planet.'"

—**Father Emmerich Vogt, OP, editor of *The Twelve-Step Review***

"I've admired Dawn Eden Goldstein's work for over a quarter century. From her music journalism to this fascinating account, her writing has always been marvelous: intrepidly perceptive and impeccably researched, with an unfailing eye for precise detail. You don't have to be a 'friend of Bill' to appreciate this passionate account, which touches on some of the most important developments of twentieth-century history and spirituality."

—**Glenn Kenny, film critic, author of**
Made Men: The Story of "Goodfellas"

"A must read for all who are interested in Alcoholics Anonymous history. Dawn Eden Goldstein's research is original and sheds light on a relatively neglected guiding light of A.A. She shows that Father Ed believed in the divine inspiration behind A.A. and how it touches its sober followers.... This book deserves the widest possible readership."

—**Ian McCabe, author, *Carl Jung and Alcoholics Anonymous***

"*Father Ed* tells the riveting personal history of a humble, deep-thinking priest who relentlessly cared for the suffering, including alcoholics and others falling on hard times. Readers will be delighted by Goldstein's fascinating storytelling and perspective on the miraculous growth of Alcoholics Anonymous through the lens of Father Ed Dowling."

—**Scott Weeman, founder, Catholic in Recovery, and author,**
The Twelve Steps and the Sacraments

"From the time I could recognize Father Dowling as the man who pointed out the gravesite of Dred Scott for my family, I have always admired that he cared about that and did something about it. His sense of rightness about race relations and lack of fear to engage his culture when it was not as popular to do so speaks volumes about his moral compass. We could use a lot more Father Dowlings in the world today.... This is an excellent treatment of his life and one long overdue."

— **Lynne Jackson, great-great-granddaughter of Dred Scott, president and founder of the Dred Scott Heritage Foundation**

"My late husband, Ernie Kurtz, [author of *Not-God: A History of Alcoholics Anonymous*] would be overjoyed to see and read this wonderful biography by Dawn Eden Goldstein. *Father Ed: The Story of Bill W.'s Spiritual Sponsor* tells the life of Father Ed from his 1898 birth in St. Louis, MO, to his death in 1960. Goldstein's study of one of Bill W.'s closest friends and advisors, truly a spiritual sponsor of his, would have been a book that Ernie wished for. Her careful examination of Father Ed's childhood and development into the man who was loved by hundreds if not thousands of people reveals the path that the Jesuit took to arrive at the place he held in history."

—**Linda Farris Kurtz, professor emerita, Eastern Michigan University**

"Dawn Goldstein's chronicle of Father Dowling is nothing short of tremendous. Through her meticulous research, she has brought to light never before known details of Father Dowling's life and works. This is a book I shall not only read, but treasure and pass on to my friends."

—**Carl B., Archivist**

"What a wonderful biography this is! Dawn has captured my uncle and made him come to life.... I have heard the story of Bill Wilson's first meeting before but never in such rich detail. For anyone who has suffered from chronic addiction and has found recovery through the twelve steps, this is a pivotal moment in the history of the recovery movement. She has truly done it justice. I loved reading this book and I know Uncle would have loved it as well. He would have said, 'Dawn, you hit this one out of the ballpark!'"

—**Mary Dowling, certified addiction counselor and niece of Father Ed**

FATHER ED

FATHER ED

The Story of Bill W.'s Spiritual Sponsor

DAWN EDEN GOLDSTEIN

ORBIS BOOKS

Maryknoll, New York 10545

Founded in 1970, Orbis Books endeavors to publish works that enlighten the mind, nourish the spirit, and challenge the conscience. The publishing arm of the Maryknoll Fathers and Brothers, Orbis seeks to explore the global dimensions of the Christian faith and mission, to invite dialogue with diverse cultures and religious traditions, and to serve the cause of reconciliation and peace. The books published reflect the views of their authors and do not represent the official position of the Maryknoll Society. To learn more about Maryknoll and Orbis Books, please visit our website at www.orbisbooks.com.

Manufactured in the United States of America

Library of Congress Cataloging-in-Publication Data

Names: Goldstein, Dawn Eden, 1968– author.
Title: Father Ed : the story of Bill W.'s spiritual sponsor / Dawn Eden Goldstein.
Description: Maryknoll, NY : Orbis Books, [2022] | Includes bibliographical references and index.
Identifiers: LCCN 2022026592 (print) | LCCN 2022026593 (ebook) | ISBN 9781626984868 (trade paperback) | ISBN 9781608339488 (epub)
Subjects: LCSH: Dowling, Ed, 1898-1960. | W., Bill—Friends and associates. Catholic Church—United States—Clergy—Biography. | Jesuits—United States—Biography.
Classification: LCC BX4705.D675 E34 2022 (print) | LCC BX4705.D675 (ebook) | DDC 282.092 [B]—dc23/eng/20220718
LC record available at https://lccn.loc.gov/2022026592
LC ebook record available at https://lccn.loc.gov/2022026593

To my parents, stepparents, sister, brother, and all my family,
with gratitude for your love and support
throughout life's joys and challenges,
and for your showing me what it means to be family;

to the family of Alcoholics Anonymous and everyone in recovery,
with gratitude for your courageous witness to healing and hope;

to everyone who has become family to me in faith
and in seeking the good, the true, and the beautiful;

this book is lovingly dedicated.

CONTENTS

PART III
A Servant until the End

INTRODUCTION

The Lord did not come to make a display of himself, but to heal and to teach suffering people.

— St. Athanasius[1]

Late on a January night in 1925, Eddie Dowling, SJ, sat at the wooden desk in his room at the St. Louis University Jesuit residence with a pen in his right hand—and tried not to think about how empty his left hand felt without a cigarette. It had been more than five years since he stubbed out his last one before entering the doors of the novitiate—a green twenty-one-year-old with little idea of the penances, interior and exterior, that awaited him beyond those stone walls.

On the desk before him, a gray metal lamp illuminated the sheet of notebook paper bearing the fruits of his past few minutes' labor. The scholastic adjusted his wire-rimmed glasses to read his cursive script, marred as it was by a couple of cross-outs and a stray inkblot. "Quotations are like some canned goods. People mistrust them unless they were there when they were made. In a recent issue of the *Modern Schoolman*..."[2]

Eddie paused. A corner of his mouth—on the side that should have been the destination of the absent cigarette—ticked upward, amused by the formality that had flowed from his pen. "A recent issue of the *Modern Schoolman*"! In fact, the article of his for which he was now composing an apology—not an "I'm sorry" apology, he thought, but an apology in the sense of *apologia*, explaining a word or Word—had appeared in the *only* previous issue of the *Modern Schoolman*.

This apologia was due to appear in issue number two, and it had to reach the typist by morning. It wouldn't need to go through any other pairs of eyes, since the journal's rotating editorship had been passed to Eddie himself.

How appropriate, Eddie thought. Here he was, the only Jesuit student in his program with professional journalism experience, just the sort of person to show his peers how to harness the power of print to bring scholastic philosophy to the masses. Instead, on this, his first and last opportunity to belch out a few words under the grand headline, "EDITOR OF MODERN SCHOOLMAN," he had to fill the space with a shame-faced accounting for himself. . . .

No, not shame-faced, he reminded himself. He had done nothing shameful—imprudent, perhaps, but not shameful. No one should have been scandalized by what he wrote.

Even so, he felt humiliated.

Eddie turned his gaze to the crucifix on the wall above his bed. The memory of his long retreat—the thirty-day Spiritual Exercises he had made as a young novice—came to him, and with it the prayer that Ignatius pre-scribed for retreatants who wished to make the greatest possible offering to God. He had made that prayer, asking Christ the King, if only it be to His greater service and praise, to let him imitate Him "in bearing all injuries and all abuse and all poverty of spirit." And he had likewise followed Ig-natius's suggestion to seek "the most perfect humility"—choosing "oppro-brium with Christ" rather than honors.

The thought consoled him. Yes, this present humiliation was minuscule compared with even the smallest part of Christ's sufferings—but even so, it stung. And for that very reason, it provided him with something to offer the Lord as proof of his devotion.

"All for Thee," Eddie said softly.

Turning back to his draft, he read on.

I referred in an article on "Dum-Dum Thinking" to St. Thomas calling his lordly Summa "rubbish." The authenticity of the quota-tion has been questioned by several of my friends, and in justice to them and to the Editors I offer this explanation.[3]

Eddie had appropriated the term "dum-dum thinking" from an editorial he read in *Scientific American*.[4] There, "dum-dum" was meant in the sense of an expanding bullet. But at this moment, the young Jesuit felt like the other kind of dum-dum.

As an experienced journalist, he should have known that even intelli-gent readers can find it difficult to grasp an unfamiliar concept when it is presented to them. Within the space of a brief article, he had not only intro-duced the idea of dum-dum thinking but also tried to apply it to the great St. Thomas. Of *course* that would elicit confusion among budding heresy hunters—especially when he threw in the part about how Aquinas, after a supernatural experience, likened his *Summa Theologiae* to chaff.

What he had meant to do in writing the article (titled "Salvage the Dum-Dum Thought!")[5] was to convey something of the wonder he felt when he first read the *Scientific American* editorial and found himself described in it.

Now as he sat at his desk, with nothing to distract him apart from the radiator's syncopated knock and the whine of a distant ambulance, Eddie tried to recall what it was about the article in the science magazine that moved him.

The *Scientific American* editorial had described two types of thinkers, comparing each of them to a type of bullet. First were the "armor-piercing" thinkers—"those whose minds pursue a thought straight to its conclusion, with no difficulty in concentration." That was clearly not Eddie's brand of mental munition.

Where Eddie recognized himself was in the second type. He was, in the *Scientific American*'s words, "the man whose mind strikes a subject like a dum-dum bullet."

"A dum-dum," the editor wrote, "tears a big hole, but it doesn't get very far. The dum-dum mind finds difficulty in finishing what it starts, because the impact starts associations laterally in all directions instead of straight ahead."

"Finds difficulty in finishing what it starts"! Indeed! That was Eddie's problem in a nutshell—or, rather, a bullet shell. His brother Jesuits joked that his purgatory would consist of finishing his uncompleted sentences.

The *Scientific American* editor went on to explain that the dum-dum mind "is distracted by the push and pull from all sides, and perhaps has an unconscious resistance against going ahead."

That last phrase gave Eddie much to contemplate.

From his high-school days, and especially during his past two years in the Jesuit philosophate, he had struggled to master Aquinas's scholasticism, which was the official philosophy of the Church. He wanted to understand it, for it was the Church's chief intellectual weapon against the atheistic and paganistic philosophies that were forever popping up in new guises. But when he was in the classroom, try as he might, he found it excruciatingly difficult to attain the level of concentration necessary to think the way Aquinas thought.

St. Thomas's method involved taking several disparate strands of philosophical thought, filtering out what was untrue or unnecessary from each, and then, finally, converging them into a single, unified understanding. Following his logic was like following a Gothic cathedral's architectural lines as they extended upward from the marbled floor of its nave to the gold-embossed interior of its uppermost spire. Each thought traveled in a glorious line until it joined with three or four others at a piercing endpoint.

Eddie's mind worked in a decidedly different manner. Granted, like St. Thomas, he set his heart on things above. But unlike the Angelic Doctor, the young Jesuit could not follow a single topic for very long without making a connection... and another connection... and another. As long as he remained on the path to truth—a path illuminated by prayer, sacred scripture, and the teachings of the Church—he wasn't impatient to tie up the various connections into a neat resolution.

Perhaps that was why Eddie loved baseball. With its array of interactions between multiple actors in multiple locations within and without the diamond, the game contained enough lateral movement to keep him interested. But more than that, a good baseball game served as a theater of human experience as well as a model of a functioning society. Each player had a unique role, and a team's success depended upon its members' pooling their individual talents for a goal greater than themselves.

Scholastic philosophy was more like tennis. Its motions were constrained to a single back-and-forth interaction on a single plane. And spectators didn't focus their attention upon people so much as upon an impersonal ball.

Outside the classroom, Eddie's dum-dum thinking and his love for all things human served him well on the social level. But in class, only those capable of following Aquinas's armor-piercing arguments made the grade.

That was why the *Scientific American* editorial so affected him, for its point was that the humble dum-dum thinker could be a valuable catalyst for scientific progress.

"The armor-piercing mind," the editorial said, "would frequently fail to get its initial impetus and direction if it were not for some explosive, variant idea" from a dum-dum thinker.[6] "Very often such a stimulus comes from the combination of two widely different and previously separated elements. It is among such elements that the dum-dum mind is at home."

Hence, the writer added, among the ranks of dum-dum thinkers were major philosophers—men such as Nietzsche, Pascal, and Marcus Aurelius, whose random inspirations, for better or worse, changed the course of world history. The writer's point was that the "flashes and glints" that such minds produced deserved some sort of place in scientific literature—even if they didn't yet rise to the level of proven conclusions.

That was the insight that set off flashes and glints in Eddie's own mind, leading him to write the op-ed that so confused his confreres.

The radiator's rhythms sputtered to a halt. It was late. Eddie glanced up at the crucifix again and turned his gaze back down to put pen to paper once more. He added a paragraph of historical references to back up the story he'd cited about St. Thomas having an epiphany that led him to say that, in comparison, his *Summa* was as rubbish.

Shouldn't that be enough? Or, Eddie wondered, was a *mea culpa* necessary?

A moment's reflection sufficed to convince him it was better to err on the side of apology. After all, not only his schoolmates but also his superior would be reading. Eddie had heard that a certain scholastic was delayed from entering into minor orders just because he had been caught smoking. If that was true, what would the provincial superior do to one who disparaged the greatest mind of the "Thirteenth, Greatest of Centuries"?[7]

Eddie sucked in his pride. "Despite the possible authenticity of the quotation," he wrote, "I admit that the context in which it was used left it open to just criticism on the score of giving too much room for a misreading."[8]

But it was still necessary to spell out what he had really meant to say. "The point I tried to make," he wrote,

was that even the *Summa* was eclipsed in St. Thomas's mind by a siege of "lights" which seem to be very like what Professor Eliot of Northwestern was calling "dum-dum" thinking. And the very force of my point was weakened if the *Summa* was really disparaged.[9]

All he had meant to convey was that perhaps God could use dum-dum thinkers like himself to inspire others. Perhaps the very quality of his mind that seemed to be a weakness could become a source of light to an armor-piercing thinker. After all, St. Thomas's own dum-dum thought, lit by a divine spark, enabled him to pierce the mysteries of heaven.

The instruction that St. Ignatius of Loyola gave to St. Francis Xavier came to Eddie's mind. Perhaps, Eddie mused, a dum-dum thought whose time had come—if it encountered an armor-piercing mind open to the Holy Spirit—could accomplish what the Jesuit founder urged that great missionary to do: "Set the world on fire!"

The efforts of Edward Dowling, SJ (1898–1960), to show his brother Jesuits the value of associative thinking, and the misunderstanding that ensued, have never before been recounted in print. Even Robert Fitzgerald, SJ's slim 1995 book *The Soul of Sponsorship*, which until now was the only work to draw upon Dowling's archived papers, omits the *Modern Schoolman* episode. So I was surprised to discover it while doing initial research for this book. It made me wonder how much more there was to learn about Father Ed's life. The answer was far greater than I could have imagined.

In 2008, I read *The Soul of Sponsorship* for the first time after discovering Father Ed through an online essay by an alcoholic who was inspired by his story.[10] Fitzgerald's book focuses on the friendship between Father Ed and Alcoholics Anonymous co-founder Bill Wilson, which lasted from 1940 until Dowling's death. Although the author notes that Bill repeatedly said the priest deserved a biography, he admits *The Soul of Sponsorship* "is not that biography."[11]

The Soul of Sponsorship's account of Father Ed's life before meeting Bill—which is to say, his first forty-two years—amounts to little more than a précis. Fitzgerald writes that when Father Ed was twenty, he lost a younger brother to influenza. A few years later, as a Jesuit novice, he began to feel joint pain and was diagnosed with incurable arthritis. He wanted to be among the privileged number of Jesuits who entered into doctoral study, but his hopes were dashed when he muffed a theology examination.

Beyond those basic facts, Fitzgerald provides only a handful of other tidbits about Dowling's background. He writes that Father Ed had a lifelong interest in social and political activism, and particularly in improving democratic systems. Before entering the Society of Jesus, he worked as a reporter for the *St. Louis Globe-Democrat*. Father Daniel A. Lord, SJ, who was one of the Society's greatest evangelists of the era, took note of Dowling's editorial talents and, after his ordination, employed him at The Queen's Work, a national media apostolate.

When I first read those scattered factoids about Father Ed's activities prior to his association with A.A., getting to the heart of the man required an almost heroic effort of imagination. Those data points provided me with a general idea of why Bill Wilson was drawn to Dowling, but they revealed little about why Dowling was drawn to Bill.

Over the next several years, I searched for all the published information I could find about Father Ed—reading biographies of Wilson, A.A. histories such as *Pass It On* and Ernest Kurtz's *Not-God*, the few items about Dowling that were available online, and A.A. historian Glenn Chesnut's self-published *Father Ed Dowling: Bill Wilson's Spiritual Sponsor*. None of those sources provided any biographical information about Father Ed beyond what Fitzgerald had uncovered.

Given the vital role Father Ed played in popularizing A.A. among clergy, as well as the spiritual fatherhood he provided to Bill Wilson, I couldn't understand why more wasn't known about him. Why was such an important figure in A.A.'s history always presented as an enigmatic *deus ex machina* figure, dropping into Bill's story like the biblical Melchizedek—without father or mother or ancestry?

I was also struck by how the story of Bill's and Father Ed's fateful first meeting was always narrated from Bill's perspective alone. In Bill's account, Father Ed arrives unannounced at A.A.'s Manhattan clubhouse on a sleet-stricken night in November 1940. The maintenance man—clearly annoyed at being made to answer the door late at night—heads upstairs to tell Wilson: "Some old damn bum from St. Louis is here to see you." Then, aided by his cane, Father Ed painfully plods up the wooden staircase toward the A.A. co-founder's bedroom, poised to change Bill's life forever.

That last part fascinated me. I wondered if it held the key to the mystery of who Father Ed truly was and where he came from, for when Father Ed first encountered Bill Wilson, there was a strange reversal of the usual order of things. It was the normally disabled, chain-smoking Dowling—whose spine had, in his words, "turned to stone" from arthritis—who became a pillar of strength. He was literally "working the steps"; nothing could stop him from ascending upward to attain his goal. And it was the normally robust former high-school athlete Bill W., Mr. A.A. himself, who was in the position of a disabled person—crashed out on top of his bed, unable to move.

Wilson himself brought out the contrast between the two men when he recounted the story. He spoke of how he was in his bedroom alone, his wife Lois being "out somewhere." As he lay in bed, he felt "full of disappointments," "consumed with self-pity." His stomach hurt with what he imagined was an ulcer (it wasn't). He didn't even rise from his bed to help his visibly stiff-boned guest remove his coat.

Not until Bill saw Father Ed's clerical collar did he summon the energy to sit up. It was then, as the priest excitedly began to share the connections he had found between A.A.'s Twelve Steps and St. Ignatius's Spiritual Exercises, that Wilson felt himself strengthened with spiritual energy as well.

Each time Bill described that first encounter with Father Ed, he used superlatives. Addressing a conference of clergy a few months after Dowling's death, he recounted the transformation that took place within him once he sat up to converse with the Jesuit:

> I began to be aware of one of the most remarkable pairs of eyes I have ever seen. And, as we talked on, the room increasingly filled

with what seemed to me to be the presence of God which flowed through my new friend. It was one of the most extraordinary experiences that I have ever had. Such was his rare ability to transmit grace.[12]

Although Bill had a number of supernatural experiences over the course of his life, he typically reserved the word "presence" to describe one of his three great epiphanies—occasions when he encountered a spark of the divine that dramatically regenerated his interior life.

During Bill's first two epiphanies—at England's Winchester Cathedral as a soldier in 1918 and at Manhattan's Towns Hospital as a recovering drunk in 1934—no other person was present. He was alone with God.

Only the third epiphany took place in another human being's company. On that November night in 1940, Father Ed and Bill W. shared an encounter with the living God.

At least, that was Bill's impression of what transpired. But, I wondered, how could I find out for certain whether the experience was transformational not only for Bill but for Father Ed as well? Just as Bill felt that Father Ed awakened in him a new sense of mission, might Dowling have felt that, in encountering Bill, he received a kind of call within a call? Could he have perceived in it a divine invitation to enter more deeply into his Jesuit vocation?

That is why the *Modern Schoolman* story was a revelation for me. It showed me that the young Eddie Dowling, SJ, felt deeply that he was different from many if not most of his brothers in the Society of Jesus. He realized he had a mode of thinking that would make it difficult, if not impossible, for him to advance to the esteemed ranks of Jesuit academics. But he also realized God could use this very weakness to accomplish his plan—by bringing him into contact with a mind whose insights would complement his own.

Bill Wilson proved to be that mind. More than eight decades since his and Father Ed's first encounter with each other, the mutual illumination remains aglow. It shines in the hearts of the millions of people around the world who benefit from the spirituality of twelve-step programs—a spirituality deepened and enhanced through the gifts Father Ed brought to A.A.

Father Ed was not an alcoholic, but he so admired Alcoholics Anonymous that he referred to non-members such as himself as the "underprivileged."

As a nonalcoholic myself, I have long felt the same way, being in awe of the holiness, joy, and conversion of life that I have witnessed in people in recovery.

I can also identify with Father Ed's background as a journalist who, in following his religious vocation, underwent a radical change of lifestyle. But there the similarities end, for whereas Dowling was born into an Irish-American Catholic family, I was born into a Reform Jewish one. During my twenties, in the 1990s, I was a rock and roll historian, interviewing oldies artists such as Brian Wilson, Del Shannon, and Harry Nilsson. Later, I worked for the *New York Post* and the *Daily News* until 2007 when—after writing my first book, *The Thrill of the Chaste*—I left the newspaper world in hope of finding some way to put my abilities at the service of my new-found Catholic faith.

My journey led me to become in 2016 the first woman ever to receive a doctorate in sacred theology from the University of St. Mary of the Lake/Mundelein Seminary (a school that I would later learn figured into an episode of Father Ed's life).[13] Along the way, I found a new mission in writing books on healing for readers who, like me, had suffered childhood sexual abuse or other traumas: *My Peace I Give You: Healing Sexual Wounds with the Help of the Saints* and *Remembering God's Mercy*. It was gratifying to see each of them find a global audience; *My Peace* alone was translated into six languages.

In late 2019, after being downsized from a seminary-teaching position, I found myself at a new vocational crossroads. A friend suggested I consider what book I most wanted to write if given the opportunity. And I realized that, more than anything, I wanted to write Father Ed's biography—if only so that I myself, who am always in need of healing, might better know that extraordinary Jesuit whose passion was to help people with problems.

To my great joy, my proposal for *Father Ed* found a home at Orbis Books, whose editor-in-chief and publisher is Robert Ellsberg. The choice of publisher seemed providential, for Ellsberg was mentored by Dorothy Day, who counted Father Ed among her own mentors. (Writing in the *Catholic Worker*, Day called Dowling "our dear Jesuit friend.")[14]

My research entailed traveling to Father Ed's hometown of St. Louis to peruse his papers, which are divided between the Father Edward Dowling, SJ, Archive at Maryville University Library and the Jesuit Archives & Research Center. I also consulted archivists at Stepping Stones, which houses Bill and Lois Wilson's personal papers, and A.A.'s General Service Office. Online newspaper archives turned out to be another major source of information, for Dowling's public-relations skills earned him hundreds of media mentions. The many descriptions of him given by reporters, along with photographs and audio recordings of Father Ed that I uncovered, helped me imagine what he was like in person.

Most excitingly, I was able to interview a number of people who were close to Father Ed and had never before shared their memories of him. These included his niece and nephew, as well as a secretary in his office; a man whom he helped guide to a priestly vocation; children of his former students; and even the daughter of the man who first told him about Alcoholics Anonymous. Their personal stories made Father Ed come alive for me in a new and profound way.

In any research project, there is a risk that the researcher may find that his or her subject proves less interesting or important than at first glance. But as I began to piece together Father Ed's story from thousands of sources, I found the opposite to be the case. The more I learned about him, the more compelling his story became.

Although I knew Father Ed had undergone illness and loss, his personal papers and my interviews revealed a depth of suffering beyond anything I could have imagined. At the same time, they bore evidence of his tremendous will to work continually to overcome his personal limitations and woundedness so he could be an ever-more effective instrument of healing to others.

A note about the structure of this book: In part one, my information is drawn mainly from documents, including Father Ed's own letters. But in part two and especially part three, I add interview material to the mix. For some readers, the personal observations and anecdotes about Father Ed may make those later chapters easier to penetrate than the early ones.

Personally, as a devoted reader of biographies, I believe you will find Father Ed's story most impactful if you read this book straight through. However, since I realize some may wish to skip ahead, I have provided context in later chapters so readers who bypassed previous ones (or have forgotten details from them) won't find themselves lost.

As you read the following pages, my prayer is that Father Ed will come alive for you as he has for me, and that your encounter with him will light a spark that will draw you closer to the true light that enlightens everyone.[15]

PART I

A SPIRITUAL FATHER IN THE MAKING

1

ᴄ⁓ᴠ

Beginnings in Baden

The only advice I want you to accept is: DON'T BE AFRAID TO
MAKE A MISTAKE. Listen to this bit of horse-sense I have before
me. We learn wisdom from failure much more than from success.
We often discover what will *do by finding out what will not do; and*
probably he who never made a mistake never made a discovery.
　　—Edward Dowling, SJ, letter to his sister Anna, July 4, 1920[1]

When I speak of failure, tho, I mean the failure of a Galileo, a
Casement, a Light Brigade,...a MacSwiney.
　　—Edward Dowling, SJ, letter to Anna, November 20, 1920[2]

Edward Patrick Dowling was born into an Irish-American family whose history was marked deeply by failure—glorious failure; heroic failure; deep suffering, endured with equally deep faith; failure that resulted not in despair but in the hope of resurgence.

From earliest childhood, young Eddie—born September 1, 1898, to second-generation Irish-American parents in St. Louis's Baden neighborhood—drank in tales of the courageous resistance his ancestors showed against Ireland's English rulers. In the evening after dinner, his father would sit at the kitchen table with pipe in hand and, in a soft voice with a hint of a brogue, would spin tales of relatives such as his lineal ancestor Ffarrell Dowling, whose candor got him banished to Connacht by Cromwell.[3]

Ffarrell's courage impressed Eddie deeply; the image of it never left him.[4] During the final weeks of his life, he mentioned it to a reporter in what would be his last interview. (The reporter wrote that Father Ed, had he lived in Cromwell's time, "would no doubt have received the same fate—and for the same reason.")[5]

Another of Eddie's father's favorite stories was that of the Maher brothers. He told the story so often that Eddie knew it by heart.

"Eddie," the elder Dowling would say, "did you know that our own family boasts of three martyrs?"

There was no need for Eddie to respond; his father would continue with the story just the same. "It's the truth. Three of them, there were, brothers. Born in Tullow and raised by their saintly mother, Molly Maher."

The Maher brothers—who were in the ancestral line of Eddie's paternal grandmother, Ann Maher—joined the late-eighteenth-century rebel group United Irishmen. During the Irish Rebellion of 1798, the brothers were captured by the British, who tried to make them inform on their cousin, Seumas Dowling. "The British gave them one hour," Eddie's father would say, "to decide whether to inform on their cousin or be put to the noose."

At that point, the elder Dowling would pause for dramatic effect, taking another puff from his pipe.

"When the English soldiers returned after an hour to the boys' cell, the eldest lad said, 'If it's informers you're looking for, to be sure ye haven't them here. We will die like Irishmen and brothers for the cause of holy liberty.'

"The soldiers set about torturin' them to make them tell, but they encouraged one another and finally the English saw that the information was not to be got out of them. They left them in the prison cell all night, and the next mornin' they hung them. They say that the dyin' words of the youngest boy were, 'My country and my God!'"

Eddie's father would pause again at that point, this time with an attitude of contemplation. Then he would add quietly, "A neighbor woman of Molly Maher's swore that, at the very hour of the brothers' death, she saw three white doves fly into the Maher house."

Exciting tales such as these, shared within a devoutly religious home —neighbors said they could set their watch each morning by Mrs. Dowling's passing by on her way to attend eight o'clock Mass[6]—impressed upon Eddie a sense of moral responsibility for those less fortunate. His parents reinforced that sense through the many ways they put their faith into action, in deeds that were humble yet concrete. Their home was known to the poor who lived in or passed through their neighborhood; hungry men would appear at their back door in the evening, trusting they would receive a meal and a room in the basement where they could sleep.[7] Eddie thus grew up believing his Irish-Catholic heritage carried with it the imperative to manifest courage and integrity, to fight for justice and take the side of the oppressed.

Although Eddie shared his father's first and middle name, he was never known as "junior"—just Edward or Eddie, until some point in childhood when his upturned nose earned him the nickname he would retain for life: Puggy. (As a young adult, when he first began giving public talks, he found he could win laughs by making jokes about his nose. He continued using such self-effacing humor in his speeches as a priest; when upturned noses were the fashion in Hollywood, he quipped that his own nose was "retroussé.")

The name Edward had been in the Dowling family for many generations; it had also been the name of his paternal grandfather, a farmer's son from County Roscommon, Ireland, who immigrated to the United States in 1847, during the potato famine.[8] Upon landing in New York, the future Grandfather Edward Dowling took a job as a day laborer with the New York & Erie Railroad. Family lore has it that a few days after he began wheeling dirt, his foreman insulted him and he replied in Gaelic. The surprised foreman exclaimed, "You must be an educated man!"[9] And then, in Father Ed's words, "The foreman promoted him from a pick to a pencil, and my grandfather said that he never worked a day in his life after that."[10]

Indeed, Grandfather Edward had been well educated in Ireland and moreover had outstanding skills in business. By 1854, he had risen to the role of a subcontractor for the railroad-building firms. He moved that year to Carondelet, on the southern edge of St. Louis, and in the fall he formed the firm that would eventually—after he partnered in 1864 with another Roscommon man, Thomas Donnelly—become known as Dowling, Donnelly & Co., railroad contractors.[11]

"Thereafter," according to a St. Louis historian, Edward Dowling *grand-père* was for thirty years "continuously engaged in railroad construction, on the Iron Mountain, the Missouri Pacific, the Wabash, and other important lines and systems in the West, employing thousands of men and building hundreds of miles of railway."[12]

In 1869, Grandfather Edward purchased a farm of one hundred acres in St. Louis, thus becoming one of the earliest settlers in a neighborhood then known as New Baden and later simply as Baden.[13] At that time, Baden was predominantly German—hence its name, after Baden-Baden, Germany— but it did have a significant Irish minority.

In the late summer of 1870, Grandfather Edward was attending Mass at Baden's lone Catholic parish, Holy Cross, when the thirty-one-year-old Westphalian pastor, Father Herman Wigger, requested prayers for the success of the Prussian Army against Napoleon III. This was too much for the Irish parishioners; local lore has it that Edward Dowling rose up during

Mass and led an exodus of his fellow Irish men and women out of Holy Cross.[14] What is known for certain is that Dowling was a leader among those who, in the wake of the offending incident, complained to St. Louis Archbishop Peter Richard Kenrick.

The archbishop made peace by establishing a new parish just three hundred and fifty yards down the street for Baden's Irish Catholic community: Our Lady of Mount Carmel, dedicated May 4, 1873.[15] Its pastor, Father David Samuel Phelan, only thirty-one, was well known as the sharp-witted editor of the *Western Watchman*, a newspaper that fought energetically against the anti-Catholic prejudices of the day. He would in later years become one of the most controversial figures in the American Church—and a formative influence upon Father Ed.

It was within this parish, this environment, these cultural tensions, that Edward Dowling *grand-père* would raise his family with his second wife, the former Ann Maher (his first wife having died in 1869, leaving no children). In 1884, Dowling, who had by then fathered eight surviving children (another four died in infancy), dissolved his firm and retired to his farm in Baden. His oldest surviving son, Edward Patrick—who would become Eddie's father—was given the responsibility of managing the land; it became his life's career.[16]

Edward Patrick Dowling *père* was twenty-five in January 1897 when he married Annie Cullinane, who was four years his junior. Annie came from St. Louis royalty: it was popularly said that her father, James Cullinane, had been the elected King of St. Louis's Irish-immigrant neighborhood Kerry Patch. (In truth, he was only Prince Regent, having been elected to rule the Kerry Patch "kingdom" until the late king's son came of age.)[17]

But James Cullinane was known for more than kingship. Like Edward Dowling *grand-père*, he too was a first-generation Irish immigrant and a successful businessman who gave back generously to his community. When he died in 1891, a *St. Louis Post-Dispatch* reporter, noting that he served as the county Poor Commissioner and as a member of the St. Louis Board of Charity Commissioners, wrote with reverence, "He never held an office to which a salary was attached."[18]

James Cullinane's wife, the former Anastasia Newman, shared his desire for civic engagement. Upon her death in 1883, the *St. Louis Globe-Democrat* commented that she "had quite a bent toward politics, and was a constant reader of the daily papers, keeping well informed on all current events." In fact, it said, "one of her last acts was to read a newspaper." Those same interests—politics and journalism—would be shared by Eddie, the grandson she would never meet, whose first full-time job would be as a reporter for the *Globe-Democrat*.

On September 6, 1898, Edward Patrick Dowling and Annie Cullinane Dowling brought five-day-old Eddie to Mount Carmel to be baptized by Father Phelan. Fourteen months later, the couple would have a daughter, Anna, followed by three more children: James, born 1903; Paul, born 1905; and Mary, born 1907. They lived in a sturdy two-story brick house on 8224 Church Road that can still be seen today.

Several men on the Cullinane side of Eddie's family played on local soccer or baseball teams, and it wasn't long before Eddie himself took an interest in sports.[19] In the summer, he would organize sandlot baseball games in the neighborhood and would take the position that no one else wanted to play, which usually was that of catcher.[20] Friends would remember "the great care [he] took of all the younger children in his own family as well as the neighbor youngsters."[21]

Eddie's care for his siblings is evident in a photo of him at age six with his mother (then pregnant with Paul), Anna, and James. As his mother and sister try to keep toddling one-year-old James on his feet by holding up the back of his gown, Eddie holds up his brother's right hand with a firm but gentle grip. And whereas Anna is looking at the camera—probably held by her father—Eddie's eyes, like those of his mother, are fixed solidly upon James, with a gaze both loving and calm. It is unusual to see such a fatherly expression on a young boy.

During the winter, Eddie would steer a toboggan down the long hills on the Dowling-owned farmland, giving rides to his younger siblings and to neighborhood children who wanted to join the fun. Some would remember how "[he] even installed an old railroad bell at the front [of the toboggan], which he tolled delightedly as the sled and its passengers went down the hill."[22]

In a school paper he wrote during his Jesuit seminary studies,[23] Dowling recalled that his Aunt Lena Cullinane gave him his earliest introduction to literature. The Irish-born Lena, who never married, lived with the Dowlings when Eddie was a child. At bedtime, she recited poems to him in a lilt that made them sound like music. The one Eddie enjoyed most was Tennyson's "Crossing the Bar," with its gentle and mysterious foreshadowing of a world beyond the blue horizon:

Sunset and evening star,
And one clear call for me!
And may there be no moaning of the bar,
When I put out to sea . . .

In 1904, Eddie entered first grade at Baden School, the local public school. His parents chose to send him there rather than to a Catholic school, as Mount Carmel did not have a school, and they were emphatically opposed to having him study at Holy Cross, where students had to learn German. But as soon as he was old enough to take the streetcar by himself, in the fall of 1908, they sent him to Holy Name School, three-and-a-half miles south of his home.

Although Eddie was known for being warm-hearted to other children and was good at playing on teams, he suffered from acute shyness. His sister Anna would remember that he was more stubborn than most children in refusing to take dance lessons.[24] But his interior life was deep and imaginative. As he began to read, he was taken with what he would later describe as the "realistic fantasies" of the Grimms' *Fairy Tales*. He also enjoyed a certain "modern fairy tale," as he called it—*The Wizard of Oz*, set in Missouri's neighboring state of Kansas. "The yarn seared my imagination, and I have yet to read a more remarkable adaptation of an author's powers to children's capacities and tendencies."

Another author who enlivened Eddie's fantasy life was Horatio Alger, who penned tales of poor boys transforming their lives through hard work and service to others. Although he couldn't have known it at the time, his future friend Bill Wilson was also reading those same stories and likewise drawing encouragement from them.[25]

Toward the end of Eddie's first year at Holy Name, in May 1909, he was confirmed at Holy Name Church by St. Louis Archbishop John J. Glennon. He made his First Communion there the following May, in line with the then-common practice of delaying First Communion until children were eleven or twelve.

Although the American Catholic experience in general at that time—with Latin liturgies, parish-centered neighborhood life, and laity viewed as passive subjects of the clergy—differed considerably from that of today, it would be misleading to assume that no change was afoot. In fact, Eddie Dowling's childhood coincided with two revolutionary changes in Catholic liturgical practice.

Both of the changes were enacted at Pope Pius X's direction and both concerned increasing the faithful's access to the Eucharist. The first was the Sacred Congregation of the Council's 1905 decree on frequent Communion, *Sacra Tridentina*. Pius X intended with that document to wipe out the last remnants of the Jansenist heresy from the minds of the faithful—a heresy that had led many to believe that very few were worthy of receiving daily Communion. In exhorting the faithful, and particularly laity (who had been made to feel morally inferior to priests and religious), to receive the Eucharist daily, the pope was implicitly acknowledging the laity's dignity and their fundamental moral agency.

The second change took place when the Sacred Congregation of the Discipline of the Sacraments, through the 1910 instruction *Quam Singulari*, lowered the age of First Communion to the time when a child could distinguish between Communion and ordinary bread—about seven years old. Eddie just missed being able to benefit from the change, for the Vatican document came out three months after he made his First Communion. When he saw how all his siblings subsequently made First Communion at a far younger age than had been permitted him, it affected him profoundly. Years later, as a priest, he would lament,

> As late as 1909, American Catholics were gripped in a moral heresy of Jansenism which kept people away from Holy Communion—in fact, I myself was kept away from Holy Communion for six or seven years during which I should have been receiving it. That is a horrible thing.[26]

As Eddie progressed through Holy Name, despite the devout example of his favorite teacher, Sister Mary Florentine,[27] sports and pleasure reading remained his preferred daily devotions. The 520-page bestseller *The Crisis* by Winston Churchill held a special fascination for him, as he would recall: "I used Churchill as a breviary during the last year or two of parochial school." (Churchill, born in Missouri, was such a popular novelist in his day that a certain British statesman wrote as "Winston S. Churchill" to avoid being confused with him.) The novel's familiar location—Civil War-era St. Louis—made it particularly exciting for young Eddie. Each school day as he walked between the streetcar stop and Holy Name, he would feel a thrill as he passed by the antebellum mansion on 1410 East Grand Avenue that was the inspiration for Bellegarde, the country estate of the novel's Colfax family.

On the sports front, in addition to playing sandlot games with neighborhood boys, Eddie became involved with the Baden Business Men's baseball team, first as a batboy and eventually as a player. At least two young men who joined Puggy on the sandlot, Ray Schmandt and Charlie Grimm, went on to play in the major leagues. Schmandt later said, "Eddie could have done the same if he wanted to. He was a terrific catcher."[28]

Baseball was not the only activity that excited young Eddie. He had another passion that, unlike his favorite sport, he could fully enjoy whether indoors or out.

"Undoubtedly," he later wrote,

> one of the strongest influences my environment threw into my life during this period was the newspaper. I burnt a devout Epicurean's incense to my morning daily, and the last rays of a perennially dying sun often blurred the numbers in the box-score. Nor was it all the sport-sheet—this diet of mine. Even now I can recall with an embarrassing vividness many of the sordid details of the notorious Thaw trial.[29]

Eddie was just eight years old when he began following the trial of Harry Kendall Thaw for the murder of renowned architect Stanford White—two trials, in fact (for the first resulted in a deadlocked jury)—and its details were sordid indeed.[30] Newspapers called it "The Trial of the Century" as they breathlessly reported vivid testimony of the celebrated beauty Evelyn Nesbit's sexual exploitation and assault at the hands of White; her subsequent marriage to the troubled Thaw; and Thaw's murderous fury after Nesbit told him how White had abused her.

But crime, justice, and baseball were not the only topics young Eddie followed, for he also picked up on his family's interest in politics. "I was just as absorbed in the actions of [Missouri Democratic Congressman] Champ Clark as I was in those of [baseball great] Nap Lajoie. The troubles of [New York] Governor [William] Sulzer I found just as interesting as I did those of [boxing champion] Jack Johnson."

Another periodical, one of the most controversial journals of its time, also caught Eddie's interest. It was helmed by his own pastor.

Father Phelan's editorship of the *Western Watchman* gained him national notoriety as a controversialist. It has been said that "perhaps no priest in American history survived so many major condemnations from higher churchmen—including his own archbishops."[31] For young Eddie, this ecclesiastical maverick was a hero. He later would class Father Phelan with his beloved Aunt Lena as "two awfully human and personal influences that served as molders of my literary and spiritual tastes."[32]

Although Phelan might superficially resemble the modern-day culture warrior who battles secularists with one arm and perceived traitors to the faith with the other, he was no garden-variety reactionary. He enjoyed targeting fellow Catholics he felt made the moral law burdensome, and he frequently said that the bishops were the "natural enemies" of the Catholic press.[33] In 1893, nearly thirty years into his editorship of the *Western Watchman*, Phelan wrote:

> Contrary to the general impression, I am not at all a contentious individual. I have been in conflict nearly all my journalistic life, but I have always had for antagonists silly bishops and stupid editors who insisted on making our people more Catholic than the Holy Father and more orthodox than the Church....
>
> My style, if it can be dignified with the name, is epigrammatic, often sharp and bitter. But I have never said an unkind thing of any man who showed a particle of that modesty which would characterize the utterances of a man who speaks for the great Catholic Church.[34]

In the first week of January 1914, at a time when fifteen-year-old Eddie was reading the *Western Watchman*, Father Phelan initiated what would be one of the last—and certainly most memorable—of his great controversies: a defense of the tango.[35]

The Latin American dance was at that time a flashpoint of an international moral panic. Six weeks earlier, newswires had reported that Kaiser Wilhelm II banned the tango from being performed at functions where the royal family were present.[36] Bishops from Verdun, France, to Nashville, Tennessee, were lining up to denounce the dance.[37] The very week Father Phelan's editorial appeared, Cardinal Basilio Pompili, vicar general of Rome, was preparing a pastoral letter for the approval of Pius X that would denounce the tango as part of the "new paganism."[38]

But when Phelan looked at the tango, he saw a way for women, "who were sent into the world to get married and have children," to "make themselves attractive to the sterner sex."[39] So, instead of denouncing the dance, he denounced "the army of crusty bishops and crabbed priests" who set themselves against it. And he went so far as to declare that "the bewitching young miss who disports her charms in the ballroom is doing God's work as emphatically as the Bishop at his orisons."

The press could not have been more delighted to see Phelan assert himself against the hierarchy. As wire services sent the priest-editor's comments around the world, St. Louis papers kept the story going for days on end by interviewing irate local Catholics and giving Phelan the opportunity to issue sharp-witted retorts.

What did Eddie Dowling take away from Phelan's public performance, coming as it did from his own pastor? The answer would become clear after his ordination, when he would display his own gifts for making headline-worthy declarations (which sometimes would result in his being called to explain himself to his Jesuit superior).

Even while he was yet in formation for the priesthood, Dowling recognized that he owed something of himself to the *Western Watchman* editor. "I listened to eight years of his sermons and read his inimitable editorial page in the *Western Watchman* for about as long," he wrote, "and while all that I heard and some that I read made little impression on me, still I can't escape that there is a residue of Phelanism in my make-up."[40]

But it was not only Phelan's contrarianism that stayed with Dowling. The pastor's warm humor also set an example for him, one that he would draw upon in his own priestly ministry. In 1944, Dowling recounted one of Phelan's anecdotes while giving a conference to married couples:

> A devout old lady said to our pastor, Father Phelan, "Father, terrible the way they're raising children today. There's my little grandson, five years old, Davy—already he's cursing." And she says, "Really, Father, for the life of me, I'll be damned if I know where he learns it."[41]

2

❧

A DISTANT CALL

I was wondering if you read à Kempis's Imitation of Christ. *I like it very much. In the novitiate I used to pit each of the sentences against each other as in a tennis tourney, then winners against winners until I got what I considered the best sentence in the book. I decided that the best thing there was the sentence "as much as thou canst go out of thyself, so much wilt thou be able to enter into me."*

— Edward Dowling, SJ, letter to his sister Mary,
November 10, 1929[1]

Although Father Phelan's bold personality inspired young Eddie, his priestly vocation did not—at least, not for a long while. Throughout Eddie's grade-school years and even as he entered high school, although he dutifully served at Phelan's liturgies, he had no interest in entering the priesthood or religious life. He later wrote to his sister Mary,

When I was eight years old, two Passionists gave [a] mission at Mt. Carmel. They convinced Auman, C. Schergen, the Godfreys, and a few other altar boys that they should become Passionists. But I felt not the least inclination to go. . . .

Out of my graduating class at Holy Name, seven out of twelve boys went to Kenrick Seminary. I had not [the] slightest desire to follow them.[2]

After completing his studies at Holy Name, Eddie entered the St. Louis Academy, one of three high schools then operating under the aegis of the Jesuit-run St. Louis University.[3] (Today it is known as St. Louis University High.) Classes were held in the university's majestic DuBourg Hall, next to the St. Francis Xavier College Church. Eddie—or, rather, Puggy, for his nickname had taken hold—would attend the academy for three years before transferring to the junior division of St. Mary's College in St. Mary's, Kansas, to finish out his high-school studies.

Dowling did so little reading during his high-school years that he later called them his "Babylonian Captivity"—a period of "little inspiration and necessarily less achievement." His one literary experience during that time that remained with him was a year-long study of the short story that acquainted him with Hawthorne, Poe, Maupassant, Conan Doyle, O. Henry, and Paul Leicester Ford.[4]

Instead of reading, Puggy spent his energies in sports fields and pool halls. A classmate of his at St. Louis Academy recalled that he was considered the least likely to enter the priesthood: "He was a slicker at pool and billiards and always ready with a wisecrack. In fact, I figured he was the type to grow up and wear a brown derby and be something of a sport."[5]

Yet, despite his worldly interests, Puggy in high school was gradually being drawn to the Jesuits, although he was still a long way from believing he had any hope that the Society would accept him.

In the robust, Irish-American strain of Catholic faith practiced in the Dowling household, men of the Society of Jesus were viewed as the Catholic Church's most elite corps of intellectual and spiritual masters. Some of their priests, beyond making the usual vows of poverty, chastity, and obedience, were called to make a fourth vow of special obedience to the pope with regard to missions—agreeing to go wherever they were sent. For that reason, they were sometimes called "God's soldiers" (which later became the nickname "God's Marines"). Jesuits were teachers, operating most of the highest-ranked Catholic high schools and colleges. They were spiritual guides, whose expertise in the Spiritual Exercises of their founder St. Ignatius Loyola made them natural leaders in the burgeoning lay-retreat movement. And they were missionaries, fearlessly entering into remote territories to bring new converts into the faith or to sustain native Catholic populations who lacked their own priests.

Given the great value that the Jesuits' ministry held within the global Church, the Society of Jesus attracted many of the most dynamic, most intelligent, and most disciplined young men of the Catholic world. It could afford to turn men away—and often it did. Would Puggy even have a chance of getting in? He wondered.

One evening during his sophomore year, Puggy made a visit to his Uncle Paul and Aunt Ellen Dowling. Over supper, as he told the couple how things were going at school, his aunt laughingly suggested he might become a Jesuit. Years later, as a Jesuit scholastic, Dowling could still remember his uncle's response. "Uncle Paul said he would be mighty proud to see me a Jesuit. I recall now that at the time the remark made something of an impression on me, and even then I must have been starting to think of it."[6]

On the field, Puggy played on St. Louis Academy's baseball team as catcher, as well as on its football team. "He was short, but solid muscle," a friend said.[7] "He could fire a baseball from home plate to second base without getting off his haunches."

In the fall of his junior year (1914–15), Puggy was a tackle on the football team during an outstanding season. The team won five out of six games, scoring 98 points to its opponents' 7 points.[8] When spring arrived, Puggy likewise excelled at baseball. The *St. Louis Globe-Democrat*'s dispatch from the team's spring training reported that, among "one of the largest squads in the history of the school, ... Dowling [was] the best at bat."[9]

Although Puggy was spending far more time on the playing field than in the library, St. Louis Academy's librarian, Father Aloysius McCormick, SJ, noticed something special about him. The thirty-eight-year-old priest, like his saintly namesake, was a deeply spiritual man with a strong Marian devotion. He understood vocation as a call to total self-giving to serve the poor in spirit, as he explained in a homily to religious sisters taking their first vows:

> The pronunciation of the vows is a consecration of the soul to God—a holocaust in which the victim is entirely consumed. The life of a religious is to work for Christ's poor. It was the religious Christ had in mind when he said, "Whatsoever you do unto the least of these, you do unto me." You who have left all you had to follow the call shall be doubly compensated for the sacrifice.[10]

One day, Father McCormick asked Puggy if he had ever thought of the priesthood. The teen replied, "Who would ordain a lazy slob like me?"

McCormick, Dowling writes, was unswayed: "He said that my slobbiness and indolence were not enough to keep me from being a priest."[11]

"I gave him no satisfaction," Dowling adds, "but the chat was a definite link in the chain of events that brought me to [the Jesuit novitiate at] Florissant."[12]

Apart from school, sports, and socializing, there was another activity that made significant demands upon Puggy's time as a teenager and helped form him for his future work—albeit in a negative way. In 1912, Puggy began to do occasional paid work as a factory hand at the Star Bucket Pump Company, which was owned and operated by his uncles on his father's side—Paul, Dennis, and Patrick Dowling. The following summer, when he was not yet fifteen, he worked there full time. It would become his regular summer job for three years, through the summer of 1916, and he put in some hours there during the summers of 1917 and 1918 as well.[13]

The firm manufactured bucket pumps for use in wells and cisterns, helping people in rural America gain access to clean water during an era when they lacked access to public water systems.[14] Its newspaper advertisements offered the guarantee, "Our Star Bucket Pumps will purify the water in any well or cistern in a short time."

What exactly were Puggy's responsibilities at Star Bucket Pump? Given that he had strong muscles and was athletic, his work likely involved lifting and other manual tasks, though his uncles might also have enabled him to gain some experience in office work.

In 1957, some forty years after Puggy Dowling worked at the factory, his nephew Paul Murphy Dowling[15] likewise worked there over the summer. The company, then called Star Pump and Cooler, was still owned by members of the Dowling family, including Puggy's Uncle Dennis (Paul's great-uncle).

"Working in the factory was a sort of rite of passage for the young men in the Dowling family," Paul recalls.

> For me it was a good summer job: I learned some carpentry skills, was paid an hourly wage for five days a week, and above all gained a sense of mature responsibility from learning on my own how to work as a high school student. There were no special protections for children of shareholders. The largest shareholder, Dennis Dowling, greeted me the first and last day of work that summer. But when I broke a metal tape measure, as I did that summer, the cost came out of my weekly paycheck.[16]

Paul adds, however, "My satisfaction with that job was not shared by Father Edward Dowling. He viewed his summers at the company as dirty and dangerous, something he did not look back on favorably." It was Father Ed himself who expressed those sentiments to Paul, as he was close to his niece and nephew, whose own father—Edward's brother Paul Vincent Dowling—died in 1955.

"Perhaps he was right," Paul writes;

> Working in that factory was both dirty and dangerous. The floor I worked on was hot and dirty, with saw wood and fibers for insulation. There was of course no air conditioning on the work floors. And the machines we used were not for children. One of the workers on my floor lost a thumb on a power saw while I was there.[17]

But Paul also suspects "there was something else about [Star Bucket Pump] that blighted Fr. Dowling's recollections":

> The company's workers were not unionized. If they had been, perhaps they could have forced management to improve worker-safety conditions....
>
> Fr. Dowling was a strong supporter of unionized labor, and both he and my father spoke in support of unions in (for instance) the newspapers they both worked for. In family discussions, right-to-work state laws were viewed as terrible things.[18]

Paul's memories provide an important insight into why Father Ed, throughout his adult life, was so passionate in his support of organized labor. As a twenty-year-old cub reporter making ten dollars a week at the *St. Louis Globe-Democrat* in 1919, Eddie Dowling made an initial, unsuccessful attempt at co-founding a union with fellow reporters. Fourteen years later, when St. Louis newspaper workers finally got a local union off the ground, Eddie—by then, Father Ed—advised them and agreed to represent them at American Newspaper Guild conventions. Later on, he became a spiritual guide to national union leaders and would even lead one of them, Heywood Broun, into the Catholic Church (see chapter 7).

Father Ed's negative impressions of his time at Star Bucket Pump may also help illuminate another aspect of his mature thought. In his most famous speech, at the 1955 Alcoholics Anonymous International Convention, he made a humorous analogy concerning how plumbing, although unpleasant, is necessary for "good drinking water":

> A great many sincere people say, "I like Christianity, but I don't like Churchianity." I can understand that. I understand it better than

you do because I'm involved in Churchianity and it bothers me too! But, actually, I think that sounds a little bit like saying, "I do love good drinking water but I hate plumbing." Now, who does like plumbing?[19]

In light of his experiences at Star Bucket Pump, this becomes a tacit acknowledgment that, from the beginning of his working life, it was Father Ed's cross always to be on the "plumbing" side of things—whether in a factory or a rectory. Yet, just as his factory experiences led him to become a great friend of organized labor, so too his insider perspectives on the Church—however much they "bother[ed]" him at times—proved to be providential. Through them, he gained knowledge and connections that he would use to win support for Alcoholics Anonymous from the Christian community at a crucial time in the movement's development.

Just as Puggy was approaching the pinnacle of athletic achievement at St. Louis Academy, his parents transferred him into the high-school division of his father's alma mater, St. Mary's College in the tiny town of St. Mary's, Kansas, for his senior year, beginning in fall 1915. Perhaps they wished to remove him from pool and billiards halls, or from other urban temptations. And perhaps too, given his lack of interest in academics, they wanted to place him in a school that imposed greater discipline.

Puggy's father, as an alumnus, would have known St. Mary's as a tightly regimented environment whose graduates often went on to the priesthood. A Jesuit historian of the 1930s described what the school aimed to accomplish:

> Traditions are an invaluable asset in any school, big or little, and in traditions St. Mary's was peculiarly rich. The picturesque historical background of the place; the intimacies, cordial yet dignified, between faculty and student body; the happy amalgam of studiousness, athleticism, and manly personal piety bred in the typical St. Mary's "boy"; out of such factors as these did the St. Mary's tradition grow up.[20]

Perhaps unsurprisingly, those on the receiving end of St. Mary's efforts to breed studious and athletic boys of manly piety told a different story. Although Dowling never spoke ill of his alma mater, the students' perspective of life at St. Mary's survives in a diary he kept during his first year there, as well as a memoir by the theologian John L. McKenzie, who entered the school nine years later.

McKenzie wrote that he once told a colleague that the discipline at St. Mary's was "medieval"—but the colleague, who was a medieval historian, "rejected the adjective as unfair to the Middle Ages."[21]

"The situation can best be grasped," McKenzie explained, "if one realizes that a student who could not be precisely and instantly located at any hour of the day or night was seriously out of order. This demanded constant supervision and complicated charts, managed by a large staff of Jesuit scholastics."

Puggy probably had some idea of how radically his life would change as he moved from the comparatively cosmopolitan St. Louis University Academy to the minutely regulated, geographically isolated St. Mary's on the prairie. Yet he went willingly—partly because some of his friends were there, and partly, no doubt, because he would have a chance to shine on the school's strong baseball team. Baseball was the biggest sport at St. Mary's; the college was a stop for major-league teams doing spring training, and the coach scouted for the major leagues.[22]

Playing sports, sleeping late, eating candy,[23] relishing the easy camaraderie of his poolroom buddies—Puggy was making the most of his teenage years. But beneath his fun-loving exterior, he wondered whether he might be called to leave the world behind.

3

⌒つ⌒

PROBLEMS ON THE PRAIRIE

*I often sigh that I could undo my classroom schooling, though I
have high hopes that the Lord will not charge against me the in-
roads made upon my character by a system which I had neither the
rights nor the guts [to] rebel at.*
—Edward Dowling, SJ, letter to his sister Mary,
March 30, 1930

Puggy had an inkling that his first year away from home was something he
would want to remember. So he began keeping a diary on the night he departed for St. Mary's—September 6, 1915.

From his account of his last night in St. Louis, it is clear that Puggy was
well loved by family and friends. He enjoyed a "series of entertainments"
that day, including a poker party, before heading to Union Station for an
11:31 p.m. departure. Despite the lateness of the hour, no fewer than five
family members were there to see him onto the train—"Mam and Pop" (as
he called them in his diary), Uncle Dennis and Aunt Maud, and Uncle Pat.

The train was to take Puggy to Kansas City, where he would switch to
a special train that would take him all the way to the front entrance of St.
Mary's College. In the meantime, he would enjoy the company of forty
other St. Louis boys heading to the same place, many of whom he already
knew. And on top of that, his best friend Joe Touhill and four other pals
caught a ride on the train to enjoy fifteen minutes more with Puggy before
getting off at the Delmar Avenue station in the city's West End. Two of the
friends gave him three boxes of candy, which he later shared with other
friends before enjoying a pillow fight that lasted until the conductor entered
the car in the morning.

Puggy found the transition to life at St. Mary's smoother than he had
expected. On his second night there, he wrote in his diary, "I like this place
better every day. No one has got pew rent, fraternity fees, or anything like
that out of me yet." On the downside, he had to adjust to the school's pun-

ishingly early hours. Prefects rousted students out of bed at six a.m. every day except Sundays and holidays, when the boys were granted the luxury of sleeping until six-thirty.

Before long, the pages of Puggy's diary became filled with names of new friends. Dowling visited the luxurious new dormitory, Loyola Hall, and dreamed of the days when he would join the college students who enjoyed single rooms there. By the end of his first week, he had begun a movement to start a soccer team at the school—presaging the successful campaign he would wage as a Jesuit to convince St. Louis University to do the same.

Perhaps the most unforgettable person Puggy met during his first week at St. Mary's was Pat Woods, an Irish-born centenarian with the leathery, weather-beaten face of a true pioneer. Puggy had heard stories about Woods from his father and marveled to discover that he was still alive.[1] The Jesuits housed the old man on St. Mary's campus in gratitude for his long years of service as a rancher there. Before he departed for the United States at the age of eighteen, Woods was active in opposing British rule in his homeland. At the time Puggy met him, he was the last living person at St. Mary's who could remember the campus's earliest days as a mission school educating the Pottawatomi Native American tribe.

Woods's greatest joy was in telling stories from his extraordinarily long and eventful life to the boys at St. Mary's who, in the words of a local newspaper reporter, "ever thronged eagerly about him."[2]

Puggy's diary entry for September 10, 1915 recounts shaking hands with this remarkable pioneer. "[Woods] claims to be 109 but...must be nearly 115," the teen marveled. Judging by the exactitude of Puggy's estimate, it seems he calculated Woods's age based on the stories that the old man told of his involvement in the struggle for Irish independence. Already Puggy was developing the passion for Irish history that he would maintain throughout his life.

Woods apparently delighted in Puggy's interest, for six days later he received the teen for a visit after supper. Puggy wrote in his diary that the old man showed him his medals and recounted his participation in one of "the Liberator" Daniel O'Connell's legendary meetings.

Although the diary doesn't give further specifics, Woods probably told Puggy the same story about O'Connell that he told a local reporter in an article published two weeks later: "[Woods] had the honor of seeing the 'cross of hair' with which the 'Kerryman' was endowed—hair growing down the middle of his back and across his shoulders, thus forming a 'living' cross, and he believes this cross had much to do with his success."[3] If Puggy did hear that story from Woods (or read it in the *St.*

Mary's Star, which is also highly likely given his love for newspapers),
the image of the Irish hero becoming a living cross would have made a
great impression upon him. As a Jesuit, he would develop a spirituality
of joyful suffering that was centered upon becoming a living image of the
crucified Christ.[4]

A few days after Puggy's visit to Woods, the teenager opened a newspaper to find some sad news: Father Phelan had died. Although Phelan's
passing was not unexpected—he had been hospitalized for several weeks—
Dowling was nonetheless shaken to learn of it. He wrote in his diary,

> I will sure miss him. He was a man who in my estimation held a
> position which none can fill.... When I heard the news I had a feel-
> ing of homesickness and blues.... It will pass over[,] I am sure, tho,
> the memory of Father Phelan will remain with me forever.

Schoolwork seems to have been incidental to Puggy's first year at St.
Mary's. In his diary, he wrote laconically of a visit to an administrator:
"Hauled before V.P. who suggested I study." Yet there are signs that he was
beginning to make an effort to emerge from the "Babylonian Captivity"
during which he avoided serious literature. He studied Shakespeare's *Macbeth* and wrote a character sketch of Lady Macbeth for the school magazine, *The Dial*. (The Shakespeare play remained meaningful to him decades
later; in the 1950s, he would cite it in his letters to Bill Wilson as a source
of wisdom on discernment of spirits.)[5] He also joined a Dickens Fellowship
Club where he "formed a pleasant acquaintance with [the characters] Sam
Weller, Micawber, and Mr. Pickwick."[6]

Although Dowling later wrote that he never read an entire Dickens
novel, his diary shows it wasn't for lack of trying; he got "jugged"—the Jesuit version of detention—for reading *Pickwick Papers* in study hall. Although such punishment may seem unreasonable, it was par for the course
at St. Mary's. Dormitory students were required to spend four hours in
study hall each day, where they were monitored by a prefect to ensure that
they were doing nothing but assigned coursework and readings. Only students in the college division—specifically, those whose parents could afford to put them up in a single room in Loyola Hall—could escape such a
massive imposition upon their daily schedule.[7]

During the rare moments when Puggy was not in class, in study hall, or
playing sports, he and his schoolmates schemed to find ways of dodging
the prefects (at least one of whom was sadistic)[8] so they might gain a
change of scenery and catch glimpses of the fairer sex. One Tuesday after-

noon in October, he and about a dozen schoolmates got ahold of a "flivver" and rode seven and a half miles down the road to Rossville, another small town. Upon their arrival, they had but half an hour to enjoy ice cream and cigars at the pharmacy before walking quickly back to campus to return in time for supper. "I like Rossville better than [the town of] St. Mary's," Puggy wrote in his diary. "Saw [a] dame divine in auto and a chick in telephone exchange."

Although Puggy's diary provides details of his social activities, it reveals little of his inner life—with one notable exception. Dowling began nearly every entry by mentioning that he received Communion that day. It was not unusual for St. Mary's students to receive daily Communion; what is telling is that Puggy felt moved to record every time he received it. Indeed, his words reveal that he felt a gentle pull towards the Eucharist. He praised the "beautiful ceremony" of the school year's opening Mass of the Holy Ghost. And he wrote that, on the morning of All Souls Day, after he received Communion, he remained in the chapel to hear the same celebrant celebrate two more Masses; all three were completed within an hour. (The priest was taking advantage of a newly granted privilege from Pope Benedict XV, issued in light of the "Great War," that permitted priests to celebrate two additional Masses for the dead that day.)

As important as faith was to Puggy, he also had a secular object of devotion. Its liturgical year, so to speak, began February 1, 1916. That was the day when baseball returned to St. Mary's, providing Puggy with a new goal to which he could aspire. He wrote in his diary, "Though I have a big bunch up against me for catcher, I am going to work like hell for the job."

Puggy succeeded in becoming the team's catcher, as well as one of its best batters. By the time he left St. Mary's in 1918, he would be the team captain. One day he hit a ball so far that, decades later, an eyewitness was still talking about it. William Dowd, SJ, who had by then become a seminary professor, told his students he didn't think the ball had ever landed.[9]

One of Puggy's best performances during the spring of 1916 was in the biggest game of the season: an April 6 matchup against the Chicago White Sox,[10] who stopped over on their way home from spring training.[11] It would prove to be one of the last White Sox games pitched by future Hall of Famer "Big Ed" Walsh, who would retire from the team later that year due to trouble with his pitching arm. Dowling managed to score a triple off Walsh before the pitcher, his arm exhausted, switched to outfield at the end of the third inning.

After the game, Puggy was offered a tryout with the White Sox.[12] The opportunity surely must have been tempting, but he declined. He was starting to gain a clearer picture of his future, and it was different from the one he had dreamed about during the summer walks of his childhood with Ray Schmandt and other sandlot friends.

The humidity was stifling when Puggy awoke on the first day of June, 1916, but he couldn't let it slow him down, for he had a jam-packed day ahead. First would be the Solemn High Mass for the Feast of the Ascension; in the afternoon would come the final ballgame of the season, a matchup against Emporia College's team.[13]

Puggy's innermost thoughts on that day can only be guessed; by then he had stopped keeping a diary. But with the help of St. Mary's staff members' diaries and contemporary news accounts, it is not hard to imagine what would have been on his mind at Mass that morning. When he heard the prayers of the Collect beseech God that the faithful might ascend with Jesus in spirit and continually dwell with him there, Puggy would have been praying for Marty O'Toole and wondering how close he was to joining Jesus that day.

Like Puggy, Marty—an eighteen-year-old freshman in the school's college division—had transferred into St. Mary's the previous fall. He hailed from tiny Seventy-Six Township in Muscatine County, Iowa, where his father owned a sizable farm. Although Puggy hadn't had much opportunity to spend time with Marty, as the two were in different years, he felt a certain kinship towards the small-town teen, for his and Marty's fathers were old friends. Moreover, as an avid fan of team sports of every kind, Puggy had followed Marty's progress on St. Mary's basketball team. Just a few weeks earlier, he had noted in his diary that O'Toole and six other hoopsters earned varsity letters that season. On that humid June morning, however, while Puggy and his schoolmates prayed at Mass, the formerly robust O'Toole boy was lying comatose in St. Mary's infirmary, suffering from a serious head injury he received two days earlier on the baseball field.

It was while playing for the local Union Pacific League team (named for the railway linking St. Mary's with the outside world) that Marty was struck on the head by a pitched ball.[14] "The blow did not seem to bother him much at the time," a school faculty member later reported in the *St. Mary's Star*.[15] But later in the day, "he complained of a violent headache."[16]

Marty was taken to the infirmary; a doctor was called and he was found to have suffered cerebral hemorrhage. At about six p.m., he lost consciousness. He clung to life for another day and a half until he finally died Ascension Thursday morning at ten minutes before noon,[17] just as crowds were starting to gather on St. Mary's baseball field for an afternoon matchup against Emporia College.[18]

St. Mary's rector tried to withhold the news of O'Toole's death from the boys until after the game, but word leaked out toward the game's end. "The boys seemed dazed when they realized it," the senior-yard prefect wrote in his diary that evening.[19] For the rest of that day and through the next, when the college held a Requiem Mass for O'Toole, they remained shellshocked. "The students are like retreatants," the prefect marveled. "They go about with serious and thoughtful faces and have no inclination to talk." A schoolmate of Puggy's wrote that it was "one of the most sorrowful incidents that has ever occurred" at St. Mary's.[20]

Sadly, Father Phelan and Marty O'Toole weren't the only people in young Puggy's world whose deaths would give him an early taste of sorrow. Worse was to come. In experiencing such losses, he grew to sense ever more strongly the fragility of earthly existence. Four years later, when he decided to enter the Society of Jesus, he would confide to a friend that he had weighed his vocational options in light of eternity.[21]

The week Marty died, Puggy—who was just days from graduating from St. Mary's high-school division—received a letter from his father. Knowing that Puggy had little interest in academics, the elder Dowling suggested he forgo college and begin working full time.[22]

Puggy's reply, although not shocking for a teenage Catholic boy studying at St. Mary's, was likely not what his father was expecting. "I wrote him saying that as there was a vague possibility I might sometime want to study for the priesthood, I thought I should continue."[23]

At the start of the summer of 1916, Dowling barnstormed as a semi-pro baseball catcher in South Dakota, where, through the efforts of St. Mary's athletic coach Steve O'Rourke (later a scout for the Detroit Tigers and the New York Yankees), he gained an audition for one of O'Rourke's former classmates—Jack Barry, the newly appointed manager of the Boston Red Sox. However, Barry did not believe Puggy was ready for the majors. The disappointed teen returned home to finish out the summer working at Star Bucket Pump.[24]

Puggy returned to St. Mary's that fall to enter the school's collegiate division. He envisioned himself "possibly entering some kind of seminary" at the end of his freshman year—whether diocesan or religious, he did not know.[25]

Long before June rolled around, however, something happened that not only dashed Puggy's hopes but also damaged his spiritual life. Five years later, he described the experience in a letter to his sister Mary,

> Trouble with the faculty that nearly resulted in my expulsion drove
> all thoughts of vocation out of my mind, and colored my views of
> religion....At end of freshman year I had decided to quit school
> and work.[26]

Although Dowling's letter doesn't specify the nature of the trouble, a clue can be found in the official diary of St. Mary's College's Prefect of Studies. On February 8, 1917, Puggy committed an infraction so serious that St. Mary's administration punished him by depriving him of his dormitory room, a prized single-occupancy space at the beautiful Loyola Hall. His crime? He overslept one too many times.[27]

Although Dowling was likely guilty as charged, a closer look at the prefect's diary reveals that the teen had good reason to feel that his punishment was unjust.

The diary shows that, since the start of the month, the weather at St. Mary's had been excessively cold. Beginning on February 1, when the mercury hit below zero, students were instructed to take "long sleeps" (meaning, until six-thirty a.m.) each day through February 6.[28]

One can imagine how hard it would have been for the eighteen-year-old Puggy—for whom waking up on time was always a struggle—to readjust after sleeping in for six days straight. If, as is likely, he slept in on both February 7 and February 8, those infractions would have been added to any previous infractions he had from earlier in the school year. Three strikes and he was out of Loyola Hall.

Losing his Loyola Hall room wounded Puggy on many levels. No more could he enjoy the many luxuries that Loyola Hall offered—including a residents-only billiard hall. He would once again be forced to remain in study hall for four hours a day along with other students not fortunate enough to have a single room. Worst of all, he would have fewer hours to spend with his friends, many of whom were Loyola Hall residents.

The odds are that Puggy did not go down without a fight. Throughout life, Puggy was unafraid to advocate for himself if he felt he was being treated unfairly; no doubt he did so on this occasion as well. Perhaps that is why, two days after Puggy was deprived of his room, the prefect of studies wrote in his diary that another boy was sent out of Loyola Hall "for [the] same reason as Ed. Dowling."[29] The administration may have cracked down on another late sleeper to counter the impression that Puggy was being singled out.

However the crisis unfolded, one thing is certain: Puggy's punishment left him feeling spiritually disillusioned. But even so, once he returned to St. Louis at the end of the school year, he found that he was unable to clear his mind of the thought that he might have a priestly vocation.

"When I asked Uncle Pat for a job at the factory, he demanded to know what I was going to make of myself," Dowling later recalled.

> Pushed to the wall, I admitted to him that there was a vague possi-
> bility of my becoming a priest.... I would hardly have mentioned
> it unless I was forced to, as my intentions were by no means sure.
>
> He took very kindly to the idea, and I sometimes think that the
> fact that I had so committed myself to him made me slow to give
> up the idea as I was often tempted to do.[30]

Puggy had been back at the factory only a few weeks when St. Louis was shocked by horrific events that erupted across the river in East St. Louis, Illinois.

A number of factories in East St. Louis were doing bustling business for the war effort. During recent months, union laborers at several plants, who were white, had gone on strike. The factories' management responded by hiring Black migrants, largely from the South. Once the strikes ended, many union members found themselves unable to regain their jobs.[31]

On July 2, the whites' resentment erupted into a full-scale riot, leading the governor to call in the National Guard. Before calm was restored, scores of Black people were dead, with many more injured; nine white people were dead as well.[32]

Puggy would have heard of these terrible events through the word on the street and on the factory floor, and through the local newspapers that he continued to follow with great interest. He would have seen the *Globe-Democrat's* front page, with its headlines screaming of a "race war" and "blood orgy." On page 8 of the same edition, he would have read a harrowing account of a middle-aged white man who rushed to the defense of an older Black woman who was lying in the street after having been beaten by a mob of white men and women. When the man tried to interfere as a white woman was hitting the helpless Black woman with a bolt, the mob attacked him, compelling him to get down on his knees and "apologize" for trying to save the poor victim. Throughout the incident, a group of National Guardsmen and policemen looked on, doing nothing.

Another report that Puggy would have seen was the *Post-Dispatch*'s eyewitness account of a "massacre of helpless Negroes" perpetrated "in daylight by citizens of the state of Abraham Lincoln." He likewise would have heard about the more than seven thousand Black refugees from East St. Louis who had arrived in St. Louis by crossing the Eads Bridge, which was just over a mile east of the Star Bucket Pump factory.

How did living through that tumultuous time affect Dowling? A comparison of his attitudes on race before the 1917 riot with those he expressed afterwards may provide an answer.

Prior to 1917, the only existing record that gives any indication of the young Dowling's views on race is his diary from his junior year of high school at St. Mary's. There, he uses the n-word offhandedly on two occasions in entries from December 1915. One entry describes a movie program as featuring "one reel of birds and n———."[33] The other tells of how, at a Kansas City breakfast eatery, a friend of Puggy's knocked a "n———" and coffee over himself (perhaps meaning the friend accidentally bumped into a waiter).[34] In both instances, the context does not indicate that Dowling intended the term to be pejorative. Nonetheless, he should have known that such language was offensive and inhumane, however common it might have been among his schoolmates.

Later in life, Dowling would be repulsed to hear the n-word used in conversation. In fact, over the course of his entire life, the only people he is known to have gone out of his way to shun were racists.[35] But at the age of seventeen, like many whites in St. Louis—where voters in 1916 passed a segregation ordinance by a three-to-one majority[36]—he thought of Black people (however unintentionally) as "other."

There is little else in the record prior to 1917 to suggest that Dowling gave much thought to the status of Black people in American society— save, perhaps, his appreciation for Winston Churchill's novel *The Crisis*, which paints a reverent picture of the abolitionist movement. But following that year—at least from 1920 onwards, when, as a Jesuit novice, he gave catechetical talks at a Black parish—Dowling's life and ministry testifiy to his great passion for racial justice. He would manifest that passion with increasing intensity during each successive decade of his priesthood. In 1957—three years before his death—he would make national headlines for his efforts to have a marker placed on Dred Scott's grave.

In his work for racial justice, Father Ed had before him the pioneering example of fellow Jesuits. Prominent among them were the brothers William and John Markoe, SJ, and Austin Bork, SJ, who together signed a pledge in August 1917—one month after the East St. Louis riot—to dedicate their lives and all their energies to the salvation of Black Catholics in the United States.[37] Nonetheless, Dowling's experience of living through the time of the East St. Louis riot was an influential moment in his personal journey. It awakened him to issues that would become deeply important to him in his Jesuit vocation.

As the summer of 1917 drew to a close, a Jesuit scholastic who was an instructor at St. Mary's reached out to Puggy and urged him to continue his studies there.[38] William Dowd, SJ, was a gifted young academic who shared Dowling's interests in writing and baseball; he was faculty advisor to the school magazine, *The Dial*, and a devoted fan of the Cincinnati Reds.[39] When Puggy spiraled into crisis following the loss of his dorm room, Dowd had been his greatest ally among the teaching staff. Now, as the teen's future studies hung in the balance, Dowd convinced Puggy that his presence on campus would be a help to his brother James, who was entering St. Mary's high-school division. (It is also possible that Dowd advocated for Puggy to the faculty in a manner that led the teen to feel more comfortable about returning.)

Dowd's care for Dowling made a great difference in the young man's life. More than forty years later, when Dowd was a professor of sacred scripture at the University of St. Mary of the Lake, Dowling wrote to him, "I shall never forget your discerning and kindness to me during my emotionally upset year at St. Mary's."[40]

Puggy would later write that, after he returned to St. Mary's in the fall of 1917, he "had a fine year, and gradually the vocation idea reappeared."[41]

4

~ ✑ ~

THE RELUCTANT SOLDIER

Obedience is the greatest cross in life and for that reason it is to be cherished.
  — Edward Dowling, SJ, letter to his sister Mary, July 5, 1929[1]

During the 1917–18 school year, Puggy finally had his time to shine at St. Mary's. He played on the football team in the fall and was so popular with his fellow players that they had him officiate at their annual banquet as "Chief Wielder of the Forked Stick."[2] In January, before classes restarted, he went with his fellow members of the basketball team and Coach O'Rourke on a six-day, six-hundred-mile pre-season tour playing college teams in western Kansas. Even though they won only one out of the five match-ups, Dowling had fond memories of the tour. "It was great stuff— good hotels and train rides, etc."[3] And in the spring, St. Mary's athletic board named him captain of the baseball team.[4]

But what Puggy remembered most about that school year was that "for the first time," he "was warmed by the genial rays of an inspirer"—Leo H. Mullany, SJ, a thirty-one-year-old scholastic in his first year of teaching at St. Mary's.

Mullany could connect with teenagers because he understood their awkwardness, their longings, and their fears, having himself overcome an emotional crisis during his youth. In the spring of his senior year of high school, he was expelled after being accused of strewing matches on the schoolroom floor. Prior to that incident, Mullany had been an outstanding student. But the shame of expulsion led him to forsake his books in favor of pool halls and bowling alleys. He sank so low that he briefly ran away from home.

Yet, within six months of his expulsion, Mullany managed a stunning re-bound. He returned to high school, this time at St. Mary's College, and he continued on to the school's college division, where he excelled in debate, drama, and oratory. After graduating from St. Mary's, he attended law school in Chicago for a year before giving up that career for the Jesuit novitiate.

Something had clearly happened in young Mullany's life to bring him back on track. But what was it? A possible clue lies in a book he published in 1915, while he was still a Jesuit scholastic: *Dream of the Soldier Saint*. Although Mullany wrote the book as a reflection on the life of Ignatius Loyola, who founded the Society of Jesus (that is, the Jesuit order), his words have an autobiographical ring:

> God allows many of His chosen souls to dip into the tide of worldli-
> ness only to claim them the more surely for His own when they
> have learned the limits of human enjoyment and its inadequate com-
> pensations. There is a great deal of the stuff of sanctity concealed in
> young hearts that show to the world nothing but giddiness. Boys and
> girls who love pleasure and seem to think of nothing but the gew-
> gaws of the moment may have, at the same time, depths of serious-
> ness within them not suspected by the rest of the world, and only at
> rare moments known to themselves. These are much more likely,
> when grace flashes the great truths into their souls, to turn to God
> and be true to Him than those pitiably comfortable people who take
> their pleasures as they come and merely as a matter of course.[5]

Puggy almost certainly read those words and took from them encour-agement in his hope that he too, despite his worldly interests, might be called to the priesthood.

Above all, Mullany would have helped inspire Puggy's vocation through his joyful witness. He had a whimsical smile and a gift for comedy. Father Daniel A. Lord, SJ, who entered the Jesuit novitiate in Florissant, Missouri, one day after him, wrote in his memoir that Mullany "could have been the country's greatest humorist. He had a natural wit and sparkle that was a blend of Will Rogers and the later Bob Hope."[6]

Puggy first came under Mullany's tutelage in a fall 1917 humanities class where the young Jesuit rushed through the musty required textbook on rhetoric so he could take time analyzing the wit of popular *Chicago Tribune* columnist Bert Leston Taylor. Later in the school year, when St. Mary's of-fered an elective course in journalism taught by Mullany, Puggy eagerly en-rolled. The dynamic young Jesuit's enthusiasm for newspapers made such a great impression on Puggy that he resolved to enter that field himself.[7]

However, a single teacher, however inspiring, was not sufficient to convince Puggy that it was worth the effort and expense for him to continue his studies at St. Mary's. Once the school year ended in June 1918, he moved out of St. Mary's for good and returned to St. Louis in hope of a newspaper job.

An editor at the city's leading morning paper, the *St. Louis Globe-Democrat*, being loath to take on another copy boy, offered Puggy a position for the insultingly low salary of ten dollars a week. To his surprise, the eager young man accepted, grateful for the excuse to avoid another summer toiling at his uncles' factory. For the rest of the summer, Puggy took the streetcar each weekday morning from his family home in Baden to the *Globe*'s headquarters downtown at Sixth Street and Pine. There, city editor Joe McAuliffe, the legendary newsman known for exposing the 1903 "Baking Powder Scandal," would bark assignments at him, sending him wherever an extra reporter was needed—whether at a police court, a political rally, or a crime scene.[8]

The *Globe* was truly a new world for Puggy. He had long been interested in politics, government, and the democratic process. Now his interests coalesced into a passion that grew as he witnessed local and national politicians orate and debate.[9]

There was still time for his former passion too. The *Globe* had an in-house baseball team, and Dowling soon became known as one of its best hitters.[10] He even gained a tryout for Jimmy Burke, the St. Louis Browns' new manager, but was told he wasn't ready for the majors.[11]

Often at day's end—which was usually one-thirty a.m., after the *Globe*'s final edition was put to bed—Puggy would head around the corner to Childs Restaurant on Olive Street. His close friend Henry Kinealy (then a reporter at a rival paper under the pen name Mike Henry) would join him, and together they would enjoy ten-cent griddle cakes before catching the night-owl trolley. Sometimes, Kinealy recalled, they would meet up there with a pair of female friends, "Myrt and Flo."[12] Those early-morning pancake meals, which were chaste, were the only times Kinealy saw Puggy with women other than his family members.

Although Puggy thrived in his new position at the *Globe*, inside he was torn over whether to continue working there into the fall. Unbeknownst to anyone else, he had decided at the end of the school year that he would join the Jesuits in September—if he had the nerve.

"My nerve was lagging towards the end of the summer," Puggy later told his sister Mary in a letter. But then "an odd thing happened."

Puggy had spent much of his free time that summer with his St. Mary's school friend Clarence Merkle, both in Merkle's hometown of Alton, Illinois—an easy trolley journey—and in St. Louis. "One day," Dowling recalled,

> on [the] Olive streetcar, he told me he sometimes thought of becoming a Jesuit. I congratulated him and only appeared mildly interested.
>
> For two weeks, he talked feverishly over his new life, which he hated to face. He felt he should do it as a duty, but the life had little appeal to him. He never suspected I was thinking of the step.
>
> About three weeks passed and I, to buoy him up, told him I was going out to [the Jesuit novitiate at] Florissant also. Unconsciously he had bolstered my resolution.[13]

Come September, Dowling and Merkle went together to St. Louis University to apply to enter the Society of Jesus—only to be told that, owing to the military draft, they should wait a year before applying. Since the two friends were about to become eligible for conscription, they opted instead to enter SLU's Student Army Training Corps, which was just getting off the ground. Dowling's boyhood friend and fellow *Globe* newsman Joe Touhill signed up as well.

On paper, Puggy was enrolled in St. Louis University's School of Law. However, given that he never showed any interest in a law career before or after that time, it seems more likely that he was simply looking for a way to ride out the war. An in-joke at the time was that the initials SATC really stood for "Safe at the College."[14]

SATC trainees were considered active-duty military. Once Puggy took his military oath, he would become Private Dowling. However, after the start of classes but before he could take his oath, the influenza pandemic intervened. St. Louis's health commissioner, seeing the devastation that the disease was wreaking east of the Mississippi River, took proactive measures to prevent the flu from spreading in the city.[15] On October 8, SLU suspended classes on the order of St. Louis's health commissioner. Not only were schools to be closed, but all public gatherings of twenty people or more were banned.[16] The commissioner also ordered the closing of movie houses and other amusement facilities, including pool halls, as well as other public places where people might gather.[17] Even houses of worship were temporarily forced to suspend services. Catholic Archbishop John J. Glennon, after failing to persuade the authorities to permit the public celebration of the Mass, had no option but to dispense Catholics from their Sunday obligation.

Puggy took advantage of the break in classes to hop a train to St. Mary's to spend the weekend with his brother James, who had just turned fifteen on October 2. Although it was James's second year at St. Mary's, it was his first semester there without his brother's companionship. Puggy must have been glad for the opportunity to check up on his little brother. But it proved to be the last time he would see him alive.

The atmosphere at St. Mary's was tense when Edward arrived on Saturday, October 12, 1918. There, as in St. Louis, public authorities had just ordered that all public gatherings cease. That meant the cancellation of the football game as well as the Columbus Day and Liberty Loan parade that had been scheduled for that day. Puggy and James were thus left with more time than they had expected to spend with only each other for entertainment. They surely took the time to walk around campus and enjoy the autumn foliage; perhaps, too, they practiced some baseball as they used to do in the yard of their Baden home. James, like Puggy, had inherited the sturdy constitution of the men on their mother's side of the family; just two months earlier, in a citywide St. Louis swim competition, he had placed second in his age bracket for the 25-yard breast stroke.[18]

What the brothers talked about with each other can only be guessed. There are no records among Father Ed's papers or those of his family that tell of James's interests or of the nature of his relationship with Puggy. But there is no question that Puggy looked with special fondness upon James as the first of his two younger brothers. During their weekend together, the five years' difference between them would have seemed narrower than ever before. James would have been eager for news of their relatives and friends in St. Louis. Puggy's description of the pandemic restrictions turning the city's downtown into a ghost town would have fascinated the teen. He also would have listened with interest as Puggy described his life at SLU and the newly built Student Army Training Corps barracks there.

One thing is certain. Amid the tensions of a world war and an impending pandemic, Puggy and James would have wanted, and needed, the spiritual refreshment that their weekend together provided.

On Sunday morning at eight-thirty, before Edward returned to St. Louis, he and James took part in a remarkable spectacle not seen at St. Mary's since the college's nineteenth-century origins as an Indian mission: an outdoor Mass. Although the location was necessitated by health concerns, St. Mary's administration sought to make the event as exciting as possible, perhaps to make up for the loss of the usual weekend entertainment. An improvised altar was set up on the baseball field. Then, four hundred students, led by the St. Mary's division of the Student Army Training

Corps, marched in formation to the field and formed an infantry square to witness the holy sacrifice.[19] In addition to infusing the liturgical celebration with extra pomp and circumstance (not to mention patriotism), the square had the added benefit of preventing outsiders from crowding the field. St. Mary's senior-yard prefect wrote in his diary that thirty visitors were turned away—probably neighbors who were accustomed to attending Sunday Mass at the school.[20]

Puggy returned to St. Louis either late Sunday the 13th or early Monday the 14th. On Monday or Tuesday, James began to develop symptoms of influenza.[21] Thursday the 17th saw him take a turn for the worse; he developed bacterial pneumonia, which, in those pre-penicillin days, was the primary cause of influenza deaths.[22]

Although James was fighting what one witness described as a "a splendid battle" to stay alive,[23] by Saturday he was doing very badly. The school administration sent a telegram to his parents; his mother arrived at St. Mary's the following morning by train. That same day—Sunday, October 20—James received the last sacraments.[24] Another telegram went out from St. Mary's, this one summoning James's father.

On the morning of Monday, October 21, for a short while, it seemed as though James's condition might be improving. "He rallied at 8 a.m., asked for something to eat, and was very cheerful," the senior-yard prefect later wrote.[25] But before long, his strength began to fail him, until he finally lost his fight against the deadly disease. At nine-thirty a.m., he breathed his last. "Beautiful death," wrote the prefect of studies in his diary that evening.[26]

Before the clock struck ten a.m., Vincent Burns, a college student in St. Mary's Student Army Training Corps, picked up pen and paper to write to Puggy,

Dear Ed,

About fifteen minutes ago, I walked across the yard to the clothes-room. A game of indoor [handball] was in progress at the upper end of the [collegian] yard. At the lower end a football was being kicked around. About the same thing was going on in the small [high-school] yard.

Just now when I came back everything was quiet. All the fellows were sitting on the benches; a few were talking. I didn't have to ask what was the matter. I knew. But I asked anyway and they said, "Jim is dead."

Ed, these words may seem hard to you and to all of us. But look at it as I try to do, and try and let our Christian faith and feeling overcome our natural feeling. Jim was a daily communicant and just as pure as could be. I know that the innocence that was his at baptism has not so much as been blurred. I never heard anything spoken by him except innocent expressions. Can he be anyplace but heaven? Ed, let us be thankful he died so young and do not begrudge him his lawful place.

Sincerely,
Vincent[27]

The letter affected Puggy so deeply that he kept it for the rest of his life. His choice to preserve it is particularly significant because, when his personal papers were archived at Maryville University following his death, it was found that he had either lost or discarded every other personal letter that he had received prior to entering the Society of Jesus. Only Vincent Burns's letter remained.

It is possible that the letter survived because Dowling carried it on his person for nearly the rest of his life. What is known is that, by 1959, the year before he died, he had unfolded and re-folded it so many times that its creases wore out and it separated into several pieces. That year, his sister Anna (who was his assistant at the time), noticing the letter's sorry state, laminated the fragments to preserve them.[28]

About two hours after Vincent mailed his letter, Puggy and James's father, the senior Edward Dowling, arrived by train at St. Mary's. Coach O'Rourke was there to meet him.

The father blurted out, "How is Jim?"

O'Rourke responded, with a sense of calm that impressed onlookers, "Jim went to heaven this morning."

As the afternoon wore on, somehow the senior Edward Dowling and his wife Annie managed to remain outwardly composed. What they were going through interiorly can only be imagined. The senior-yard prefect observed, "Both Mr. and Mrs. Dowling's resignation [is] a source of great edification. Coach O'Rourke takes care of their wants and will send [the] body to St. Louis tomorrow." A funeral was hastily arranged for Wednesday, October 23, the speed probably necessitated by government restrictions requiring that influenza victims be buried quickly.[29]

James's death traumatized his mother Annie so much that she insisted the family move out of their home on Church Road in Baden, perhaps to avoid being surrounded by memories of him. They did move to a house on Maryland Avenue, near the cathedral, for a time, but eventually returned to the family home.[30]

Among the three surviving Dowling children, Puggy, as the eldest, would likely have felt James's loss most profoundly—especially if he wondered whether he had infected his brother with the deadly disease.

And he may well have wondered. Although asymptomatic transmission of viruses was not well understood in 1918, the medical community nonetheless recognized that even outwardly healthy people might need to be quarantined to stop the flu's spread—hence St. Louis's citywide shutdown.

If Puggy did turn his mind to consider whether he was the source of James's infection, he would have found many reasons to suggest that he was. First, he had prior immunity thanks to an encounter with a previous version of the flu. That much is clear from his schoolboy diary, where he wrote that from Christmas Day, 1915 through New Year's Day, 1916, he was laid up with "the grippe," which was a popular term for influenza prior to the 1918 pandemic.[31]

Second, Puggy's participation in SLU's Student Army Training Corps program likely placed him in close contact with military officers who resided in Jefferson Barracks—which was ground zero for St. Louis's flu pandemic. On October 8, whereas St. Louis had 164 known influenza cases, Jefferson Barracks had nearly one thousand men ill from the disease—one-sixth of the outpost's population.[32] Puggy, having endured military brass barking orders in his face on a daily basis, was thus at a greater risk of infection than was the general population.

Third, the dates of Puggy's visit to James coincided with the dates when James would have been exposed to the virus. Normally the incubation period for influenza is about two days, although it can range from one to four days.

Fourth and finally, James, despite being healthy enough to have placed in St. Louis's swim meet just two months earlier, was the only high-school student in St. Mary's to die of complications from the flu. At the first news of the disease, St. Mary's had taken a number of public-health precautions—sending home nonresidential students, suspending daily Mass, and keeping boys out in the open air as much as possible. Despite these efforts, on Monday the 14th, the senior-yard prefect wrote in his diary, "The dreadful 'flu' has arrived."[33] James was among the first to enter the infirmary.[34] It is therefore highly possible that he caught the virus from Puggy.

Whether or not Puggy was haunted by the possibility that he infected James, or experienced any other kind of survivor's guilt, the loss of James shattered him and his entire family. One particular effect it had upon Puggy was that it forced him to grow up more quickly. After the period of mourning, although he returned to favorite pastimes such as sports and socializing with a wide circle of friends, inside himself he wrestled with existential questions.[35]

To an observant Catholic family such as the Dowlings, James's dying a "beautiful death"[35] at fifteen, his baptism unstained, marked him forever as having lived a perfect life. He was offered a participation in the Cross, and he accepted the offer in the truest Christian manner, placing the love of Christ above his natural love of his family and friends.

From then on, Puggy would carry in his memory the example of the purity of James's life and witness. It makes sense, therefore, that, for years to come, beneath the generosity of spirit that he displayed to others, he was torn between his hope that God was calling him to serve as a Jesuit priest and a near-overpowering fear that he was unworthy of such a lofty calling. He wrestled with that fear throughout his vocational discernment. It dogged him during the months before he entered the Jesuit novitiate and during the years leading up to his first vows. Even as he prepared for priestly ordination, he wrote to his sister Mary, "A depressing sense of unworthiness sort of swamps a person at the prospect."[37]

Over time, with the help of prayer, spiritual reading (particularly Thomas à Kempis's *Imitation of Christ*), and spiritual direction, Dowling would learn to face his sense of unworthiness with a humble attitude of surrender to God's will. In this way, he developed the spirituality that he would later bring to his work with Alcoholics Anonymous, when he would teach that "the shortest cut to humility is humiliations."[38]

On October 28, 1918—five days after James's funeral—Puggy returned to St. Louis University and took his military oath of enlistment. The presence of his friends Clarence Merkle and Joe Touhill with him in the Student Army Training Corps helped ease his transition back into life at SLU.

From nearly every perspective, Private Dowling's Army career was forgettable. For one thing, he was hardly military material; looking back on the experience years later, he quipped that he was "allergic to brass."[39] On top of that, he barely had enough time to get his boots dirty before the Armistice ended the war on November 11. After that, the new joke on campus was that SATC stood for "Stick Around 'Til Christmas."[40] And indeed, once the fall semester ended on December 20, SLU disbanded the program.

Yet, for all that, the SATC program gave Puggy a great gift, one that he would treasure for the rest of his life. It was the gift of being taught by a thirty-year-old Jesuit scholastic who in years to come would be his supervisor and beloved friend—Daniel A. Lord, SJ.

Lord was a humanities instructor in SLU's College of Arts and Sciences in the fall of 1918 when his dean thrust him into the position of secretary of the SATC and assigned him to teach a course in "military English." Private Dowling was surely excited to find himself among Lord's students, knowing that the scholastic was good friends with his former teacher Leo Mullany.

Like Mullany, Lord was an inspirer. During the ensuing decades, his voluminous energy, easy command of language, and exuberant love for the faith would make him one of the most sought-after Catholic lecturers in the country.

In his memoir, Lord recounts that he was advised to teach from a textbook that had been hastily composed for the program, but chose instead to base his course on a book of President Woodrow Wilson's speeches: "[I] taught them the old Princetonian's dream of a democratic and united world."

Lord's lectures—both in their content and in the instructor's contagious appreciation for his subject—reached Dowling at a critical time in his intellectual development. Growing up in a civic-minded Irish Catholic family, Puggy had long been interested in the workings of democracy. That initial interest grew exponentially as he had firsthand encounters with local and national political figures during the previous summer at the *Globe-Democrat*. Given that Dowling would ultimately become a nationally known expert on democracy (as well as a key consultant to Bill W. as he crafted a lasting democratic structure for Alcoholics Anonymous's General Service Conference), the importance of Lord's influence upon him at that particular moment cannot be underestimated.

Although Lord projected confidence in the classroom, interiorly he struggled at having to babysit "toy soldiers." It struck him that his real job was "largely one of keeping the unit from tearing the school to bits." With the best and brightest military commanders needed at the front, the two officers sent to command the SATC were unsuited to the task. "Their control over these play soldiers who didn't want to drill and who resented the interference of the military training with their education was that of a small boy in a cage of Clyde Beatty's less docile animals," Lord writes. "I soon discovered that the classes began at full complement and ended with a corporal's guard, while the rest of the young men had climbed out of windows and slipped along ledges and water pipes."

Making matters worse, there were "no organized plans for recreation," Lord adds. "The sketchy program of the SATC did little to take up the time of the men, though it expected them to be in the barracks at sundown and to be checked at regular intervals."

Lord sensed that the situation was a potential fire keg. Fortunately, he possessed personal gifts that made him uniquely equipped to lighten the burden of students who were dulled by routine and annoyed by efforts to whip them into military shape. He had patience, genuine concern for the men's well-being, and—not least of all—a background in musical theater:

> Knowing that young fellows with nothing to do were likely to rip the barracks apart, knowing too that they simply gave the sentries a wink and came and went as they pleased, it became my self-imposed duty to drop over after supper—mess, if you prefer—roll a light piano into the center of the floor, and gather the crowd around for a song fest. Or I would bring my books over and relax with them while I kept an eye open for the frisky and noisy students who so often disturbed the serious students who wanted to study. Or we'd call the sergeants to line them up and march them back to the auditorium for an impromptu variety show or a motion picture.

When Puggy was in the presence of Daniel A. Lord, whether listening to classroom lectures or singing along in the mess hall as the scholastic played "It's a Long Way to Tipperary," he knew that he was in the presence of a man who had fully given himself over to serving God as a Jesuit. Lord, like Mullany, had something about him that Puggy longed to possess. He had wisdom. He had faith. Most of all, he had true Christian joy.

On December 20, 1918, a Friday. the SATC officially ended. Puggy, with great relief, hung up his Army boots for good and prepared to return to the *Globe-Democrat*. When he arrived back in the newsroom—which was perhaps as soon as December 21, given his eagerness to get back in the game—city editor Joe McAuliffe assigned him to the paper's real-estate division.[41]

It didn't take long for Puggy to get back into the groove at the *Globe*, where he impressed the editors with his dedication. By the time he left the newspaper in September 1919, he was making $24.50 a week—nearly two and a half times as much as his starting salary the previous summer. To all appearances, he was an energetic and capable young reporter who could look toward a bright future in journalism. But inside, he was marking time until the fall, hoping against hope that the Missouri Province of the Society of Jesus would accept him into that year's novitiate class.

As the early months of 1919 turned to spring and then summer, Puggy became increasingly anxious with the fear that the Jesuits might not accept him. For the most part, he avoided telling his close family and friends of his plans to enter Florissant, to avoid embarrassment in case nothing came of it.

However, keeping a secret from Joe Touhill—the co-worker who was his best friend from boyhood—proved to be more than Puggy could bear. One day in May, as the two friends, having wrapped up their shifts at the *Globe*, were enjoying midnight griddle cakes at Childs Restaurant, Puggy opened up about his intentions of trying his vocation at Florissant.

Joe gasped. "Do you know any other funny ones?"[42] he asked. Puggy let it drop.

During that same period, Rapp Miller, a schoolmate from St. Mary's, invited Puggy to visit him at his family's mansion in Moberly, Missouri. Rapp's mother, a widowed society matron who was rather strict, was concerned that the boys were staying up talking past nine. To alleviate her anxiety, Rapp came up with a creative solution, as Dowling would recall:

> He made up a story to his mother that I was going to become a priest. He figured his mother would not object to late hours chaperoned by a future cleric. All during my stay, Mrs. M and [Rapp's sister] Lora spoke about my becoming a priest as Rapp laughed up his sleeve. So when the news came out, Mrs. M and Lora were not surprised, while I suppose Rapp got a paralytic stroke to see his cock-and-bull story actualized. He never dreamed that I would become a priest.[43]

Indeed, a common thread running through Dowling's and his friends' recollections is that his peers never pegged him for the priesthood. It wasn't that he had any great vices to speak of, but simply that he was gregarious and real. His feet were planted not in heaven but on the solid earth of the baseball diamond. He enjoyed staying up late with his friends and sleeping in, and he seemed to love the life he was living as a newspaper reporter in an exciting city. There was nothing about his manner to indicate he might be attracted to the highly disciplined life of the priesthood, let alone that he might thrive in such a vocation.

Over time, the tension of hiding his vocational plans, as well as his fear that the Jesuits might turn him down, began to eat at Puggy. Three years later, looking back on that period of his vocational discernment, he would write to his sister Mary, "My, but that last August and September were wi-i-ld months. . . . I was nervous and wanted to forget everything."[44]

Only one family member knew of his plans—the uncle to whom he had already confessed his hope of entering the priesthood.

> Uncle Pat in my chats with him at the factory was perhaps the biggest influence [upon my vocation] during that summer. He is a warm admirer of the Jesuits and I caught the contagion of his enthusiasm and it helped to keep alive in me my lagging resolution. I could just as well have talked it over with Mam and Pap, but it was a thing I did not care to discuss, and as I had been forced by circumstances to mention it to Uncle Pat, I thought I might as well keep it as quiet as possible.[45]

At the *Globe*, Puggy kept at his job as though nothing had changed. He kept up his baseball playing too, scoring three hits and driving in one run in the newspaper's annual Printers vs. Editorial game.[46] No one knew that, in his off time, as the deadline for entrance into the fall novitiate class approached, he was scrambling to acquire the documents he needed to bring with him to Florissant—records attesting to his baptism and confirmation—and to fulfill other requirements of the Society of Jesus's admissions process.

On September 3, 1919, Puggy met with a panel of four Jesuit priests at St. Louis University who interviewed him to ensure that he met the requirements of canon law for entrance into the Society of Jesus as a candidate for the priesthood. His responses satisfied the panel, so the university's president, Father Bernard Otting, SJ, gave him a typed letter addressed to Archbishop Glennon requesting the testimonial letter for Dowling that was required by canon law.[47]

Dowling hastened on foot to the archbishop's residence to deliver Otting's request personally. Then he headed downtown to begin his shift at the *Globe*—and to begin long days of waiting for Glennon's response.

One evening the following week, as Puggy walked by the copy desk in the *Globe* newsroom, a copy editor who was a member of the anti-Catholic American Protective Association took the opportunity to mock him. Dowling later recalled to his sister Mary, "Knowing I was a Catholic, [he] sarcastically asked me why I didn't become a priest, as they had a good living. He little dreamed I would take his advice so soon."[48]

While he continued waiting for Glennon's response, Puggy wrote a letter revealing his hope for a Jesuit vocation to his friend Tony Harig, who had just begun his junior year in the collegiate division of St. Mary's College. Harig responded that he had shared the news with St. Mary's prefect of studies, Father Benedict Rodman, SJ (which was not happy news to

Puggy, who was still trying to be discreet), and that he himself was curious to know what brought Dowling to make such a radical choice.

Puggy's reply, written on or about September 18, provides an invaluable window into his state of mind as he prepared to make the leap into religious life. Using frank language, he unblinkingly describes why a man would choose the joy of the priesthood over sex and marriage.

The letter begins trivially enough; Puggy offers positive thoughts on Tony's current love interest and on the Cincinnati Reds' winning the National League pennant. Finally he works his way to the topics that clearly are at the front of his thoughts:

> You ask about my plans and say that you might get a little inspiration from me about your own ideas on such a move. I consider it as much of a mistake to push a guy into that thing as I do to hold a fellow out. Do your own thinking. [...]
>
> As for myself, I haven't thought long on the Jeb idea,[49] but I've thought frequently of it in the last 3 years. I see a perfect analogy between the physical and the spiritual. Airplaning appeals to the average young fellow.[50] To my way of thinking, the Jebs for several centuries have been airplaning in a higher and, from a hedonistic viewpoint, a more exhilarating sphere.
>
> I refer to philosophy. You kissed girls, Tony. Was that pleasure near as great as the feeling that came from the successful working-out of an arithmetic problem? There are three reasons why a fellow considers marriage, Tony—money, companionship, or lust. The most sensible, money, has yet to bring genuine pleasure, if we are to believe those that have. You can only drink so much, you can only eat so much, you can only sleep in one bed. So what the hell good is money. It's a means, not an end. Companionship—a high motive, but the simpering stage wears off and you have the blasé hus and wife if not the openly fighting mates. In the Jebs, you have the companionship of clever ducks without the obligation of sticking to them when their line gets old. Lust—hell, Tony, you're worn out in ten years, you're as dry as a eunuch.
>
> Seriously, tho[ugh], Tony, the end of every Jeb's thought is a high one, the highest possible, or our belief is a sham. The end of the average fellow's thought is right between a girl's legs—just the same as a dog's.[51]

Perhaps Puggy feared that his language sounded too worldly, for immediately he added,

Tony, please don't think that I have not given the proper thought to the spiritual and ennobling end of the game. I have, and in the last analysis, it is the impelling force that is bringing me into the order (if they let me in). Consider the confessional and the Mass from the priest's viewpoint, Tony, and weigh any worldly achievement with three minutes during the Mass, and you have your answer. I can never be conservative, Tony. If Catholicism is worthwhile, then I want to partake of the best that it has to offer.

Incidentally, throughout all of my life, I have developed the power of quitting anything that was not in my estimation right for me. If I'm not cut out for the job, I'll drop out of the order in 2 years with an experience. I'll know better then than I do now what's in my guts. I'll study myself, a highly remunerative study, and — —— but I rave, Tony. Don't let anyone talk you into the Jebbies, it is your own funeral. If you get to the point where it worries you, why, take a crack at it for two years. I'm not afraid to put up two years as my side of a bet that promises so much for the winner. Men play bigger odds than that at Churchill Downs and lose without a whimper. Two years! Hell, Tony, they ain't finished counting the years in eternity and it looks to me as we'll both get our share of them. So we can afford to [be] prodigal.

Puggy's thoughts then returned from heaven to earth. Hitting the caps-lock key on his typewriter, he wrote,

BUT DON'T MENTION THAT AGAIN as you did to Father Rodman, because, as I said before, I may not be able to get in. I've not been living in a plaster caste *[sic]* during the last years and they don't let every roué in. If I am discarded I want to walk the streets as if nothing happened and then try next Sept.

I'm going to loaf for the next two weeks. If you want to loaf, drop up. I might get to Louisville and Davenport, etc. Write.

Despite his intention to loaf, Puggy found he could neither spend his last days in St. Louis away from the *Globe* nor could he delay his arrival at Florissant for two full weeks. On the one hand, he wanted to spend his last pre-Jesuit days doing the things he loved with the people he cared about. On the other, he realized that he had to make his move as soon as Archbishop Glennon's testimonial letter came through—otherwise he might lose his nerve.

It appears that on Friday, September 19, the day after he mailed his letter to Harig, Puggy learned that the testimonial would be ready for him after the weekend. That Sunday night, most likely after the usual post-shift supper at Childs Restaurant, he rode the streetcar with friend and *Globe* co-worker Henry Kinealy and stayed at Kinealy's home in the St. Louis suburb of Ferguson. Perhaps Puggy was trying to avoid having to answer questions from his parents, for word of his vocation had begun to leak out of St. Louis University.

In the morning, as Henry's mother served breakfast to Puggy, Henry, and Henry's sisters, Clarence Merkle's name came up in conversation. Merkle had stayed at the home recently, and Mrs. Kinealy and her daughters "were very impressed by him," as Dowling later recalled.[52]

Puggy told the Kinealy women that, only two weeks earlier, Merkle had entered Florissant. "They were horrified, and Mrs. K said she thought it was 'horrible.' I agreed with them and told them he had made a great mistake. Two days later, I made the same mistake."[53]

Upon leaving Kinealy's house that Monday morning, September 22, Puggy probably stopped home to change. Then he took the streetcar down to the archbishop's house to pick up the testimonial letter before doing one final shift at the *Globe*.

After work, Puggy and a few co-workers, including Touhill, headed over to Childs. There—perhaps with Myrt and Flo looking on—Puggy astonished everyone present with the sudden announcement that he was entering Florissant the next morning.[54] Somehow, Touhill managed to collect his thoughts sufficiently to offer to drive him there.

Puggy returned home during the wee hours of September 23 to find that Kinealy, whose shift had ended earlier, was spending the night there. At breakfast-time, he told Kinealy that he wouldn't be able to commute downtown with him to the *Globe*, for Joe was taking him to Florissant. "When I told him, he nearly got a headache," Dowling would remember, "and [he] said with real conviction that he would rather be dead than do it."[55]

But Puggy's mind was made up. Not even Touhill could change it—despite his trying, during the hourlong ride to Florissant, to convince Dowling to let him turn around.

Finally, Touhill pulled up at the seminary's central edifice, a venerable limestone structure known as the Rock Building. Puggy emerged from the car, his fashionable striped silk shirt standing out against the monastic surroundings. He carried no luggage save for the archbishop's letter and a pair of white duck trousers tucked under his arm.[56]

5

DARKNESS AND LIGHT

*And then came two years' diligent search for canonical impediments
in the storied Florissant valley. With it there came struggle and the
carnage that must always accompany revolution.*
                        —Edward Dowling, SJ, writing of his novitiate
                                    in a class assignment, circa 1922[1]

*The letter on Obedience of Ignatius is a KO but it took me two
years to accept it.*
                        —Edward Dowling, SJ, to his sister Mary Dowling, RSCJ,
                                                            May 7, 1930[2]

When Puggy entered Florissant—or St. Stanislaus Seminary, as it was officially known—he hoped to find the peace of mind that would come from
the certain knowledge of whether or not he was called to the Jesuit priesthood. But what he actually found was quite different.

Crossing the Rock Building's threshold marked the start of the greatest
spiritual crisis Puggy would ever experience. The next two years would see
him spiral downward until a point when, just prior to professing his first
vows, he felt utterly bereft. In the very place where he had hoped to find his
path to heaven, he descended instead into a personal hell.

Yet, in years to come, as Father Dowling immersed himself in ministry
to alcoholics, he would refer to his time in the novitiate as "the most important months of my life."[3] For it was there that he had his own personal experience of what his future friend Bill Wilson would call "deflation at
depth[,] . . . a cornerstone principle of A.A."[4] From then on, for as long as he
lived, the memory of that experience would ground the deep sense of empathy that empowered his ministry to alcoholics, drug addicts, spouses in
troubled marriages, people with anxiety disorders, the incarcerated, and
anyone with a problem.[5] More than anything else—even more than the

crippling arthritis that would calcify his spine—that memory would enable him to speak with authority about how God awaits us in the depths of our suffering.[6]

A week after Puggy entered Florissant, he saw someone using his prized silk shirt—the one he had worn upon his arrival—to polish wooden floors.[7] The image would remain with him, viscerally impressing upon him that, as a member of the Society of Jesus, his life was no longer his own. Whatever qualities he possessed in the outside world that made him stand out among his peers—be they his athletic prowess, his journalistic talents, his debating skills, or his gift for friendship—none of them could define him anymore. His duty now was to submit his personality—and indeed his whole self—in all humility to God under the judgment of his superiors, so that the Jesuits' formation process might transform him into the priest he hoped he was called to be.

Ironically, and almost certainly unbeknownst to Puggy, at the same time that his Jesuit formators were helping him learn to become small, the Society of Jesus was telling the world that it had reeled in a major catch. On September 27, the very day he was clothed in his novice cassock,[8] the Missouri Province's press office sent an item to Catholic newswires about the Society's accomplished new recruit. Dozens of newspapers throughout the world picked up the story, including the Cincinnati *Catholic Telegraph*, where it made the front page: "Edward P. Dowling, Jr., former member of the *Globe-Democrat* staff, has entered the Jesuit novitiate at Florissant, Mo., to study for the priesthood."[9] The story also noted Puggy's achievements as "an athlete of some local prominence."

Indeed, the former reporter had left behind an exciting life in the world for the austere life of a Jesuit-in-training, and no one was more conscious of his change of environment than Puggy himself. Although it was not his first time living under regimentation, Florissant presented challenges unlike any he had ever faced.

For starters, he had to forsake his nickname for the duration of the novitiate. He could no longer be called Puggy, nor even Eddie or Edward. Until he made it to the juniorate level of formation, he was to be addressed under a Latin title: *Carissime* ("Beloved") Dowling. To an Irish populist such as Dowling, the aristocratic-sounding honorific was embarrassing. Later on, he recalled his revulsion to the term in a letter to his sister Mary, by then a Religious of the Sacred Heart, as he commented on the title she received in her own order, "Madame":

We call our novices Carissime and that is more difficult yet. These renaissance conceits that give worldly-smacking titles to clerics and *religieux* doth grate my narrow soul. I often sigh for the simpler open days when Paul was Paul and Peter was Peter and Moses was Moses. How offensive to the nostrils of sane Paul would have been some rigamarole such as Your Elevatedness or some such lily-painting.[10]

Even as Carissime Dowling's "worldly-smacking" title placed a layer of unwanted formality between him and his fellow novices, the unforgiving schedule at Florissant—and the plethora of rules that governed it—militated against his having anything resembling a normal social life.

In the past, even when he was bound by the quirky traditions of St. Mary's College or the quasi-military discipline of the Student Army Training Corps, Puggy could always find time to enjoy the companionship of his peers. Some of his happiest memories at St. Mary's were of conversations with friends during outdoor walks. But at Florissant, he and his fellow novices had to maintain silence, save for two hour-long recreation periods each day. And even those recreation periods could not be taken entirely as free time; they were subdivided into smaller periods when novices had specific tasks to fulfill.

During each recreation period, Dowling and his fellow novices had to spend forty-five minutes of time in common, with the other fifteen spent either walking in groups of three (during the afternoon recreation hour) or conversing in Latin (during the evening recreation hour). If it was necessary for them to speak outside of the recreation periods, they were permitted to speak only Latin, to discourage unnecessary conversation.[11]

What would Dowling have made of all this? His first reaction might have been like that of Joseph T. McGloin, SJ, who entered Florissant the following decade. McGloin writes,

I recall the first time I answered one of our second-year novices in English when I should have been speaking Latin. You can imagine his shocked surprise when, to his demand, *"Latine, Frater"* ["Latin, Brother"], I asked him simply, "What the hell for?" I soon learned what for![12]

Taking walks with two other novices afforded Carissime Dowling some opportunity to socialize. But his enjoyment of those walks was limited by his being unable to choose his walking partners. Walking partners were assigned on a rotating basis, for the Society of Jesus, like other religious orders of the day, discouraged "particular friendships."[13] He also had to keep "modesty of the eyes," which had a wide meaning in the Jesuit understanding. It encompassed not only avoiding looking at women (not that there were any to see at Florissant) but also avoiding making eye contact with men if possible.

As if that weren't constricting enough, the Society's rules barred physical contact of any kind between novices; they could not even shake hands or pat one another on the back. For a man as gregarious as Dowling, it must have felt isolating to be surrounded by "brothers" and yet forbidden from making friends.

Beyond the psychological challenges that he faced due to Florissant's restrictions on socializing, Dowling also faced the challenges of conforming to the novitiate's timetable. Never had he been made to endure so many bells during the course of the day. The daily order at Florissant, McGloin writes, "was such that we never found ourselves with any time on our hands. In fact, you could never do anything at all for more than fifteen minutes without a bell sounding and starting you off in some other direction."[14]

A particularly vivid picture of Florissant daily life from the novice's perspective comes to us from Father Daniel A. Lord, SJ, who entered the novitiate eleven years before Dowling.

The order of the novitiate was a masterpiece of accomplishment and frustration. The assigned order of the day, indicated by a constant series of bells, began at five o'clock, always an intolerable hour to most of us. It ended with the striking of the *De Profundis* [bell] at nine-forty-five. There was time for all that the training demanded of us—prayer, manual work, meals, common recreation. And there were exasperating little slivers of time when we made a transition from one assigned duty to another. Following Mass, meditation, and breakfast, there was about twenty minutes. Amazing, now that I regard it in retrospect, what I crammed of physical necessity and care into twenty minutes.

After the manual work, fifteen minutes were permitted to wash up, put one's tools away, and be in place for the spiritual reading which followed. Of these fifteen minutes one might, with skillful manipulation, manage to save five minutes for some pursuit of one's own. After noon recreation we got a delightful half-hour, from one-thirty to two o'clock, to ourselves. Then or at some

other time a good novice made his Stations of the Cross, said his
Little Office of the Immaculate Conception or his rosary. But with
skillful management of time it might be that he could get to take
care of these in shorter intervals and know the splendid luxury of
thirty minutes to read, to write, to study, to walk in the open air,
just to be free and on his own.[15]

Another valuable source of information about the Florissant novitiate
comes from Dowling himself. Hardly six months after moving on to the juniorate stage of formation, he published an unsigned article in the March
1922 issue of the *Jesuit Bulletin*, "The Training of a Jesuit."

The article acknowledges the novitiate's hardships but is careful to
frame them within the larger perspective of the spiritual growth that they
are intended to foster. To a reader familiar with what was going on behind
the scenes in Dowling's own novitiate, the author appears to be speaking to
his younger self, explaining the meaning behind practices that he wishes he
had appreciated when he was a novice.

"No one," Dowling writes, "not even the novice himself, knows the
real story of the novitiate until he grasps the motive behind it, the soul un-
derlying the humdrum activity of the novice's day."[16]

The article shows how, after professing vows, Dowling was able to reflect upon novitiate life with a serenity that frankly is absent from his writings during the time when he was actually living that life. Although he
writes the article as an anonymous observer, the reader familiar with his
story can see that, having made it to the juniorate, he has come to appreciate what he calls the "spiritual militarism" of novitiate life.[17]

"The two-year Jesuit novitiate period is a practical course in the spiritual life," Dowling writes. He explains, that

[it] aims to develop in the novice both persistent longings and
consistent efforts to reproduce in himself the life of Christ, into
whose society he desires to be peculiarly admitted.[18] Its methods
train to self-examination, a requisite for understanding others; to
self-mastery, a condition for directing and controlling others; to
self-realizing, the *sine qua non* for the molding of an effective
personality.[19]

It is significant that Dowling highlights how the work that the novice
does upon himself is geared toward helping others. His words provide an

early indication of the profound other-directedness that would come to be the mark of his personal vocation and his priestly life as a whole.

Between the lines of his reverent and overall glowing depiction of the novitiate, Dowling provides glimpses of the mental stress he suffered during that time of his life. After describing the "strenuous round of activities" that constitute the novice's highly regimented day, he adds, "The monotony is punctuated by long 'hikes' on Tuesdays and Sundays through the Florissant valley and along the Mississippi River. Thursday afternoons find the novice on the campus, forgetting in a ball game the strain of his busy life."[20]

Despite the loneliness he likely felt under Florissant's social constraints, as well as the "monotony" and "strain of his busy life," Dowling's greatest challenge in the novitiate arose not from external rules but rather from his own internal fears.

When he considered his fellow novices, he assumed, rightly or wrongly, that they were confident in the knowledge that they were called by God to belong to the Society of Jesus. But he himself felt no such security. In February 1922, five months after his novitiate ended with his profession of vows, he wrote to his sister Mary from his new quarters in Florissant's juniorate,

> I came here pretty nearly convinced that I would not stay for a few weeks. In a sense I came to satisfy myself that I did not belong here. Even to this day, I have not a trunk here, as for nearly two years I still could not bring myself to believe that I belonged here.[21]

Dowling's sense of being out of place was likely reinforced by the many opportunities that the novitiate gave him to learn about his faults. One such opportunity was the *Exercitium modestiae*—a weekly meeting at which a few novices knelt while their fellow novices identified their failures to behave properly in community.[22] In addition, Dowling, like every novice, was assigned an "admonition partner." A fellow novice would meet with him once a week for a few minutes in the late afternoon to tell him the ways in which he needed to correct his behavior in order to better follow the rules.[23]

Among the personal papers Dowling preserved from his novitiate are two single-page handwritten notes from Jesuits offering him such corrections. The first one, dated May 6, 1920, states at the top that it is from "A Kind Brother" and is signed with the initials "W.J.T." Those clues point to William J. Thirolf, SJ, one of the Jesuit lay brothers who managed nearly all the day-to-day operations of Florissant.[24] Brother William held the humble yet vital position of *custos vestium*—keeper of the clothes. Although he wrote with the tone of a grizzled elder, he was only four years Dowling's senior.

Brother William's note is folded over several times and is torn at the creases. It is likely that Dowling kept it in a pocket of his cassock and reviewed it often. The lay brother writes,

Notice

Please clean your room and make it a little tidy.

Don't forget to shine your shoes.

Walk a little slower. Take larger steps. Hold your head erect. [...]

The main fault with you is, you do not take enough time to do that which you are doing. You do things in a sloppy manner and therefore the boys get a bad impression. They are waking up to the fact that you [don't] comb your hair and brush your cassock.[25] If I were you, I would not be seen *scratching* any part of my body, especially in the chapel. It shows a lack of bringing up. *Mortify* yourself. When St. Peter Claver was working among the Negroes, his face was always filled with biting insects. He never so much as raised his hand to strike them but let them be. If he did that, we could so too.

W.J.T. (Will let you know faults)[26]

Another note of admonition that has survived suggests that, months after receiving Brother William's frank criticisms, Dowling continued to struggle with maintaining the poise, neatness, and general savoir-faire that was expected of him. The note is from Frank Mehigan, who was a year behind Dowling in the novitiate. He was a childhood friend of the actor Pat O'Brien (and perhaps an inspiration for his onscreen depictions of priests). In late 1920 or early 1921, during a period when he was assigned to be

Dowling's admonition partner, Mehigan passed Dowling a sheet of loose-leaf paper on which he had jotted some advice in pencil. His admonitions included the following:

1. Walking
Don't rest your chin upon your breast.
Keep erect and keep your eyes lowered.

2. Eating
Don't play with anything on table.
See what you can do for others. *Be alert.*
Don't eat anything that has fallen from your lips, especially if it has fallen on your cassock.

3. Dress
Be more careful about your hair. Rearrange your underwear so that it is not visible, especially over your trousers. This is inexcusable.

Mehigan's advice to walk erect with "eyes lowered" indicates that, more than a year into the novitiate, Dowling was still trying to grasp what was expected of him with regard to basic rules of Jesuit conduct such as posture and modesty of the eyes.

❧

Dowling evidently placed great value in the admonitions he received, for he preserved them for the rest of his life. Yet, given that he suffered mental distress from feeling he did not belong in the novitiate, it is possible that they reinforced his sense of being out of place.

What exactly was it that prevented Dowling from feeling he belonged at Florissant? From his correspondence and personal papers, this much at least is clear: Dowling envisioned the Jesuit priest as possessing an unstained holiness that was, humanly speaking, all but impossible to attain.

Just prior to entering Florissant, Puggy wrote to his friend Tony Harig, "The end of every Jeb's thought is a high one, the highest possible, or our belief is a sham."[27] He could maintain such an elevated view of the Jesuit mind as long as he felt that, by entering Florissant, he was merely trying out the Jesuit vocation. However, once he began to realize that God truly was calling him to be a priest of the Society of Jesus, Dowling was faced with a crisis of faith.

The things he had enjoyed in the world, such as reporting for a newspaper, playing baseball, tracking the minutiae of local and national politics, and hanging out with friends (and friendly waitresses) in all-night diners—none of these were sinful in themselves, but they weren't compatible with the Jesuit priesthood. If he were truly called to the Society of Jesus, he would have to sacrifice his hopes of being able to do those and a thousand other things he enjoyed. Yet here he was in the novitiate, longing for the things he left behind. How, then, could he truly be called to the Jesuit priesthood if "the end of every Jeb's thought" was "a high one, the highest possible"? Under the limits of his own logic, he was forced to confront the possibility that Catholic belief was "a sham."

Dowling refrained from revealing the depth of his anguish to his family at the time. But later on, both in personal correspondence and in talks, he often reflected upon the years when he doubted his vocation and even faith itself. To him, it was the critical growth period of his life. In April 1944, nearly a quarter-century after he entered Florissant, he gave a talk at an A.A. gathering in which, as he described the pain of spiritual confusion, he related his novitiate experience to that of alcoholics who struggled with the notion of surrendering to their Higher Power:

> But here, tonight, [I am] discussing a problem to which I am not entirely alien. Up to about the age of twenty-one, my spirituality, my religion, my faith was a comfortable, unchallenged nursery habit. And then, over a course of some twenty-four months—the most important months of my life—I saw that faith, that religion, drift away. It began to make demands. And when it ceased to be comfortable and comforting to big, important I—when it ceased to "yes" my body and my soul—I found I moved away from it. I am not utterly unacquainted with atheism. I know and respect agnosticism, and I have been a bed-fellow of spiritual confusion—not merely the honest, sincere kind but the self-kidding kind.[28]

The most comprehensive account available of Dowling's spiritual crisis appears in the letter he wrote to his sister Mary during Lent 1922 in which he shared his vocational journey. He begins by describing the thoughts that led up to his "black hours":

> During the two-year novitiate effort to determine a course in life, I had many black hours. Most men have made up their mind that they belong here when they come—while in my case half of my reason

in coming was to convince myself I did not belong here. Gradually
the idea began to force itself on me that I was in the right place, and
when I began to see the sacrifices and difficulties involved in such a
"cross-carrying" as a Jesuit life would be, I wavered.[29]

When did Dowling begin to believe he was in the right place? Most
likely, it was during his first full month at Florissant. From the evening of
October 1 to the evening of October 31, 1919, he went through his first
Long Retreat, making the Spiritual Exercises of St. Ignatius along with the
rest of his novitiate class.

In his article on the novitiate for the *Jesuit Bulletin*, Dowling described
the Long Retreat as "by far the greatest trial the novice undergoes, the real
eye of the needle," owing to the physical, mental, and spiritual effort that it
required.[30] It was no exaggeration. Decades later, one of Dowling's fellow
novices said of the Long Retreat that they made together, "Those thirty
days were the most difficult time of my life. They came close to being
agony."[31]

Yet, in that atmosphere of asceticism, Dowling found divine intimacy,
as he described in the *Jesuit Bulletin*:

In silence and solitude and by meditation on the basic thoughts of
reason and revelation, with all distracting intellectual or manual
work cut off, the novice spends a month alone with God. No man
can come away from such an experience unchanged.[32]

Dowling's novice class had for its retreat master Father Patrick J.
Phillips, SJ, an administrator at St. Louis University. A gifted spiritual director (he would become the retreat master at SLU's retreat house), Phillips
lit a spark that would eventually go around the world, as Dowling under his
guidance became deeply taken with the Spiritual Exercises, eventually writing his master's thesis on the topic. And, twenty-one years after that Long
Retreat, Dowling would share his insights about the Spiritual Exercises
with Bill Wilson—transforming the way Bill understood the role of discernment in the spiritual life.

In addition to the Long Retreat, Jesuit scholastics (that is, seminarians), including novices, made two three-day retreats each year and, and as
with all Jesuits, they also made an annual eight-day retreat. These shorter
retreats were far less taxing than the Long Retreat and made for a refresh-
ing break from the novices' daily responsibilities. As Dowling's first year
in the novitiate wore on, he found himself longing for the respite they

offered. He wrote to his sister Anna, "I thoroughly enjoy those days of quiet —of progress—of irresponsible reveries. I do look forward eagerly to those retreats."[33]

Despite his enthusiasm for retreats, when Dowling completed his first Long Retreat, he sensed that something was missing. He knew from his experience that the thirty-day Spiritual Exercises were intended to guide him to a point where he would be ready, with the help of God's grace, either to choose a particular vocation ("making an election," in the terminology of the Exercises) or to enter more deeply into the vocation he had already chosen. Therefore, if his Long Retreat had gone according to plan, he would have returned to the outside world feeling renewed and confident of his path in life—regardless of whether he elected to continue as a Jesuit.

But all had not gone according to plan. Although Dowling emerged from the retreat with a greater sense that God was calling him to a Jesuit vocation, he failed to receive the strength and consolation from above that the exercises were intended to facilitate.

Faced with such a situation, Dowling, despite not feeling like a model Jesuit, nonetheless did exactly what a Jesuit is supposed to do: he "manifested" his state of mind to those who were responsible for his formation. Perhaps in response to his manifestation, a spiritual director in late 1919—either Phillips or the novice master, William Mitchell, SJ—instructed him to write a self-assessment. Dowling took out a scrap of St. Mary's College stationery, sat at a desk, and hurriedly jotted down the following:

> Lack of system, careless in small things. Usually versatile[34] and seldom reliable about keeping appointments. Generosity, self-sacrifice, spontaneity, sympathy. Affectionate warm nature. Animation. Easily speeded up to meet sudden emergencies. Generous & somewhat extravagant nature with a rather weak power of concentration. Restlessness. Apt to generalize. Good conversationalist. Cleanness of ideas. Energy, initiative, acuteness, perseverance. A quick thinker. Always on the go either mentally or physically. Sagacity, aggressiveness, spirituality, & refinement. Quiet, modest tastes & unobtrusive manners. Simplicity & high sense of honor. A changeable nature. Reticence. Sincerity. Sometimes logical, sometimes intuitive. Usually good judge of character. Simplicity of taste. Modesty. Physical weakness.[35] Energy & mental activity with an inclination towards impulsiveness & intuition, curiosity & inquisitiveness. Procrastination. Apt to be obstinate[,] contrary & persistent about having own way. Firmness, determination, self-

assurance, will power. Sudden temper which explodes & dies down. Independence & fond of children.[36]

Two things about this self-assessment stand out. First, Dowling shows a remarkably mature level of self-knowledge for a young man of twenty-one. Second, although his temper perhaps lost its edge over the years (and in any case rarely surfaced), the man he describes has all the salient qualities of the man he would be in later life—save for a sense of peace in his Jesuit vocation. That security would come in time—but as 1919 came to an end, it still seemed a distant hope.

Although the sense of vocation Dowling received during his first Long Retreat did not bring him strength or consolation, it was strong enough to impress upon him the need to deepen his walk with God.

He knew from his Jesuit training what he was supposed to do when he sensed that Christ was calling him to make a greater gift of himself. The Spiritual Exercises themselves gave him the answer, in one of St. Ignatius Loyola's greatest prayers, the *Suscipe*. He was to pray with his whole heart—

> Take, Lord, and receive all my liberty, my memory, my intellect, and all my will—all that I have and possess. Thou gavest it to me: to Thee, Lord, I return it! All is Thine, dispose of it according to all Thy will. Give me Thy love and grace, for this is enough for me.[37]

But those words, as beautiful as they were, proved daunting for Dowling. "I was afraid of that prayer," he later wrote. "I feared that if I made that offering to God at eight o'clock in the morning I would have taken it back by ten o'clock."[38]

In his letter to Mary on vocation, as he recounts when he "began to see the sacrifices and difficulties involved in such a 'cross-carrying' as a Jesuit life would be," he says his thoughts took him to a frightening place:

> I began to go to the root of things and see why I should be asked to give up the fun in life and become a drab religious. And the only answer I could get was that it was the will of God as explained to me by the Catholic Church.

In desperation I began to doubt the truth of the Catholic Church and even of the existence of God. (I tell you these things not because I feel they won't shock you but because I believe it is good that you be aware of the facts so that you can guide your own course. Out of my difficulties in regard to faith, there has arisen a stronger and more burning faith that I appreciate all the more because I came nearly [to] losing it at one time.) There were weeks in the novitiate when I felt that I could not honestly remain a Catholic. I thought I had just been fooled by a lot of pious fairy tales and if I wanted to be honest with facts as I saw them I would have to become an atheist or a skeptic. I sometimes think if I had gone on much further I would have gone insane. (That may explain the hysterical tone of the letters I used to write.)[39]

One thing Dowling does not mention in describing his mental and spiritual trials to Mary—for Mary already knew them well—is the comfort he received when family members came to see him, as they were permitted to do on Sundays during his first year of novitiate. His immediate family was deeply attached to him and visited him at least every two weeks.

In fact, Dowling's family visited him so often that Father Mitchell considered transferring him to the New Orleans province's novitiate in Grand Couteau, Louisiana, to prevent his being subject to such frequent distractions from novitiate routine. However, Mitchell—who, as novice master, was also his spiritual director—was a kindly man, and ultimately his concern for Dowling's mental health won out. Not only did he permit him to remain at Florissant and continue to enjoy family visits, he even permitted Dowling to reserve a parlor for visits with his friend Henry Kinealy and to take walks with him along the nearby Missouri River.[40]

Although the visits brought Dowling comfort, the troubled novice continued to struggle interiorly. Only Mitchell was privy to the extent of Dowling's sufferings. Dowling later described to his sister Mary how a gentle word from the novice master provided him with the beginnings of the hope that he was seeking:

One night, things came to a crisis and the Spiritual Father told me I would have to stop going to the sacraments unless I could throw off the ideas I had. I told him it was hopeless and he let the whole thing hinge on my answer to one question: "Do you believe in God?" I told him that I could not actually say that I did, but I was afraid to say that "I actually did not believe." In other words, I doubted the existence of God, but I wasn't ready to say that "I was sure there was no God." The priest told me to keep praying and, in view of my nervous and confused condition, that my answer was satisfactory.[41]

With Mitchell's guidance, Dowling gradually opened up to the possibility that God was not truly absent but rather was patiently awaiting the novice's "yes." In this way, his journey to a mature faith began through what theologians call the *via negativa*, that is, the negative path. He had to develop the wisdom to recognize the dark places where his own mind and will had excluded God, and gain the humility to ask God to illuminate them.

Dowling would carry his experience of the *via negativa* into his work with A.A. In his first meeting with Bill Wilson, he said, "If you can name it, it's not God."[42] The same sentiment would underpin his address at the 1955 Alcoholics Anonymous International Convention, when, commenting on A.A.'s use of the phrase "we agnostics,"[43] he said,

> There is a negative approach from agnosticism. This was the approach of Peter the Apostle when he said, "Lord, to whom shall we go?"... I don't think we should despise the negative. I have a feeling that if I ever find myself in Heaven, it will be by backing away from Hell.[44]

In writing to Mary of his novitiate experience, Dowling wrapped up the story of his spiritual crisis with the observation,

> To conclude—I had the experience of feeling that Catholicity might be false, and believe me, it is a harrowing feeling. Watch your faith, Mary—live up to what you believe.[45]

At the time Dowling wrote those words to Mary in 1922, the message to "live up to what you believe" had become extremely important to him. It expressed a personal epiphany he had received—the fruit of a spiritual experience he underwent during the second year of the novitiate that transformed his understanding of God.

Dowling's spiritual experience appears to have taken place in or around October 1920, when he made his second Long Retreat, for the letters he wrote afterwards testify to his personal transformation.

A second Long Retreat for a Jesuit novice in 1920 was practically unheard of. Then as now, the Society of Jesus required that Jesuits make their second Long Retreat during their final stage of formation—which, for those on the clerical track,[46] comes after they complete their studies and are ordained to the priesthood. But Dowling's first Long Retreat had left him feeling he had some unfinished business with the Lord. Perhaps, he thought, the divine confirmation and assurance that he longed for was to be found by making the thirty-day Spiritual Exercises a second time.

Dowling did not have an easy time winning Father Mitchell's support for the idea, but he kept pushing for it, and eventually his persistence won out. And so, on October 1, 1920, he wrote to his sister Anna with a prayer request for her to pass on to the rest of the family:

> After being refused twice, I finally obtained my request that I be permitted to make the Long Retreat this year. I start tonight, so I thought I would drop a line before I went in. You need not write during the month but I would like to have a good breezy note waiting for me November 1st.
>
> I am certainly congratulating myself on getting to make the retreat. It should be as beneficial as a year in Europe or a couple of terms at Oxford. They are great things, these months of quiet seclusion, and if I had my way I would spend one month that way every year. However, I must ask that you all pray for me— that I may do my best to take advantage of the opportunity offered me. As pleasant as things are in this life, still there are a few obstacles that might make it impossible for me to live it. These I feel should disappear this year and I intend [on] putting in as good a year as I can. I would like to feel you all remember daily to ask God to guide me aright when I come to the "parting of the ways."[47]

In the text of the Spiritual Exercises, at the end of the instructions for the first week of daily prayers and meditations, Ignatius writes, "During the Second Week and thereafter, it will be very profitable to read some passages from the *Imitation of Christ*, or from the Gospels, and from the *Lives of the Saints*."[48] So it was likely in the second week of his October retreat that Dowling began to delve deeply into the *Imitation of Christ*, which he had previously read only in brief bites. (Novices were required to read the book for seven-and-a-half minutes each day; one bell rang to tell them when to begin reading and another to tell them when to stop.)

From its very first pages, *Imitation of Christ* captured Dowling's imagination. Unlike the theological works he had encountered in his Jesuit education—abstruse manuals that sapped the life out of St. Thomas Aquinas's *Summa Theologiae*—Kempis's book was written for the common man. Dowling's democracy-loving heart was immediately won over by the biting words Kempis reserves for scholars who thought that book-smarts alone could get them to heaven:

> For high words make not a man holy and righteous, but it is virtuous life that maketh man dear to God.
> I desire rather to know compunction than its definition.
> · If thou knewest all the Bible without book and thesayings of all the philosophers, what should that avail thee without charity and grace?[49]

However, as Dowling read further, he realized that the *Imitation of Christ's* objective was not to critique Catholic education (however much he might have enjoyed such a critique). It was rather to call him to conversion of heart through a personal encounter with Jesus Christ.

A letter Dowling wrote to his sister Anna the following June, three months before he was to make his vows, gives the best impression we have of the dramatic impact that Kempis's book had upon him. "I almost know the *Imitation* by heart,"[50] he said. "[It is] a book that has helped me a great deal."[51] And, unable to keep the good news of the book to himself, he added,

> By the way, have you ever read Thomas à Kempis? Like all the classics—Shakespeare, Mozart, Da Vinci, Heifetz, and so on— the *Imitation of Christ* is about as interesting at first sight as is one of those stray prayer books printed in German that you occasionally find in the last pew at Mount Carmel. But being a true classic, its worth becomes more apparent as acquaintance with it grows. George Eliot, that chilling writer, in her *Mill on the Floss* allows the *Imitation* to afford about the only gleams of happiness and hope that ever brightened poor Maggie Tulliver's life. Get acquainted with that little book which has helped so many.

With his typical honesty, Dowling then confesses to Anna that the *Imitation* made him realize his failure to walk the Christian walk in sincerity and truth:

> You know Protestants were first to discover [the *Imitation*'s] beauty. Ever and anon it has some rare humor—deep as eternal verity itself. The humor comes from standing in the white glare of the great truths of life (with which à Kempis abounds) and realizing how awkwardly and grotesquely we are playing our roles.[52]

If Dowling's spiritual experience could be pinned down to a single moment, it would be the moment he read in the *Imitation of Christ*, "If thou dwell in my way thou shalt know truth and truth shall deliver thee and thou shalt have everlasting life."[53] Ever after—in his preaching, in his letters to Bill W., and in his guidance to people who came to him with problems—he would center his message in the simple yet profound advice, "Dwell in my way and you will know the truth."

Those words had such meaning to Dowling that when he read them in the *Imitation*, he felt as though Jesus were speaking them to him personally. They brought him to realize that, for all his desire to grow in the spiritual life, he was still clinging to an immature faith. He was forced to admit that his faith had become, as he said in the talk quoted earlier in this chapter, "a comfortable, unchallenged nursery habit."[54] And he came to see that, by limiting his spiritual outlook, he had left little room for the action of God's transforming grace.

But that was just the beginning of the epiphany Dowling received.

Over the next four decades, Dowling referred many times in his letters and other writings to the message he received from *Imitation* and the "dwell in my way" passage. From those writings, it is possible to envision with some degree of accuracy what Dowling believed Jesus was saying to him. The message he heard was something like this:

> I am the way, the truth, and the life. You cannot understand me and your place in me by acting on the basis of your preconceived notions. A leap of faith is necessary.
>
> Accept my offer of grace, and you will no longer intellectualize yourself into your beliefs and convictions. Instead, you will *live* yourself into your beliefs and you will *live* yourself into your

convictions. In this way, you will become transformed into my image.

It is no exaggeration to say that this insight from *Imitation of Christ* provided the fuel that would power Dowling's spiritual outreach for the rest of his life. A decade later, in one of his early sermons, he drew upon it as he preached on Jesus's words in Matthew 11:29, "Learn of me, for I am meek and humble of heart":

> Christ always emphasized the heart over the head. Even in this age of intellectualism he emphasizes his Sacred Heart rather than his Sacred Intellect. We, whose education has taught us to aim at shrewdness and acumen of intellect, find this a strange emphasis. Truly "My ways are not the ways of the world."
>
> And lest we should find ourselves outside of Christ's way, let us acquaint ourselves with his technique in order that in our homes and in our daily life we may supplement our inadequate education and counter the vicious emphasis of an intellectual fetishism. To do so is an integral part of the whole allegiance we owe to Christ. To shape our educational policy in view of the suggestions of Christ is to avail ourselves of the Christ outlook and perspective on the significant issues of life. For most of us this may mean the substitution of faith for sight, but a faith which will anticipate for us by years the findings of sight—yea, will enable us to catch the light of some large truths, which otherwise must have fallen unnoticed for all eternity into the ultraviolet regions of our limited mental spectrum. [...]
>
> Christ's emphasis upon the heart does not involve a denial of our soul's urge toward intellectual satisfaction, but rather affords the shortest cut to it. The surest way of enlightening the mind is to purify the heart.[55]

Dowling went on to describe how the heart becomes purified "in the school of Christ."[56] At the heart of the sermon's message is that "men live and love themselves into their convictions far more than they reason themselves into them."[57]

That same message would echo down through Dowling's letters to Bill Wilson and all the way to his final months of correspondence. In December 1959, when a woman in A.A. wrote to him that she was in a "strange, frightening, no-man's-land, unsure of what to think, feel, or believe," he reached back nearly forty years to the spiritual sufferings of his novitiate so that he might descend to meet her in her agony.

> You are like a thoroughbred in a burning stable; the best chance to get out of it is to let the stableboy put a wet towel over your eyes and be led out.
>
> I know what I am talking about on the horrors of the quick-sands of lack of Faith.
>
> We live ourselves into our doubts and we live ourselves into our beliefs. Christ's "dwell in My way and you will know the truth" is the route to truth.[58]

In early July 1921, with less than three months before he and his fellow second-year novices would be called to make their vows, Dowling wrote his mother asking once again that all his family pray for his discernment. Again, too, his characteristic straightforwardness is evident as he humbly admits, "I really need a great deal of light from God":

> We start our eight-day retreat July 22nd and come out July 31st. Please forestall any visitors. I look forward to the retreat very much as I found last year's a most fascinating period of studying that most interesting thing under God—*Myself*. I hope you will all pray for me that eight days. Is it asking too much that at least one of you go to Communion each day for the successful outcome of that period? I am of a hesitating disposition and I really need a great deal of light from God to see what fork to take in September when they tell me to take my perpetual vows or leave.[59]

Dowling's next words indicate how far he has come from the "black hours" of his dark night of faith. Although remnants of his former trepidation remain—particularly his elevated view of Jesuit holiness—it is now counterbalanced by a sincere effort to resign himself serenely to God's will for his life.

> It is a big step either way because, as I view it, for me to become a Jesuit means nothing less than a life of sanctity, and it is not easy to believe that one is called to live such a life as it is mapped out in the Society of Jesus. I have long ceased worrying about the deci-

sion, realizing that to take the proper step I must be helped very much by God. And it is for that reason I want you all to say a little prayer daily for me during my retreat.[60]

The letter shows how hard Dowling was trying to absorb one of the main lessons that the Jesuit novitiate was intended to teach. Decades later, he would recall that lesson with appreciation:

The great distinction made in religious training—I remember [it] in my novitiate, which was typical, I guess, of a great many [methods of] asceticism training—is a first distinction between feelings and the will. You have that in the Agony in the Garden; Christ's feelings were all opposed to going on, and that never stopped him there.[61]

Yet, as the date of his novitiate class's profession of vows grew closer, Dowling's feelings once again became hard to ignore. Despite having told his mother he had "long ceased worrying about the decision,[62] he was trying desperately to reconcile the Jesuit vow of obedience with his love of democracy and his accompanying aversion to monarchic authority.

In an effort to sort out his thoughts—perhaps at Father Mitchell's request—Dowling drew up several pages' worth of notes under the heading, "I don't feel I should take vows." Written in an intense, even feverish voice that testifies to Dowling's agitated mental state, they read in part,

Because I was told that this was not a theologate but a novitiate, and my difficulties did not fit into the Procrustean bed. [. . .]

Because my attitude on Faith has not been helped by S.J.'s, but from S.J.'s attitude toward imparting knowledge [it] has been hurt.

Because not having Faith[63] to fall back on or not knowing what Faith's role would be in such a case, I don't know [the Society of Jesus's] Constitutions and don't see how I can honestly vow "juxta Constitutiones" ["according to the Constitutions"] [. . .][64]

Because [a] vow requires exact knowledge.

Because for any undertaking, if not enthusiasm, at least conviction is necessary. I lack this.

Because obedience does not appeal to me. [...]

Because [the] appeal from God's will seems like French action in League of Nations.[65] [...]

Principles in [Jesuit] Constitutions not clear. (1) Superior holds God's place. (2) His voice is God's Voice. (3) I see I have to accept sans reservation but I don't know it [i.e., the Constitutions]. I haven't read it. [...] I am not convinced that whatever [the Society of Jesus] commands is best. [...]

Am at loss to know what is meant by "sin" in connection with obedience. I fail to see that I am offering it to God. "He that heareth you [heareth me]"[66]—don't see how this applies to my superiors, and if it does, why the appeal? [...] Are rules to be taken literally or interpreted?

It is hard not to feel sympathy for Father Mitchell, who clearly had his hands full in guiding the agonized novice. One of the things that Mitchell likely recommended to Dowling was that he read John Henry Newman's meditation on vocation. Dowling internalized Newman's words and took strength from them; years later, he would draw upon them to encourage Bill Wilson at their first meeting.[67] The meditation reads,

God has created me to do Him some definite service; He has committed some work to me which He has not committed to another. I have my mission—I never may know it in this life, but I shall be told it in the next. Somehow I am necessary for His purposes, as necessary in my place as an Archangel in his—if, indeed, I fail, He can raise another, as He could make the stones children of Abraham. Yet I have a part in this great work; I am a link in a chain, a bond of connection between persons. He has not created me for naught. I shall do good, I shall do His work; I shall be an angel of peace, a preacher of truth in my own place, while not intending it, if I do but keep His commandments and serve Him in my calling.[68]

But, although Dowling prayed that God might show him what was the work that God committed to him and whether it was to be done in the Jesuits, he still could not decide. Ten years later, he would tell his sister Mary, "I just reached a point where I had to join up or get out. It was terrible."[69]

And so, Dowling, on the night before vow day, once again approached God through the *via negativa*—finding himself in heaven through backing out of hell. But this time, he made a leap of faith—accepting the cross of obedience that he had so dreaded.

> So I told the confessor that I wanted to do whatever he said. I have never felt that I made a mistake. It would have been more dramatic and statuesque if I had decided myself—but the other was more humiliating and consequently better. I abdicated my own reason except for that little sector of the reason which said that it was reasonable to obey more experienced and older heads.[70]

Although Dowling was years away from his work with twelve-step groups, there is no mistaking the voice of the man who would write in his endorsement of A.A.'s Big Book, "The shortest cut to humility is humiliations" (which is itself inspired by the Spiritual Exercises).[71] But what was it exactly that led him, finally, to back out of the hell of indecision and enter the life that he believed God intended to be his path to heaven? Dowling's memory of that time was still fresh when, five months after professing vows, he detailed his deliberations in his 1922 letter to Mary on vocation:

> Mary, I think every man's or woman's vocation can be learned from Christ's direction of how to "follow" him. He said, "If any man will come after (follow) me, *let him take up his cross daily.*" And that simply means, Mary, accepting patiently the hard and difficult things and gradually getting the habit of choosing the difficult rather than the easy things—in other words gradually getting an attitude of mind that embraces and thoroughly enjoys the very things that the rest of men and women recoil from in fear. To such a person nothing is hard or unpleasant. Now do you see why Christ points out the cross (which stands for difficulty) as the means of making us perfect—for who is more perfect than the man or woman who can laughingly endure or studiously seek occasions of enduring things which the majority of people (being imperfect) are afraid even to think of.[72] ...
>
> I concluded that *everybody's vocation is to take up his difficulties (either patiently or eagerly) daily.* And tho I could not decide until the last [minute] to become a Jesuit, still I knew my vocation. It was DAILY to take up my difficulties, and I figured that if I did that for two years, I would be in a position to judge about joining

the Jesuits. And just before my vows, I saw that the Jesuit life for me was just a great big life-(instead of daily) cross that I had the chance to take up.

So I did it. And because of the eleventh-hour decision and its relation to the cross, I took for my vow name (some saint's name we take on [the] occasion of our vows) Dismas, the Penitent Thief who got in at the last moment.[73]

Dowling professed his vows on September 27, 1921. At Florissant, September 27 was celebrated as the Society of Jesus's "Confirmation" day—the anniversary of Pope Paul III's approval of the Jesuits in 1540. But to Dowling it would always be the day when he, like St. Dismas, stole heaven.

6

◈

BECOMING A TEACHER

Get the Christ outlook! Don't stop in your admiring at the disciples
(e.g., Aquinas, [Francis of] Assisi, Leo XIII, or any of the great
churchmen of our day)—no, go on and gaze full in the eyes of the
Master and there you will find much more of deeper interest.
—Edward Dowling, SJ, letter to his sister Anna, June 19, 1921

Joy, peace, consolation—these were Puggy's dominant emotions as he
headed into October 1921, his first full month in the juniorate. The weight
of indecision was off his shoulders and the grace-filled memory of his vow
day was fresh in his mind. And although he was still at Florissant and subject to its unforgiving bells, he now had greater stimulation for his insa-
tiably curious intellect—a course of studies in classics.

A host of new privileges added to Puggy's pleasure. No longer did he
have to endure the aristocratic title of Carissime. From now until ordination, his public form of address was simply "Mr. Dowling" (though his
brother Jesuits had long been calling him by various nicknames—Eddie,
Ed, Puggy, or simply Pug). During the daily recreation period, he could
begin his recreation inside the house. (A fellow Jesuit recalled, "Thus, we
had the inestimable privilege of speaking as we changed our shoes, an unheard-of phenomenon in the novitiate.")[1]

Best of all, Puggy could take more of the nature walks he loved, and
could choose his own walking companion. One such walk, taken with a
companion whose name has not come down to us, would become so important to Dowling that its date would become a kind of personal feast day for
him—an occasion to celebrate Mass in thanksgiving for God's granting him
a new way to share in Christ's sufferings.[2]

In 1950, Father Ed told the story of that walk to a writer who was composing a radio play about his life. Although the interview has not survived,

the script has, and Dowling vetted it for accuracy, so it will guide our image of what transpired.[3]

The scene began on an unseasonably warm day in late October—Indian summer, as it was known then. Dowling had a special fondness for that wistful time of the year, when the golden sunlight hits at a slight angle, its warmth mitigated by an occasional cool breeze that hints at the coming winter. In later years, he often commented in letters to his sister Mary that the Indian summer had a "wine-like" effect on him. Fresh air, he wrote, was a "sacramental"; its power to restore the soul placed it in the same category as blessed medals and Church-approved devotions.

Since Thursday was the day juniors usually went out for walks, Puggy and his companion probably went for their walk on October 20 or October 27. They chose a path that took them over a "Camelback"—a truss bridge that afforded them a view of the fall leaves overlooking the Missouri River.[4] As Dowling gazed at the trees with autumn colors and their shimmering reflections, his thoughts likely turned to memories of his brother James, for that week marked three years since James's death.

The two Jesuits were walking leisurely across the bridge, surrounded by the grandeur of creation, when Puggy suddenly stopped, stiffened, and gave out a little cry—startling his companion.

"Oh, I've got a funny twitch in my leg," Puggy said. "It's nothing. . . . I guess I strained my leg or something."

Although he did not realize the cause of his pain at the time, Dowling would remember that as the day he first noticed his arthritis.

Over time, the twitch turned to a strange feeling of stiffness. It is not clear when Dowling finally sought medical help. Although the radio script says he was diagnosed in 1923, his earliest extant medical diagnosis dates from 1933. That same year, he wrote in a letter that his back, which had become significantly calcified, had only "gradually (twelve years) glided toward its present futility."[5] Doctors would eventually conclude that Puggy's arthritis was a severe form of ankylosing spondylitis that was causing the bones of his spine to fuse together.[6] In any case, after that October walk in 1921, years would pass before Dowling would become aware of the progressive nature of his disease.

Among the dozens of Puggy's surviving letters from his time in the Jesuit scholasticate, he makes little mention of his disease until early 1931,[7] when doctors began to treat it aggressively.[8] However much the effects of his illness may have encroached upon his daily life, he never admitted to feeling physical pain.

Typical of the way he handled his physical sufferings was a letter he sent his sister Mary in the early 1930s, after his disease had significantly progressed.

> In your last letter home you said that someone told you that I was in pain all the time. I laughed quite heartily at that. Do what you can to spread the impression, because there are few postures I more enjoy than martyrdom, provided that it involves no pain.[9]

Yet, between the lines, Dowling's letters made it clear that his illness was tutoring him in the school of suffering, as when he wrote to Mary in Lent 1922 that taking up one's cross daily meant "gradually getting an attitude of mind that embraces and thoroughly enjoys the very things that the rest of men and women recoil from in fear."[10] Those words, written four months after his arthritis first manifested itself, provide an early indication of how Puggy—who was the best soccer player of his novitiate class—was striving to find joy amid his new limitations.

In that same letter, Puggy offered his sister an insight that was highly unusual for the time, if not outright shocking. Writing about the importance of discerning one's personal vocation, he added, "And by 'vocation' I do not mean only 'priesthood or sisterhood.' The married state and the single state in the world are as truly vocations as the other two."[11]

There was no precedent in contemporary Catholic literature for such a claim—quite the opposite. The Council of Trent in 1563 had stated, "If anyone says that the married state excels the state of virginity or celibacy, and that it is better and happier to be united in matrimony than to remain in virginity or celibacy, let him be anathema." Catechetical materials of Dowling's time interpreted that doctrine to mean that the priesthood and the vowed religious life were the only true paths to sanctity. Not until the Second Vatican Council's 1964 Dogmatic Constitution *Lumen Gentium* did the Catholic Church state clearly and definitively that "all the faithful of Christ of whatever rank or status, are called to the fullness of the Christian life and to the perfection of charity."[12]

But Puggy was adamant that the lay vocation was a true one. He went on,

> The Blessed Virgin, St. Joan of Arc, and countless saints were not religious. It is well to realize this when you begin the study of your own calling. One's vocation is simply "the kind of life God wants

me to lead." Don't be afraid to begin to find it out. It will make you a happy and powerful woman.[13]

Dowling's respect for his sister is striking—he wrote to her as though she were a peer rather than a fifteen-year-old schoolgirl. He proceeded to present an account of vocation that demonstrated the gentle and plain-spoken wit that would become a trademark of his in years to come.

> Everybody has a vocation, as surely as everybody is the object of God's interest. The way I doped out my vocation was [that] God wants me to be "perfect" because Our Lord said, "This is the will of the Father, that you may be *perfect* as your Heavenly Father is perfect." And to further convince myself, I laughed at the opposite of that wish—God wishes me to be "*im*perfect."
>
> But how be "perfect"?[14]

The answer, he wrote, lay in following Christ.

On Thursdays and most Sundays, juniors at Florissant had the luxury of being able to relax at Charbonniere, a villa overlooking the Missouri River about two miles away from the seminary. There they could cook their own meals and, if the weather permitted, enjoy swimming or hiking. Although Dowling normally enjoyed visiting Charbonniere, on one Sunday in January 1922 he chose to forgo such refreshment in order to do something that was meaningful for him. Along with another junior, he traveled about eight miles to Sandtown, an unincorporated community consisting of a handful of impoverished families, most of whom were Black or mixed-race. Some of them were descendants of slaves who had been owned by the Jesuits.[15]

Sandtown comprised a thin line of territory stretching about five miles along the Missouri River across from St. Charles, Missouri. A chronicler described the residences there as "stranded houseboats, abandoned box-cars, and huge boxes with thatch."[16] There, in 1919, the Jesuits built a small log chapel, twenty-eight by fourteen feet, that they named St. Mary's ad Ripam—literally St. Mary's by the Bank, although it came to be called Our Lady of the Wayside.[17]

Dowling's visit to Sandtown, where he and another scholastic gave catechetical talks, marked an early sign of his interest in outreach to

Black people. Three years later, he would list the plight of Black Americans among potential research topics for the doctoral dissertation that he hoped to write.[18] And once he began to give public lectures in the 1930s, he often sought to shake white listeners out of their complacent belief that Black people in the United States enjoyed the same freedoms as white people. He would point out that slavery still existed in principle throughout the South,[19] and he would criticize white Northerners for congratulating themselves on their racial tolerance while maintaining prejudiced attitudes.[20]

About two weeks after Dowling's Sandtown talk on January 15, 1922, Florissant was graced by the return of a thirty-three-year-old former resident who, although not yet ordained, was already well on his way to becoming one of the Missouri Province's most visible and energetic evangelizers. It was Daniel A. Lord, SJ, sent to the seminary by the provincial for a period of enforced rest to recover from tuberculosis, with the hope that he might heal in time to be ordained the following year.

Puggy was excited at the opportunity for reconnecting with his former St. Louis University instructor. He wrote to Mary that the two of them had a "fine chat" one evening.[21] The admiration Puggy felt for Lord is palpable in his letter. It is particularly touching given that, in time, he would spend most of his priestly life working under Lord's direction at the Jesuit apostolate The Queen's Work.

During Puggy's two years in the juniorate and his ensuing three years studying philosophy, his fellow Jesuits came to see him as a confident and charismatic figure, and even as a leader of sorts. The juniorate beadle's diary for October 1922 tells of Puggy's taking charge when the seminary's superiors, after five years of pleadings from scholastics, finally consented to have a new athletic field built at Florissant—provided that the scholastics would help build it.

The morning after it was announced that permission had been granted to build the field, Dowling, who managed the juniorate's soccer team, held a mass meeting in the rec room to whip up the juniors' enthusiasm for work. His skilled oratory paid off, as the beadle excitedly scribbled in his diary the following evening: "Work began on the new field tonight. Thirty-three volunteers answered Mr. Dowling's stirring call, and much more work was accomplished than had been even hoped for."[22]

On the academic side, although Puggy did well in the classics courses he took in the juniorate, his grades slipped once he began his philosophy studies at St. Louis University in the fall of 1923. The subject matter's difficulty no doubt had something to do with it, but Dowling's new environment was also a factor. Although he still lived among Jesuits—the Society had its own student residence on campus—he was no longer isolated in the country. Instead, he was back in the heart of the city he loved. That meant, among other things, that he could return to his beloved pastime of reading daily newspapers, which had been forbidden at Florissant.

One exciting consequence of Dowling's relative freedom was that he was free to walk into a police station to get fingerprinted—and that is exactly what he did after class one day shortly after the start of the spring semester.

The previous day had marked the beginning of a new era in the annals of criminal justice in St. Louis. Thomas Skinner, an associate of the notorious criminal gang Egan's Rats, was indicted for robbing cash from a safe—the first time in St. Louis history that a criminal indictment was obtained based on fingerprint evidence alone. On the afternoon of January 17, 1924, an article ran in the *St. Louis Star* relating how John M. Shea, superintendent of the St. Louis Police Department's Bertillon Bureau,[23] oversaw a massive research operation that matched a thumbprint found on the safe to a print of Skinner's left thumb.

The *Star* article would certainly have caught Dowling's eye as he read the newspaper after class. Shea—who was known around the world as "the man with the camera eye" for his remarkable ability to remember faces—was Puggy's first cousin, the son of his mother's sister Margaret Cullinane.

And that, it seems, is why Puggy—who thrived on curiosity, delighting in new experiences—headed over to his cousin's office at the police department and got himself fingerprinted, to see what it was like.[24] The police likely had no small amusement at the sight of the eager young Jesuit in a cassock asking to receive the treatment they usually gave to a perp.

Perhaps, in addition to his scientific curiosity, Dowling sought to be fingerprinted as part of his pastoral training, so he might have greater sympathy with those accused of crimes. His vow name was Dismas, after all.

During the same period that Puggy was receiving his philosophy education, he was also gaining informal pastoral experience of a kind that would prepare him for his future work accompanying people with problems. Some of the people he loved the most needed his help.

James Dowling's death in 1918 had cast a long shadow over the Dowling family. Among the children, Edward, the oldest, and Mary, the youngest, proved the most resilient. Those born closest to James, however—Anna, who was two years his senior, and Paul, who was two years his junior—wrestled most intensely with the effects of the traumatic loss, particularly as they entered young adulthood.

The children's father, the senior Edward Dowling, had always been quiet and reticent, leaving important family decisions to his intelligent and assertive wife Annie. But in Irish Catholic families of the time, a son who entered religious life was accorded significant moral authority—especially one who, like Puggy, clearly had a special wisdom. Thus, by the time Puggy was in his mid-twenties, he found himself in the position of being a spiritual father to his own parents and siblings.

On June 8, 1924, the day after Puggy received his bachelor's degree in philosophy from SLU, he composed a letter to Paul to congratulate him on graduating from high school and to ask him his future plans.

"Naturally," Puggy wrote, "I wonder if your choice has hit on the Jesuits. I have always refrained from urging that step or hindering it. That's a matter between oneself and Christ."

Between the lines, Puggy appeared to be conscious that Paul, who took after his father in being shy and sensitive, looked up to him. Recognizing the influence he held over Paul, he was concerned not to sway him toward a direction in life that might be against God's will. So he wrote that the most important thing was that Paul seek to serve Christ, regardless of his specific calling. "I urge you most strongly to say frequently and fervently 'Go to Hell' to every consideration other than Christ's wish and to follow His apparent wishes no matter where they lead. If Jebbies, okeh.[25] If not Jebbies, just as okeh."[26]

Puggy then offered a detailed list of steps for discernment. It ended with the question, "At hour of death, what step would I wish I had taken?" He closed out the letter suggesting a possible college—Holy Cross, the Jesuit university in Worcester, Massachusetts—in case Paul decided in favor of continuing his schooling.

But Paul did want to enter the Jesuits, and so, at the age of nineteen, on August 8, 1924, he crossed the threshold of Florissant as Puggy had done nearly five years before. Unlike Puggy, however, Paul's novitiate experience was not merely stressful. It was disastrous.

By the time Paul left Florissant in the summer of 1925, he had begun to manifest the symptoms of what would later be diagnosed as manic depression (now known as bipolar disorder). The rigors and austerities of novitiate life—the insistent urgings of the bells, the punishing winter cold, the manual labor, the multitude of minute rules, the frequent admonitions to do better and be better—all those things took their toll on a fragile teen who liked to stay indoors and read poetry.

It seems that Paul's desire to conform to the novitiate's daily routine and formation program led him to push himself to the limit. Five years later, he was still recovering. As Puggy observed to Mary, "[t]he effort [Paul] made in the novitiate at Florissant is enough work for two ordinary lifetimes.... Paul is back from the wars and deserves a rest."[27]

Although Puggy had done his best to avoid pushing Paul into a Jesuit vocation, he still seems to have felt responsible for his brother's plight. At the least, he wanted to do what he could to help his brother get back on his feet. But what could he do? There was no rule book, no script for helping a former religious novice readjust to life in the outside world.

Puggy initially approached the problem in a manner befitting his curious nature and his journalistic instincts. He wrote to a leading Catholic intellectual, Dr. Austin O'Malley—one of the few American laymen to have studied at the Jesuits' Pontifical Gregorian University in Rome—to ask if he knew of any former Jesuits who had made successes of their lives.

O'Malley responded that he knew few ex-Jesuits, adding as an aside, "Dr. James [Joseph] Walsh of New York has been fortunate, but he is especially talented and he had money left to him."[28]

That offhand comment, far from discouraging Puggy, led him to take a step that presaged the outreach that he would later make on behalf of alcoholics and others seeking healing. He wrote to Walsh, who, like O'Malley, was a highly accomplished Catholic author and academic. Instinctively, Puggy knew that if he could find someone who had gone through the same experience as his brother and had emerged in a better place, that person's story could encourage Paul.

Walsh replied quickly, offering much hope for Puggy to pass on. "I am quite sure," the doctor wrote, "that if your brother has anything in him"—meaning virtue, talent, or character—"it will come out, and I think the difficulties of the situation will do him good rather than harm. Fortunately we cannot preserve our friends from trials that come to them. We would surely do them much harm if we could."[29]

Puggy's brief exchange with Walsh made a lasting impression on him. Decades later, when counseling a young woman who had just left the Religious of the Sacred Heart novitiate, he recalled how he had once "made a study of some people who took the same step."[30] In some small way, the correspondence opened his mind to the therapeutic possibilities of communication between a person who was undergoing some personal trial and one who had made it through a similar trial.

In May 1924, as Puggy neared the completion of his bachelor's degree in philosophy, he was eager to map out his academic future. He wrote to the province's prefect of studies, Father Michael O'Connor, SJ, that his overarching research interest was the Spiritual Exercises of St. Ignatius of Loyola.[31] His letter listed no less than nineteen topic headings under which he wished to study the Exercises, including "Relation to Education," "Adequacy of Exercises as a philosophy of life," and "Comparison with well-known 'efficiency courses.'"

Most interesting in light of Dowling's future work with Alcoholics Anonymous was the final entry on his topic list: "Orientation and classification of a number of the Arts, all focusing to bring out [the] fact that life is a true Art and that the Exercises give rules of this Art."

Puggy thus saw the Spiritual Exercises as providing a set of principles that could be practiced in every area of life—much as Bill W., ten years later, would see the Twelve Steps as a set of principles that should be practiced "in all our affairs."[32]

After listing possible topics, Dowling outlined a "pet plan" for his course of study. He wanted to begin by earning a master of science degree in the "science of the generation process, with a special reference to its moral implications"—a timely subject, given the then-current debates over birth control. Then he would obtain a master of arts degree in education, focusing on "the educative value of the aims and methods of [the] Spiritual Exercises."

But that was just the beginning. Dowling's ultimate desire was to "get [a] PhD on the Spiritual Exercises" after his priestly ordination, at the end of his tertianship—that is, the final stage of Jesuit formation. To accomplish this, he intended to use his regency—the stage of his formation when he would likely teach at a high school—to do "survey work, questionnaire work, etc.," and to use his theology studies to "ramify [his] knowledge of the dogmatic aspects." Even his retreats, he wrote, would serve to prepare him for this project.

O'Connor agreed to let Puggy do a master's degree on the Spiritual Exercises—but it would have to be in philosophy, not in education. Dowling, eager to show what he could accomplish if given the opportunity to pursue his interests, worked on his thesis over the summer so that he could complete the degree in a single year.

Before his master's degree was even complete, Puggy renewed his push to continue toward a doctorate. In January 1925, he wrote to James I. Shannon, SJ, secretary of the Board of Graduate Studies at SLU, with a list of five possible subjects for his doctorate—including one on the Spiritual Exercises. He now proposed to "study [the Exercises] from philosophical, theological, sociological, [and] educational angles, as well as from [an] ascetical viewpoint" and to "study means of popularizing their principles in these various fields."[33] Again he displayed the intuition that the Exercises contained valuable "principles" (!) that people could practice in all their affairs.

Given that, when Dowling read A.A.'s Big Book in 1939, he noticed parallels between the Spiritual Exercises and the Twelve Steps, his views on the universality of the Spiritual Exercises point to the attitude he would take toward A.A.'s spirituality. After he encountered A.A., he devoted much of his pastoral work to adapting the Twelve Steps to help people with any type of problem. His final article, published after his death, was on "A.A. Steps for the Under-Privileged Non-A.A."[34] It is all the more impressive, then, to see how, long before Puggy met Bill W.—and before he was even ordained—he already envisioned his future ministry in terms of equipping laypeople with practical spiritual tools to change their lives.

In the spring of 1925, Dowling submitted his master's thesis, "A Psychological Study of the Spiritual Exercises of Saint Ignatius." He intended it to show, from a psychological standpoint, how the Spiritual Exercises provided an ideal method for educating a person's will. However, in his enthusiasm for his subject, Puggy took on more than he was able to accomplish. He had set out to write a three-part study but had to turn in the thesis after completing only the first two parts: "Spiritual Exercises [as] a Will Education" and "Psychology of a Will Education in General."

Dowling's intentions for the never-completed third part of his thesis are intriguing in light of his future work with Alcoholics Anonymous. Its title would have been "Psychology of a Definite Will Education—the Spiritual Exercises." In a postscript to his thesis, he explained,

This [third] part was to have paralleled Part II. In a general way the purpose was twofold:

(1) [to] show the psychological steps in the Exercises, as well as to indicate evidence of St. Ignatius having utilized the findings of psychology

(2) [to] study the cardinal ascetical points of the work in light of their psychological implications[35]

Dowling thus had intended to increase understanding of the Exercises by outlining how their "psychological steps" enabled exercitants to train their will so they might gain the virtues they needed to effect positive change in their lives. When he discovered the Twelve Steps and recognized their similarity to certain principles of the Exercises, part of him must have felt as though Bill W. had brought his own unfinished research to fulfillment.

Between the spring of 1925, when Puggy received his master's degree, and the spring of 1926, when he wrapped up his third and final year of philosophy studies, Dowling was forced to give up his plan to do a doctorate in the Spiritual Exercises. His interest in psychology seems to have made his religious superiors uncomfortable. On a draft copy of his thesis that is in the Dowling Archive, an adviser crossed out the word "psychology" at various points and substituted the word "philosophy." Much of the Jesuit educational establishment was suspicious of contemporary psychology because of the discipline's dependence upon the teachings of Sigmund Freud, whose approach was seen as fundamentally incompatible with Catholicism.[36]

In May 1926, Puggy wrote a letter to the provincial, Father Francis X. McMenamy, SJ, to manifest his desire for a new focus for his apostolic efforts.

"The question I would like to ask," Dowling wrote, "is, 'Ought I to specialize in Journalism?' and if so, 'How, in a general way, should I go about it?'"

Although he realized that any decision about his area of specialization would have to be made by his superiors, Puggy argued that he believed that journalism would be a good fit for him:

Journalism is organic with [my] interests, abilities, and, if Obedience sanctions, with my secondary life aims. My style and sympathies are journalistic and philistinic rather than classical. Just now I know of no other work in which [I] could so naturally enlist my ardor and interest. I see in journalism a central channel thru which to express my interests in the Spiritual Exercises, Scholasticism,[37] Education, and to such tertiary but intense interests such as the Negro, Politics, the Sodality,[38] Newspapermen, and Journalism itself.[39]

But Puggy didn't want to stop at merely writing news articles about his areas of interest. His real interest, as he explained to Father McMenamy, was to mobilize lay Catholic newspaper journalists into joining the Sodality of Our Lady so that they might establish within it a section for the press apostolate. And then, he imagined, the press apostolate might in turn spawn a journalism school along with a bi-weekly news syndicate. And the bi-weekly news syndicate might eventually become daily, with a circulation that could reach "four or five million."

Having sketched out his plan, Dowling seemed to realize how grandiose it appeared: "Now you can see, Father Provincial, why I was afraid to start talking to you about this; I'd never stop." He closed his letter on a note of obedience, emphasizing that he only intended to present his desires, and would submit his will to the provincial's judgment. "I feel that I have done full duty to my promptings when I have manifested them to you. They have been so urgent that I felt you would approve of my doing so."

It is a curious letter, to be sure. On the one hand, journalism was certainly a natural field for Dowling to desire for his specialization, given his background and interests. On the other, his desire to create a Catholic media empire, and particularly his vision that it would reach up to five million people, suggests that, at that point in his development, his measure of pastoral success came down to sheer numbers.

There is no record of a response from Father McMenamy. Perhaps the provincial knew that, come fall, Dowling would learn to measure his success by his ability to reach one teenager at a time.

As school bells rang at the opening of the Fall 1926 semester, a class of high-schoolers at the all-male Loyola Academy were greeted by a new teacher: Mr. Dowling, who was sent there to fulfill the three-year regency stage of his formation. The Jesuit-run high school was the preparatory division of Loyola University, with which it shared its campus by the shore of Lake Michigan.

It was evident to Dowling's students that their new instructor was not a master of the fine art of Jesuit pedagogy. Father Ed later admitted, "As a teacher of youth, I never got any offers to come back and teach after my first effort."[40] Although he cared deeply for his students, he was vexed by the one-size-fits-all approach that classroom teaching required. In his letters to family, he often discussed how, if he had the power, he would convert schools to a tutoring model.

But Dowling gave the students something more valuable than the subjects he taught. He gave them himself—his warmth, his humor, his listening ear, and his spiritual accompaniment. And the students responded—so much so, that, after he moved on, dozens of them remained in regular contact with him for the rest of his life.

Puggy expressed his teaching philosophy in a January 1927 letter to his sister Anna: "Second semester starts tomorrow morn. English, Latin, Catechism, and Algebra—rather, kids, kids, kids. I like to look at it that way. I hate to think of the subject standing between me and a boy."[41]

In the summer of 1927, Puggy was assigned as a remedial tutor for Joe Cahill, a Loyola Academy student who had flunked his freshman year of Latin. Nearly sixty years later, Cahill retained clear memories of how Dowling brought him hope at a time when he was straining under parental pressure to succeed.[42]

The tutoring sessions took place in Mr. Dowling's room at Loyola's Jesuit Residence. Although Cahill entered the sessions feeling dismayed, having never failed a course before, Mr. Dowling's relaxed demeanor immediately put him at ease. Unlike other Jesuit teachers, who always wore their cassock around students, Mr. Dowling dressed informally. He would chew cheap cigars—"Jesuit stogies," he called them—from both ends; his conversation was punctuated by frequent pings as he used a spittoon that was a couple of feet from his chair.

Cahill soon came to look forward to the sessions and felt a personal bond with his teacher. "I learned some Latin—and a lot more," he recalled.

One day while chewing on a stogie, [Mr. Dowling] looked out the window and said, "You know, I never wanted to become a priest,[43] but I always had this feeling [for] some time, until I began to feel guilty about it. Finally, I decided to go into the order for one year and break every rule they had and convince myself that I shouldn't become a priest. And here I am. Well, the Lord chooses strange followers. Look at the twelve ignorant fishermen he started out with."

Even at this time, only six years since Dowling felt the first sign of arthritis, the twenty-eight-year-old Jesuit "walked as though he had a steel rod extending from his neck to his tailbone," according to Cahill.

Another student had Mr. Dowling for first-year Latin during his freshman year at Loyola Academy in the fall of 1928. He wrote to Anna Dowling after Father Ed's death in 1960 to share his memories from both inside and outside the classroom:

> I was a horrible Latin student and he wasn't much better as a teacher. But it was through my failures that I got to know him and received the help he so freely gave to others....
>
> I can truthfully say that, more than any other individual, Father Dowling influences me in the kind of life I've tried to live. As in first-year Latin, I have had many failures since, but now, thanks to his encouragement and belief that I could do better, I have been blessed with a happy life for which I am deeply indebted to him.[44]

Although Puggy took joy in providing spiritual accompaniment to his Loyola students, he was not yet free from the feelings of unworthiness that dogged him during his novitiate. On August 9, 1928, while back at Florissant for a retreat at the Charbonniere villa, he made a general confession. Afterwards he wrote in his retreat diary that he had told his confessor of having "practically nightly sad thoughts." Sadness was his predominant passion, he said; he also confessed "sensuality"—which, in the terminology of the time, meant too much attachment to worldly pleasures[45]—and "impatience."

The following morning, trying hard to grow in the life of grace, he arose at five a.m.—half an hour before the villa's morning bell—and smoked cigarettes and coffee to gain the energy to stay awake during the morning meditation period. "Problem for some time is to be awake," he wrote in his diary. "Good prayer is a long way off."

If his letters to family, his personal writings, and the testimonies of those who knew him are assessed in their entirety, it becomes obvious that Dowling the scholastic was far more advanced in the life of grace than he realized. Yet the dark night was reluctant to leave him. He carried the burden not only of his own personal sadness but also of that of his family—his bipolar brother Paul, his depressed sister Anna, and his mother, who was forever mourning James. Not until he began his work with Alcoholics Anonymous would he attain the lasting sense of interior peace that came with knowing he was exactly where God wanted him to be.

A year later, Puggy drew from his personal experience to offer advice to his sister Mary on the eve of her entering the novitiate of the Religious of the Sacred Heart:

> TRY to learn how to pray. At the end you will have the healthy feeling that you have botched the job. But not so. God spares us the sight of our progress lest we run up too big a bill for bonnets. St. Teresa [of Avila] used to savagely shake her hourglass to hasten the end of her prayer period, and yet she must have done tolerably well.[46]

During Puggy's regency, although he no longer had an admonition partner as had been required during the novitiate, he remained subject to periodic evaluations from superiors. In the files at the Dowling Archive is a handwritten analysis of him from that period. Its origins and purpose are somewhat mysterious, but it appears to be a draft of a report to be sent by his Loyola Academy superior to his provincial. The priest who wrote it, a "Fr. M _____" (only the first initial is legible), said of Dowling,

> He is trustworthy, dependable, and a very honest character. Is conscientious in his work. Thinks clearly, logically, and also fluently. He has business ability above the average, and would probably succeed in an executive position because of the above qualities and also because he is ambitious, wants to get ahead, possesses a great deal of shrewdness in getting what he wants from people and from circumstances in which he is placed.
>
> Though possessing some aggressiveness, a lot of physical energy, considerable will power and firmness, he is apt to procrastinate at times and to excuse himself on practical grounds for small lapses in conduct, though he is in no sense dishonest or hypocritical. He is modest and also reticent about his own affairs.
>
> He has a very good physique and constitution. Is fond of outdoor sports—probably has played them a good deal.
>
> Is gifted along scientific rather than artistic and literary lines. Comparatively weak imagination, though some constructive ability is indicated.[47] Has a gift for mathematics.

He is eccentric. Is a very distinctive and original personality. He is careless about small things and is very absent-minded. He is self-conscious at times, and somewhat sensitive.

He is a man of simple tastes, and though he has some strong likes and dislikes, he is quite generous, humble, and modest.[48]

Whatever may have been the intended purpose of this analysis, it is an interesting document of how an ordained Jesuit viewed Dowling during his teaching years. Dowling saved it and no doubt took its criticisms to heart.

∽⌒∼

"Dear Loyolan," Dowling typed on July 1, 1929, beginning a mimeo-graphed letter that he sent to dozens of his former students. "Tonight I am leaving Loyola after spending the three most happy years of my life with the finest group of boys in America. . . ."

Puggy added that he was to begin his theology studies at St. Louis University in the fall, and would likely be ordained in June 1932. But before arriving back in his hometown, he said, he would spend the rest of July at "The Island," the Society's vacation house on Lake Beulah, near Mukwonago, Wisconsin.

As it turned out, his summer experience proved neither as bucolic nor as relaxing as he had planned. Puggy ended up arranging a stay for his brother Paul at a Catholic-run health spa, Sacred Heart Sanitarium in Milwaukee—paid for by their uncle Pat—in the hope that it might calm Paul's anxiety.[49] He himself decided to lodge at Marquette University, the Jesuit college in Milwaukee, rather than Lake Beulah, so he could visit Paul and monitor his progress.

The experience of bringing his brother to the sanitarium made such an impression on Dowling that he could still recall his feelings clearly twenty-five years later. At a 1954 event promoting the mental-health support group Recovery, Inc., he said,

I remember when a member of my family entered a mental hospi-tal. It was one of those ambivalent places, partly [a health spa and partly] a sanitarium. I said, "Doctor, could this lead to insanity?" He said, "This is insanity."

There are people in this room who know how I felt; fright-ened, stigmatized, futile, poor. It was a bachelor uncle's benefac-

tion which enabled us to pay the hospital bill. Recovery[, Inc.], if
I'd had it then, wouldn't have made me feel so bad.[50]

At the same time that Paul and Edward were in Milwaukee, the
youngest Dowling sibling, twenty-two-year-old Mary, was beginning her
first month at Kenwood, the novitiate of the Religious of the Sacred Heart
in Albany, New York. Puggy wrote to Mary on July 5 to let her know that
Paul was at the sanitarium, and to share the good news that their sister Ann
(also known by her full name, Anna) was coming out of her own depression.

> From all reports, Ann has found herself. I hope she doesn't overtax
> herself now that she has gotten control. Pray for Paul and Ann and
> Mam. The best prayer for them is to come closer to Christ and his
> blessed and kind Mother. The closer you come to them, the more
> you can do for the rest of us. And to come close to Christ, *forget
> home.*

Between leaving the students he loved, caring for his troubled brother,
monitoring his fragile sister Anna from a distance (as well as his mother,
who had difficulty weathering Mary's departure for religious life), and cop-
ing with his worsening arthritis, it was a challenging summer for Puggy.
Yet his letters to Mary were consistently bright and encouraging.
"You are right in forgetting St. Louis," he wrote to Mary on July 18.

> The constantly recurring thought of old haunts and old yoke-
> fellows, if it is frequent enough, will afford you a fine pleasant ex-
> ercise in concentration. Substitute some engaging thought for it
> and whenever it comes up, meet it with an ejaculation for repose
> of James's soul or call up some interesting picture such as a base-
> ball game with some portly Reverend Mother striking out.[51]

In another letter, he counseled Mary as she strove to meet the novitiate's demanding regimen of prayer: "Nobody can do better than they can
do. In matters like prayer, etc.—the effort is what we give to God, the success is what He gives to us. Prayer, etc., without the 'pay' of success is
more unselfish and unselving."[52]

With Puggy's return to St. Louis in the fall to begin his theology studies at SLU in late August 1929, his old temptations to distraction returned. He wrote to Mary on October 1 as he prepared to go into a retreat,

> Say a little prayer for me during retreat. I rather like those days. The theologate is bethlehemic after the babylonic teaching, and I hope to profit [from] the chance of silence and prayer. One of my great difficulties is spreading my efforts, and during these days I hope to develop some won't-power.

Dowling's greatest distraction was his newfound interest in the Hare system of proportional representation (known today as single transferable vote or multi-winner ranked-choice voting). Just prior to arriving back in St. Louis, he wrote to his family, who were active in local politics, urging them to research that system:

> I always thought it would solve the problem of minority represen-tation in St. Louis.[53] ...If Mam would read up on it and through the Cullinanes and her precinct and ward leaders start an agitation for it, something might be done. The present law is unjust and con-ducive to corruption and stagnation.[54]

Now that he was back in his hometown, there was nothing to prevent him from continuing his research on proportional representation and promot-ing it on the local level. Nothing, that is—except his full schedule of theology courses at SLU. But that didn't stop him. By early 1930 he was writing to Elsie Parker, secretary of the Proportional Representation League in Philadel-phia, to request information on how the Hare system functioned in Ireland.

> Miss Parker, I am in the graduate school of St. L. U. with about 200 Jesuits who will later have considerable spheres of influence in the ministry and in colleges. If you have a surfeit of pamphlets at any time, I can guarantee you a discriminating circulation of them. I can't pay for them. I am broke, irrevocably a vowed pau-per. But I have a tongue and a typewriter and, until I can find something better than the Hare system for a hobby, both these clumsy instruments are at the command of the Cause.[55]

Indeed, over the remainder of his life, Puggy would frequently use his tongue and typewriter to spread the gospel of proportional representation.

In time he would direct his interest in ways that would help effect positive change both in St. Louis politics and—through the inspiration he gave Bill W. —in the governing structure of Alcoholics Anonymous. But in those early months of 1930, Dowling was simply firing off letters in all directions, trying to interest every influential local politician and every local media outlet in proportional representation.

Four days after writing to Parker to volunteer his service to "the Cause," Puggy wrote a frenzied letter to his old friend Joe Touhill, who was then an editor at the *St. Louis Star*. He put forth an ambitious proposal to increase the *Star*'s circulation by making it a vehicle to promote proportional representation nationally. Black people and women would support such an editorial move, Dowling wrote, for "proportional representation is the political salvation of the Negro" and "proportional representation is the kind of voting that will make women's suffrage operative."

After outlining his plan to Touhill, Puggy added, "The best part of the scheme, Joe, is that it would be propagandizing for simple justice in our election methods. It would be an insane drive for the sake of sanity."[56]

Although Dowling's desire to promote proportional representation was noble, there is something unnerving about the level of enthusiasm in his letters on the topic during this period of his life. As with the letter he wrote to his provincial proposing to launch a mammoth press apostolate, Puggy's tone has an air of desperation. He seems at times to be groping in the dark, believing he must find some way to use his talents to improve people's lives on a grand scale.

Puggy struck a similarly discomfiting tone in a speech he wrote in March 1931 on the need for Catholics to be active in political life. It is not clear whether the speech was ever delivered; if it was, the man who delivered it is hardly recognizable as the future Father Ed. In it, Dowling took his cues from radio priest Father Charles Coughlin, whose denunciations of the extremes of communism and predatory capitalism had made him a household name.[57]

The speech began,

A week from next Tuesday in St. Louis there will be held an election to determine the personnel of the city's law-making body and of its board of education, more important elections than which I find it hard to conceive. Eligible to vote are 270,000 Catholics. 258,000 or 97% will not vote. Over half of the members of this parish are not even registered. I have their names here. As a result, in this Rome of the West, the laws are made and administered, the education is molded, by our separated brethren, the Scottish Rite sect.

Dowling proceeded to argue that without Catholics involved in politics, the field was left to Satan, who used political tactics to undermine the Church. If Catholics stopped thinking of politics as a dirty word, they could enact laws that would reinforce Catholic standards of morality, such as making divorces more difficult to obtain.

The speech was not without humor. Echoing the intentionally outrageous style of his childhood pastor Father Phelan, Dowling wrote,

> I suggest that we start agitation for a Missouri law that will make any person responsible for a divorce (by adultery, abandonment, cruelty, etc.) automatically guilty of a felony punishable by a penitentiary sentence at least as long as we assign for a pint of liquor. Think that over. I think that the person who breaks up a family is doing as much harm to the state as the possessor of a pint of whiskey.

This modest proposal was a sly jab against Protestants, given that those who were being jailed for possessing a pint of whiskey included many Irish Catholics.

As he wound down the lengthy speech, Dowling reeled off a list of Catholics who were models of political courage, including Simon Bolivar, Blessed Thomas More, Daniel O'Connell, Archbishop John Carroll, Father Phelan, and, last of all,

> Father Coughlin of Detroit talking weekly to more people than Peter the Hermit in a lifetime, a venerable [John the] Baptist howling in the wilderness, translating the political principles of Leo's great encyclicals and saving the Church from the stigma of being the lackey of capitalism.

In reading Puggy's admiration of Coughlin for reaching more people than the Crusades preacher Peter the Hermit, one senses again the familiar hint of desperation. It was not enough for Dowling simply to become a good priest; he had to be a great one, and the way to become a great one was to reach as many people as possible.

It is difficult, with the distance of a century, to discern the source of Puggy's desperation, but it is possible that the psychological stress of his crippling disease played a role. Dowling was always a man of enormous vitality. Even in his later years, it was said that if one spent a few minutes with him, one forgot that he used a cane. If he had so much physical energy when in the depths of his illness, one can only imagine how much he had when he was at the peak of his powers—right when his illness first struck him at age twenty-three.

Perhaps Puggy's occasional tendency during this period to make proposals that were a bit too grand, and to push them a bit too hard, reflected his need to find an outlet for the pent-up energy that he could no longer expend on the baseball or soccer field. He may also have feared that, with the progress of his illness being uncertain, he had to make his mark upon the world while there was still time.

Yet, even amidst his obsessive study of proportional representation, Dowling never lost his interest in ordinary people and their problems. In October 1930, he wrote to Mary that he had stayed in Chicago during much of the summer, where his time "was spent largely in chatting with boys" he knew from Loyola. "It is most amazing to come to learn the problems, the phobias, the aspirations that young folks have," he wrote.

Dowling then related a story of an encounter that showed him, perhaps more than anything else he had yet experienced in his apostolate, the healing power of empathy:

> One case I can't get out of my mind and whom I wish you would pray for occasionally was unforgettable. Cultured to his fingertips, widely traveled, twenty years or thereabouts, I had always found this fellow remote, elusive, fugitive, though unfailingly polite.[58] For several months he has been in a nervous morose condition. His doctors and older priests couldn't reach him, though the boy was desperately anxious to get relief. A chance remark to him indicated to him that I had several friends who were in his boat, and the result was a conversation that lasted from 10 o'clock at night until 20 minutes to 5 in the morning. My experience with Paul and a couple of similar cases made it so easy for the boy to talk, [whereas] he would have found it impossible to talk to men who had not walked so closely with these depressions and their odd vagaries.[59]

With this story, we see the familiar image of Father Ed taking shape—a man who walked closely with depression and whose empathic spirit made the depressed feel at ease. His encounter with the Loyola student reads like a preview of the consolation that he would give Bill W. ten years later at their first meeting—when Bill, like that student, was in a nervous, morose condition, desperately anxious to get relief.

The year 1931 marked a decade since the onset of Puggy's arthritis. In February, his superior sent him to St. Mary's Infirmary in St. Louis in the hope that the doctors might be able to make his calcified back more flexible. There he endured treatments that, although standard for the time, seem medieval by contemporary standards.

"They prescribed a diet of three glasses of sulfuric acid daily with regular meals," Dowling wrote to Mary. "The whole thing is such a joke. If I didn't enjoy the change, I'd never come."[60]

Puggy's claim that the discomfort of the infirmary was an enjoyable change from his theology studies speaks volumes about his emotional state as he drew closer to ordination. After he returned back to campus from the infirmary, he wrote to Mary,

> I may be ordained on June 24 and then again I may not.... All those whom the war held back [from entering the Society] were granted a privilege of being ordained at [the] end of [their] second year of theology. I may get in on the privilege. *Please* pray not that I get it, but that I be considerably less unworthy of it when it comes, no matter when it comes. A depressing sense of unworthiness sort of swamps a person at the prospect.[61]

Although Puggy did not tell Mary why he felt unworthy, he wrote in his meditation diary that his continuing struggle with sadness left him uncertain as to whether he was fit to be ordained.

Between the end of March and the middle of May, Dowling confessed his sadness and uncertainty to no less than four Jesuit priests. According to his notes, each one of them told him his sadness didn't "specify." It seems they meant that it did not fall under any specific category of canonical impediments that would prevent him from being ordained. Of those four, Father Laurence J. Kenny, SJ, a wise and gentle priest in his late sixties, was the one whose opinion mattered most to Puggy. Kenny assured him that he had done the right thing by being frank, and that he should not go back on his resolve to be ordained that year.

And so Puggy became Father Edward Dowling, SJ, on June 25, 1931, ordained along with forty other men—nearly all of them Jesuits—by St.

Louis Archbishop John J. Glennon at SLU's St. Francis Xavier (College) Church. Relatives and family friends traveled long distances to be there, and all his siblings were present save for Mary—now Sister Mary—whose religious order did not grant her leave to attend.

During the run-up to his ordination, Father Ed's arthritis caused quiet concern among those who knew him. Sister Mary confided to her fellow novice Sister Mary Louise Scott, a family friend, that she was afraid that once her brother made the ritual prostration—laying himself face down before the altar as the bishop and congregation chanted the Litany of the Saints—he would be unable to rise unaided.

Whether or not an acolyte had to extend a hand to Dowling after his prostration, one thing is certain: Father Ed's ordination brought him an abundance of consolation. The following Sunday, he had the joy of celebrating his first Solemn Mass at his family's home parish, Our Lady of Mount Carmel, where many parishioners remembered him from his days serving Father Phelan's Mass.

Father Ed then prepared to take the train to Chicago to celebrate with his friends from the Loyola community. But before leaving town, he sent an ordination announcement to one of the Jesuits he most admired: Father Daniel A. Lord, SJ, editor at The Queen's Work, the U.S. headquarters of the Jesuits' international Sodality of Our Lady. Dowling likely still longed to be assigned to The Queen's Work, as he had told his provincial five years earlier when proposing to specialize in journalism.

Father Lord's warm reply must have had special meaning for Father Ed, for it is one of the only incoming letters from this period that he preserved. In it, Lord showed just how far back his memory of Father Ed went—all the way to Puggy's time in the Student Army Training Corps. "It gives me the greatest joy to see the men I had known at the University reach God's altar as priests," Lord wrote.

On July 2, Father Ed arrived in Chicago, where he was taken to a dinner at the City Club in honor of him and another former teacher who had been ordained. One hundred Loyola Academy alumni were there. He told them, "The ordination week has been a honeymoon. Unforgettably sweet."[62]

The following morning, July 3, Father Ed celebrated his first Mass at Loyola. Some of his former students were present for the occasion. But the best was yet to come.

He wrote his family about what happened next. "[Then] began the trek of old students to my room. This is my idea of my paradise."[63]

For all Father Ed's fantasies of becoming a media apostle and reaching millions through his tongue and typewriter, he had one conception of paradise—and it wasn't journalistic fame. The pastoral activity that gave him the greatest joy was simply sitting at his desk and ministering one-on-one to a steady stream of people with problems. Although he couldn't have known it at the time, within just a few short years his vision would become a reality. The personal accompaniment of wounded souls would become the core of his ministry, the dynamic center around which all his activity revolved.

7

⤻⤳

A HEART FOR DEMOCRACY

*The biggest obstacle to democracy in the United States is the
delusion that we are a democracy. . . : Did we beat Italy to Fascism
by over a century? Has Hitler in his treatment of the Jew caught up
with our Founding Fathers' treatment of the Negro?[1] Has Mussolini's treatment of the Ethiopian yet reached the hoodlum sav-
agery that marked our democratic consideration for the Americans,
or, if you know them better by their other name, the Indians?*
— Father Ed, addressing the General Federation of Women's
Clubs, Kansas City, Missouri, May 12, 1938

In St. Ignatius of Loyola's "Letter on Obedience," the Jesuit founder urges
members of the Society to follow the example of such obedient saints as
Abba John, one of the Desert Fathers, who "did not examine whether what
he was commanded was worthwhile or not, as when he laboriously watered
a dry stick for a whole year."[2]

The Abba John story inspired Father Ed, with his reporter's knack for
coining unique expressions, to refer to obedience in his letters as "dry-stick
watering." It was his tongue-in-cheek way of acknowledging how often the
idea of subordinating his own desires to those of his religious superior
seemed futile to him. Yet he believed with his heart that it was through obedience—especially when it was difficult (as it so often was)—that God
wished to perfect him. Above all, Father Ed believed there were certain
graces God wished to give him that he could receive only if he practiced
the virtue that was for him "the greatest cross in life."[3]

His first year after ordination gave him more than one occasion for
dry-stick watering. As he began the third of his four required years of theological studies in the fall of 1931—now at the familiar campus of St.
Mary's College[4]—his superiors handed him the greatest disappointment of

93

his Jesuit life. A low-level student prefect informed him that the higher-ups had moved him down from the Long Course—the program for Jesuits destined for careers in academia—and into the Short Course, which was for everybody else.[5]

The change was no mere academic demotion. Its effects would stretch all the way to the solemn vows that Father Ed would make after his formation was completed. Only those in the Long Course were permitted to make the fourth vow of "special obedience to the Sovereign Pontiff with regard to the missions"—professing their absolute willingness to put themselves entirely at the Church's service wherever the need was greatest. Upon making their final vows, they would thus gain the noble title of "professed of the fourth vow." Those in the Short Course, upon solemn vows, would have only the lesser title of "spiritual coadjutor."

Father Ed believed he knew why his superiors authorized the demotion. Although he did reasonably well in his second-year theology courses, he faltered during the end-of-year oral examination, when the examiner asked him "what note the Church assigned to the problem of whether angels had subtle corporeal bodies."[6]

"As soon as the question came up," Father Ed wrote afterwards in a letter, "I told the examiner that I had not the faintest idea whether there was an ecclesiastical note on the matter. The fact of the non-corporeality of the angels I felt sure."[7] But that was not enough to satisfy his examiner.

In addition to having to accommodate himself psychologically to his newly reduced status in the Society, Father Ed also suffered physical stress during the fall of 1931. His arthritis was worsening—so much so that he spent his Christmas vacation receiving inpatient medical treatment from a doctor who thought he could arrest the disease's progress.[8]

Two months after returning to St. Mary's from the hospital, Father Ed received another occasion for obedience—this time directly from his provincial superior. Father Samuel H. Horine, SJ, wrote him a letter ordering him to curtail every activity apart from his theological studies—especially his correspondence, which Horine said had grown "too large and frequent."[9]

Although Father Ed recognized that the order was probably in his best interest, he was deeply wounded by the reasons Horine gave for it. The provincial asserted that the order was necessary because Father Ed had lost interest in his theology studies completely:

> You are at present giving an altogether disproportionate amount of your time and energy to questions outside your present studies which have been assigned you by obedience. There is in your case

the question of whether you are doing the right thing at the right time. The answer as your elders see it is clearly that you are relegating theology altogether out of your interest.[10] Even if you are later assigned to political science, you will, as a priest in the Society, need your theology, both Dogma and Moral. For a long time you have paid too little heed to it.[11]

Since Father Horine instructed him to speak about the matter with St. Mary's prefect of studies, Father Ed wrote to the prefect, Father Aloysius Kemper, SJ, expressing his hurt with typical candor.

Two remarks in the letter make me feel like a pariah: "...clearly that you are relegating theology altogether out of your interest" and that "for a long time you have paid too little heed to it." This is a portrait of a man who is welching on his vow of obedience because assignments are hard. It is a sordid, mean, small type that is depicted—a parasite who will take his meals and bedding from the Society and then not put his shoulder to the wheel to help the Society as obedience directs.[12]

Father Horine's words hit Father Ed particularly hard because he was still smarting emotionally from having been demoted to the Short Course. Until then, he had kept his feelings about the demotion to himself. But now he felt compelled to tell Father Kemper what it had done to his self-esteem:

You know of the danger in some cases of sourness and resentment that can be germinated at that transition [from Long to Short Course]. The Province is not without its examples who are thereby precluded from becoming what Father General called during the last Triduum reading "*veri*" [true] Jesuits and later become emotional misfits.[13]

Father Ed added that he believed he could avoid such a bitter fate. But he still longed for some understanding from his superiors:

It was [a] hard semester, Father, and my health was never poorer. I say this to try to remove an impression that seems to exist that I discount the significance of theology.... Please charge my critical and smallish spirit in this letter to an urge to open up on the matter with you, whom I have found unfailingly sympathetic and something of a shock-absorber. I am the better for getting rid of some bad blood and apologize for victimizing your patience.[14]

But he realized that the only answer was dry-stick watering:

Basically I am glad of Father Horine's interest. I am convinced of the appositeness of his observations and directions. I intend to conform and will find a good deal of natural pleasure in that conformity. Your help to this end I know I can count on.[15]

The letter was a true *cri de coeur*. Father Kemper met it with wisdom and understanding. Since the provincial had left it to him to determine the specifics of how Father Ed was to focus on theology, Kemper chose not to forbid political correspondence altogether. Instead, he met personally with Father Ed to give him practical suggestions on how to budget his time so he could balance his studies with his personal interests.

Dowling, reporting back to the provincial on the meeting, was unable to hide his joy: "[Father Kemper] assured me of the theological character of interest in the social sciences."[16] He added, with honesty,

I must confess that my interpretation of your letter is a different one than the one Father Kemper puts on it. He puts a less drastic and less literal meaning into it than I do. Since you told me to consult Father Kemper about it, I will follow his interpretation unless I hear from you to the contrary.[17]

From Father Ed's perspective, God was enabling his dry-stick watering to bear fruit. It would not be the last time.

As Father Ed immersed himself in his theology studies, he continued to share in his family's concern for his brother Paul. On Paul's twenty-seventh birthday—November 5, 1932—Father Ed wrote him a long and hope-filled letter. Paul's past trauma, Dowling wrote, gave him a providential opportunity to enter into the "heroic" work of rebuilding his identity:

In my mind your biggest achievement is still going on—it is a life work and is not to be produced in a day or a year—it is the rehabilitation of yourself after your experiences at Florissant which almost dynamited your foundations. Few men get the opportunity to go through this trial. Fewer still succeed in it. Keep up the slow, patient, and heroic work.

In these words, it is possible to discern the same supportive voice that would, within ten years, lead people with personal crises to line up outside Dowling's door. Father Ed developed his empathy for people with problems in the school of his own family.

"So," Dowling added as he continued his letter to Paul, "keep fighting along." His next words show him feeling self-conscious over his tendency to throw various ideas at Paul about ways he might improve his life. The most important thing, he wrote, was that Paul grow in imitation of Jesus:

> You will forgive and laugh at my constantly using you as a target for my suggestions as to what to do.... Instead of doing, BE. And instead of being Paul, be more and more, gradually, Christ. This is slow work, but it is better to be muddling along at a masterpiece like that than mass-producing a lot of trinkets such as I suggest.

Even at this early stage of his priesthood, the great patience that would characterize all Father Ed's outreach to the suffering was evident. Here was a priest who did not hesitate to walk with those who were doing the "slow work" of recovery.

Throughout Father Ed's theological training, he continued to follow the career of his former teacher Father Daniel A. Lord, SJ, with admiration. In 1925, Father Lord was made national director of The Queen's Work, the U.S. office of the Jesuits' international Sodality of Our Lady, a network of youth groups (sodalities) spreading devotion to Jesus through Mary.[18] By 1930, the energetic editor had so transformed the once-sleepy apostolate that he had become the Missouri Province's most visible media apostle— writing and directing musical pageants,[19] authoring inspirational pamphlets that sold in the hundreds of thousands, and advising Hollywood moviemakers. At the center of all these activities was the *Queen's Work* magazine, which Father Lord and his staff used to inform and motivate the Sodality's tens of thousands of members.

Some of Father Lord's work for the movie industry was well known— Cecil B. DeMille engaged him as a consultant for his 1927 epic *The King of Kings*—but he made his most important contribution behind the scenes. In 1930, industry executives, who were then under pressure from government officials to reduce the explicit content in films, enlisted him to write a code of morality for movie-making. Hollywood's hope was that, by exercising self-censorship, it would ward off official attempts at censorship.

Lord responded to the request by drawing up what would become known as the Motion Picture Production Code, which would influence filmmaking through the 1950s. Although Lord's authorship of the Code was not revealed to the public at the time, Father Ed learned of it through his brother Jesuits and took great pride in it, as he wrote to his sister Mary in February 1930: "I expect [the Code] to have an unnoticed but tremendous effect on the movies after about six months."[20]

Father Ed also admired the large-scale educational outreach that Lord initiated in 1931: the Summer School of Catholic Action (SSCA). It was a traveling school that the Sodality conducted in different cities over the course of each summer to educate laity, members of religious orders, and priests in applying their faith to every major area of life and societal engagement. "The approach," one commentator has said,

> was to make the human side of Christ so real, so irresistibly attractive, and so pertinent to the lives of the students that they would be eager to imitate Him in their personal lives and to carry His spirit into their homes and parishes, their schools and colleges.[21]

It appealed greatly to Father Ed, who had long believed that the way to holiness was to "get the Christ outlook."[22]

In the spring of 1933, as he completed his theology studies, Father Ed received his first post-ordination work assignment from his provincial. He was to support Lord as the public relations manager for The Queen's Work and the coordinator for the SSCA.

How are we to imagine the excitement with which Father Ed took the news of his Queen's Work assignment? An anecdote relayed by one of his friends may provide a clue.

The story comes via Sam Lambert, a Protestant staff member of the *St. Louis Post-Dispatch*. Two years after Father Ed's death, Lambert wrote to the Jesuit provincial to suggest that Dowling be considered for sainthood. He related several examples of Father Ed's humility, the last of which was rather mysterious:

> Father Dowling once said that his condition—he called it arthritis—may have had its origin when he entered the priesthood and, early in it, was given a position or task that he prized but had hardly considered himself a possible candidate. He was extremely

elated, and this emotional response, he said, may have had something to do with his condition.[23]

At first glance, Lambert's account of Dowling's words does not appear
to make sense, because its timeline is off; Father Ed's arthritis began well
before he became a priest. But if we assume that Dowling was referring not
to the *origin* of his arthritis but rather to its *intensification*—then this story
sheds light on not one but two significant events in his life: his acquisition
of the Queen's Work assignment ("a position or task that he prized but had
hardly considered himself a possible candidate") and the health news he received after.

To appreciate the story's full significance, it is important first to understand what Father Ed meant when he told Lambert he was "extremely
elated" upon receiving the new position. Although Lambert did not realize
it, Father Ed, who had deeply internalized the Bible's teachings on suffering,
was referring to St. Paul's words in 2 Corinthians 12 about being afflicted
with some type of infirmity: "And to keep me from being too elated by the
abundance of revelations, a thorn was given me in the flesh, a messenger of
Satan, to harass me, to keep me from being too elated" (2 Cor 12:17 RSV).

As the scripture passage continues, Paul explains how God brought
him to understand that the "thorn" that so grieved him was in fact an invitation to grow in grace:

> Three times I besought the Lord about this, that it should leave me;
> but he said to me, "My grace is sufficient for you, for my power is
> made perfect in weakness." I will all the more gladly boast of my
> weaknesses, that the power of Christ may rest upon me. For the
> sake of Christ, then, I am content with weaknesses, insults, hard-
> ships, persecutions, and calamities; for when I am weak, then I am
> strong. [2 Cor 12:8–10]

If that verse is what Father Ed had in mind when he told Lambert about
his feelings upon gaining the Queen's Work assignment, then it is possible
to understand why he said "this emotional response...may have had something to do with his condition." To keep Father Ed from being too elated,
God sent him a thorn—permitting his arthritis to intensify to the point
where, for the first time, doctors pronounced it incurable.

Father Ed learned the true seriousness of his condition in October
1933—only a few months after he started at The Queen's Work. Dr. Arthur
Krida, a specialist whom Dowling saw while in New York, detailed his
opinion in a letter:

Your condition is called spondylitis deformans,[24] a process which results in the stiffening of the spine and the stiffening of the joints between the ribs and the spine. This latter has the effect of impairing your respiratory activity and is in itself a matter of great importance with regard to your future welfare.

I would strongly advise you to make your home and do your work in a dry, sunshiney climate without too great altitude, such as is afforded in Arizona or New Mexico. This will not only serve to relieve you of your discomfort, but it will give you the best opportunity of resisting any respiratory infection, which in your case would be rather more serious than with the average individual....

I hope you will let me know where you eventually settle and how you get on.[25]

Krida's apparent confidence that Father Ed would take his advice and move south is not surprising, given the conditions in St. Louis at that time. The city was famous for having the sootiest air in the nation, due largely to the type of cheap coal that was burned by industries and homes.[26]

But Father Ed had no intention of moving. The Queen's Work was where he believed God had placed him. His task now, he felt, was to be like St. Paul and live with his thorn, trusting that God's power would be made perfect in weakness.

At The Queen's Work, Father Ed had the joy of working for and with a boss who was a true kindred spirit. "Father Lord," in the words of a fellow Jesuit who worked with him,

> thought of his staff as a family. He never tried to mold them into a tightly disciplined team. He let each pursue his own special interest and talents in addition to sodality promotion. He encouraged his co-workers to collaborate with existing associations in a wide variety of fields. He was one of the first business leaders in the community to breach the color bar, an accepted part of local life at the time. He urged the formation of a credit union among the lay staff.[27]

The atmosphere at The Queen's Work was thus ideal for a creative person with Dowling's qualities of strong initiative, diverse interests, a love of social justice, and a desire to engage with people from a variety of backgrounds, races, and even faiths. At a time when ecumenism was regarded with suspicion in official Catholic circles, both Lord and Dowling frequently joined with Protestant and Jewish leaders to speak out publicly on social-justice issues.

In addition, although Jesuits made up the executive leadership of The Queen's Work, Father Lord made it a point to involve lay staff, both men and women, on an equal level wherever possible. And, at a time when nuns rarely left the convent to attend institutes or conventions, he encouraged nuns to participate in the Summer School of Catholic Action.[28] Father Ed once observed that "the greatest thing Father Lord ever did was to discover the American nun."[29]

As Father Ed began work as publicity manager for The Queen's Work, he eagerly set about renewing his old contacts in the St. Louis newspaper world. They in turn were eager to reconnect with him and to draw upon his organizational expertise as they embarked upon a new enterprise: founding a local chapter of the newly established American Newspaper Guild. Father Ed was honored when the St. Louis Newspaper Guild invited him to join as an at-large member. In years to come, he would assist the guild by representing it at regional and national meetings—thereby saving it money as well, since as a clergyman he could travel the rails at half fare.

In June 1934, Father Ed's travels took him to Chicago, where, in addition to reconnecting with some of his former students, he met up with his old friend Henry Kinealy to visit the 1934 World's Fair, "A Century of Progress." Kinealy would later recall that Father Ed was fascinated by one of the attractions at the Ripley's Believe It or Not Odditorium: Harry J. Overdurff, billed as "Ossified Harry, the Man Who Turned to 'Stone.'"[30] Father Ed returned several times to ask Harry questions about his illness, as he feared (mistakenly)[31] that he was suffering the same ailment.

Contemporary accounts of Overdurff describe a man whose attitude toward his condition would have made a deep impression upon Dowling. Although his sufferings were clearly far worse than Father Ed's, he maintained a bright and peaceful disposition. A reporter who met him a few months later called him "a model of patience and philosophy."

> Weighing originally 165 pounds, he is now a piece of human concrete weighing seventy pounds. Yet he has no aches and pains, bodily or spiritually. He takes his affliction on the chin and says he enjoys himself, as going from place to place he meets so many pleasant people. . . . One can never forget the genial twinkle of his dark mountain eyes, or the cheery optimism of his voice.[32]

The image of this warm-hearted man remained with Dowling. In later years, he would often joke that he was "turning to stone" or that he was becoming his own tombstone.

Now that Father Ed was coordinating the Summer School of Catholic Action, the event became larger in every way—more lecturers, more courses, and a more comprehensive range of social-justice topics covered during its six days. One of those who attended the SSCA in New York City during that 1934 season was Dorothy Day, who just the previous year had begun the Catholic Worker movement with Peter Maurin. Through her work promoting peace, nonviolence, and a radical, Gospel-inspired commitment to serving Christ in the poor, Day would eventually be recognized as one of the twentieth century's greatest lay Catholic activists.

Day likely met Father Ed for the first time at the New York City SSCA; either he or Father Lord convinced her to give a talk about her apostolate. Decades later, Day recalled the event as the first time she learned about many of the areas of social justice that she would champion in the *Catholic Worker*:

> It was there I first heard of cooperatives and credit unions and of the liturgy[33] and it was there, too, that I first saw enthusiasm. It was like a revival in a way, but it was not emotional, but of the mind. Good food for the mind and heart was dispensed with ready generosity, and one could not help but respond. It was there I was first persuaded to speak,[34] and I was so petrified with fear that I sat in the chapel (too weak to kneel) saying the *Memorare* over and over again until one o'clock when my time came, and lo and behold, I've been doing it ever since, though always with qualms. But if you love your brother, you want to talk to him, to convey to him, too, some of your enthusiasm.

Father Ed became good friends with Day and Maurin and made it a point to connect with them when he traveled; both of them visited him in St. Louis as well. Day referred to him in a 1945 column as "our dear Jesuit friend, Father Dowling, who often has often come to us and talked to us of proportional representation."[35]

Father Ed had been at The Queen's Work for just over a year when, in September 1934, he had to take ten months off for his tertianship, the last stage of Jesuit formation. At that time, the Missouri Province's tertianship was at St. Stanislaus in Cleveland, Ohio, a four-story brick building that doubled as a laymen's retreat house when the tertians were away. Coincidentally, just six years later, Sister Ignatia—"the Angel of Alcoholics Anonymous"— would begin sending recovering alcoholics for retreats to that very house.[36]

The tertianship is directed toward helping the Jesuit enter more deeply into the Christ-centered spirituality that is to ground his ministry, so that his priestly actions will spring from a heart that loves like Christ's. As part of this "school of love" (as the tertianship has been called),[37] the Jesuit makes the Spiritual Exercises for thirty days—his first Long Retreat since the novitiate.

A letter Father Ed wrote to his sister Mary in early November shows how seriously he sought to enter into the spirit of the tertianship.

> The Long Retreat was calm and simple. No strain. Devotion to the Sacred Heart, against which I had a confused prejudice (as complicating and distracting from devotion to the Person of Christ and [the] Blessed Sacrament) took on a new value....
>
> Frustrations and ineptitudes are so prominent in my pattern that humility should be easy (though vanity is such a resourceful intruder). And the Exercises put humility as among the highest moral achievements—so fertile a soil for Love. I am counting much on Christ's promise to make tepid souls fervent if they are devoted to his Sacred Heart. I wish I could be more faithful in this matter. It simplifies.

Father Ed's admission of his "frustrations and ineptitudes" presages his later comment to a clergy conference on alcoholism, "You and I know that in the depths of humiliation we are in a natural area."[38] His tertian experience helped him understand more deeply how he needed God's grace to raise him out of his natural shortcomings and into the realm of supernatural love.

In June 1935, Father Ed returned to The Queen's Work with renewed zeal, eager to collaborate with Father Lord in promoting Catholic social teaching. It was around this time that he began using a cane for balance, since his disease had progressed to the point where his hips had become uneven. Yet he continued to have such great physical energy that somehow, in his hands, the cane became a symbol of perpetual motion rather than infirmity. When he gave lectures at the blackboard at the Summer School of Catholic Action, it made a handy pointer.

Once the SSCA's season was done, Lord, for his part, wasted no time in engaging Dowling as a close collaborator in a new initiative: Social Order Mondays, a fall lecture series at the St. Louis University Auditorium. The series was an ideal vehicle for Lord's and Dowling's talents as charismatic communicators who believed that Catholic social teaching offered solutions to the problems of communism, materialistic capitalism, and the threat of dictatorship. It proved wildly popular, with a total of eight thousand people attending its ten lectures.

Father Ed participated in four Social Order Mondays, giving two lectures on his own and participating in two debates with Father Lord. He viewed his lectures as precious opportunities to tutor audiences about proportional representation, and so he planned them in sequence. In the first, "Is Democracy Doomed?", he would lay out the flaws in American democracy that proportional representation sought to solve. Part two would be "Votes the Bosses Fear," in which he would outline the process by which proportional representation could be introduced into a city.

Whether or not Father Ed's audience grasped the intricacies of the complex voting system that he sought to describe for them, they surely enjoyed the original way he presented it. In "Is Democracy Doomed?," he sought to counter the prevailing wisdom that dated the "crawl toward democracy" to ancient Greece, which in fact denied the vote to most of its population. Democracy's true origin, Father Ed said, lay in the Sermon on the Mount:

> The Apostles had asked Christ how to deal with God, or as the ecclesiastical slang has it, "How shall we pray?" Slang is such a lazy obscuring thing. The God-Man told them two things. First, not to pray as an individual, "My Father—*Me und Gott*," but rather as a social, polite or political group—"Our Father"—and, in defining this social or political arrangement in dealing with Him, he counseled avoiding monarchic forms of address. "My Father and my subjects' step-Father" or "My step-Father and my most serene corpulence's Father"—no, just "Our Father." The purest human soul God ever created and the one closest to God Himself can say no more, and the lousiest human skunk that ever lived need not, due to the awful mystery of God's love, say less. Any other basis of distinction, be it Mayflower passage, pigmentary coloration, or Dun & Bradstreet rating—any other distinction you can mention in comparison to this basis of relationship of our common Father

doesn't mean a damn and it doesn't mean a Beatitude, if I may use scriptural language.[39]

Priests did not speak that way in 1935. Father Ed, with his streetwise humor and journalist's gift for wordplay, had a remarkable talent for conveying orthodox truths in a way that made them seem as up-to-the-minute as tomorrow's editorial page.

With "Votes the Bosses Fear," Father Ed criticized Father Charles Coughlin and other prominent figures, accusing them of proposing superficial economic fixes for problems that required deep changes in the political system:

> You remember the experiment in your physics laboratory in which a plate of glass about two feet square was sprinkled with iron filings, underneath which was placed a strong electromagnet. The iron filings are wealth. The electromagnet is political power. The more you fidget with those filings or that glass, the more concentrated do those filings become right over the electromagnet.
>
> Now, almost without exception, all the men who are urging cures for our present depression, the Communist and the Capitalist, Hoover and Stalin and Long[40] and Coughlin are all fooling with some arrangement of those iron filings without getting down to that magnet. The way to distribute those filings and keep them distributed equitably is to break up that electromagnet into many (125,000,000 in this country) electromagnets equitably distributed under the glass. Power is more basic than pelf,[41] the state more fundamental than industry, and politics more radical than economics. And that is the reason why in that great central sentence in that great encyclical *Quadragesimo anno*, Pius XI says, "When we speak of the reform of the social order, it is principally the state we have in mind."[42]

Father Ed clearly put his heart into writing "Votes the Bosses Fear." It is worth examining this lecture closely, as it gives us the best insight into his political philosophy. He is greatly concerned with the rights of Black people and other minorities, of women, of the poor, and—most of all—the right of all the people to determine how their government is to represent them.

At a time when the United States was struggling to emerge from the Great Depression, Father Ed argued that the Catholic faithful were morally obligated to use their vote to remedy social ills:

Except for those who can't see the forest for the trees and except for those who think that God created depraved hearts that must await human education to make them fit, there is only one answer to our social problem and that is that money is not equitably and justly distributed. Oh, we make jerry-built adjustments like old-age doles to old-age wrecks, paid for by a sales tax that hits the poor sixty times harder than it hits the wealthy. We cry peace, peace, and there is no peace.[43] And the Holy Father from the watchtower of the world warns men that "conditions have come to such a pass that vast numbers of men can only with the greatest difficulty attend to the one thing necessary."

This question of distribution of money, apparently an economic question, is radically a political question. We will never share the wealth until we share the political power. And a political share is called a vote. And voting is an official duty of every member of the state. Catholics know or should know that, except for the invincibly ignorant, one can sin by not voting....

What is a vote? A vote and the possession of voting power is as true and sacred as the possession of wealth, and there will come a day when we'll answer for its use.[44]

Father Ed assailed elections in St. Louis, "with their lack of secret ballot [and] their practical disenfranchisement of great sections of the poor," and in the United States in general. He proposed three improvements. The third, which was in line with the proportional-representation plan that he sought, has yet to take off nationally, but the first two are familiar today: "First, suffrage should be dropped to 18 years old. Second, we should have registered-mail voting instead of polling-place voting. Third, we should have weighted voting."[45]

The goal of proportional representation, Father Ed explained, was true representation, which meant representation of women, of racial minorities, and of all the other groups that constitute the voting populace. "The Board of Aldermen of St. Louis should represent, mirror, St. Louis," he said. "Suppose I had a mirror that always left off 11 percent of my face. Our Board of Aldermen has never represented our Negro population."[46]

Father Ed added that that the Board of Aldermen consisted entirely of Democrats, and so failed to represent the 50 percent of St. Louisans who were either Republican, Independent, or Socialist. "Here we are dealing not with representation but with caricature," he said.

And the price of caricature is revulsion by the caricatured. Our election method is really a rejection method, and the rejected pay in kind by obstruction and rejection. Hoover smearing Roosevelt, as the Democrats smeared Hoover, and the country suffers a perpetual civil war, which you think is bloodless, because you don't count the suicides, the starvations, and the abortions.[47]

It is striking that Father Ed chose to identify abortions (which were then a felony in every U.S. state) among the symptoms of a society that failed to care for the poor. He did not see the problem of abortion as an isolated issue but rather as part of an entire culture of political dysfunction that Catholics were obligated to counter.[48]

As Father Ed wound down the lecture, he encouraged his listeners to have faith that they could effect positive political change. "Hammer away at the weaknesses of the present system and people will back into good things even as you and I will back into heaven trying to keep out of hell."[49]

Already the image of backing into heaven had become a trademark phrase for Father Ed. Although he used it as a laugh line, it expressed something fundamental about his personality—a recognition that God's grace was active even in his most difficult, painful, and humiliating experiences.

Father Ed's interests in democracy and Catholic social teaching and his reporter's gift for making connections led him to cross paths with many of the era's leading voices for social justice. January 1936 saw him having lunch at Catholic Worker associate Dorothy Weston Coddington's home in Manhattan, where guests included Jacques Maritain and Dorothy Day. Father Ed wrote in a report to Father Lord, "Through a Fordham University interpreter—Maritain knew very little English—we discussed papal encyclicals, continental social doctrines, democracy, corporative state, etc."[50]

It would be wrong to assume that, because Father Ed associated with many progressives, his views comported neatly with the Catholic progressivism of yesterday or today. As with many Irish-Americans of his generation, his opposition to American involvement in European wars stemmed not from pacifism so much as isolationism. That same attraction to isolationism drew him to Senator Joseph McCarthy, whom he appreciated as "a catalyst for the anti-Ivy Leaguers, for the populace, for the Anglophobes, for the non-interventionists."[51]And he raised his voice against communist efforts to gain control of labor unions—and this despite maintaining a warm friendship with Simon W. (Si) Gerson, the former *Daily Worker* reporter who was the Communist Party USA's leading expert on electoral politics.

With that said, many of Father Ed's public comments from this period reveal an imagination well ahead of its time. In his "Is Democracy Doomed?" lecture, he argued that the American Revolution failed to bring true democracy, in part because "it wasn't a vertical revolution—the rising of poor against rich." Instead, he said, it was a horizontal revolution in which "aristocrats like Hamilton and Charles Carroll and Baron de Kalb, and slave-master Washington and Count Pulaski and banker [Robert] Morris [Jr.] fought against Rothschild's Hessian cattle and the lowest of the Cockney rabble."[52] Although Father Ed's frank analysis of the Founding Fathers—particularly his criticism of George Washington as an aristocrat and slave-master—would not be out of place today, in 1935 it would have struck listeners as edgy, if not outright shocking.

Similarly, despite his opposition to communism, Father Ed did not hesitate to speak out against the threats that right-wing ideologies posed to the Catholic Church's witness. In December 1936, he and Father Lord each addressed a capacity crowd of 2,200 at Rochester, New York's Columbus Civic Auditorium in an evening titled "The Catholic Faces Communism." Although a local Catholic newspaper headlined its account of the evening "Jesuits Riddle Red Flag of Communism," and certainly that was the event's general thrust, Father Ed's comments were, as usual, nuanced—and prophetic:

> Answering the question as to whether the Church favors Fascism, Father Dowling quoted the Rev. James M. Gillis, the noted Paulist, who said that within the next century it will have been established that the Catholic Church has "suffered more from the friendship of Fascism than from the enmity of Communism."[53]

The Rochester event was part of a move by Lord and Dowling in 1936 to expand their popular Social Order Monday lectures to other cities, including Chicago and Detroit. In St. Louis, the series continued with events such as "The United States Will Have Dictatorship by 1941," a debate between Lord and Dowling. Father Lord argued in the affirmative; having recently visited Europe, he was pessimistic that democracy would survive in the polarized U.S. political climate. But Dowling could never lose hope in democracy. The *St. Louis Star-Times* captured some of the pair's exchanges:

Dowling: "The point is the United States sets the fashions. It's sixty years ahead, whether in autos, vice, or economics. It's tempting to describe everything by a cycle theory. We see the tides, the seasons, and so on, but where human nature is concerned, cycles may not apply. I believe in history proceeding in a straight line; I'm a fundamentalist. I believe the first great democratic idea was the Sermon on the Mount, which leveled emperors and the lowliest, and that the direction of history—so far as democracy is concerned—has from that day been straight and up."

Lord: "Democracy is the most difficult form of government ever attempted. The world has come to distrust it. If the currents now prevailing continue, a dictatorship is inevitable."

As always, Father Ed's faith in democracy didn't mean he believed the U.S. political system was above criticism.

Dowling: "We should end, first of all, the separation of power [between the legislative, executive, and judicial branches of government]. It won't work. I think the movement to abolish the Supreme Court is a healthy one."

Lord: "Goodbye, Constitution; goodbye, Supreme Court; hello, fascism. Frankly, I can no more think of our getting along without a Supreme Court than I can think of a baseball game without an umpire."

Dowling: "It seems to me that, like the crawfish, we progress toward democracy backward. I've always said the only way I'll get to heaven is by backing out of hell.... We should stop reading about the hoodlums in Europe and make ourselves part of the irresistible tide of democracy—irresistible because of Him who started it."[54]

"Hoodlums" was a favorite term of Father Ed's for European dictators and their political parties. Before the decade's end, it would get him into trouble.

Although it was not until Father Ed began to work with Alcoholics Anonymous during the 1940s that he became widely known for helping people with problems, in the 1930s many people already looked to him as a lifeline. It is difficult to uncover examples of his pastoral accompaniment from that period, because those who approached him usually were troubled about some private matter that would cause them shame if it were known. There is, however, a folder of correspondence in the Dowling Archive that gives a fascinating window into the great lengths to which Father Ed went to help people resolve a crisis.

The parents of "Carl,"[55] one of Father Ed's former students from Loyola Academy, were supporting his studies in an elite and highly demanding graduate program at an East Coast university—on condition that he would not marry until he graduated. But Carl and his girlfriend "Susie," who lived with her parents in Chicago, decided they couldn't wait. So they secretly wed during Carl's Thanksgiving break—but, being observant Catholics, they followed canon law and were married by a priest in a church rectory.

At the time of their clandestine nuptials, the couple optimistically imagined they could find a way to make their long-distance union work until Carl graduated. But once the reality of being husband and wife sank in, their frustration at being unable to live together became unbearable. Making matters worse, Susie's mother learned of the wedding and was furious at Carl for refusing to publicly acknowledge the marriage. She urged her daughter to have the marriage annulled.

And so, in February 1937, Susie poured out her problems to Father Ed in a tear-stained letter. "Dear Father," she pleaded, "my respect for your judgment is, at this point, the only thing I can cling to as a possible means of unraveling this mess. Please write me."

Within a week of receiving Susie's letter, Father Ed was at a soda fountain in Chicago's Union Station with Carl and Susie, working out their problems over hot-fudge sundaes. That was Father Ed's normal mode of operation: when one of his "Loyola boys" was in trouble, his first instinct was to make the five-hour train ride from St. Louis, meet with the former student at the station, and then catch a train back home.[56]

Dowling worked out a tentative plan with the couple: Carl would try to convince his father to accede to his and Susie's marrying. If that could be accomplished, then perhaps the Archdiocese of Chicago might permit the couple to have a "nuptial" Mass at which they would renew the vows they had already made. To Carl's parents, and to Susie's father as well, it would appear to be an actual wedding. Only the couple themselves, Susie's mother, and the priest would know it was a renewal.

Carl followed through on Father Ed's suggestion and managed to gain his father's permission to wed. But there remained the question of whether the rest of Father Ed's plan was permissible under canon law. Father Ed therefore wrote to the Missouri Province's foremost liturgical expert, Gerald Ellard, SJ, a professor at St. Mary's College.

"May I lean on your kindness," Father Ed began, "for some information which is a mixture of canon law, moral theology, and fast foot-work?"

Dowling proceeded to explain the couple's dilemma, adding, "I, of course, would favor making a clean breast to the parents, but I suspect that there is a good deal to the contention of the young man that any chance of help, financial, from the folks would be blasted by a revelation of the elopement."

Father Ellard, after consulting an authority in canon law, responded with a hearty *"nihil obstat"* ("nothing stands in the way"): "They may go through the whole ceremony, understanding, however, that they are already married, and regarding it as a sort of renovation and completion."

That should have settled the issue—but it didn't. Once Father Ellard's reply made it back to Father Ed, and through him to Carl and Susie, and through them to their pastor, and through him to the lead canonist of the Archdiocese of Chicago, a new problem came up. The canonist was scandalized at the idea of the couple's renewing their vows during a nuptial Mass—and was not convinced when the pastor told him, "Some priest from St. Louis, a Jesuit, says it's okay."

When Father Ed learned of the archdiocesan canonist's opposition, he did not give up. Instead, he turned his efforts towards approaching the resident canon-law expert at the Archdiocese of Chicago's Mundelein Seminary in hope that he might believe that the vow renewal would be permissible. After all, the Archdiocese couldn't say no if its highest academic authority supported the idea. Thankfully, Father Ed knew a sympathetic Chicago Jesuit, Father Martin Carrabine, SJ, who was willing to make the hourlong car trip from the Windy City to Mundelein to sound out the seminary's canonist.

In reading Father Ed's correspondence with Carl and Susie during what proved to be a lengthy saga, four things stand out that are emblematic of his outreach to those who came to him with problems. There is, first of all, Father Ed's strong initiative; he does not delay reaching out to the couple in crisis. Second is his resourcefulness in discerning creative solutions. Then there is his inexhaustible warmth. He never displays the slightest hint of impatience with the couple, even though many other responsibilities make demands upon his time.

Finally, there is Father Ed's deeply felt desire that Carl and Susie use their crisis as an occasion to grow in intimacy with Jesus. As with the letters he wrote to his brother Paul and sister Anna when they were going through difficult times, he urges the couple to receive Holy Communion daily. Typical are these lines from a letter Father Ed wrote to Carl and Susie:

> There have been sacrifices and hardships in the past months, and there may be some in the next weeks, but I feel sure that as the months and years roll on, you will never want to have been without them, because it has welded you two so much closer together, and you both closer to the Divine Lord. [...]
>
> I really feel unable to worry, as long as I hear that [Susie] is going to daily Communion. I do hope that [Carl] makes a daily visit, at least.[57] [...]
>
> [Carl] promises the first boy to the Jesuits if this goes through. That promise I would like to amend to permission for the boy or girl—whichever is the first one—to marry their choice, when or if. Twenty years from now, you will understand your parents better. [...]
>
> I know that if you keep praying, everything will be all right and will be all right in a measure of which you can't dream. As the time narrows down, do keep me in touch with developments.
>
> I assure you that you make me very happy in sharing with me this trial and your plans. May the Holy Family bless you both.

All told, it took Father Ed more than three months of phone calls and correspondence to resolve Carl and Susie's crisis. But he did it, and they had their vow renewal under the guise of a nuptial Mass. The couple remained together for nearly six decades, until Carl's death, and had several children.

One night in May 1937, during a visit to the New York City area for Queen's Work business, Father Ed found himself at dinner with two of the country's most popular newspaper columnists and their wives: Westbrook Pegler, who played host at his home in Fairfield, Connecticut, and Heywood Broun.

The newsmen were wildly opposite in both politics and personality; Pegler was an acid-tongued, anti-Roosevelt reactionary, whereas Broun was a gregarious, progressive social-justice crusader who championed the New Deal. Yet they had managed to forge a shaky friendship over their shared background in sports journalism, and they often met for dinner and poker.

Father Ed would write in his travel report for Father Lord that he "talked over the national and labor situations" with the two columnists. Broun, who was raised Episcopalian but was married to a Catholic, was intrigued to hear a Jesuit priest speak so astutely about democracy and labor—even about the Newspaper Guild, of which Broun was president and co-founder. Years later, Pegler would remember the dinner as the night when Broun "really pricked up his ears for the first time" to consider the Catholic Church's perspective.[58]

Over the next couple of years, Broun became increasingly interested in the Catholic understanding of what was then called "the brotherhood of man."[59] In January 1939, while vacationing in Florida, he told a Catholic friend, Al "Hollywood" McCosker, that he was looking for a priest to help him study the catechism.[60]

Once McCosker caught his breath, he offered to connect Broun with the then-Monsignor (later Archbishop) Fulton J. Sheen once the journalist returned to his Connecticut home. But before McCosker had a chance to introduce him to the monsignor, Broun had a conversation with another priest—one that would mark the turning point in his journey into the Catholic Church.

On February 6, Broun stopped in St. Louis to meet with Father Ed. The columnist was traveling home from San Antonio, where he had gone to interview a Jesuit pastor, Father Carmelo A. Tranchese, who was receiving death threats over his advocacy for fair housing.

Father Ed ventured out to see Broun at the Statler Hotel and spent five or six hours speaking with him and answering his questions.[61] A month later, Broun recounted the main thrust of their conversation in one of his columns, referring to Father Ed as "a newspaper friend of mine who is now a priest."

> I said to him that I wanted to know if there was anything in Catholicism which stood in the way of any person who believed in political and economic progressivism. And my friend smiled and answered: "Don't you realize that you're a little naïve, Heywood? You like to call yourself a radical, but the doctrines of the Church to which I belong imply so many deep changes in human relationship that when they are accomplished—and they will be—your own notions will be nothing more than an outmoded pink liberalism."[62]

Shortly after Broun returned home from St. Louis, the call came from Monsignor Sheen. The monsignor found him eager to receive instruction in the Catholic faith. Surely he was the easiest convert that the celebrated evangelist ever made.

Initially Broun met weekly with Sheen, but soon he asked if they could meet twice as often, so that he might complete his instruction as soon as possible. "I have a strong premonition of death," he explained.[63] It was a surprising statement, given that he was only fifty years old and did not have any serious illness.

In May, Archibald MacLeish invited Broun to Harvard to witness a new educational experiment that he was helping guide there—the Nieman Fellowship, a yearlong learning opportunity for working journalists. Broun arrived in time to attend a May 11 dinner MacLeish hosted for the Fellows, where he became fast friends with Edwin A. Lahey, star reporter for the *Chicago Daily News*.

The two afterwards disappeared for a few days. Lahey's classmates assumed they spent it consuming copious amounts of alcohol and swapping stories of journalistic exploits.[64] Although there was truth in that—some of Lahey's anecdotes turned up in Broun's next column[65]—in fact, the men had other things to discuss as well. Lahey, unlike many newspaper reporters of his stature, was a prayerful Catholic—and a longtime friend of Father Ed.

Was it, then, mere coincidence that Broun connected with Lahey? Or did Father Ed speak with him before his Harvard trip and urge him to seek Lahey out, knowing that the Chicago newsman would encourage him in his Catholic journey?[66]

Broun was received into the Catholic Church on May 24, 1939. He made his first Holy Communion four days later on Pentecost Sunday—and died of pneumonia a week before Christmas.

Two months after Broun's death, Father Ed paid tribute to him in a lecture in St. Louis. As he recounted his late friend's political and religious shifts, he said,

Yet through all these years, there was a consistency that lesser men missed. He loved his fellow man, and like true love, it burned in pity when that fellow man was the underdog. Too sincere to make the right-wing mistake of thinking that inaction meant security, he did for a time fall into the left-wing delusion that extremism is true radicalism.

   It was Catholicity in the role of the underdog, I suspect, that first made a challenging appeal to Heywood Broun. It found there a nostalgic longing for the peace he had learned in his Episcopalianism.[67]

How typical of Father Ed to acknowledge subtly—and subversively for a Catholic priest in those days before Vatican II—that Episcopalians too knew something of the peace of Christ!

Father Ed's friendships with newspaper journalists ensured that wherever he lectured, a reporter was there to cover the event. Knowing his strong opinions, his searing wit, and his sheer fearlessness, they could be confident of returning to the newsroom with a good story.

At the August 1939 Summer School of Catholic Action in Washington, DC, a *Washington Post* reporter (whose name has not come down to us) decided, rather than going to the official lectures, simply to follow Father Ed around until he said something headline-worthy. And Dowling did not disappoint. The next day's *Post* featured the headline on page six, column one, "U.S. 'Elective Monarchy,' Says Cleric." Not until readers made it to the second paragraph did they find that Father Ed made his comments "to a small group of schoolgirls from Richmond, Va., who had 'cut' the afternoon seminar of the Summer School of Catholic Action [...] to discuss student government with him."[68] It is difficult to imagine another Catholic priest, either in 1939 or today, who could gain feature coverage in the U.S. capital's largest daily for remarks made on politics to high-school students.

Unbeknownst to Father Ed, however, the *Post* reporter wasn't the only person tracking what he said at the SSCA. Shortly after he returned to St. Louis, his provincial's assistant forwarded him a letter from Mother Mary Angela, SND, provincial superior of the Sisters of Notre Dame in Covington, Kentucky. The nun was greatly disturbed by a report she received from a member of her religious order who was present at one of Father Ed's talks.

"Upon me devolves the very unpleasant task of making a complaint," Mother Mary Angela wrote to the provincial, Father Peter Brooks, SJ:

At the School of Catholic Action which convened in Washington recently, Father Dowling made the most derogatory remarks about our [high] school, our system of student government, our Congregation. He made these remarks publicly at the session on student government.

With regard to the congregation itself, Mother Mary Angela claimed Father Ed said, "The [Sisters of Notre Dame] community is not prosperous, the Motherhouse is in Germany but has been removed to Holland. In fact, one of the Sisters has been in jail for four years for smuggling money out of the country."[69]

It was the mention of the jailed nun that particularly irked the mother superior:

> Worse still is the disclosure of a situation of which very few people are aware, and about which the Sisters do not even speak among themselves. It is entirely uncalled-for. What has the imprisonment of a Sister abroad to do with student government here?[70]

The provincial's assistant, in forwarding Mother Mary Angela's letter to Father Ed, asked that Dowling reply to the provincial rather than directly to the nun.

Father Ed began his response with a tone that neared, but did not quite reach, contrition: "I am quite distressed that a friend of Notre Dame Academy feels that I spoke in derogatory manner about a school to which I am attached and indebted, and I am sending you this explanation at your request."[71]

The mother superior's allegations were not entirely unjustified. Father Ed admitted he had indeed made some offhand comments that could be taken as disparaging the Sisters of Notre Dame's high school, as when he commented that it had narrow stairwells. But, he said, he had only praise for its student government, which, by bestowing practical experience in democracy, was "preparing the girls against dictatorship."

Finally, Father Ed addressed the main issue of Mother Mary Angela's complaint. He explained that, during his visits to the high school, administrators told him that Adolf Hitler had jailed an elderly nun of their German motherhouse for sending money out of the country to pay community debts. His intention in highlighting her story was not to embarrass the Sisters of Notre Dame but rather to praise the congregation's prisoner as a model for students.

> Her plight is a slow martyrdom for Christ at the hands of [an] anti-democratic state, and I do think the firsthand experience the community has with anti-democracy throws a strong light on their work for democracy through the tool of student government. If student government is merely for a faculty to make a

school function, then there is little connection between a nun in jail and it, but if it [is] viewed as an educational laboratory to train girls to be effective against the jailing of priests and nuns, there seems to be a connection with and an inspiration in the story of this heroic nun.[72]

The contrast between Mother Mary Angela's embarrassment over the imprisoned nun and Father Ed's admiration of her "slow martyrdom for Christ" reveals the extent to which Dowling was ahead of the political drift of many U.S. Catholics at the time. During those weeks after Mussolini and Hitler's "Pact of Steel" and before Nazi Germany's invasion of Poland, many in the U.S. church were uncomfortable calling attention to Nazi persecution of Catholics. But Father Ed didn't hesitate to condemn injustice wherever it appeared. And he saw clearly that, where it did appear, civil disobedience—and the willingness to suffer the consequences—was a vital part of Christian witness.

Five months later, in January 1940, Father Ed was again called to explain comments he had made against European dictators. This time, the complaint came from the provincial himself.

The controversy stemmed from an aside Father Ed made in a November 1939 speech to the National Municipal League on proportional representation. In the course of criticizing party government as practiced in the United States, Father Ed said he thought "the hoodlum parties of Europe" were "vicious."[73] After he gave the speech, he adapted it into an article that ran in one of The Queen's Work's publications.

Although several U.S. dailies ran an Associated Press story on the speech, Father Brooks took no notice until he read a news item in the London Catholic paper *The Universe* quoting Father Ed's ensuing article.[74] It was one thing for Dowling to point out the dysfunctions of American and European governments from the safety of a midwestern lecture hall. But when his comments were published in Europe, they risked turning global sentiment against the Society of Jesus.

And so, Father Ed was called in by Father Brooks and ordered to write a letter explaining himself once more. In his ensuing letter, he showed even greater boldness than he had in his response to Mother Mary Angela, arguing that the U.S. church had a duty to speak boldly against threats to democracy both at home and abroad.

Dowling did concede one point: his phrase "hoodlum parties" was "indefensible on the point of tact."[75] But he added, "I do think worse things have been said by reputable priests [about] the National Socialists and the Bolshevik parties."

Given the political situation, Father Ed wrote, perhaps tact should not be the Church's primary concern:

> Untactful remarks do a great deal of harm. Tactful silences, however, can get frighteningly like the tactful omission described by Christ in his picture of the Last Judgment.[76] . . .
>
> As any Jesuit, I desire to do whatever Superiors wish in this matter. I regret adding worries to your already arduous responsibility. I ask that what I write be construed as requested exposition and not as argumentative defense. I believe that the issue raised may well become important.

Father Ed's closing words to the provincial were unyielding and prophetic: "Surely, on a thousand fronts, today, Christian social concepts will shock and disturb and always be folly and a stumbling block to some." Here was a priest unafraid to "shock and disturb" listeners with the social teachings of the Church.

PART II

A PRIEST FOR PEOPLE WITH PROBLEMS

8

⊷ↄ⌒∾

Finding fellowship

The A.A. program is a slow seeping of God into the thirsty soul of the alcoholic.

— Father Ed[1]

At the start of 1940, although Father Ed did his best to maintain his usual cheerful disposition, the world weighed heavily upon his increasingly stooped shoulders.

The first recent blow to Dowling's well-being was self-inflicted—a missed opportunity to improve his health. Just over a month earlier, after the Thanksgiving holiday, Father Ed had caught a train to San Antonio to escape St. Louis's smoke pollution, which had gotten so bad that drivers had to use their headlights at midday. Upon his arrival, he checked into a local Catholic hospital, where he was put under the care of a doctor who claimed that, given three months, he could arrest Father Ed's arthritis.

The doctor's optimism intrigued Father Ed. He wrote about it in his travel report to Father Lord, venturing that perhaps he could renew his railroad pass and commute down to San Antonio twice a month for treatment.[2]

Father Lord's reply was swift and forceful, as though he felt he must seize the moment in the hope that, for once, Father Ed—who seemed always to be on the move—would pause and put his health first.

"I guess that crack about the pass and the necessity for a return was meant as a joke," Lord wrote. "If so," he added,

> it ain't no joke. YOU STAY until you feel it's just what you've gone to get....Take your time. There is no job as important right now as your giving the doctor a chance to work on you and with you. SO TAKE IT EASY...and stay on just as long as you feel you are getting good...days or weeks or months...And the pass stuff is a mere waste of words.

Let me know how it all progresses, and God bless and keep you always.[3]

But by the time Father Lord's letter reached Santa Rosa Hospital, it was too late. Father Ed had already caught the Missouri Pacific Railroad's Sunshine Special back to sooty St. Louis. The temptation to take time out for himself had passed. There were people with problems who needed to see him, and talks on proportional representation lined up that only he could give.

Father Ed had been back in St. Louis for two weeks when the next blow came—Heywood Broun's death on December 18. The loss was all the more painful for him because he knew how much Broun's conversion to Catholicism had cost him during his final months. Many of Broun's old friends from the progressive movement had ostracized him for his faith, while many Catholics who should have welcomed him instead expressed embarrassment to find him in their ranks. Father Ed commented acidly that such unkindness from radicals and "sterilely orthodox and orthodoxically sterile Catholics" was the true cause of the great columnist's death.[4]

Finally, around New Year's Day, when Father Ed at least should have been able to enjoy the relief of saying goodbye to 1939, came the phone call from Edwin A. Lahey—or Eddie, as Dowling called him.[5] Lahey, who had returned to his *Chicago Daily News* post after completing his Nieman Fellowship, had a wife, two young daughters, and a future filled with promise. But now he was on the brink of losing everything for which he'd worked so hard—because he couldn't stop drinking.

Just how Father Ed came to be friends with Lahey is unknown, but there are many ways their paths could have crossed. They could have met during Father Ed's time teaching at Loyola Academy, when Lahey was taking classes at Loyola University. Or they might have connected through the Newspaper Guild, or through Father Ed's friend Dempster MacMurphy, who was for a time Lahey's colleague at the *Chicago Daily News*.

In any case, Lahey, like so many others, relied upon Dowling for fatherly assistance during difficult times. And so when his wife of ten years—unable to take his drinking any longer—took the children and went to stay with relatives in Texas, he telephoned his Jesuit friend and poured out his pain.[6]

As Father Ed sat in his Queen's Work office listening to Lahey's tortured voice over the crackly long-distance phone line, he felt conscious of his limitations. Lahey likely required the help of a doctor who specialized in alcoholism, and maybe even a psychiatrist. All Dowling could do was help him sort out the spiritual side of things. But perhaps even that might be enough to get Lahey on the right track. At least, it might arrest his downward spiral.

"Eddie," Dowling said, when Lahey's flow of words finally ebbed, "why don't you take a few days off and come down to St. Louis? I can get you a room at the White House Retreat. It'll give you a chance to get some rest, be with the Lord, and start putting yourself back together from the inside out."

There was a moment's silence on the line. Lahey was thinking. Father Ed took the opportunity to add, "Plus you'll get three squares a day." Probably Lahey was eating terribly with Grace gone, Dowling thought. "And the White House is far enough outside the city that you'll be able to enjoy some fresh air. A walk along the Mississippi will do you good."

"Will you be there, Father?"

"Of course I'll be there! I'll come by each morning to celebrate Mass, and we'll have plenty of time to talk."

By the end of the conversation, Father Ed was able to convince Lahey to set a tentative date for a weekend retreat starting on Friday, January 12.

A few days later, however, Father Ed was at The Queen's Work when his telephone rang. It was Lahey, calling to say he needed to push back the retreat to the middle of the following week. Father Ed said he understood. The 16th through the 18th would be fine.

Once he put down the receiver, Father Ed penciled in Lahey's name on those dates on his desk calendar. As he did, he noticed he had already written "Heywood Broun month's mind"[7] in pen on the 18th. It was a happy coincidence—providential, even. His remembrance of Broun at the altar would be sweeter in the presence of Lahey, given that Lahey shared his affection for the columnist.[8]

But would Lahey follow through with the retreat? Father Ed wondered as he opened the drawer under his desk to replace his pencil. His eyes fell upon a slip of paper he kept there. On it, he had typed a prayer to his patron St. Dismas that he had found in a magazine.[9] It was, he thought, another providential sign—a reminder that his friend and Lahey's, Dempster Mac-Murphy, who had done so much to spread devotion to the Good Thief, was with Broun in heaven praying for Lahey's recovery.

Dowling remembered Dempster's unforgettable description of Dismas —"this hoodlum saint, who roams the outfield of eternity, making shoestring catches of souls."[10] Surely, he thought, this hoodlum saint would help him make a shoestring catch of dear Eddie Lahey before it was too late.

And, lifting the slip of paper closer to his eyes, he began to pray: "O great saint, whose unutterable privilege it was to die by the side of our Blessed Savior expiring on the Cross to atone for the sins of all mankind...."

When he was done, he picked up the telephone receiver again and dialed a Chicago number.

"Hello, Sister Mary Alice? It's Father Ed....Keep those prayers coming!... Yes, Eddie called me...."[11]

Sister Mary Alice Rowan wore the "butterfly nun" headpiece of the Daughters of Charity of St. Vincent de Paul. But to Father Ed, she might as well have worn angels' wings. She was his secret weapon against the forces of darkness that threatened to bring down his alcoholic friend.

Although Father Ed had never met Sister Mary Alice in person, he felt she was a kindred spirit. Certainly she cared about Lahey as he did, for she had secretly alerted Dowling to the newsman's troubles before Lahey himself had the courage to tell him.

To Eddie and Grace Lahey, Sister Mary Alice was practically part of the family, for it was she who, as director of social services at Chicago's St. Vincent's orphanage, had enabled them to build a family of their own. When they approached her at the end of 1934 after five years of unsuccessfully trying to have children of their own, she guided them through every stage of the adoption process. Through her caring assistance, they now had two little girls, four-year-old Jayne and two-year-old Judith, each adopted shortly after birth.

Sister Mary Alice was a large, jovial woman with a powerful voice—people joked that she had little need of a telephone—and a deep, hearty laugh that made her body shake.[12] But, as with Father Ed, beneath her cheerful exterior, she carried great concern for those who were dear to her. Her seriousness was evident as she wrote Father Ed on January 16, 1940, to update him on the Lahey situation:

> When our friend was here a week ago Saturday I tried to persuade him to get straightened out physically before he made the retreat. He would not agree and said he would rather start from the inside out. I told him to do anything, try anything, go anywhere, but to *do something*. He expected to go into retreat this last weekend and promised to call before he left. I was delightfully surprised to receive a note from him last Thursday from Hot Springs saying the

retreat would not start until this week and he suddenly decided to go to the Springs, and that he was sure it would bring him a lot of good. Well, here's hoping.

I assure you I am storming heaven, and while my prayers may not be so good, I have so many truly holy friends who are helping me out.[13] We are all praying that the cure may be permanent....I feel nothing should be left undone to help them keep their home together, for they are indeed a grand couple.

But even as Sister Mary Alice sealed the letter, Lahey's plight had taken a new and troubling turn. Unbeknownst to the nun, the newsman's trip to Hot Springs, Arkansas, had devolved into a tour of the spa town's saloons. And he had already written to Father Ed saying not to expect him at the White House Retreat.[14]

When Father Ed received Sister Mary Alice's letter, he replied immediately, updating her on Lahey's situation.[15] Sister Mary Alice responded on January 19, writing that she heard from Grace's sister that Lahey wrote his wife saying he was in Hot Springs and suggested she call for him. Grace refused.

The nun added,

[Lahey] has written and wired [to Grace] that he is through, that he is not going to St. Louis to make the retreat, etc., that she failed him when he needed her most. Of course, I know he does not mean a word of it, but it hurt [him] when she did not run back at the first line [from] him. To me, this is a good time to wake him up, and I do not blame her one bit.

Of course, I am not supposed to know that he did not go to St. Louis. I have written a nice letter welcoming him out of retreat and telling him everything is lovely. I sent the letter in care of you and ask that you just forward it to Hot Springs. I think that he will be ashamed when he gets the letter, as he made such wonderful promises to me.

I assure you, dear Father, that I have never been so interested in folks' private lives as I have been in this case, for I am very fond of the Laheys, and then too, I still have to be interested in our babies. Although [the children] no longer belong to St. Vincent's, still I feel I helped them select the both of them and it seems a responsibility that is mine. Then too, what about Catholic Action, eh? Could there be any better than to help someone who is wrecking everything just through human frailty when prayer and a little time may straighten out everything?

Thanking you, dear Father, and assuring you that prayers are being offered by the wholesale, and knowing you are praying too, I am,

Sincerely,
Sister Mary Alice

The January 20 mail batch that brought Sister Mary Alice's letter also brought the letter that she wanted Dowling to forward to Eddie. Father Ed had to smile at the nun's cunning in writing to Lahey as though she were unaware of his decision to forego the retreat. He put the sealed letter inside a Queen's Work envelope to be sent to Hot Springs, saying a silent prayer that it would prick the reporter's conscience.

Before he put Sister Mary Alice's letter to Lahey down his office's mail chute, however, Father Ed had two more letters to write. Neither of those letters exists, but the replies to them do, so it is possible to guess at their contents.

The first letter was to Eddie. Given the way Father Ed had written in the past to people who were suffering crises—especially his letters to his brother Paul—he likely offered a few practical suggestions for how Lahey might begin to get his life back together upon his return to Chicago. In a P.S., he added that, before Eddie did anything else, he would do well to go to Confession so he could truly start afresh with strength renewed from above.

Then Father Ed typed a letter to Grace Lahey. It was time he let Grace know that he and Sister Mary Alice were together trying to find a way to bring Eddie back to sobriety. He also wanted to learn how she was holding up amid the strain of the separation, and to assure her that he was there for her as well as for her husband.

Two days later, when the afternoon mail arrived at The Queen's Work, Father Ed was excited to find replies from both Eddie and Grace. He opened the envelope from Eddie first. Inside was a single sheet of stationery from the Maurice Baths & Therapeutic Pool in Hot Springs, covered on both sides with Eddie's cursive scrawl—

Dear Father:

This morning there comes a letter, forwarded from your office, which is ironic, to say the least. It is from Sister Mary Alice (of St.

Vincent's), full of holy pictures and felicitations on a "successful retreat." Sister had fondly supposed that upon receipt of her kind note, I would have had emerged bright and shining from the White House.

It looks as though I'll have to do some high-class lying when I get back to Chicago, and make the good sisters think that their chubby little wards still enjoy a good Christian home.

I appreciated your letter, and readily conceded the wisdom and correctness of your remarks, particularly your postscript on Confession.

However, a month of bitter isolation, plus the recriminations to which the post office and Western Union have been parties, has got me talking to myself, and walking and thinking in circles. The two hours every afternoon I spend in the bath house being my only approach to a state of repose, I look forward to them each day as sort of a pagan ritual.

I'm leaving here Saturday night, in the expectation that you will be available in St. L. Sunday. Probably will arrive in St. L. by bus about 10 a.m. on Sunday. Will get in touch with you soon as I'm cleaned up.

> Cordially—
> Ed L.

When Father Ed read the end of the letter, his heart raced. Please, Lord, let it be true! Let Eddie leave behind his "pagan ritual" of Hot Springs' bath houses to visit him and receive the true cleansing that could come only from a sincere Confession.

Dowling knew he must tell Grace. But first he would read her letter, which bore the postmark of Edcouch, Texas, where she and her daughters were staying with her sister. It ran for three pages, written in neat Palmer script.

"Dear Father," she wrote,

It was good to receive your kind letter, so full of interest in the Laheys.

I had thought that by this time Ed would be with you in St. Louis and already so much the better mentally for the meeting. It was a great shock to learn that he was passing up you and the White House.

[I] presume that Sister Mary Alice outlined our trouble, which, of course, is due entirely to drink. As Ed and I had reached a point where trying to talk it over would be in vain, there was nothing I could do but leave. And after three weeks I still feel that was the only course open to me.

Nobody appreciates more than I what a great person [Ed] is basically, and besides reaching an all-time low in unhappiness myself, I just couldn't see him go on for the next ten years as he has the last.

Grace explained that, beyond the problems that her husband's drinking caused for their marriage, his work was suffering as well. She had learned that just after she left, his boss had called him to account for himself. It was in fact his boss who suggested Lahey avail himself of Hot Springs' baths, and he had extracted from the newsman the promise that he would drink nothing while on vacation.

"Despite all my worry and fear," Grace went on,

I really do feel that all will turn out well and we can be together again. I still have a lot of faith in Ed and his love for us. Am sure that if he gives up liquor he will become less selfish and more kind and considerate of me. Can you imagine Ed unkind? That was what I couldn't bear....

It was more than Father Ed could bear too. But Grace's next words renewed his hope, for she wrote that she intended to drive back to Chicago as soon as the weather permitted.

[I] feel that many obstacles would be removed if you, Ed, and I could have a visit together....

Thank you muchly for being so interested in us. [I] know if we could talk, you could help, and I think we both need help.

What did Father Ed do after reading Grace's letter? The answer to that question comes to us directly from Dowling himself. In a March 1944 *Queen's Work* article, he detailed the Lahey saga—changing the names and identifying details of all involved, including Sister Mary Alice[16]—and told how it led to his discovery of Alcoholics Anonymous.[17] (Amazingly, until now, all other published accounts of Father Ed's first encounter with A.A.—even those of Robert Fitzgerald, SJ, and Ernest Kurtz, who researched Dowling extensively—have overlooked both the *Queen's Work* article and the Lahey correspondence that it describes.)

Father Ed (who, in his article, renames the Laheys "Jim and Jane") picks up the story at the point where he receives Eddie's and Grace's letters:

> In answer, I wrote [Eddie] saying that I would be glad to see him, and [...] I wired [Grace] that [Eddie] was passing through St. Louis the next Sunday.
>
> That next Sunday morning, [January 28, 1940,] at *The Queen's Work*, I was startled to answer the door and failed to recognize the really pretty [Grace] after her twenty hours in a day coach and twenty days on the brink of the crash of her home. I didn't think that she could look worse, but she did when I answered her that [Eddie] had not come but that "buses are often late."
>
> About an hour after we started our chat in my office, the doorbell rang. As I led the grim [Eddie] to the back of the building toward my office, I stopped at the intervening washroom, told [Eddie] to go back to my office and that I would be there in a few minutes, and then loudly and ostentatiously locked myself in the washroom.
>
> Five minutes later, when I entered my office, I found two happy people who had learned what so many couples sometimes find out—that if it is hard to get along with each other, it is impossible to get along without each other. The next morning, [Eddie] and [Grace] went to Communion together, and in the four years since that morning, it has been a very rare week when [Eddie] has missed Communion more than one or two days.[18]

Once again we see Father Ed mention the importance of daily Communion, just as he had in his letters to family members who were going through difficult times. Whenever he gave spiritual guidance to Catholics, that was his first recommendation.

After Father Ed celebrated Mass for Eddie, Grace, and their daughters on the morning after their reunion, the family returned together to Chicago. The next morning found Eddie making a visit to the very woman who, unbeknownst to him, had played a hidden role in the Laheys' reunion.

Sister Mary Alice's joy is tangible in the letter she wrote to Father Ed the following day—January 31, 1940:

Dear Father Dowling,

The prodigal returned, thanks to the dear Lord and good Father Dowling. I hadn't heard a word from either side since I spoke with you last Thursday, and on Tuesday morning was trying to picture just what would happen. Yesterday morning about ten o'clock I was told Mr. Lahey was here, and when I saw his happy boyish grin I knew all was well.

After asking our good friend how he enjoyed his vacation and retreat, he informed me that he had made a one-man retreat. Asked him what this meant and he said he thought best to remain in Hot Springs a while longer. When he told me he had two hectic weeks there, I appeared much surprised and asked why. He said that it was home trouble and that when one writes, things always sound differently than when you talk. He knew there were many in Chicago who were interested, and that if he returned without Grace, he would have to be embarrassed or lie. He also said that he didn't like to talk about it, that it had already gone over the dam. I did not ask many questions as I was afraid I would betray myself.

He said when he came into your office he found Grace there, that you were very kind to them, giving your time, which he knew was precious for you are a busy man. He sang your praises and said, "Gee, Sister, he is swell, how I wish you could meet him." He promised the next time you came to Chicago he would bring you to St. Vincent's. I also told him you were a *real friend*.

He informed me my letter was forwarded to him and said it was a source of disturbance as I thought he was making the retreat when he was not. In my own mind I was saying, that's just what I wanted it to do.

He went to Holy Communion and intends to go daily, let us pray that he does. [...]

St. Vincent [de Paul] tells us we should spend as much time thanking God for his favors as we do [in] asking them. If this is true, my poor spirit of prayer will improve considerably, for I have certainly been talking plenty to the Lord since Ed Lahey's slip. Last week, when things looked so dark, I thought I might be disappointed in Eddie Lahey (though I knew I would not), but was definitely sure I would never be let down by our Changeless Friend. [...]

Asking you to sometime say a little prayer for me and looking forward to the pleasure of meeting you, I am,

Sincerely,
Sister Mary Alice

Although Sister Mary Alice did not point Eddie Lahey to Alcoholics Anonymous, her letters to Father Ed reveal her heretofore unknown role in Lahey's recovery. It was not merely a Jesuit priest, but a priest and nun in union of prayers and action who together helped save Eddie's marriage, his sobriety, and, in all likelihood, his very life. From a Catholic perspective, Sister Mary Alice's and Father Ed's collaboration is a model of the spiritual parenthood that is possible when people who have vowed themselves to God live what they believe.

Father Ed writes in his *Queen's Work* article that, one month after the Laheys' reunion, he went to Chicago to visit the couple.[19] The trip was most likely on or about February 23, as he would have had an opportunity to pass through Chicago by train on his way to New York City, where he was to give lectures on the 25th and 26th.[20]

When Dowling met up with Eddie, he was delighted to find that the journalist was still sober. However, his delight turned to concern as Eddie told him that the very people who were helping him avoid drinking were themselves active drinkers until very recently. In fact, they included some of his former barroom companions from the *Chicago News*.

"I was rather confused and apprehensive," Dowling says,

> to learn that [Eddie] was spending a good deal of time with some of his old saloon friends who had started a rather strange fellowship called Alcoholics Anonymous. At best it sounded cockeyed.
>
> My misgivings were not removed when at [Eddie]'s invitation I attended a meeting of this crowd and sat through a rather poor meal and tried to size up some thirty or forty vapid-looking and uninteresting people. Poor [Eddie]. This looked just like the family entrance to skid row.
>
> Then the talks started. And so did my amazement. In the four years since that moment, I have been transfixed in the fascinating

stories of Alcoholics Anonymous. The greatest drama in America today.[21]

There is so much meaning packed into those few brief paragraphs. It is worth taking a moment to examine what Father Ed said to his *Queen's Work* readers about Alcoholics Anonymous and how he said it.

"At best it sounded cockeyed." Father Ed's colloquial language is a fine mask for the classic rhetorical technique that he is employing—the fruit of his many years learning the art of persuasion from great Jesuit teachers. He is aware that *Queen's Work* readers—who, as observant Catholics, are already inclined to be suspicious of extra-ecclesial fads—will have a hard time accepting the idea that sobriety can be attained through a group of former drunks. So he skillfully gains their trust by showing that he once shared their perspective. And it works, because the reader never doubts Father Ed's honesty. He *would* want the best for his alcoholic friend, and he *would*, as a Catholic priest, be "confused and apprehensive" at Lahey's seeking help for a serious addiction within a fellowship that was both amateur and secular.

"At [Eddie]'s invitation I attended a meeting of this crowd." What a powerful statement this is, for those who know what came next! Father Ed did not learn of A.A. from a doctor; neither did he learn of it from a priest or bishop or from any professional organization. It was a Catholic layman (an alcoholic, no less, to whom he himself had ministered) who introduced Father Ed to A.A., thereby changing Father Ed's life, and Bill W.'s life, and ultimately A.A. itself—forever.

Along with Edwin Lahey, Father Ed himself deserves credit for his discovery of A.A., for he attended the meeting out of his great fatherly love and concern for the reporter. Even today, not every priest has the humility, let alone the interest, to attend an open meeting of Alcoholics Anonymous and learn for himself what the fellowship has to offer to people in need of recovery. In humbly accepting Lahey's invitation to experience an A.A. meeting for himself, Father Ed showed himself a true "shepherd with the smell of the sheep" (to borrow a favorite expression of Pope Francis).[22]

"...and sat through a rather poor meal." These words serve a dual function. On the one hand, Father Ed begins to establish his point that A.A.'s are ordinary people—a point he reinforces by describing the members with seeming harshness as "vapid-looking and uninteresting people." These are not wide-eyed enthusiasts trying to win newcomers' favor with expensive food. Neither are they bored elites, as were many (though not all) of those who dabbled in 19th- and early 20th-century occult trends such as

seances and theosophy. There is, in fact, nothing that could distinguish them from the reader's neighbors or co-workers. Hence, anyone could attend an A.A. meeting and feel as though they belong.

On the other hand, in describing how the gathering included "a rather poor meal," Father Ed implicitly connects the meeting with the poverty and the meal fellowship of the early Christians. It is a beautifully subtle way of indicating to Catholic readers that—although he did not yet realize it—in sitting among A.A. members, he was in the presence of holiness. He was like Jacob who, upon waking from his dream of the ladder with its steps leading to heaven, exclaims, "Surely the Lord is in this place; and I did not know it" (Gen 28:16). And the comparison for Dowling went both ways; later on, speaking to an A.A. convention, he would describe the "mystical body" (a Catholic term referring to the faithful)[23] as "a sort of Christians Anonymous."[24]

"I have been transfixed in the fascinating stories of Alcoholics Anonymous." This passage is not only key to understanding A.A.; it is also key to understanding Father Ed himself. Father Ed did not approach alcoholics— or anyone with a problem—as though he had something to give them. His perspective always was that, however much the Lord might use him to help people, he himself had something to *receive* from them. In the case of A.A. members, Father Ed especially appreciated receiving their "stories"—testimonies given at meetings by people who were striving, each in his or her own way, to remain sober.

To say that Father Ed was inspired by A.A. members' stories would be an understatement. He *thrived* on them.

Once he came to know Bill Wilson, Father Ed would write to A.A. headquarters in advance of his travels, requesting the times and locations of meetings in the cities where he would be staying. According to Robert Fitzgerald, SJ, he and Bill "seemed to have some unspoken agreement that Dowling could attend A.A. meetings as a special friend or 'fellow traveler,' a common practice in the early days of A.A."[25] Father Ed's gratitude for the arrangement showed in a letter to Bill where he wrote, "I have been shameless in my use of A.A. in my travels as a Lonely Heart Club."[26] Being around members of the fellowship and hearing their stories brought him joy, pure and simple. Paul H., an A.A. member, observed, "Those in the Fellowship were always his 'pets,' so to speak—you could tell that by the way his eyes lit up when we came in the room."[27]

What was it about A.A. members' stories that so encouraged Father Ed? Paul H. heard the answer from the man himself, toward the very end of his life, when Father Ed was introducing some of his A.A. friends to

members of the marriage ministry with which he was involved: "He
wanted to emphasize how A.A.'s faced their problems and spoke about
problems and about 'God directly, and not as if the word were immodest
like "legs" in the Victorian age.'"[28]

A.A. members' humility, their recognition of their need for constant
conversion, and their dependence upon God's grace to strengthen them
amid temptations and suffering—all these things left Father Ed in awe. He
came to rely upon his regular contact with A.A.'s to help him remain hopeful, strong, and faithful in his own personal trials.

9

∽᠈᠁

BEFRIENDING BILL

I had had some opportunity to observe religious experience such as Bill had. I think my respect for him was the initial cement of our friendship.
— Father Ed on his first meeting with Bill Wilson[1]

He became just about the closest friend I shall ever have—and my spiritual adviser, too. He took me through some of my rough going, which, without his counsel and love, I might never have survived.
— Bill Wilson on Father Ed[2]

At the Chicago meeting, Father Ed bought a copy of the fellowship's recently published official text, *Alcoholics Anonymous*, popularly known as the Big Book. Once he caught the train out of town, the book, along with his breviary, was his companion for the next leg of his travels—a journey to New York City, where he was to give lectures on democracy. By the time he returned home, at the end of February, he had finished the book and was in awe of its spiritual depth.[3]

Having come of age during the era of Prohibition, Father Ed would have been familiar with Protestant temperance literature, which typically bore down upon alcoholics with warnings about the sinfulness of their behavior. He also would have known of Catholic temperance movements such as the Dublin-based Pioneer Total Abstinence Association of the Sacred Heart, which, although refraining from applying the language of sin to alcohol, praised abstinence as a "heroic offering to God." But nothing he had read or heard from temperance advocates prepared him for the Big Book's intense call to self-examination, conversion, and trustful surrender to God's transformative grace.

Although Father Ed did not immediately connect the Big Book with the Spiritual Exercises of St. Ignatius Loyola, he instinctively recognized in it some of the same spiritual principles that had drawn him to the Exercises. It was his fellow Jesuit Father John Markoe—a priest of outstanding ability (and a trailblazer in interracial justice) who struggled with alcoholism—who, when Father Ed showed him the book in April or May of 1940, pointed out to him connections between the Twelve Steps and the Exercises. Markoe's insights increased Father Ed's interest in A.A. even more, and he resolved to find the author or authors of the Steps.[4]

A sad occasion was in store for Father Ed upon his return to St. Louis—the funeral of his uncle Paul M. Dowling, one of the owners of the Star Bucket Pump factory where Father Ed worked during his teens, who died on February 28.

The first of Father Ed's uncles to die during his lifetime (others had died before he was born), Uncle Paul was only sixty-one when he passed away. And the last seven years of his life had not been active ones; he had suffered from Parkinson's disease.

Although Father Ed's own illness was not Parkinson's but ankylosing spondylitis, he recognized in his uncle's sufferings something of his own future.[5] He was now forty-one. Time was running out. If he wanted to fulfill the path that he believed the Lord was showing him—a path that now included spreading the word about A.A.—he had to stay on the move, cane and all.

But first he had to find some alcoholics. At that time, Alcoholics Anonymous was barely out of its infancy. Just five years earlier, in December 1934, Bill Wilson was lying in a treatment bed at Towns Hospital in New York City when he had the transformative spiritual experience that confirmed his faith in God—and gave him the strength to quit alcohol forever. Eager to share the healing he had received, Bill tried to help other alcoholics, but was unsuccessful until his fateful encounter with Dr. Bob Smith, who would found A.A. with Bill in Akron, Ohio, in June 1935.[6]

By the time Father Ed discovered the fellowship, Alcoholics Anonymous had about one thousand members nationwide. Its only chapters in the Midwest were the original Akron group and those that had recently formed in Cleveland and Chicago. If Father Ed were to minister to A.A. members in St. Louis, he would have to start a chapter himself—or, rather, convince some drinkers to do so.

And so, Dowling, ever the connector, reached out to Eddie Lahey and the Chicago A.A. leaders he had met to let them know to encourage any alcoholics from St. Louis who approached their group to contact him. And they did. On May 11, 1940, Father Ed took his contact with A.A. to the next level, with a letter to its New York office, the Alcoholic Foundation (today known as the General Service Office):

Gentlemen:

I had the rare privilege of attending the business meeting of the AA and later a social open house in Chicago, at the invitation of one of the members who consulted me on his last escapade. I am deeply impressed by what I saw and heard.

Dowling wrote that, in addition to the Big Book, he had obtained a copy of A.A.'s recent pamphlet—its first, containing reprints of articles about the fellowship from the *Houston Press*. "I enclose $1.00 and ask that you send me all of the A.A. pamphlets, April 1940, that this will cover." And he added, "I know, personally, nine or ten prospects here in St. Louis."

In closing, he encouraged the Alcoholic Foundation to "continue on the splendid work" and said he was thinking of writing about A.A. in *The Queen's Work*.

At some point not long before or after Father Ed reached out to the Alcoholic Foundation, he made a visit to the Akron group, where he met Dr. Bob Smith and Henrietta Seiberling.[7] He also visited Dr. Bob at his home. The doctor told him how he "had not had a completely sober day in twenty years" until Bill W. worked with him.[8]

It was likely during Father Ed's visit to the Akron group that he said something to an A.A. member that affected Seiberling so powerfully that she could still recall the Jesuit's words clearly thirty years later: "This is one of the most beautiful things that has come into the world. But I want to warn you that the devil will try to destroy it."[9]

According to Mary Darrah, the biographer of Sister Ignatia (whose work among alcoholics earned her the title of "Angel of Alcoholics Anonymous"), Father Ed sought to learn from the Akron group whether the author of the Twelve Steps had consciously adapted them from the Spiritual Exercises. "However, in Akron his spiritual inquiries yielded no results. Most of the early A.A.s there were Protestant and had never heard of St. Ignatius or his Spiritual Exercises." It was they who directed him to seek his answers from Bill W., the primary author of the Big Book.[10]

Darrah's account seems fundamentally accurate, particularly in light of comments Father Ed made in a May 1942 letter to Bill Wilson about his and Dr. Bob's impressions of each other when they first met in Akron. Father Ed diplomatically described how Dr. Bob expressed discomfort with a certain brand of Catholic spirituality (and received a delightfully Dowlingesque reply):

Doc Smith is so real and I would feel bad if I didn't have a well-grounded hope of coming to know him better. In our Akron talk, Smith seemed to have a sincere respect for the Jesuit Order because of its social activities, but he was a bit scandalized at the thought of the Trappist Order which spends most of its time in silence and prayer. I suggested that trafficking with God in prayer is a pretty high society and a very influential social activity—that these people are our lobbyists before the divine legislature.[11]

Although Father Ed did not make a note of his Akron visit on his desk calendar (which is unsurprising, as he kept few records of his appointments), his calendar for Friday, May 24 through Sunday, May 26, 1940, does show an A.A.-related engagement. He marked down that Cleveland Indians catcher Rollie Hemsley would be in town with his team that weekend for games against the St. Louis Browns. A month earlier, Hemsley had made national headlines when (with much goodwill but no regard for anonymity) he credited the Akron chapter of Alcoholics Anonymous with enabling him to recover from alcoholism. It is not known whether Father Ed actually had the opportunity to meet with Hemsley; if he did, he would likely have been eager to learn about the catcher's experiences in A.A. and his advice for starting a St. Louis chapter.

When Bill Wilson received Father Ed's letter, he mailed him ten copies of the pamphlet he requested. Four weeks later, on June 11, he directed his secretary, Ruth Hock, to follow up with a letter. Thanking the priest for his interest, Hock typed (perhaps following Bill's dictation),

For quite a few months we have been receiving inquiries for information and assistance from St. Louis and vicinity and we would, therefore, appreciate an opportunity to correspond with you and those working with you in the A.A. Fellowship so that we may extend the possibility of personal assistance to those in the vicinity of St. Louis who desire it.

The letter's businesslike cordiality likely reflected Bill's discomfort at interacting with a member of the Catholic clergy. Although Bill saw Catholics at A.A. meetings, he had never been good friends with any Catholic, let alone a priest, until he met Father Ed.

Hock's reply reached Father Ed at a busy time; the Summer School of Catholic Action was about to launch its 1940 season. A few days later, on June 18, he found a moment to reply.

"I am spreading the good word of the fine work being done by the A.A.," Father Ed wrote. "I have had two or three callers."

He added,

In general, I run into the difficulty of the unwillingness of the people concerned to admit they are alcoholic. I know this is not a new difficulty and can gradually be overcome.

Mr. [K.] of this city who has visited the Chicago A.A. group is going to have a gathering next Sunday. He is the only one who has visited an established A.A. group. I would have preferred to have at least several local alcoholics visit with Akron or Chicago groups before doing much in an organized way.

However, I am deeply happy to cooperate in any way I can. If any literature other than the Houston Press pamphlet and large book is available, I should appreciate getting it.

Upon receiving this second letter from Father Ed, Bill Wilson recognized that the priest's interest in A.A. was more than casual. Here was a non-alcoholic with some influence in his community who was sincere about wanting to spread the fellowship's message. Bill therefore spent more time composing his response than he did in replying to Father Ed's first inquiry. (This second letter, unlike the first, was clearly written by him personally, despite bearing Hock's signature.) He also took a warmer tone, although his lack of familiarity with Catholic clergy remained evident, for he began the July 9, 1940, letter with "Dear Sir":

Thank you very much for your recent letter in response to ours.

We can well appreciate the difficulty which you find in that many drinkers think this is a fine movement but not for them. We feel that one of the reasons for the success of this work is the fact that one alcoholic spreads the word to another, for almost invariably an alcoholic will admit his condition more readily to another alcoholic. Of course, even so, many alcoholics will not admit the fact. We do not try to convince them, knowing that if they are truly alcoholic, the time will come when they will be forced to admit it.

Bill then switched topics to request details of the incipient St. Louis fellowship: "In an indirect way, it has come to us that there are five alcoholics working together in St. Louis at the present time. Can you tell us if this is a fact and, if so, what progress has been made?"

He then added a question that hinted at his real concern: "Also whether any religion is represented in addition to the Catholic?"

The question reflected the tensions that were then going on within A.A. as it began to come into its own, having only recently severed its ties with the Oxford Group, the Protestant movement that had provided it with its initial spiritual moorings. In the face of members' disagreements over the place of religion in A.A., Bill was insisting that the fellowship had to be open to people of all faiths and even of no particular faith—hence the Twelve Steps' references to "God as we understood him." So he was concerned at the prospect that the St. Louis chapter might be a Catholic-only fellowship. If that were the case, it could threaten the universality that the Alcoholics Anonymous name was intended to represent.

Bill's letter went on to assure Father Ed, in answer to a concern the priest had expressed, that new chapters had managed to thrive even when their members had not witnessed existing chapters in action. In response to Dowling's request for additional literature, Bill enclosed a new pamphlet, this one reprinting articles on A.A. from the Washington *Star*. And in valediction, he wrote, "Awaiting your reply with interest." But he still had his secretary sign the letter, perhaps as a means of preserving anonymity during those early days before his identity became well known.

Father Ed responded on July 17 with answers to Bill's questions about the St. Louis group. To the one concerning religion, he responded, "The only one of the group who is a Catholic is a Mrs. [C.]. I do not know Mr. [K.]'s religion, though it is not Catholic. Two men, Mr. [F.] and Mr. [J.] are Episcopalians, I think." Although Dowling did not intend to mock Bill, his offhandedness is a humorous counter to the seriousness of Wilson's query. Throughout Father Ed's priestly life, he never judged people who came to him for help according to whether they were Catholic or not. He was interested in them simply because they were people, and people interested him. Years before Pope Francis used a maxim of the Roman playwright Terence in his preaching, Dowling lived the message of its words: "I am a man: I regard nothing human as foreign to me."[12]

The Alcoholic Foundation did not respond to Father Ed's letter, which was just as well. He had work to do, teaching at the Summer School of Catholic Action and, when that was done, helping the St. Louis chapter of A.A. find its footing. It was during this summer's SSCA that newspapers reported what would become his most famous quotation: "The two biggest obstacles to democracy in the United States are the widespread delusion that we have democracy and the chronic terror among the rich lest we get it."[13]

By October, plans were well underway for the St. Louis A.A. group's official launch, with Eddie Lahey and three other key members of the Chicago group coming down to assist. Father Ed helped the lead organizer, Fitz F., prepare for the meeting spiritually, directing a retreat at the White House on October 17 for him and the four visiting members of the Chicago group.[14]

The first regular meeting of the St. Louis A.A. followed on October 30, 1940, at the home of one of the members. Father Ed would have found special meaning in that date, as it was the feast of St. Alphonsus Rodriguez, the patron saint of Jesuit lay brothers, who was known for his humility—the very virtue that he saw as foundational to A.A. In his first *Queen's Work* article on A.A., he would write,

> The essential dynamic of the program is based on the scriptural teaching that while "God resists the proud, He assists the humble." Secondly, that the shortest road to humility is through humiliation, and the Alcoholics Anonymous yield to few other groups in their capital stock of humiliations.[15]

As Father Ed joyfully witnessed the St. Louis chapter settle into a regular rhythm of meetings, A.A. members' humble openness to grace continued to impress him. And he still wanted to learn whether Ignatian principles lay behind the creative work of Bill Wilson when he composed the Twelve Steps. Soon, thanks to a providential opening in his travel schedule, he would finally have the opportunity to find out.

On the same day that Dowling thanked God for enabling the St. Louis A.A. chapter to begin its healing work, Bill Wilson wrote to his friend Fitz M., one of the fellowship's earliest members, expressing feelings of depression, frustration, and even hopelessness.

Bill had put his heart, his hopes, and all his and Lois's money into bringing Alcoholics Anonymous to a wider audience. And, for a while, it seemed as though God was rewarding his good intentions with worldly success. Back in 1938, the Rockefeller Foundation expressed interest in A.A., the Big Book was readied for a first printing of nearly five thousand copies, and the editor of *Reader's Digest* expressed interest in running an excerpt of the book once it came out. But the Rockefeller Foundation's funding proved far smaller than Bill had hoped,[16] and the *Reader's Digest* editor's initial interest fizzled. In the fall of 1940, a year and a half after the Big Book's publication, more than half of its first printing remained unsold, piled up in a warehouse. Making matters worse, Hank P., the first alcoholic Bill had ever sponsored, who had been his closest collaborator in A.A., had resumed drinking and was spreading vicious and untrue rumors about him.

Uppermost on Bill's mind as he wrote to Fitz M. was his sense of failure in not having been able to support himself and his wife Lois. It was because of his single-minded dedication to A.A., to the point of being unable to take an interest in other lines of work,[17] that he and Lois had been homeless since April 1939, having lost their house—Lois's inheritance—to the mortgage company. An official Alcoholics Anonymous history says the couple were living as "vagabonds, first with one A.A. family, then with another."[18] Bill, in his letter to Fitz, put it in starker terms: "As usual, we are living nowhere at all—just floating around—and I don't know when it will stop, if ever."[19]

Bill also felt under strain as A.A. members pressed him to explain why the fellowship had cut ties with the Oxford Group. The same day he wrote to Fitz, he wrote to an A.A. member in Richmond, Virginia, McGhee B., offering a lengthy list of reasons for the split.

In the eighth point and final point on the list, Bill acknowledged that A.A.'s religious makeup had changed since its early days—more Catholics were coming in: "Were we to make any religious demands on people, I'm afraid Catholics would not be interested. As matters now stand, I suppose A.A. is 25 percent Catholic."[20]

Although Bill was heartened to see the fellowship's appeal extend to an ever-more religiously diverse membership, the influx of Catholics placed additional pressure upon him. More Catholics in the fellowship meant more questions from Catholic clergy and bishops wanting assurance that A.A. was not a Protestant temperance group in disguise, or even a religious sect of its own. Until and unless Bill could find someone within the Catholic clergy to be a true friend of the fellowship, it would be difficult for A.A. to answer the Church's concerns in a convincing manner. However, as of October 1940, although some Catholic priests were quietly supportive of A.A., none was yet willing to be an ambassador to other Catholic clergy on the fellowship's behalf.

Shortly prior to Bill's first meeting with Father Ed, one Catholic priest did reach out to Bill in a personal way. Bill later related the story in A.A.'s *Grapevine* magazine:

> Speaking at Baltimore, I ran on at a great rate about the terrible sufferings we alcoholics had endured. My talk must have had a

strong flavor of self-pity and exhibitionism. I kept referring to our drinking experience as a great calamity, a terrible misfortune.

After the meeting I was approached by a Catholic clergyman who genially remarked, "I heard you say you thought your drinking a great misfortune. But it seems to me that in your case it was your *great good fortune*. Was not this terrible experience the very thing which humbled you so completely that you were able to find God? Did not suffering open your eyes and your heart? All the opportunity you have today, all this wonderful experience you call A.A., once had its beginnings in deep personal suffering. In your case that was actually no misfortune. It was your great good fortune. You A.A.s are a privileged people."[21]

Robert Thomsen, the most authoritative of Bill Wilson's biographers, writes that the priest's words led Bill to take the kind of "fearless moral inventory" that he himself prescribed in the Fourth Step. He knew that some of his fellow A.A.'s were saying he was on a "dry drunk"—engaging in the same distorted and self-destructive thinking as when he was drinking.[22]

Bill "examined his too-famous drive," Thomsen writes,

and he saw that it served to cover his failures, his impatience, and his eternal frustration at not being able to move things as he knew they must be moved. In turn, this stock-taking led to a depression which, in its prolonged intensity, was worse than any he had experienced since Towns Hospital.[23]

Towns Hospital was where Bill in December 1934 underwent his final bottoming-out as an alcoholic—feeling the despair of being unable to quit drinking on his own power. But it was also where he, in the midst of that terrible crisis, had the spiritual experience that freed him from his addiction.

Where now was the peaceful wind that he had felt during that transcendent moment as he sat in his bed at Towns Hospital—a wind "not of air," but "a wind of God, the grace of God"?[24]

In chapter 4 of *Not-God*, Ernest Kurtz's magisterial history of Alcoholics Anonymous, the author relates "how Bill Wilson habitually recalled that moment" when he met Father Ed. Kurtz begins:

It would seem that, on a chilly, rain-pelting early winter evening in late 1940, as Wilson almost tangibly felt himself being wrapped ever more tightly in a gloomy pall of spiritual darkness, he sat forlorn in the sparsely furnished clubhouse rooms in which he and Lois were then living.[25]

The tentative words "it would seem" reflects Kurtz's awareness that Bill, a master raconteur, was known for altering details of stories to make his desired impression upon listeners. When describing events of his life that had significance for Alcoholics Anonymous, he typically was not as concerned with maintaining historical accuracy as he was with conveying the spiritual truths that the events taught him.

In this case, when Bill remembered that "it was a sleety, bitter night"[26] when Father Ed came to meet him, his memory altered the weather to fit his mood. For, according to Dowling's desk calendar and his speaking schedule, Father Ed visited him late in the evening on Saturday, November 16, 1940. And, on that night, according to contemporary newspaper reports, Manhattan's temperature was indeed chilly—just above freezing—with some wind gusts, but there was no precipitation.

What Bill sought to convey with his images of Father Ed's "coat... covered with sleet" and his "hat...covered with snow"[27] was the courage with which Dowling selflessly sailed straight into the storm of the A.A. cofounder's embittered mind. The meaning of the story was that it took a weak, "crippled"[28] priest to enter into his interior turbulence and carry him back into the warm light of regeneration that he had received at Towns Hospital. As in the Book of Acts, when the gentle touch of the meek Ananias of Damascus caused the scales to fall from Saul's eyes,[29] God used a humble instrument to restore the deflated and depressed Bill to a state of grace. At least, that is how Bill saw it; he referred to his first meeting with Father Ed as his "second conversion experience."[30]

Father Ed planned his trip to New York City as a one-night stopover on his rail journey to Springfield, Massachusetts, where he was to address a meeting of the Proportional Representation League on November 18. His calendar does not indicate that he had any business in New York; it seems his only reason for spending the night there was so he could visit the Alcoholics Anonymous clubhouse and, he hoped, meet Bill Wilson.

It was eight p.m. on November 16 when Father Ed's train pulled into Pennsylvania Station.[31] From there, he went to a taxi stand and caught a cab for the five-minute ride to the place where he was staying—most likely the Jesuit community house at St. Francis Xavier High School on West Sixteenth Street between Fifth and Sixth Avenues. There, he dropped off his bag and perhaps had a late dinner.

Finally, as the ten o'clock hour approached, Father Ed put his coat and hat back on and stepped outside to take another five-minute taxi ride—this one to the Alcoholics Anonymous clubhouse on West Twenty-Fourth Street between Eighth and Ninth Avenues. He would have learned the clubhouse's address from Earl T. or another A.A. leader in Chicago, or possibly from having made a telephone call to Ruth Hock at the Alcoholic Foundation.

Just twelve days prior to Dowling's visit, Bill and Lois Wilson had moved into one of the two tiny upstairs bedrooms of the clubhouse. The room was only ten feet square; Lois tried to make it look larger and brighter by painting the walls white with red trim.[32] It was dominated by a bed that had no footboard so that Bill, who was six-foot-three, could stretch out comfortably.[33]

As a Checker Cab carried Father Ed to the clubhouse, Bill was lying in that bed with his feet hanging off the end, listening to the wind blow on the tin roof above his head. He was exhausted not just physically but emotionally as well. In his words, "It had been a hectic day, full of disappointments."[34]

For the past few days, he had been shepherding *Saturday Evening Post* writer Jack Alexander to meetings.[35] Alexander's editor had asked him to investigate Alcoholics Anonymous for a story that, if it came to pass, could bring the fellowship the large-scale national publicity that Bill had been dreaming of. But although Bill had tried to put on a cheerful face for Alexander, inside he feared that the *Saturday Evening Post* story, as with the hoped-for *Reader's Digest* publicity, might come to naught—for it was clear that the seasoned reporter was skeptical of what he saw. To Alexander, the alcoholics' tales of recovery seemed too perfect; he suspected he was being conned.[36]

After Alexander left the clubhouse that day, a number of alcoholic visitors had kept Bill busy until well after dark.[37] When they left, only Bill and the live-in caretaker Tom M., a crusty retired fireman, remained; Lois was out somewhere.

Nearly twenty years later, when Bill gave a talk to Catholic clergy days after attending Father Ed's funeral, he offered a vividly detailed account of what happened next.

> I lay upstairs in our room, consumed with self-pity. This had brought on one of my characteristic imaginary ulcer attacks....
>
>   Then the front doorbell rang, and I heard old Tom toddle to answer it. A minute later, he looked into the doorway of my room, obviously much annoyed.

Then he said, "Bill, there is some damn bum down there from St. Louis, and he wants to see you."[38]

Despite Bill's mistaken recollection that it was snowing, there are two solid reasons to accept the rest of his account of the evening. The first is that he told the story of it at least once in Father Ed's presence, at A.A.'s 1955 International Convention in St. Louis. The second is his recollection that Tom M. mistook Dowling for a "bum." He was not the first to do so, and he would not be the last.

Even in his youth, Father Ed had been somewhat careless about his personal appearance, as the admonitions he received in the novitiate attest. He took his vow of poverty seriously and paid no mind to the age of his clothes. There are stories of people buying him a new hat or a new pair of shoes in the (often vain) hope of convincing him to replace his old one.

Once his arthritis set in, Father Ed's grooming habits worsened as it became more difficult for him to neaten himself up during the course of his workday. He also had to adapt his clothes to his disability; he would split his socks at the top so he could put them on more easily and they would not hamper his circulation. And, like many sufferers of ankylosing spondylitis, he also suffered from psoriasis, to the point that flakes of dry skin would be evident on his black clerics.

So, when Father Ed spoke about humility arising from humiliations, he was not speaking theoretically. The humiliation of being taken for a street person was part of his daily life. Particularly at the end of a long travel day, it is completely plausible that Tom M. would have thought he was just "some damn bum."

Bill, in his weariness, resented having yet another drunk show up expecting to see him—and at such a late hour. With a sigh, he said to Tom, "Oh well, bring him up, bring him up."[39]

After Tom headed back downstairs, the next sound Bill heard was that of the wooden stairs creaking as his visitor plodded painfully and haltingly upward. Bill, reluctant to arise, remained stretched out upon his bed as he mused to himself about the stranger, "This one is really in bad shape."[40]

With Bill lying down, the first things Father Ed saw as he approached the top of the stairs were the white walls and red trim of the cramped bedroom. The color combination would have been familiar to Father Ed; it was like that of the candy-striped silk shirt he wore when he entered the Jesuit novitiate at Florissant—which he last saw being used by a Jesuit brother to wipe the floors. Ever since, that shirt had symbolized for him everything he gave up in order to share in the poverty of Christ. Now, twenty-one years later, God was giving him back the colors that had been missing from his life, in a way that would bring him more joy than he could have ever imagined.

"Then," Bill said as he recalled that moment,

> balanced precariously upon his cane, [Father Ed] came into the room, carrying a battered black hat that was shapeless as a cabbage leaf.... He lowered himself into my solitary chair, and when he opened his overcoat, I saw his clerical collar. He brushed back a shock of white hair and looked at me through the most remarkable pair of eyes I have ever seen.[41]

Somehow Bill, without realizing it, had finally sat up on the edge of his bed to face his guest. Father Ed leaned forward in his chair; he stood his cane up in front of him so he could rest his hands upon its grip. It was in fact an old-fashioned shillelagh. Dowling's left leg remained extended; Bill could tell there was something wrong with it, some kind of stiffness.

Once the two men were finally face to face, what did they discuss? Bill, in telling the story publicly, shared how Father Ed made him feel, but gave few specifics of their conversation. Robert Thomsen was able to learn a bit more about it from a tape recording that Bill made of his recollections. But the best account comes to us from Ernest Kurtz, for he, in addition to consulting Bill's writings, interviews, and speeches, also interviewed Lois Wilson and Nell Wing, both of whom recalled to him how Bill would tell the story of the meeting. What is more, Kurtz learned details of the meeting from John C. Ford, SJ, who recalled how Father Ed would tell the story.[42]

"Father Dowling," Kurtz wrote,

> introduced himself as a Jesuit priest from St. Louis who, as editor of a Catholic publication, was interested in the parallels he had intuited between the Twelve Steps of Alcoholics Anonymous and the [Spiritual] Exercises of St. Ignatius.... That he showed delight rather than disappointment when Wilson wearily confessed ignorance of the Exercises at once endeared the diminutive cleric to Bill.[43]

Then something extraordinary happened. Bill described it as a kind of divine inbreaking:

We talked about a lot of things, and my spirits kept on rising, and
presently I began to realize that this man radiated a grace that
filled the room with a sense of presence. I felt this with great intensity; it was a moving and mysterious experience. In years since,
I have seen much of this great friend, and whether I was in joy or
in pain, he always brought to me the same sense of grace and the
presence of God. My case is no exception. Many who meet Father
Ed experience this touch of the eternal.[44]

When Bill described the evening in the recording he made for Thomsen, he said that at the end of his and Dowling's conversation, which went
on long into the night, he "felt for the first time completely cleansed and
freed."[45] As the author of the Fifth Step— "Admitted to God, to ourselves,
and to another human being the exact nature of our wrongs"—Bill recognized this as a Fifth Step experience. But, more than that, as Kurtz has
noted,[46] it was Bill's *first* Fifth Step experience. Although Bill had composed the Twelve Steps, he himself had not made all of them; they were an
adaptation and expansion of the approach that had brought him healing
when he was in the Oxford Group.

And so, Kurtz writes,

[Bill] told Dowling not only what he had done and had left undone—he went on to share with his new sponsor the thoughts and
feelings behind those actions and omissions. He told about his
high hopes and plans, and spoke also about his anger, despair, and
mounting frustrations. The Jesuit listened and quoted Matthew
[5:6]: "Blessed are they who do hunger and thirst." God's chosen,
he pointed out, were always distinguished by their yearnings, their
restlessness, their thirst.

Father Ed could say that to Bill because he had lived it. Years later,
looking back on that evening in a letter to an A.A. member, he wrote that
he and Bill bonded over his respect for Bill's religious experience; this respect, he said, came about through a sense of sympathy: "I had had some
opportunity to observe religious experience such as Bill had."[47]

But in fact, Father Ed had more than sympathy. He could directly em-
pathize with Bill, for he too had experienced the peaks and valleys of the
spiritual life. He too had experienced the dark night of doubt that descended
into despair, when he went through his great time of purgation in the novitiate. He too had experienced the joy of the certainty of God's presence,
when, upon making his initial vows, he was flooded with divine consolation.

He too had experienced—and continued to experience—the hunger and thirst for a renewal of that sense of the nearness of God. And, like Bill with his Twelfth Step,[48] Father Ed had discovered that the hidden God awaited him in the form of each person who approached him with a problem.

Bill, recognizing in the priest a kindred spirit, asked him from the depths of his pain, "Won't there ever be any satisfaction?"[49] Dowling, Kurtz writes,

> almost snapped back: "Never. Never any." He continued in a gentler tone, describing as "divine dissatisfaction" that which would keep Wilson always reaching out for unattainable goals, for only by so reaching would he attain what—hidden from him—were God's goals.

Father Ed's many hours reading the *Imitation of Christ* had prepared him well for this moment. At one point in that spiritual classic, the storm-tossed disciple prays for light: "O Christ, ruler of the power of the sea and calmer of its raging waves, come near and help me."[50] Christ responds with words much like those that Dowling used to teach and comfort Bill: "How will you gain eternal rest if you look for leisure in this life? Do not choose to have rest, but patient endurance.... I will give an eternal reward for your brief toil and endless glory for your transitory trouble."[51]

But Father Ed did more than remind Bill of God's promises. He gave him, in Kurtz's words, "this acceptance that his dissatisfaction, that his very 'thirst,' could be divine." Such acceptance, Kurtz wrote, "was one of Dowling's great gifts to Bill Wilson and through him to Alcoholics Anonymous."[52] The divinization of thirst is a classic Christian message; Father Ed would have known it from Augustine's words to God at the start of his *Confessions*: "You have made us for yourself, and our heart is restless until it rests in you."[53]

When Bill asked Father Ed's opinion on another issue, the priest again drew upon ancient wisdom:

> Bill spoke of his own difficulties in prayer and his continuing problem in conveying the meaning of his "spiritual experience" to alcoholics. There was a move afoot within the fellowship just then, he told Dowling, to change that phrase in the Twelfth Step to "spiritual awakening"—it seemed to Bill an attempt to mask rather than to clarify the role of the divine in the alcoholic's salvation. Tartly, Father Ed offered a succinct response: "If you can name it, it's not God."

Kurtz, who titled his study of A.A. *Not-God*, seems to have been unaware that Dowling's words in this instance were a near-direct quote from Augustine. Father Ed—who, as we have seen, in his personal spirituality often followed the *via negativa*, the negative path to God—drew the saying from Augustine's Sermon 117, in which the saint says, "*Si comprehendis, non est Deus*"—if you comprehend it, it is not God.

Finally, after hours of conversation, Father Ed raised himself up to leave, using his cane to steady himself. Then he leaned down to meet Bill's gaze, looking intently at him. Thomsen, drawing from Bill's recorded recollections, says,

> he told [Bill] that the two of them in that little room were among the blessed of all time, for they were here, living now. Out of those who had gone before, and all those not yet born, they had been elected to stand up now and speak their piece. There was a force in Bill that was all his own, that had never been on this earth before, and if he did anything to mar it, or block it, it would never exist anywhere again.[54]

It was Father Ed's way of impressing upon Bill the message of Cardinal Newman's reflection: "God has created me to do Him some definite service; He has committed some work to me which He has not committed to another...."[55]

Then, Thomsen writes,

> [Dowling] hobbled over to the door, looked back, and as a parting shot said that if ever Bill grew impatient, or angry at God's way of doing things, if ever he forgot to be grateful for being alive here and now, he, Father Ed Dowling, would make a trip all the way from St. Louis to wallop him over the head with his good Irish stick.[56]

Bill was left feeling a great calm—and great hope. He would tell Thomsen "there was no way of describing what Father Ed did for him, the doors he flung open before him; after absorbing the impact of their first encounter, he awakened to a new reality, a totally altered view of himself and his place in the world."[57]

This meeting, Bill said in his talk to Catholic priests after Dowling's death, "was the beginning of one of the deepest and most inspiring friendships that I shall ever know. This was the first meaningful contact that I had ever had with the clergymen of your faith."[58]

As for Father Ed, perhaps the best indication of how he felt after meeting Bill was in a letter where he wrote that the inspiration he received in his work with alcoholics in A.A. was comparable to that which he received when he was ordained.[59] When he published a pamphlet on the fellowship, he dedicated it "in gratitude to the women and men of A.A."[60]

A month after Father Ed visited Bill, Jack Alexander came to St. Louis to investigate the A.A. group there. It was the reporter's final stop after researching A.A.'s activities in New York, Philadelphia, Akron, Cleveland, and Chicago. In each city after New York, he had shed some of his skepticism—particularly in Chicago, where he discovered that Eddie Lahey and other journalists like himself were benefiting from the fellowship.[61]

But, as Alexander later admitted, he was not convinced of A.A.'s validity and importance until he visited the group in St. Louis—his own hometown. "I met a number of my own friends who were A.A.s," he wrote, "and the last remnants of skepticism vanished. Once rollicking rumpots, they were now sober. It didn't seem possible, but there it was."[62]

Alexander wrote his article for the *Saturday Evening Post* while in St. Louis. Its glowing tone reflected his heartfelt appreciation of what Alcoholics Anonymous had done for people who were close to him. Once the article appeared, in March 1941, A.A.'s membership numbers skyrocketed and the Alcoholic Foundation raced to publish a second printing of the Big Book.

Today, Alcoholics Anonymous recognizes Alexander's article as "a milestone in the history of this fellowship," being "largely responsible for the surge of interest that established the society on a national and an international basis."[63] And Father Ed, as the organizing force behind the St. Louis A.A. group, was a vital link in the chain of circumstances that led Alexander to find, in his hometown, evidence that—in A.A.'s phrase—"it works."

10

⧼ᔜᔜ⧽

EXERCISES IN OBEDIENCE

I am grateful to God for the A.A. virus in my spiritual bloodstream.
                                                        —Father Ed[1]

Two months before Jack Alexander's article raised the national profile of Alcoholics Anonymous, the fellowship's St. Louis membership enjoyed a public-relations boost of its own.

The media coverage bore the hallmarks of a coordinated effort. Most likely, the fledgling A.A. chapter enlisted Father Ed and his journalist friend Joe Touhill to persuade local papers to report on it so that it might attract new members. They timed the publicity campaign to launch just after Christmas—the same week Ed Lahey had bottomed out just one year earlier. And it worked: between Christmas and New Year's, all three St. Louis dailies ran stories about the local fellowship. One article included Father Ed's first published comment on A.A.: "It is soundly based and does a great deal of good."[2]

The articles reached readers who were eager for what A.A. had to offer. On January 14, Father Ed wrote to Lahey and two other Chicago A.A. members, reporting that the St. Louis fellowship had received thirty letters from prospective members.[3]

But Father Ed also had something painful to share. One of the chapter's members had relapsed and was about to be admitted to a sanitarium for treatment. Worse, the member was "convinced he [could] do it alone without group aid."

In light of that sad news, Father Ed made a gentle request of the Chicago A.A. members:

> My real reason for writing is to express a hope that some of you
> get to St. Louis some weekend soon. While God has blessed our

start in St. Louis with sincere, congenial members, some of us feel that the quick growth, the relative magnitude of the candidates compared to the members, and the tendency to feel that social example may minimize the new members' recognition of the necessity of the spiritual.[4]

Without the spiritual, slips and failures seem like catastrophes. With the spiritual, these can be capitalized as realistic bases for increased dependence on God.

Hence, if there is any inclination among any of you folks to come down to St. Louis, I believe there is real good that you can do just now.[5]

Letters such as this show how Father Ed delicately shepherded the St. Louis A.A. fellowship through its initial months. As a priest, he was normally in a position to instruct people on spiritual matters. Yet, when it came to A.A. meetings, he knew that the only people qualified to offer spiritual guidance were the members themselves. If the St. Louis A.A. group stood in need of such mentorship, the best he could do was notify the more experienced Chicago A.A. members and hope they would heed the call. It was nothing short of a role-reversal—a priest asking laypeople to give the spiritual help that only they could provide.

Later on, when describing himself in relation to A.A. members, Father Ed would adopt a humorous term he had seen in the fellowship's *Grapevine* newsletter. As a nonalcoholic, he said, he was among the "underprivileged."[6]

Father Ed also set to work spreading the word about A.A. to his fellow clergy. One of the first priests he approached outside his Jesuit circle was Father John A. Keogh, a Philadelphia priest who had recently been elected to the presidency of the Catholic Total Abstinence Union—the leading U.S. Catholic temperance group.

After Dowling reached out by mail in March 1941, Keogh responded expressing a reservation about A.A.—one that the fellowship often encountered from Catholics in its early years. He feared that the Big Book's description of alcoholism as a "sickness" would lead A.A. members to believe that they lacked free will, which in turn would lead them to lose their sense of sin.[7]

It was no small concern; rather, it was the gravest concern a Catholic moralist could express. The then-reigning Pope Pius XII, in words that would later be echoed by Pope Francis, said, "Perhaps the greatest sin in the world today is that men have begun to lose the sense of sin."[8]

But Dowling was undaunted, for he knew A.A. too well to believe Keogh's suspicion had substance. He wrote in reply, with a lightness that likely shocked the temperance crusader, "While the sense of sin would be naturally lost in institutions of secular higher learning, this is an institution of secular lower failing."[9]

Behind his delightful elegance of expression, Father Ed's words show the extent to which—only a year after beginning to accompany A.A. members—he had so deeply absorbed the fellowship's philosophy that it had become part of him.

When considering how Father Ed budgeted his time during the decades after he discovered Alcoholics Anonymous, perhaps the most striking thing is that he did the opposite of what a priest in his circumstances might be expected to do. Given that his physical illness never abated—it only became worse over time—one might expect him to slow down, or at least to narrow the range of his activities. But that was never Father Ed's way. He never let go of his old pursuits; he simply added his new interests to his old ones, and pursued all of them at once.

The evidence of Father Ed's activities—from his desk calendars and other surviving papers to his hundreds of media mentions—together presents a picture of a man of extraordinary mental energy who continually pushed himself to his limits. In his letters and conversations, he shrugged off thoughts of mortality. He said in later years that, after his various brushes with death, the remainder of his life was a "curtain call."[10] Yet, the sheer volume and breadth of his outreach suggests he felt driven to spend whatever time he had left in helping people as much as he could.

And so it was that, even as Father Ed began to assist A.A. members and promote the fellowship's mission, he did not put aside what he admitted was his "fanatic" interest in proportional representation.[11] On the contrary, in fact, he increased his political activism and became ever more sought after for his expertise in democracy. In February 1941, he accepted an invitation from former New Hampshire Governor John G. Winant to serve on the council of the National Municipal League (today known as the National Civil League), which promoted democratic reforms on the local level.

However, although Father Ed remained active in the National Municipal League for the rest of his life, he did not remain long with another group that he joined at about the same time. America First, the most visible domestic group opposing the United States' entry into what was then known as the "European war," invited his participation as it established itself in St. Louis.[12] Father Ed served on the local America First committee alongside other prominent citizens, including the deans of both of the city's law schools.

Although history primarily remembers America First for its conservative supporters—particularly Charles Lindbergh, whose anti-Semitic comments at a rally caused scandal in the movement—the group's anti-interventionist goals attracted people from across the political spectrum. Many Irish Catholics were drawn to it because it appealed to their desire that the United States avoid helping England extend its military might. John F. Kennedy, then a senior at Harvard, sent America First a check for $100 (about $2,000 in 2022 dollars) with a note saying, "What you are all doing is vital."[13]

Father Ed continued his support of America First for several months. He attended a May 3 rally at the St. Louis Arena, where hometown hero Lindbergh addressed a crowd of fifteen thousand,[14] and co-sponsored a second rally August 1 at the Municipal Auditorium.[15] However, after the August 1 event, Dowling's name disappeared from the committee's rolls. Judging by a news account of the rally, it's not difficult to imagine why.

The *Post-Dispatch*'s account describes how Senator Gerald P. Nye, Republican of North Dakota, stirred up the crowd of twenty-five hundred with his claim that Hollywood had set up the "most gigantic engines of propaganda to rouse the war fever in America."[16] Nye went on to list the moguls he held responsible for Hollywood's' "insidious" efforts to turn the United States to war against Hitler. As he called out the film producers' names—Louis B. Mayer, Darryl Zanuck, Sam Goldwyn, and others—members of the audience began to shout mockingly after nearly every one of them, "*Jews! Jews!*"

Although there is no record of how Father Ed reacted to Nye's incitements, other occasions when Dowling was confronted with hate speech leave no doubt that he would have been utterly appalled. For years, he had worked alongside Jewish leaders to promote democracy, labor unions, and other social-justice causes, and he counted many of them among his closest friends. Father Ed therefore quietly quit America First—and none too soon, for the following month, Lindbergh caused an uproar with a speech expressing similar anti-Jewish conspiracism.

In October 1941, Norman Bierman, a Jewish lawyer active in St. Louis political life, wrote to the city's mayor proposing several candidates for the local Civil Service Commission—including Father Ed.[17] Although the mayor did not act on Bierman's suggestion, the letter is evidence that Dowling's temporary association with America First did not tarnish his reputation with Jewish leaders as an advocate for social justice.

At the 1941 Summer School of Catholic Action, Father Ed spoke passion-
ately against the two-party system's chokehold on the American electoral
process. He said during the school's Pittsburgh session, "Partyism is a dangerous form of factionalism that divides a country into maniac victors and
sullen, obstructionistic losers." As usual given Father Ed's media connections, a reporter was there to take down his words, which resulted in a sen-
sationalistic headline on the Associated Press newswire: "Priest Would
Make Ballots Very Blank."[18]

A Pittsburgh radio station invited Father Ed to give an on-air address
on democracy. Dowling used the opportunity to speak about how religious
people could "sanctify their citizenship":

> Catholicity teaches that you must free a man's soul before you can
> free his body. A man must think as a free man before he can act as
> a free man. Not in Athens with 80 percent of the people slaves, but
> at the Sermon of the Mount began the freeing of men's souls—
> began democracy.[19]

It was in essence the same point Father Ed had been making since he
began speaking on the topic ten years earlier—that the true spirit of democracy was to be found in the Our Father. But at this stage of his life, the
prayer had even greater meaning for him, for he now experienced it in a
deeper way through the unity he witnessed in A.A., where members typically would pray the Lord's Prayer at the close of meetings.

A scrap of paper preserved in the Dowling Archive testifies to the way
Father Ed's understanding of the Lord's Prayer developed through his contact with A.A. It is an invocation he gave at a meeting of the fellowship,
probably in St. Louis in 1941. The emphases in the text are Dowling's own;
he underlined the words with a red grease pencil:

> *Unknown* God of the Athenians
> *Power* greater than ourselves
> God of our *fathers*
>
> Our Father—who promised to be in our midst when two or three
>   are gathered—
> In thy name, we gather in thy *hallowed* name.
>
> We admit our powerless dependence on you for today's sobriety,
>   sanity, life.
> *For* these and all that come with them, we thank thee.

Forgive us today's trespasses.
Bless our *speaker*, use his words to help us make a personal
    inventory,
improve our conscious contact with thee,
increase our knowledge of thy will
and the power to carry it out.

Bless us this evening with a spiritual experience, a message to
practice in all our affairs
"until the shadows lengthen,
and the evening comes,
and the busy world is hushed,
and the fever of life is over,
and our work is done.
Then, Lord, in thy mercy,
grant us a safe lodging,
a holy rest, and peace at the last."[20]

What stands out is the way Father Ed builds by steps from the distant and impersonal "*Unknown* God of the Athenians" mentioned by St. Paul in Acts 17:23 to A.A.'s nearer but still nebulous "*Power* greater than ourselves," to the still nearer and more concrete "God of our *fathers*," and finally to the intimately personal "Our Father." He believed in like manner that the Twelve Steps (and, indeed, the whole of A.A.'s program), if practiced diligently, would guide the alcoholic from agnosticism to interior knowledge of the love of God.

Bill Wilson, like Father Ed, was a man gifted with enormous energy, and he needed it as he sought to make the most of the newfound attention Alcoholics Anonymous had received in the wake of Jack Alexander's *Saturday Evening Post* article. The spring of 1941 through 1944 was a period of rapid growth for the fellowship. Bill spent most of those years traveling so he might provide hands-on guidance to local chapters.

On October 22, 1941, Bill flew into St. Louis while in the midst of a Midwestern speaking tour so he could make his first-ever visit to the St. Louis chapter of A.A. as it approached its first anniversary.[21] The unseasonably hot weather—it was eighty degrees when Bill's plane landed—was matched only by the enthusiastic warmth of Father Ed, who met Bill at the Lambert airfield.

Father Ed took Bill to The Queen's Work, where his colleagues were eager to meet the A.A. co-founder. When Bill recounted the experience to an audience of Catholic clergy nearly twenty years later, he said he did not know what to expect when he arrived. "I had never been in such a place before. I had been raised in a small Vermont village, Yankee-style. Happily, there was no bigotry in my grandfather who raised me. But neither was there much religious contact or understanding."[22]

The atmosphere at The Queen's Work, Bill was happy to discover, was one of "delightful informality." Father Ed's Jesuit colleagues asked him about the Big Book—"and especially about A.A.'s Twelve Steps," Bill recalled.

> To my surprise they had supposed that I must have had a Catholic education. They seemed doubly surprised when I informed them that at the age of eleven I had quit the Congregational Sunday school because my teacher had asked me to sign a temperance pledge. This had been the extent of my religious education.[23]

He explained to the Jesuits how he had picked up certain key concepts from the Oxford Group—"self-survey, confession, restitution, helpfulness to others and prayer." The Twelve Steps thus sprang from his desire "to define more sharply and elaborate upon these word-of-mouth principles so that alcoholic readers would have a more specific program: that there could be no escape from what [A.A.] deemed to be essential principles and attitudes."

Father Ed's colleagues listened attentively to Bill's account of his composition of the Twelve Steps. Then they showed him something that took him by surprise. In Bill's words—

> My new Jesuit friends pointed to a chart that hung on the wall. They explained that this was a comparison between the Spiritual Exercises of St. Ignatius and the Twelve Steps of Alcoholics Anonymous, that, in principle, this correspondence was amazingly exact. I believe they also made the somewhat startling statement that spiritual principles set forth in our Twelve Steps appeared in the identical order that they do in the Ignatian Exercises.[24]

Although the chart Bill describes has not been preserved, it was almost certainly a modified version of one that had been created more than ten years earlier by John Markoe, SJ. Published in 1930 by The Queen's Work, the chart was intended to show how the essential elements of a thirty-day Spiritual Exercises retreat could be compressed into eight days.

It was Father Markoe who first noted to Father Ed the parallels between the Twelve Steps and the Spiritual Exercises, as Dowling recalled in an interview:

> I remember the astonishment of one Jesuit, whom I believe to be wise in the ways of the spirit, when he first read A.A.'s Twelve Steps.[25] He was astounded at the great similarity between those steps and the Foundation and First Week of the Spiritual Exercises of St. Ignatius, which contains the basic and ridding-oneself-of-sin part of Jesuit spirituality.[26]

It is quite possible that Markoe—an alcoholic who almost certainly learned of the Twelve Steps from Dowling—showed Father Ed his Spiritual Exercises chart and wrote on it to point out which Steps corresponded to particular parts of the Exercises. But even if Markoe did not write anything on the chart or otherwise adapt it, the chart's treatment of the Foundation and First Week of the Exercises lends itself readily to comparison with the Twelve Steps.

The Foundation is a brief instruction in which Ignatius explains the philosophy that underlies the Spiritual Exercises. It begins,

> Man is created to praise, reverence, and serve God our Lord, and by this means to save his soul.
>
> The other things on the face of the earth are created for man to help him in attaining the end for which he is created.
>
> Hence, man is to make use of them *in as far as* [*tantum*] they help him in the attainment of his end, and he must rid himself of them *in as far as* [*quantum*] they prove a hindrance to him.[27]

Markoe's chart features a numbered list of "spiritual fruits" that correspond to different points within the course of the exercises. The first four fruits correspond to the Foundation and are listed as follows:

1. Sense of nothingness
2. Utter dependence upon God
3. Gratitude; love for God
4. Resolve to attain end[28]

A person familiar with the Twelve Steps can easily connect those fruits with the principles of self-knowledge, God-consciousness, and surrender that characterize the first three steps:

> 1. We admitted we were powerless over alcohol—that our lives had become unmanageable.

> 2. Came to believe that a Power greater than ourselves could restore us to sanity.

> 3. Made a decision to turn our will and our lives over to the care of God as we understood Him.

Markoe's chart goes on to list spiritual fruits for the First Week of the Exercises. They include "intense sorrow" for one's sins, "firm resolve to amend," and "strong resolve to throw self on mercy of God and...become reconciled by a sincere confession." These likewise parallel (in almost exactly the same order) steps four through eight of the Twelve Steps:

> 4. Made a searching and fearless moral inventory of ourselves.

> 5. Admitted to God, to ourselves, and to another human being the exact nature of our wrongs.

> 6. Were entirely ready to have God remove all these defects of character.

> 7. Humbly asked Him to remove our shortcomings.

> 8. Made a list of all persons we had harmed, and became willing to make amends to them all.[29]

Almost certainly it was Markoe himself, along with Father Ed, who drew Bill's attention to the Spiritual Exercises chart on the wall at The Queen's Work office and pointed out the parallels to the Twelve Steps. An amazed Wilson exclaimed, "Please tell me—who is this fellow Ignatius?"[30]

Bill Wilson's St. Louis trip gave him a much-needed opportunity to renew his friendship with Father Ed after an exhausting past several months. In between overseeing A.A.'s responses to the thousands of inquiries that poured in after the *Saturday Evening Post* article and his near-constant travels to local chapters, he had been refurbishing his and Lois's new home—the first one they ever owned. Located in bucolic Bedford Hills, New York, the house was just over an hour from Manhattan by train but felt like it was a world away from the city's clutter, noise, and smoke. Although the Wilsons would later name it Stepping Stones, it proved no mere stepping stone for them but a permanent residence and peaceful haven.

Before Bill departed from St. Louis, he extracted a promise from Father Ed to visit him and Lois. Dowling, with a glance at his desk calendar, saw that he was to be in New York City at the end of December for the annual meetings of the American Political Science Association and the American Catholic Sociological Society. So he delightedly agreed to stay with Bill and Lois for a few days beginning on New Year's Day.[31]

On January 6, 1942—his first day back at The Queen's Work after his visit to the Wilsons—Father Ed wrote to Bill, "I want to thank Lois for seconding your efforts to make that New Year's Day one of the happiest I've ever spent." Clearly the feeling was mutual, as Bill would write to Father Ed in January 1954 that he had thought back fondly upon their time together in Bedford Hills "a hundred times since."[32]

Father Ed's Bedford Hills visit was a time of spiritual refreshment for Bill as well as for himself. When Bill shared with Dowling about his own continuing struggle against discouragement, the Jesuit assured him that the sacrifices he was making to promote A.A. bore tremendous fruit in transformed lives.

One story Father Ed told the A.A. co-founder about a life transformed by the fellowship made such an impression upon Bill that it became a mainstay of his public talks. Almost certainly Bill added his own details to the story, starting with the place (for Dowling was visiting an A.A. chapter in Kansas City, not St. Louis, on the day in question).[33] Even so, its substance is pure Dowling:

> On the day that the staggering calamity of Pearl Harbor fell upon our country, a friend of A.A., and one of the greatest spiritual figures that we may ever know, was walking along a street in St. Louis. This was, of course, our well-loved Father Edward Dowling of the Jesuit Order. Though not an alcoholic, he had been one of the founders and a prime inspiration of the struggling A.A. group in his city. Because large numbers of his usually sober friends had already taken to their bottles that they might blot out the implications of the Pearl Harbor disaster, Father Ed was understandably

anguished by the probability that his cherished A.A. group would scarcely settle for less. To Father Ed's mind, this would be a first-class calamity, all of itself.

Then an A.A. member, sober less than a year, stepped along-side and engaged Father Ed in a spirited conversation—mostly about A.A. As Father Ed saw, with relief, his companion was per-fectly sober. And not a word did he volunteer about the Pearl Har-bor business.

Wondering happily about this, the good Father queried, "How is it that you have nothing to say about Pearl Harbor? How can you roll with a punch like that?"

"Well," replied the A.A., "I'm really surprised that you don't know. Each and every one of us in A.A. has already had his own private Pearl Harbor. So, I ask you, why should we alcoholics crack up over this one?"[34]

Apart from giving Bill encouraging evidence that his labors were hav-ing an impact, perhaps the greatest help Father Ed provided during that New Year's visit was guidance in discernment. Even at such an early point in the pair's friendship, Bill could sense that Father Ed was a problem-solver par excellence. And Bill badly needed the Jesuit's guidance, for he was at a crisis point in his work with A.A.

The problem was money. Bill was currently receiving a weekly stipend from donors who had attended a benefit dinner for A.A. hosted by the Rockefeller Foundation, and he also drew a weekly sum from A.A.'s Works Publishing company in view of the work he had done on the Big Book. Those amounts together, although quite modest in view of the full-time ser-vice Wilson was giving to A.A., were sufficient to support him and Lois. However, Bill knew he could not rely upon the Rockefeller Foundation din-ner funds indefinitely. Although A.A. did not yet have an official tradition of self-sufficiency, the guiding sentiment in the fellowship was that it should not receive contributions from outsiders.[35]

Bill also had scruples about receiving funds from Works Publishing. He knew that, if A.A. continued to grow, the Big Book's royalties alone could eventually provide him and Lois with enough income to support themselves fully. But he was concerned that if he received what he was rightfully due as the book's primary author and editor, he might be seen as breaking another as-yet-unwritten tradition in A.A.—that of receiving pay-ment for "Twelfth-Step work," which is the fellowship's crucial mission to "carry the message to alcoholics."[36]

At the time of Father Ed's New Year's visit, recent events added urgency to Bill's deliberations. Members of the Cleveland chapter had called for an investigation into A.A.'s finances after hearing rumors that the Rockefeller Foundation, Bill, and Dr. Bob had conspired to exploit the fellowship for profit. Bill and Dr. Bob were compelled to travel to Cleveland to answer members' questions; there, they presented a certified audit of A.A.'s finances that showed how outrageously wrong the accusations were.

Bill would later recall that the pain of that experience lay heavily on his mind as he asked Father Ed's advice on how he might best support himself and Lois:

> Shortly after the financial investigation episode, Father Ed Dowling, our Jesuit friend from St. Louis, turned up in New York. Still puzzled, I put the case up to him. He asked, "Do you think A.A. requires your full-time efforts?" I replied, "Yes, I think it does, perhaps indefinitely." Then he inquired, "Could you become a paid therapist, taking money for Twelfth Step work?" I told him that this issue had been settled long since. Most emphatically I could not, regardless of the consequences, nor could any other A.A. member.
>
> "Well, Bill," said Father Ed, "if you were the only one concerned, you could certainly start wearing a hair shirt and take nothing. But what about Lois? Once upon a time you made a marriage contract to support her. Suppose you put her on the charity of friends so that you can do a service organization job for A.A. free. Would that be the kind of support your marriage contract called for? I should think the royalties would be the best bet."
>
> That meant that Dr. Bob and I must certainly never accept money for Twelfth Step work but that we could be recompensed for special services. We both accepted Father Ed's down-the-middle advice and have stuck by it ever since, and I am glad to say this status for Dr. Bob and me was later accepted as correct in principle by our entire fellowship.[37]

Father Ed's astute guidance provided Bill with the discernment he needed to shape what would become the eighth of A.A.'s Twelve Traditions —the understanding that whereas it may never charge fees for counseling alcoholics, it may employ alcoholics for "special services."[38]

Bill's recollections of Father Ed reveal much of what his friendship with the Jesuit brought to his life. But what did Bill's friendship bring to

Father Ed? Although Father Ed did not reveal his inner life to others as readily as did Bill, it is possible to make a few educated guesses based on what is known of Dowling's personality and background.

First, Father Ed, throughout his Jesuit life, bore the cross of loneliness. He was built for friendship; throughout his childhood and teen years, he had enjoyed a wide circle of companions. But once he became a Jesuit, he was conditioned to avoid "particular friendships"—not only because of the threat they might pose to chastity but also (and primarily) because they might distract from the single-hearted devotion he owed God.

When Father Ed was ordained a priest, the clericalist atmosphere of his time (in which priests were looked upon as being above mortal men) further isolated him. Thus, although he made a conscious effort to remain in touch with people he cared about, including his old school friends and his Loyola Academy students, his status as a Jesuit priest militated against his being emotionally intimate with them. Bill helped fill the gap of friendship in Father Ed's life.

On a second and related note, although Father Ed had great fondness and respect for his Jesuit confreres, he remained a man of the people, preferring the company of laity. He hinted as much in his address to A.A.'s Second International Convention, when he said, "A great many sincere people say, 'I like Christianity, but I don't like Churchianity.' I can understand it. I understand it better than you do because I'm involved in Churchianity and it bothers me too!"[39]

Father Ed simply loved being around real people, and Bill was a real person. Like Father Ed, Bill was unafraid to make himself vulnerable and to meet needy people where they were.

Third, the death of Father Ed's brother James in 1918 left a hole in his heart that his surviving siblings (whom he loved dearly) could not fill. In particular, Father Ed missed the brotherly companionship that he and James had enjoyed. His surviving brother Paul, although intellectually gifted, struggled with mental-health issues that became more severe over time. He was incapable of encouraging Father Ed with hope and Christian joy in the way that James had done.[40] Bill Wilson, with his deep affection for Father Ed, stepped into the role of the adoring brother who had been missing from Father Ed's life.

Finally, Dowling and Wilson, despite the differences in their backgrounds, shared certain fundamental experiences. Each of them had hit bottom—Father Ed with his near-despair during his novitiate and Bill with his alcoholic downslide. Each of them was healed through a spiritual experience that led him to a profound personal conversion. And each of them, having had this liberation, felt inwardly compelled to dedicate his life to helping liberate others.

However, when Father Ed, as a young Jesuit, initially tried to plan a career for himself in bringing others the healing he had experienced, his superiors stymied his efforts. First they denied him his wish to do his doctoral research on the Spiritual Exercises, which was crucial to his goal of helping others find freedom in Christ. Then they removed him from advanced graduate studies altogether.

Although Father Ed would find meaning in his priestly ministry and in promoting proportional representation, he had to give up his dreams of bringing spiritual liberation to people on a large scale—until he discovered Alcoholics Anonymous. The Twelve Steps presented Father Ed with the opportunity he had been waiting for. They enabled him to bring his knowledge of the Spiritual Exercises to bear upon people's most difficult personal problems. Thus, Bill Wilson, both as author of the Twelve Steps and as his personal friend and collaborator, opened the way for Father Ed to fulfill his dreams that his superiors had deferred—and in a manner greater than he could have imagined.

Upon his return to St. Louis after the New Year's visit with Bill, Father Ed promoted A.A. even more vigorously than before. His desk calendars for the first few months of 1942 are dotted with reminders to give copies of the Big Book to various priests and laypersons he knew.

But Bill wanted Father Ed to be even more closely involved with the fellowship. When he met with Father Ed in St. Louis the previous October, he had asked the Jesuit if he might be willing to become one of the Alcoholic Foundation's trustees. Father Ed, although honored by the request, replied that he doubted his superiors would permit him to accept, given the Jesuits' general policy against having its members control funds of outside groups.

Now, in the wake of the New Year's visit, Bill renewed his invitation and continued to press it even as Father Ed attempted to demur. After putting off Bill's request several times, Father Ed mentioned the invitation to Father Lord, who, as his editor at The Queen's Work, would need to have a say on anything that might take his time away from his main job. Lord, who had great appreciation for A.A., urged Dowling to accept.

And so Father Ed telephoned his provincial superior, Father Peter Brooks, SJ, to tell him of the invitation and ask whether he should accept or reject it. Brooks asked him to make the request in a letter, which Father Ed sent on February 18, 1942.

Father Ed's letter to the provincial is interesting for the historical information it gives about A.A. and his involvement with it at that time, but most of all for what it reveals of his growing discernment with regard to how he might best serve the fellowship. Dowling began by briefly stating the facts: One of A.A.'s co-founders had asked him "five or six times" in the last several months to serve as a trustee for the organization; he had put off the invitation "with the suggestion that normally we do not accept such positions"; and he now felt he should give a definitive response. He added, "Father Lord has instructed me to say that he wants me to accept it if it is agreeable to you."

Then Father Ed described the nature of the role he was being asked to take on. A.A.'s trustees, he wrote, were entrusted with auditing the administration of the Big Book's royalties and the central office; at present, they included lawyers, businessmen, and John D. Rockefeller, Jr. (Upon reading that, the provincial likely wondered what need the organization would have for a Jesuit in such a role.)

As for his own involvement with A.A., Dowling wrote that for two years he had been in "quite close contact with the A.A.'s" and had met the two founders. He highlighted the spiritual benefits of the fellowship: "I have seen their use of gross humiliations as a bridge to humility and a consequent deluge of God's help." And he enclosed a letter from Father John Markoe, SJ, pointing out the parallel between the Twelve Steps and the First Week of the Spiritual Exercises, along with Bill Wilson's most recent letter to him. Of Bill, Father Ed wrote, "Like so many others [in A.A.], he started out as a pronounced agnostic." Dowling's message was clear: regardless of whether he should accept the trusteeship, there was no doubt in his mind that his service to A.A. had an important place in his ministry as a Jesuit priest.

Finally, in a display of classic Ignatian obedience—maintaining indifference before the manifested will of his superior—Father Ed laid out the pros and cons of accepting the invitation:[41]

> The arguments against accepting the trusteeship are the general arguments the Society had for not burdening itself with responsibilities for which it hasn't a great degree of control.
>
> The reasons that might counsel accepting the trusteeship are that Catholic thought be represented and that Catholics might feel freer to avail themselves of this deeply spiritual salvage of lives and families that are headed toward Hell here and hereafter.

If I do not accept the trusteeship, there will be no difficulty of explaining the reason on the grounds of general policy. My general feeling would be to politely ignore the request, and if it were not for the desire to be guided by obedience in the matter and also for the urgency of Father Lord's attitude, I would let the matter drop.

As soon as Father Ed completed his letter to Father Brooks, he wrote a letter to Bill Wilson confessing that the "prestige" of the proposed trusteeship appealed to him. Yet, he added,

The feeling that any pronounced institutional bias in the "officialdom" of A.A. might minimize the usefulness and frighten timid agnostics is a strong reason in my mind for its inadvisability. You must not forget the sinister suspicions that would be created by the presence of a crossback, mackerel-snapping Jesuit near the cash register.[42] I am afraid it would produce an epidemic of dry benders and spiritual shakes. However, I will feel safer in my decision if it is guided by obedience. I will let you know if Father Provincial decided to make an exception to a general policy of not undertaking trusteeships involving dispositions of money.[43]

Father Ed's concern for the universality of A.A.'s mission (and thus the need for it to avoid even the appearance of association with a particular religion) is admirable. The Jesuit knew that Bill would be sympathetic to his concern, given that Wilson himself had seen the need to sever the fellowship's ties to the Oxford Group. And Bill did sympathize—more than Father Ed would have liked. In a few years' time, Wilson would cite that same concern as one of his reasons why he could not convert to Catholicism.

The response from the provincial was as Dowling expected: no. Father Brooks deferred the decision to his assistant, who opined that, if the Catholic Church were to have an official association with A.A., the connection should be made through a local bishop rather than the Society of Jesus.

Additionally the provincial ventured an opinion of his own. Although innocent enough, it likely unnerved Father Ed.

"Since you have so many obligations of your own," Brooks wrote, "I wonder too if your future contacts with this organization are advisable. How much of your time does this require?"[44]

Given the agitation that Father Ed had expressed in the past to superiors who tried to rein in his activities, his response to Father Brooks was remarkably serene. Perhaps he had grown in his ability to resign himself to divine providence as it was expressed through his superior's will; perhaps, too, he was himself benefiting from the principles of surrender contained in A.A.'s first three steps.

Whatever the reason, Father Ed betrayed no distress as he wrote to Father Brooks to answer his questions. After detailing the amount of time he was expending on his ministry to A.A. members and to alcoholics who were not yet members of A.A., he added an assurance that must have been painful to type:

> As for future contacts with the organization, I do not foresee any certain opportunities for this and, in the light of your misgiving, I certainly shall try to avoid them. If circumstances catch me in such a situation, I shall try to be guided by what I feel are your unspoken wishes.[45]

Giving up contact with A.A. as an institution was one thing; giving up contact with A.A. members, however, was quite another. So Father Ed proceeded to provide an account of his ministry to individual alcoholics. His desire to continue such outreach showed through as he emphasized that those he assisted included "close friends":

> Some of them are very close friends and most of them seem to want to chat when they are disturbed. These close friends in A.A. amount to about six or eight in St. Louis and four or five out of St. Louis. Casual acquaintances in A.A. amount to about thirty in St. Louis and fifty outside of St. Louis.[46]

Father Ed went on to admit that "the quantity of the contact with the A.A. [might] seem inadequate to explain the offer of a trusteeship."[47] He explained that he believed that the value his spiritual guidance held for A.A. members lay in his making "a very free use of the Rules for the Discernment of Spirits for the Second Week (rules one can practice without preaching)."[48]

Of all Dowling's writings and interviews over the course of his life, those words reveal most precisely how he saw himself in relation to members of A.A. To Father Ed, the fellowship's members, whether they realized it or not, were traveling the road to perfection mapped out four hundred years prior by St. Ignatius Loyola. Once they made it through the first six steps, they had in effect completed the Exercises' First Week. In that week, exercitants are guided through what the Christian mystical tradition calls the purgative way, in which they seek to be purified from sin and from temptations to sin.[49]

Father Ed therefore saw his ministry to A.A. members as akin to the work of an Ignatian spiritual director who leads exercitants into the Second, Third, and Fourth Weeks of the Exercises. His goal was to help them ascend toward the two further states of Christian perfection—the illuminative way, in which the soul grows in virtue, and the unitive way, in which the soul enjoys peace in the love of God.[50] And he could do so particularly by instructing them in Ignatius's Rules for the Discernment of Spirits for the Second Week of the Exercises, which were designed to help people remain on the upward track. As Dowling explained to Brooks, "The spiritual life of this movement [A.A.] gradually creates problems in the illuminative way, and the tools and equipment that our Second Week [contains] give one great help in dealing with these people."[51]

In the final sentence of his letter to the provincial, Father Ed expressed in succinct terms his abandonment to divine providence: "My own best contribution to any project including the A.A. will be a contribution of obedience."[52]

Three days later, the morning mail brought a brief note from Brooks. "I am grateful to you for your letter of March 14th and your very complete report of your work with the A.A. organization," the provincial wrote. "It was not my intention to forbid you all contacts with this group." Brooks added reassuringly that his only concern was that Dowling not be overly burdened, given his current workload.

As Father Ed read Brooks's reply, his heart overflowed with feelings of consolation and gratitude to God.[53] His ministry to A.A. members, which had given new life to his priesthood, could be a contribution of obedience after all!

Given his Irish background, as well as his middle name, Dowling thought it no coincidence that the provincial's note arrived on March 17— St. Patrick's feast day. Providence had indeed smiled upon Father Ed.

11

STEPS IN A NEW DIRECTION

If you are too happy, Father Dowling will probably find you slightly boring.

— Anonymous friend of Father Ed[1]

One morning during the mid-1940s, Father Ed leaned on his cane outside the Jesuit residence at DuBourg Hall on the St. Louis University campus at West Pine and Grand, waiting for the car that would drive him a block and a half to The Queen's Work.[2] Cars and people moved briskly at SLU, and Dowling relied upon rides to get around safely.

A student, seeing Father Ed standing on the corner, thought he would do him a good turn. "Here, Father," he said, taking Dowling's free arm, "let me help you."

"Thanks, kid," Father Ed said. ("Kid" was his affectionate name for younger people.) And, with the student's help, Dowling made it across the street—to the opposite side of where his driver would be expecting to find him.

The driver came and went. Father Ed was left standing on the corner for some time until an acquaintance spotted him and drove him to his office.

Rosemary Hendron, a recent high-school graduate who was part of Father Lord's stenographic pool, breathed a sigh of relief when she saw Father Ed walk in. She was very fond of him and had become worried when he failed to arrive at his usual time. When he explained about the well-meaning student who left him on the wrong side of the street, Rosemary exclaimed, "Father, why didn't you tell him that you were waiting for a ride?"

"Oh, kid," Father Ed replied with a smile, "he was doing a work of mercy, and I wouldn't rob him of that."

Rosemary followed Father Ed into his office. Already a line of people were in the hall waiting to see him. Before he admitted them, he would want the dandruff brushed off the shoulders of his black clerical suit. She located the little brush he kept for that purpose and neatened him up, rewarded with a warm smile and a heartfelt "thanks, kid."

As Rosemary returned to her desk, she reflected sadly that Father Ed's dry skin, which she knew was one of the symptoms of his disease, was worse than usual; the red patches on his neck stood out against the white of his clerical collar. She made a mental note to stop at the Italian grocery on her way home to see if it had pure virgin olive oil.[3] Father Ed liked to use it on his skin; it was the only thing that seemed to help. Anything that had perfumes or additives only made his condition worse.

The people waiting to see Father Ed this morning looked like the usual mix—a newspaper journalist whose face Rosemary recognized, a society woman in a little velvet hat with a black mesh veil,[4] and a couple of men in suits who were together and looked to be either businessmen or politicians. Rosemary also spotted a couple of men farther down the hall who were shabbily dressed and unshaven. Undoubtedly they were waiting to see Father Ed too.

If this was like most days, the flow of visitors would continue into the afternoon. Whenever Rosemary and the other stenographers went out for lunch together and saw someone walking down West Pine Boulevard, they would wonder if the person was going to come in to see Father Ed, because he loved people.

And of those people he loved, so many were from the streets! Rosemary remembered the time when, as she and her co-workers were heading out to lunch, one of Father Ed's transient friends was heading in. Upon the stenographers' return, they discovered that two of the office's typewriters were missing.

Rosemary waited until Father Ed had a moment in between visitors and alerted him to the theft. He had no doubt who had taken the machines. "We'll get them back," he assured her.

Even when Father Ed knew that one of his friends had done something wrong, "he never, ever criticized or belittled anyone," Rosemary recalled in a 2020 interview. "But he had ways of getting things back [when] these guys would come in and they had sticky fingers."

As Father Ed gained a reputation for being something of a divinely appointed "ambassador at large to humanity" (in the words of one friend),[5]
Emilie Basel, a United Press reporter in her late twenties, ventured to his
office one day in early 1943 to experience his ministry for herself. In an article that appeared in dozens of newspapers around the country, she wrote,

> Mixing oil and water is an easy trick compared to the variegated ac-
> tivities Father Edward Dowling, SJ, blends into his contented life.
> At 44, he sits happily in his office, nibbling chocolate bars and com-
> menting keenly, sometimes radically, but accurately on any topic
> you'd care to discuss.
>
> Nominally, he is associate editor of *The Queen's Work*, na-
> tional Catholic magazine. Actually he combines that with fifteen
> other organizations ranging from the American Political Science
> Association to Alcoholics Anonymous. His friends call him "Fa-
> ther Eddie."[6] . . .
>
> Father Dowling speaks easily, pausing occasionally to punctu-
> ate his remarks with a deep, infectious chuckle. As he warms to his
> subject, he runs stubby fingers through his corn-yellow hair until it
> points stiffly to the four corners of the room.[7] A huge man, he
> lounges back in his swivel chair, coat off, sleeves rolled. . . .
>
> A steady stream of people flows into his small office for ad-
> vice, information, or simply to let off steam. Father Dowling
> greets each one with an unaffected enthusiasm. He dispenses com-
> ments and bits of chocolate freely, sending each person away
> seemingly happier for their brief contact.[8]

The article left at least one reader happier—Bill Wilson, who was delighted to see his beloved friend receive national attention. He wrote to Father Ed in March 1943, "I see by the papers that people call you 'Father
Eddie' and that you are a Jesuit of unusual promise. They will be putting
you down in the kitchen if you don't look out!"[9]

On a serious note, Bill—never one to be shy about his need for his
friends and his fondness of them—added,

> You have no idea how many times I think of our talks together. To
> me they are really treasured experiences.
>
> When will there be another?

Affectionately,
Bill[10]

Three months later, Bill would have his wish for another in-person talk with Ed when he was invited to St. Louis for a dinner that the local chapters of A.A. were hosting in his honor.[11] Among the topics the two friends may have discussed during that June visit was their mutual desire to see A.A. become racially integrated. In October, Father Ed wrote a letter to his friend Joe Diggles[12] in which he shared a story that Bill told of the time he attempted to bring a Black member into the fellowship:

> Bill Wilson, editor of the book and co-founder of A.A., brought a Negro to a downtown New York meeting about four or five years ago, with the same spirit you would expect from the man who wrote most of the quotations you sent me [from the Big Book].[13] He anticipated no difficulty because of the tolerant cosmopolitan character of A.A. and also because of his supposed leadership status. He ran into strenuous objection.[14]

Diggles, an Irish American who lived in Chicago and had been in A.A. for a year, had written asking Father Ed to register a protest with his Chicago A.A. friends over the chapter's excluding Black people from membership. In his reply, Father Ed (after relating the story of Bill's failed effort to integrate the fellowship) wrote emphatically that both he and Wilson believed that admitting Black members would be an unqualified gain for the fellowship:

> I think that Bill Wilson (he is from Vermont)[15] would feel that the poor and the underprivileged are the best guarantee of the sincerity of A.A. Without any qualification, I believe that any A.A. group could telescope months and years of spiritual progress by the presence of Negro members. I am glad you are working on that dining-car waiter, and if he comes to St. Louis on his trips, ask him to look me up.[16]

Having made his and Bill's sentiments clear, Father Ed then explained that, out of respect for the integrity of the fellowship, he could not impose his own views upon members. "The A.A. principle of self-help and policy control by alcoholics has precluded me from ever presumptuously trying to interfere with the policy of A.A. individuals or groups except in individual conversation such as we are having in this letter."[17]

Thus, the most that Father Ed could do under the circumstances was to encourage Diggles as he sought to change the Chicago fellowship from within:

Chicagoans have less excuse than St. Louisans for Jim Crowism, and even here in St. Louis I think that the few Negro alcoholics that would turn up would do the local A.A. very much good in its growth of the [fellowship's] basic spirituality.

Any use you want to make of my views, you [have], as an A.A., every right to use, since you asked me.[18]

Dowling wrote that he was sending carbons of his letter to Bill Wilson and to Chicago A.A. member John T., adding, "I am convinced that these men are as opposed to Jim Crowism as you are." He encouraged Diggles to "talk this matter over with them."[19]

In putting his support behind bringing Black people into the fellowship, and using his networking skills to connect members who shared that goal, Father Ed set forces in motion that sped the formation of A.A.'s first Black chapters. It is surely no coincidence that the first Black A.A. chapter was founded in St. Louis in January 1945. Father Ed's hand may also have been at work in connecting the chapter with its spiritual director, Father Austin Bork, SJ. The pastor of the Black Catholic parish St. Malachy's, Father Bork was a close friend and collaborator of Father John Markoe, SJ—the alcoholic who had shown Father Ed the connections between the Twelve Steps and the Spiritual Exercises.[20] And Joe Diggles, buoyed by Father Ed's encouragement, provided meeting space to Chicago's first Black A.A. group, which formed in March 1945. One year later, the speaker at the group's anniversary dinner was John T.—the very same person whom Father Ed urged Diggles to contact for help in bringing Black people into the fellowship.

But Father Ed's work to promote integration and racial justice went well beyond such behind-the-scenes efforts. He regularly used his column in The Queen's Work's eponymous monthly magazine to raise readers' consciousness on race issues. In January 1943, decades before Pope John Paul II brought Our Lady of Guadalupe to the awareness of Catholics outside Latin America, Father Ed wrote about the sixteenth-century Marian apparition's importance for racial justice. "It was as an Indian virgin that Mary appeared at a time when European exploiters from Cape Cod to Magellan's Strait were treating Indians as if they were not human. Today the Indian Virgin of Guadalupe is patroness of all Latin America."[21]

The following month, Father Ed again brought racial issues to the fore of his Queen's Work column. Its lead item juxtaposed two quotations from recent news reports. In the first, Judge Landis, the major-league baseball commissioner, claimed defensively, "There is no rule, formal or informal, or any understanding, unwritten, subterranean, or sub-anything against the hiring of Negro players in the rank of organized baseball." In the second, a newswire reported that, at a joint session of the National and American leagues, CIO delegates sought to present a demand that Black players be permitted major-league tryouts—but "Commissioner Landis stifled the movement by refusing to give the CIO representative an audience."

Father Ed presented the two quotations with no comment. But the headline he chose left no doubt about what he thought of Commissioner Landis: "ARYAN BASEBALL."[22]

Alcoholics Anonymous members and other people with problems weren't the only ones seeking Father Ed's guidance during the early 1940s. Hollywood also came calling.

Metro-Goldwyn-Mayer producer Cliff Reid had heard about Dempster MacMurphy, Father Ed's late reporter friend who had spread devotion to St. Dismas (the Good Thief), and wanted to make the journalist's story into a film. When he learned that it was Father Ed (whose vow name was Dismas) who first interested the reporter in the saint, he contacted Dowling and invited him to come to Hollywood to advise the scriptwriters as they began work on the project. Father Ed flew out in early December 1943 and stayed for two weeks.

It should be no surprise that Hollywood did not change Father Ed. He wrote to Father Lord from his studio-provided room at the Beverly Wilshire Hotel:

> As elaborate and offhand as MGM seems, the whole thing increases my respect for the personnel and spirit of The Queen's Work. On the surface, everything here [is] easygoing—but you soon realize that everyone is working under the gun and the pressure is intense.[23]

But Father Ed did change Hollywood. Although the Dismas film—which went through many rewrites before it was released in 1946 as "The Hoodlum Saint"—turned out to be, in Dowling's words, "something of a bust,"[24] he made a lasting impression upon one MGM employee: Judy Garland.

Dowling was dining with British screenwriter James Hill in the studio commissary when he first saw Garland, who was then filming "Meet Me in St. Louis." "I felt sure that I would have recognized Judy Garland," Father

Ed wrote to Father Lord. "But even after Jim pointed her out, I found it hard to realize from her champagne cocktail to her chocolate sundae."[25] Although there is no further mention of the actress in his archived correspondence,[26] Dolores Tygard, who knew Dowling well and visited him at The Queen's Work, wrote after Father Ed's death that "he and Judy Garland corresponded for years."[27]

Three months later, in March 1944, it was Bill Wilson who received a call from Hollywood. Although Bill was suffering from a debilitating depression at the time, he managed to summon the energy to type a letter to Father Ed:

> The Selznick Agency has approached us about a possible movie to be a serious picture about Alcoholics Anonymous. They say we can be warranted that the A.A. background and philosophy will be sympathetically portrayed....
>
> Do you think this idea any good for A.A.?
>
> And does your recent experience in Hollywood give you confidence that we could get a good job done?
>
> Should they settle, by any chance, on my own story, do you think I ought to back away?
>
> I know, good sir, that you don't give advice. But how about a few "curbstone" observations?[28]

Father Ed took some time to reflect upon Bill's questions. When he finally responded, in April, his tone was encouraging but subdued. "For the time being," he wrote, "there is no harm in going slow on the Hollywood thing."[29] He may have been concerned that Bill, when undergoing dry benders, was vulnerable to placing his hopes in grandiose schemes.

Even so, Dowling did not hesitate to provide the practical observations that Bill requested. "My vision of the picture would be a three-stage picture," he wrote. The first would be "the sobering stage"; the second would be "the social stage," and the third would be "the spiritual stage."

Father Ed's tripartite division provides a window into how he thought the A.A. experience could best be encapsulated to outsiders. It was about becoming sober, becoming involved with other human beings (both in accepting their fellowship and in spreading the message to those in need of sobriety), and becoming involved with God.

Although nothing came of the proposed film, Dowling continued to reflect upon how to present A.A.'s message to non-alcoholics. And the more he did, the more he became convinced that the fellowship's true purpose went well beyond sobering up drunks. As he put it in a talk at an open meeting of A.A. in Wilmington, Delaware:[30]

> In the Alcoholics Anonymous plan of life, one finds an overall plan for personal adjustment.... When the A.A. movement was founded, it just happened that the immediate problem with Bill, the founder, was alcoholism. It is a program no less effective for other things.[31]

What kind of "other things" did Father Ed have in mind? He offered some examples in a March 1944 *Queen's Work* article on A.A. and Twelve Steps:

> If you can't stop biting your fingernails, growling at your mother-in-law, or are obsessed with any other deteriorating habit, just substitute your vice for alcohol in the following twelve steps and see if you have the courage even to start the program.[32] It is very practical for men and women who are drinking too much loneliness, anxiety, and discouragement these days.[33]

In these suggestions, one point is particularly indicative of how Father Ed understood the Twelve Steps as well as how he understood "deteriorating habits" in general: his belief that the steps benefited "men and women who are drinking too much loneliness, anxiety, and discouragement." Although Dowling had never been an alcoholic, he understood loneliness, anxiety, and discouragement. Those had been his own "deteriorating habits" when he was in the novitiate, and he overcame them through the ascetic program mapped out by St. Ignatius in the Spiritual Exercises—a program whose outlines he recognized in the Twelve Steps.

Dowling's language of "drinking too much loneliness, anxiety, and discouragement" also harkened back to his first conversation with Bill Wilson, when he quoted Jesus's words from the Beatitudes, "Blessed are they who hunger and thirst" (Matthew 5:6). He explained the point in detail in a pamphlet on A.A. published by The Queen's Work that is well worth quoting at length, especially given that it is out of print and hard to find:[34]

A.A.'s great contribution to the treatment of chronic alcoholism is their concentration of effort on *thirst* rather than *drink*. . . .

The A.A. program is the slow seeping of God into the thirsty soul of the alcoholic; the alternative is a deluge of alcohol.

It is exactly at this point in the treatment of thirst that the lessons of A.A. start to have a universal application. The A.A. people know that fear, discouragement, futility, and loneliness are the four melancholy horsemen of the alcoholic apocalypse. These Our Lord contended with in the Garden of Olives, and consciously or unconsciously the A.A.'s have imitated him in his answer—the only possible answer: "Not my will but thine be done." It was only after Christ said this that the angel ministered to him and quenched his terrible thirst, ministered to his fear, discouragement, futility, and loneliness.

Such thirst is universal. It was the great Augustine's thirst for God that supplied the entire subject matter of his Confessions. The reason that it is such a great book is to be found of course in the fact that every human being in some measure sees his own experience mirrored therein. . . . That thirst is built into us, a part of our nature, and the only thing that adequately satisfies it is God. But like Augustine, most of us will try anything and everything else before we come to God to quench that thirst. . . . The alcoholic exemplifies just one type of thirst; he happens to be the kind of person who tries to short-circuit this pursuit of God by seeking a pleasurable oblivion in drunkenness. . . .

The success of the A.A. reminds me of an old saw: There must be something wrong with Christianity because of the terrible state of affairs in the "Christian world." But the real problem is that Christianity is not being tried at all, and the state of the world is the precise result of Christ's being left out of the world.[35]

The A.A.'s have tried some of the fundamental and basic tenets of Christianity, and those tenets have worked wonderfully with them.

The alcoholic problem and its A.A. solution can by analogy be applied to any chief vice that is found in human beings.[36]

Father Ed's use of the term "chief vice" is revealing. Catholic preachers and spiritual writers of his time urged the faithful to seek God's grace to root out their predominant vice so that their other vices might more easily follow. In calling the A.A. program a means of combating one's chief vice,

Dowling was effectively asserting that the fellowship was doing more than merely trying out some "basic tenets of Christianity." It was genuinely accomplishing the work of Christ in the world by bringing the goal of faith—a closer walk with God—to people who otherwise might never internalize the Christian message. That was a provocative claim for a Catholic priest to make in 1947. Not until Vatican II would the Church teach that "whatever is truly Christian"—even if proclaimed by non-Catholics—could bring Catholics "a deeper realization of the mystery of Christ and the Church."[37]

Although Father Ed often spoke of what he learned from the Twelve Steps, he was equally if not more impressed with A.A.'s social aspect. Certainly, the idea that alcoholics could find healing in fellowship with other alcoholics appealed to his democratic sensibilities. But more than that, it felt right to him because communion in suffering and healing was so near an echo of the communion Christ intended for the fellowship he founded, which was "a sort of Christians Anonymous" (as Father Ed once termed the Catholic Church).[38]

In 1944, Dowling discovered a new way to apply the social aspect of A.A. (and a hint of the Twelve Steps as well) to help people with problems. As with his discovery of A.A., it was laity who led the way. But this time, it was not just a single layman, but a lay couple, Pat and Patty Crowley of Chicago.

Pat Crowley was one of Father Ed's many former Loyola students who remained in close touch with him. Back in 1937, when Pat and Patty were preparing for their wedding, Father Ed took the train to Chicago so he could give them marriage instruction at the bar of the Bismarck Hotel.[39]

Since their marriage, the Crowleys had become active in Catholic Action—the pre-Vatican II lay movement that encouraged Catholics to bring their faith into their social and political engagement. In July or early August of 1944, a former high-school classmate of Patty's invited her and Pat to join several other couples at a "Family Renewal Day" led by Father John P. Delaney, SJ, who was prominent in Catholic Action circles.[40] Although the day included practices typical of a spiritual retreat—including Mass and Benediction—its overall focus was to help couples come to see the practical aspects of marriage in a spiritual light. To that end, it included lectures by Delaney and round-table discussions where the couples took charge. At its close, the priest led the couples in a renewal of their wedding vows.

Patty was "thrilled" by the retreat,[41] and her husband was equally enthusiastic. Knowing of Father Ed's interest in marriage ministry (he had
lectured on it at the Summer School of Catholic Action), they contacted
him and suggested he consider leading a Family Renewal Day himself.

Intrigued, Father Ed did some research on the Family Renewal movement (and likely asked Father Delaney about it, as the two knew each other
well). When he was next in Chicago during the final week of August 1944,
he spoke at the Summer School of Catholic Action on "Mental Compatibil-
ity in Marriage." As word circulated among Father Ed's Chicago friends
that he was interested in Family Renewal, a local Catholic couple invited
him to come to their home one evening to deliver that same talk to a group
of married couples. Father Ed would later thank the couple for "a beautiful
memory."[42] He was impressed to see how much the married couples benefited not only from his talk but also from being able to speak openly with
one another.

But before Father Ed was ready to host his own Family Renewal Day,
he wanted one more practice run. So he phoned his former student J. Raymond Fox, who with his brothers owned the Fox De Luxe Brewing Company, and asked him to arrange a gathering of a few of his Loyola Academy
classmates with their wives. Although Father Ed never mentioned that gathering when describing the origins of what became known as the Cana Conference movement, Fox's son Michael (who was seven at the time) says it
was the first-ever Cana Conference.[43] Perhaps the gathering was written out
of Cana's history because it took place not in a church but in the tap room
of the Fox De Luxe Brewery on West Monroe Street, which the Fox brothers purchased in 1933 from Al Capone.

After the tap-room conference, Father Ed had the confidence he needed
to bring his own version of the Family Renewal Day to his hometown of St.
Louis. It was then that, with his gift for public relations, he dubbed the
event the Cana Conference. The very name *Cana* reflected Dowling's dual
interests in faith and community. It came both from the wedding at Cana,
where Jesus performed his first miracle (John 2) and from the initials for
"Couples Are Not Alone"—an inspiration Father Ed took from We Are Not
Alone, a support group founded by former mental patients.

Father Ed, in relating Cana's history, took care to emphasize that he did
not found the movement on his own. A layman and laywoman, each with
specialized skills and experience, helped him adapt the Family Renewal
Day concept and gave him the encouragement he needed to move forward.

"During the summer of 1944," Father Ed wrote in an article for his Jesuit confreres,

Mr. Bolen J. Carter [of the St. Louis Catholic Worker community] and Mrs. Thomas J. [Harvey] Kinsella—he of public high-school teaching and she of social-service background—frequently discussed the idea with the writer.

"Let's get out of the clouds and do something about it," they kept insisting. We did something. I realized that I was standing in the way and that if I would get out of it, the venture would probably progress.

So they each got one other couple; I enlisted a third. At their first meeting, the five couples proposed to meet again a week later, each promising to bring one other couple.

Came the next week, and the ten couples decided to try a day with husbands and wives together at a central place in St. Louis.[44]

In encouraging the married couples to take the lead in organizing Cana Conferences, Father Ed took a significantly different approach than that of Father Delaney and other priests in marriage ministry. Here again, his actions presaged the teachings of Vatican II, which urged clergy to promote laypersons' dignity by encouraging them to take up apostolic work on their own initiative.[45]

When Father Ed and the Cana couples began to plan the first public Cana Conference, one of the questions they had to consider, given that St. Louis was a segregated city, was whether the event would be open to Black people. They decided to make it open to all races, and that remained the policy for St. Louis Cana Conferences from then on.

Although there is no record of how the decision-making process went, it is safe to say that Father Ed, despite wanting the laity to take the lead, would have urged that Cana be an interracial ministry. With each passing year, his words and actions in support of racial justice were growing bolder.

In August 1945, Father Ed made headlines with a fiery speech against the hypocrisy of Northerners who were content to mock racist Southern politicians while overlooking racism in their own communities. Speaking at the Summer School of Catholic Action at Chicago, he said of a Mississippi politician who was an ardent segregationist and member of the Ku Klux Klan, "I admit that Senator [Theodore] Bilbo's actions are shocking and his statements insulting."[46] Then he turned his attention to his audience:

But at the same time it does seem preposterous for the people in the Northern states with their restrictive covenants and industrial and educational discrimination to be denouncing anyone else. In effect we imply that it is all right to be anti-Negro if you are polite about it.

Periodically the people and newspapers in the rest of the country will rise up in highly publicized indignation at conditions in the South. We think that because we let the Negro ride in the streetcars with us that we have solved the race problem and that we can continue to place economic and social restrictions on him that often have tragic consequences.

Father Ed then suggested to his audience that if they and other Northerners truly opposed the racism of politicians such as Bilbo, they should take action by eliminating racial restrictions in their own communities.

As long as we have our own prejudices, anything we say about the South remains shocking hypocrisy. We must practice what we preach. The elimination of the Jim Crow car is not enough. We must remove Jim Crowism from hotels, restaurants, neighborhoods, offices, factories. When we do, then we can start criticizing Bilbo.

Dowling's perspective would have been familiar to his listeners from the Sermon on the Mount: "Why do you notice the splinter in your brother's eye, but do not perceive the wooden beam in your own eye?" (Matt 7:1–5). And certainly Father Ed, who often referred to the Sermon on the Mount in his talks, would have had Jesus's admonition in mind. But he was also likely thinking of A.A., for he was in effect calling upon his audience to take a Fourth Step approach to racism—to have the courage to make "a searching and fearless moral inventory" of themselves.

On October 15, 1944, twenty-seven couples, including two who were Black, attended the first public Cana Conference at the City House of the Convent of the Sacred Heart in St. Louis. The event went over so well that a second one was arranged for the following month at the same venue. This time, organizers admitted non-Catholic couples and those in mixed (interreligious) marriages, including Jews—a radical move at a time when the Church's Code of Canon Law still labeled non-Catholic Christians *haereticis aut schismaticis* ("heretics or schismatics").[47] Yet again, Father Ed, with his lay collaborators, was twenty years ahead of his time.

The overwhelmingly positive response to the first Cana Conference at City House so excited Father Ed that he wrote to Father Lord asking that he be shifted off his publicity duties at The Queen's Work so he could focus on Cana. When Father Lord declined the request,[48] Dowling, with help from his sister Anna (who by then had become his secretary), did as he had always done. He simply added this latest interest to his ever-lengthening list of things he was passionate about, and pursued it with an energy level that never seemed to wane, even as his arthritis continued its slow but inexorable progress. By June 1946—less than two years after Cana began—Father Ed had organized or led Cana Conferences in thirteen U.S. dioceses, reaching one thousand couples in St. Louis alone.[49] And by 1949, no less than fifteen hundred St. Louis couples had attended a Cana conference, and the Cana movement itself—with the added efforts of Archdiocese of Chicago Cana director Father John J. (Jack) Egan—had expanded to 110 cities in thirty dioceses.[50]

Father Ed's involvement alone was not enough to account for the popularity of the Cana movement as dioceses nationwide began to host Cana Conferences of their own. It clearly filled a need that Catholic married couples had for fellowship and guidance, particularly during the postwar baby boom. Although other priests such as Egan did more to organize and expand the movement, Father Ed remained Cana's most popular conference speaker.

What exactly did Father Ed discuss at Cana Conferences? Perhaps the best answer to that question, out of the handful of Dowling's Cana talks that survive in written or recorded form, is summed up in a single page of a talk he gave in 1952. "Unity in General" was Father Ed's introductory address at a daylong conference. His first words to the assembled couples were,

The spirit of this Cana conference is not to get something out of it. Rather, [it is] the spirit of a visit to Christ. When we visit our mothers and fathers, it is to give them something, and in doing so that we find our pleasure.

It is not a day in which we will discuss spiritual things as much as discuss ordinary things spiritually.

Among the many ways that marriage can be viewed, today we view it as your soul and body joined to the soul and body of the person sitting next to you, and this joined unit is joined to God who is also next to you. For he has promised that when "two are gathered in my name, I will be in their midst" [Matt 18:20].

There are secondary joint activities between you two, such as a joint house, joint recreations, joint finances, children; but the primary joinings that we would like to discuss today are the joining between you two and the joining of you two with God.

The secondary joining (finances, recreation, etc.) will work out much better if the primary joining of you two persons is successful.

When we come to this primary union of you and the person next to you, we find that marriage not only involves a union of bodies but a union of souls. What is the relation between them? Is bodily union a vestibule to soul union or vice versa?

A mother kissing and hugging her son back from a European concentration camp gives a real clue to the relationship. Anybody describing this kissing and hugging between mother and son as a bodily action would miss its larger and fuller import in the soul union there. However, if there were not these embraces and kisses between the long-separated mother and son, manifesting deep soul unity, they would be very abnormal people.

In this instance we see that the bodily union involved in the kiss or the embrace is the result of soul union. Modern or temporary [*sic*] propaganda may suggest the dangerous reverse of these two. The doctrine that physical intimacy will lead to mental intimacy is dangerous, not only morally but psychologically, because bodily intimacy can create barriers to mental intimacy....

The *extrinsic*, the *exterior* joint activities, such as finances, recreation, children, house, occupations, depend in very large measure on the successful joint activity of the *interior* and *intrinsic* joining of the bodies and souls of you two.[51]

Central to the Cana concept were three principles that Father Ed brought over from Alcoholics Anonymous. They were, as Dowling later put it,

First, that a husband and wife could share their spiritual life.[52] Second, that sanctity was not necessarily uniformed [in the garb of a priest or nun]. Third, that experienced amateurs were often more capable of handling their own non-sacramental affairs than inexperienced professionals.[53]

Although the Cana movement succeeded in applying the first two principles, it faltered at applying the third, due to the Church's prevailing clericalist mentality. Such a mentality existed among laity as well as clergy; many faithful were unused to apostolic movements that lacked the visible direction of a priest.

Still, Father Ed did what he could to ensure that Cana Conferences under his guidance afforded couples as much agency as possible. He had much the same admiration for Cana couples as he did for members of A.A. Writing to *Guideposts* editor Grace Perkins Oursler in 1949, five years into his Cana ministry, he observed,[54]

Saving marriages from serious mistakes is an occasional by-product of Cana, but this aspect of it is relatively dull—like the pre-A.A. escapades of an alcoholic (and Cana has borrowed definitely and heavily from A.A.).

For the most part, the couples who come to Cana Conferences are enjoying their marriage and want to enjoy it more. If there is a Big League in the art of marriage, I believe most of the couples who have enjoyed Cana Conferences would be in it.[55]

The admiration was mutual. Typical of the responses Father Ed received was a letter from a woman who was present when he addressed 110 couples in Minneapolis:

Last night I was a part of your spellbound audience at Incarnation Church when you spoke on Christian Marriage to the Cana couples. I'm sure that I speak for every couple there when I say I went away marveling at your insight and vowing I'd help build a happier, holier married life. For my part, the discussion could have continued all night.[56]

A man who attended the same talk picked up his pen at nearly 1 a.m. the next morning to write a thank-you to the priest who sponsored it. "[Father Ed] was everything you said he was and more," he wrote. "He had the audience in the palm of his hand throughout his talk. I think everyone would still be there if he hadn't had to leave at 10:30 to catch his train."[57]

It was not only the spiritual content of Father Ed's talks that fascinated couples. The Jesuit peppered his lectures with quotations from trendy books by Freudian psychologists on sexual unhappiness in marriage. He chose to quote Freudians because he wished to show that "materialist" psychologists (meaning those whose philosophy denied the realm of soul) could accurately diagnose married couples' sexual problems but were incapable of solving them. Cana, by contrast, taught that the reason many married couples were unable to enjoy satisfying bodily intercourse was because they lacked satisfaction in their "soul intercourse" (as Father Ed called it). If their soul intercourse was satisfying, their bodily intercourse would be too.

Among the quotations that Father Ed used to make his point were medical experts' observations concerning the difficulties many married women had in achieving orgasm. That was an unusual issue for a Catholic priest to raise, to say the least. But Father Ed was not bringing it up for the sake of being shocking. He discussed the physiological and psychological aspects of sexual satisfaction because he knew they were vital components of a happy marriage, and anything that related to a happy marriage was of interest to him. His favorite quotation on the topic was from Lewis M. Terman's *Psychological Factors in Marital Happiness*: "Our search for [the answer to this question], so hopefully begun, has been disappointing. Why one woman out of three fails to achieve orgasm, or achieves it only rarely, is still a mystery."[58]

At one Cana talk in about 1947, after reading those words of Dr. Terman, Father Ed added,

> Now, it's false to pretend that what these careful, scientific people are finding mysterious, we've got all sewed up. [But] there's room for Cana. You're apt to come and say, what would anybody else know more about marriage more than I? Maybe neither of us know much. [But] maybe with God's help we can find something.[59]

To the Cana couples, such words would have been revelatory. Even if what Cana taught them about building "soul intercourse" failed to help them increase their sexual satisfaction, Father Ed's acknowledgement of the importance of such satisfaction (particularly for wives) encouraged them in two ways. First, it let them know that they were not alone in their challenges. That sense of solidarity was a benefit of the aspect of fellowship in Cana that Father Ed drew from A.A.—the reason he said Cana stood for "Couples Are Not Alone."

Second, and more important, by saying that "maybe with God's help" the Cana couples could find a solution to their sexual difficulties, Dowling was saying that God *cared* about their sexual satisfaction. Not only should they refrain from feeling guilty for wanting their sex life to be satisfying, they should take their sexual problems—along with *all* their intimacy issues—into their prayer life. What a comfort that message must have been, at a time when many clergy continued to hold Jansenistic attitudes toward sex!

Although Father Lord, Dowling's superior at The Queen's Work, unqualifiedly supported his Cana ministry, not everyone in the Society of Jesus was so appreciative. One day while dining at table at the St. Louis University Jesuit residence where he lived, Father Ed was discussing his Cana conferences and mentioned spousal sexual relations—scandalizing his provincial superior, who told him to end his conversation. But Dowling simply went on with what he was saying. It was then that his provincial *ordered* him to be quiet—under holy obedience. From then on, Father Ed kept his Cana conversations far from the Jesuit residence's dining room—at least when the provincial was at table.[60]

Despite the considerable effort Father Ed put into leading and promoting Cana Conferences from fall 1944 onward (even hosting a weekly "Cana Conversations" radio program),[61] he always found time to assist A.A. In April 1947, he traveled to Marshalltown, Iowa, to address those attending a dinner celebrating the third anniversary of the local A.A. The talk he gave there, perhaps more than any other, gives a sense of the wonder that he continued to experience when he contemplated the Twelve Steps and the people who practiced them.[62] His awe at A.A. members' fortitude is evident from his opening words:

> A man who just came off a bad binge happened into my study while I was giving thought to this meeting—a man who has, in the last four years, had about three weeks dry, but I knew the effort he was making. Our hope was to keep that man off the street. He came in yesterday four days dry. I asked him to say a prayer for this talk. At least my words are backed by that man's prayers. You know the weight and the value of those....
>
> When Marty Mann came up to her first meeting from a sanatorium, the first chance she got when she got out of that room, she went to a telephone and called the sanatorium to say, "We are not alone anymore."[63] That sense of not being alone—it is not an occasion for self-glorification but, I think, of congratulations. I think that the *grat* in that word means the same as in the word *gratitude*—to come together in our gratitude.

As Dowling went on, he turned to what had become a favorite topic of his—the Twelve Steps' universal value. Drawing upon his knowledge of A.A.'s founding, he related a story about Ebby Thacher that he likely heard from Bill Wilson or perhaps even from Ebby himself:

Ebby, who dried up Bill Wilson, says A.A. was not founded to cope with alcohol alone, but that they picked alcohol because that was the most obvious job. A noted psychiatrist says, "I see A.A. as an organization of very humble people striving for the ultimate goal of perfection." And they are doing that successfully in a certain sense. The idea of alcoholism may have been over-estimated because it was the most obvious barrier that blocked your goal.

Maybe A.A. is striving for perfection. Perhaps we are not aware of a goal that has become apparent to others. It is in this possible seeking of personal betterment that religion is the reaching-down of God to the soul of man, and in the A.A. program we have a reaching-back of the soul of man to God. In that part of the Twelve Steps, the alcoholic and the non-alcoholic share these Twelve Steps. . . .

It is because of [the] suggestion that the alcoholic's wife and others who have the chance to watch and be affected by A.A. also have a stake in A.A., that I would like to go over the Twelve Steps as they strike the non-alcoholic.

Father Ed began his discussion of the Twelve Steps by pointing out that only three of them—the first, fourth, and tenth—applied to self. The remaining steps required the persons making them to go outside themselves—toward God or toward others.

"The First Step," Dowling said,

has the most essential description of ourselves—dependent creatures. The Second Step touches the point of belief. The man comes to God because everything else looks worse. Christ himself also points out how we may grow, because faith, unless it becomes a telescope by which we may come to truth, is a false avenue to mind.[64]

After briefly mentioning the Third Step ("made a decision to turn our will and our lives over to the care of God as we understood Him"), Father

Ed moved on to the Fourth ("made a searching and fearless moral inventory of ourselves").

> I believe an inventory is better when made by comparison. If you are comparing and using a standard, why not take the best? This inventory should be made in the presence of God. I think we fail to realize how like Christ we are. We fail to realize that the divine power tried to make Christ like us. Therefore, I think we are like Christ. His judgments are kinder and more tolerant of our actions than our own are.

If Father Ed's ministry could be summed up in a single sentence, it's unlikely that one could do any better than repeat his remark about Christ's judgments being kinder and more tolerant than our own. He knew that as a priest, and as someone who visibly carried the cross of physical suffering, he represented Christ to people. Many people came to him for help because they were being eaten away from within by guilt, shame, and despair. When they did, he brought them to hope in Christ's mercy by telling them that the Lord looked upon them with more kindness than they looked upon themselves. But, more than that, he embodied that very mercy, by gently guiding such people to take the steps—whether they were the Twelve Steps or the steps of sacramental confession and penance—that would bring them to healing and renewal.

As Father Ed continued his account of how the Twelve Steps could help nonalcoholics, he described the Seventh and Eleventh Steps in terms of what he personally had learned from them. With the Seventh Step—asking God to take away one's defects—he said, "There you are coming very close to a vision of perfection. I can't practice that seventh step myself, and yet we should if we realize how good God has been."

It was typical of Father Ed to compare himself unfavorably to A.A. members with regard to the spiritual life. In the final step that he discussed, the Eleventh, he did the same:

> Prayer is the *eleventh* step. Prayer is difficult. Prayer is the supernatural thing. And yet it has been one of the privileges in A.A. for me as a priest to find people whose success in prayer of gratitude has brought them tremendous peace.

Father Ed's writings and talks show again and again how, in the midst of hardship, he found his own peace through sharing in the "prayer of gratitude" of A.A. members as he ministered to them. And he needed that peace, for, in his desire to be present to those who sought him out, he continued to struggle against the limitations imposed upon him by his arthritis-weakened body.

By the end of 1944, those limitations included not only illness but also obesity. He had used the Twelve Steps to quit smoking at the behest of some of his A.A. friends, only to find himself rechanneling his craving towards food. In March 1946, he wrote to a Jesuit friend that his weight gain had aggravated his mobility problems:

> I have been using two canes the last few days and am going to try to go into the hospital. . . .
>
> I am like Babe Ruth; my legs are giving out on me. I think I will go on a diet so as to give them less to haul around.[65] . . .

That same week Dowling wrote to Mary Ellen Kelly, founder of the League of Shut-In Sodalists—the first-ever unit of the Sodality of Our Lady whose membership was limited exclusively to people who were bedridden.

Since the age of fifteen, Kelly had been paralyzed by rheumatoid arthritis, save for her facial muscles and a few fingers. Now twenty-three, she had recently contacted The Queen's Work to register the League of Shut-In Sodalists as a fellowship of prayer for Catholics who, like herself, were barred by illness from engaging in the active apostolate.

"Dear Miss Kelly," Father Ed wrote,

> Miss [Dorothy] Willmann[66] tells me that I can participate in the League of Shut-In Sodalists by remembering them in my daily Mass.
>
> I want you to know that I wish to take this opportunity of "honorary" membership in the League of Shut-In Sodalists by promising to remember them in my daily Mass.[67]

Thus far, the letter was pro forma; Dowling was simply notifying Kelly, in polite and almost businesslike terms, that he wished to participate in her sodality's union of prayers. But then, with one brief final line, he opened his heart to her.

"I imagine," he wrote, "it is not too far off when I can become an active member."

It was around that time that Rosemary Hendron said to Father Ed one day at The Queen's Work, as she brushed the dandruff off his stooped shoulders, "Father, I'm really praying that the Lord will heal you of this."

When she recounted the story in 2020, Rosemary observed that, although Dowling's illness made getting around a trial for him, "he never complained about anything." Still, as she assisted him that afternoon, she could not help saying to him, "I'm praying for you to be all better."

"Oh, kid," Father Ed replied, "don't do that. This is my ticket to heaven."[68]

12

SPEAKING OF THE DEVIL

God resists the proud, assists the humble. The shortest cut to humility is humiliations, which AA has in abundance. The achievements of AA, which grew out of this book, are profoundly significant. Non-alcoholics should read the last nine words of [the] 12th Step.
> —Father Ed, back-cover endorsement for the January 1946
> printing of *Alcoholics Anonymous* (the "Big Book")[1]

I was of course flattered to have my name on the cover. It looks like I did even better than the author.
> —Father Ed, letter to Bill Wilson thanking him for
> an autographed copy of the Big Book, January 5, 1946

On a May morning in 1946, Bill Wilson sat at his desk in the wood-paneled studio at Stepping Stones where he did his writing—"Wits' End," he called it—and typed a letter to his dear Jesuit friend. A deeply emotional man, Bill never shied from telling Father Ed how much he valued their friendship.

"Just now getting back from an auto trip in Vermont, find your summer-school schedule and the reminder that we shall soon see you again. Which, as always, is just wonderful."[2]

In his letter, Father Ed had shared how he was applying A.A. principles in his ministry to married couples. Bill wrote in reply, "That Cana Conference idea impresses me more and more all the time." Then he came to what was uppermost on his mind—his efforts to overcome depression:

> Little by little I seem to be getting out of the clutches of the Devil—or whatever it was had hold of me the last couple of years. The past few weeks have been the best yet.

Father Ed, having long studied St. Ignatius's teachings on discernment of spirits, would have taken Bill's reference to being in "the clutches of the Devil" very seriously. Moreover, since he had studied the Big Book as well, he knew the specific significance that the devil had for Bill. In "Bill's Story," the A.A. co-founder wrote describing his mental state as he hit bottom during his drinking days, "If there was a Devil, he seemed the Boss Universal, and he certainly had me."[3] So, when Bill felt he was in "the clutches of the Devil," it was no mere depression. He was on a "dry drunk"—not drinking like an alcoholic, but thinking like one.

With that said, the devil was no mere metaphor to Bill. Father Ed once said in an address to Catholic clergy that Wilson believed that many alcoholics were engaged in genuine spiritual combat:

> Bill, the A.A. founder, told me that he thought that alcoholism in many cases was a diseased bodily reaction to alcohol plus a psychic obsession. What Bill meant was diabolical obsession. It was a malign obsession of the devil paralleling the guardian angel's benign obsession. We visualize the guardian angel as besieging us with good suggestions. He thought the devil was also there besieging the alcoholic. Bill knew the difference between obsession and possession.[4]

This observation of Father Ed's reveals much about the conversations that he and Wilson had on spiritual topics. In Ignatius Loyola's Rules for Discernment of Spirits for the First Week of the Exercises, the saint writes of how the person seeking to lead a spiritual life must do "exactly the opposite of what [the enemy] suggests" (*Spiritual Exercises*, no. 325). Father Ed would have affirmed Bill in his belief that the devil was the source of his evil temptations and encouraged him to act directly against such harmful impulses.

Dowling's words also give a good idea of the intensity of the discussions he had with Bill about the Wilsons' efforts to contact the spirit world. Soon after Bill and Lois settled into their Bedford Hills home in 1941, they began hosting regular "spook sessions" on Saturday evenings, during which they would attempt to make contact with spirits through a Ouija board, table tapping, automatic writing, and the like.

Bill wrote of one Ouija session, "There were malign and mischievous [spirits] of all descriptions, telling of vices quite beyond my ken.... Then, the seemingly virtuous entities would elbow them out with messages of comfort, information, advice—and sometimes just sheer nonsense."[5]

Usually at some point during these evenings, Bill would lie down on a couch in the hope that some spirit might "enter in" and give him a message. He was not disappointed.[6] The Wilsons continued to participate in spook sessions (sometimes at friends' homes) into the early 1950s.[7]

If Dowling could say with confidence that "Bill knew the difference between obsession and possession," it was likely because he had quizzed Wilson on the topic. He would have wanted to reassure himself that the spirits who visited Bill were not attempting to take charge of him. As we will see, in later correspondence with Wilson, Father Ed gently attempted to warn his friend away from attempting to contact the spirit world.

In Bill's May 1946 letter to Father Ed, after writing of escaping the Devil's clutches, the A.A. co-founder wrote further about his depression, which was only just beginning to lift:

> Though I can visualize the benefits of the suffering involved, I am still unable to say that I got any great joy out of the experience while it was going on. Which fact informs me loudly that I have a hell of a long way before catching up with some of the guys I read about (and see) in that astounding outfit of yours!

By "that astounding outfit," Bill likely meant not merely the Jesuits but the Catholic Church as a whole. Recently he had begun delving into the lives of Catholic saints and mystics such as Teresa of Avila and Mother Cabrini. "Accounts of people such as these always lay powerful hold of me," he wrote to Father Ed.[8] He was also drawn to Francis of Assisi, as he loved the Peace Prayer that was popularly attributed to the saint ("Lord, make me an instrument of your peace. . . .").

Did Bill's effusive praise of the Church's saint-making power reflect a desire to impress Father Ed? His own father deserted his family when Bill was ten. Many have observed that Dowling helped him heal his father wound; certainly, Bill looked to the Jesuit for fatherly guidance. Over the ensuing months, when Bill wrote to Dowling enthusing over things he was learning about the Catholic Church, Father Ed would come to suspect that the A.A. co-founder was exaggerating his interest.

At the very least, Bill's account of trying to "visualize the benefits" of his suffering, and his sense of inadequacy for failing to get "any great joy out of the experience," suggests he was trying to emulate Father Ed's attitude. In December 1943—the month before Bill's depression took hold—Father Ed had published an article in *The Queen's Work* on "How to Enjoy Being Miserable." Bill's letter can be taken as a personal response to that article.

Father Ed began his article by limiting his focus to little sufferings, meaning petty annoyances that are brought on by providence—not personally chosen mortifications, and not major tragedies. "Little sufferings are easier to practice on in order to develop an habitual outlook and attitude toward inevitable misery."

To enjoy suffering, Father Ed wrote,

> you have to be either crazy or in love. In everyday life we see instances of people wanting pain if it helps someone they love. In carrying a trunk upstairs with your mother, you definitely want to get the heavy end of the burden. On a winter night a mother will shiver so as to give a warm blanket to her child.
>
> Hence the psychological trick of changing from resigned willing acceptance of suffering to grateful wanting to take up and enjoy suffering consists in finding someone we love who will be helped by our sufferings. St. Paul supplies that person when he points out the chance we have to "fill up those things that are wanting of the sufferings of Christ" [Col 1:24].

Dowling emphasized that the "psychological trick" was not a matter of feelings. Not even Jesus in Gethsemane could make himself feel a desire for pain. Rather, it was a matter of making a conscious act of the will to express gratitude for suffering and to desire it.

Such gratitude, Father Ed wrote, means

> NOT that I want the suffering to continue, because as far as I know I may be dead the next instant and it may be God's will that the suffering cease. Nor does it mean that I want the suffering to be worse than it is, because the amount I have is the exact amount that God wills.
>
> BUT in the specific instant, now, since I cannot avoid this suffering, I want to get the best possible use out of it.

Father Ed then turned his attention to the enemy of joy. He drew upon the wisdom of St. Ignatius Loyola's Rules for Discernment of Spirits, with a distinctively modern twist—a quote from C. S. Lewis's recent bestseller *The Screwtape Letters*, which to him was "St. Ignatius done in *New Yorker* style."[9]

"The Devil will try to frighten you by directing your attention to the future and pointing out how terrible it will be if this suffering continues," Dowling wrote.

Tell him to go to hell. Screwtape, the old business agent of the Devil's Union, says that since the present is the only point at which time touches eternity, humans should be tempted to live in the past or, better still, in the future, where most vices, such as fear, avarice, lust, and ambition draw their strength. According to *Screwtape Letters*, the Devil's delight is a human soul "hag-ridden by the future—haunted by visions of imminent heaven or hell on earth."

But, Father Ed added, whereas the Devil desires that we be dragged down by loneliness, discouragement, and a sense of anxiety or futility, God desires that those same emotions be for us a bridge to union with him in Jesus Christ:

> Strangely, these three sufferings—loneliness ("Couldn't you watch an hour with Me?"), discouragement (Isaiah said Christ took upon Himself the sickening responsibility for "the iniquity of us all"), the futility (What's-the-use?) engulfed God in Gethsemane in that rendezvous where Divinity came closest to me. Where God's loneliness and mine are bridged by St. Paul's union of suffering, I can find the closest approach to God, to power, to achievement, to happiness, to joy!

If the spiritual practice that Father Ed is striving to put into words seems opaque, it may help to imagine it as a Christian application of the consoling words of Socrates to the judges who condemned him to be executed: "[N]o evil can happen to a good man, either in life or after death."[10] Moreover, Socrates, while in prison awaiting execution, insisted that he possessed true freedom, for he remained faithful to his divinely given wisdom.[11] Dowling held a similarly paradoxical understanding of the prison of suffering: when viewed through the eyes of faith, inescapable suffering opens the door to a new experience of freedom in Christ.[12] He knew, with Socrates, that the human person's true liberty comes not through isolated self-empowerment but through self-abandonment to the providence of a Higher Power.

In that light, perhaps when Bill wrote of longing to catch up with "some of the guys [he] read about" in that "astounding outfit" of the Church, he meant that he saw Father Ed as a truly free man. As "little by little" Bill continued to make his way "out of the clutches of the devil," he realized more and more that he wanted what Father Ed had.

Years later, writing about his journey toward "emotional sobriety," Bill reflected upon the source of his innermost struggles:

> My basic flaw had always been dependence—almost absolute dependence—on people or circumstances to supply me with prestige, security, and the like. Failing to get these things according to my perfectionist dreams and specifications, I had fought for them. And when defeat came, so did my depression.[13]

During the late 1940s, Bill's quest for personal independence and freedom took him down two major avenues that ultimately came into conflict with one another: Jungian psychotherapy and instruction in the Catholic faith. It is to this period of Bill's psychological and spiritual journey—and especially Father Ed's response to it—that we now turn.

In 1947, Bill Wilson's interest in Catholicism led his friends Fulton and Grace Oursler to do for him the same thing they had done for Heywood Broun eight years earlier. They introduced him to Monsignor Fulton J. Sheen, whose fame as a Catholic communicator—as well as an instructor of prospective converts—had only grown since Heywood's conversion.[14]

It seems that Dowling expressed some doubt over whether Wilson would actually take the leap into the Catholic Church, for Bill wrote to him on September 3, 1947, "Think your intuition is correct. Don't believe I could ever make it, just looking at the 'gang plank.'" He went on:

> The net result so far is this: I'm more affected than ever by that sweet and powerful aura of the church; that marvelous spiritual essence flowing down the centuries touches me as no other emanation does, but—when I look at the authoritative layout, despite all the arguments in its favor, I still can't warm up. No affirmative conviction comes. [...]
>
> So, as you may gather, I *feel* more like a Catholic every day, but I *reason* more like a Protestant; experience is convincing but instruction is not—at least, not yet.
>
> Of Monsignor Sheen's deep conviction, great power, and learning, I'm gratefully impressed. He really practices what he preaches to a degree which ought to make me ashamed to differ

with him at all. Yet, I tremendously appreciate being with him so much. He is very generous of himself.

After writing that he was sorry he and Lois had been out of town during Father Ed's recent visit to New York, Bill signed off "Affectionately," before adding a postscript:

> P.S. Oh, if the church only had a fellow-traveler department, a cozy spot where one could warm his hands at The Fire and bite off only as much as he could swallow.
> Maybe I'm just one more shopper looking for a bargain on that virtue—Obedience![15]

Father Ed's reply is remarkably beautiful. In *The Soul of Sponsorship*, Robert Fitzgerald, SJ, felt it was worthy of being reproduced in its entirety. I can only do the same (with slight corrections to Fitzgerald's transcription):

September 8, 1947

Dear Bill:

Of course there is a fellow-traveler department, even as A.A. has a fellow-traveler department.

Christ's church is not for the just and the good, but rather for sinners. "I came not to save the just." And of course the biggest boobs in the world are sinners. Just as A.A. is not for the sober and the good but rather uses the weak and the bad for its work, so Christ has always been associated with the weak, the sinner, and the human, from his nine-months stay in the womb of his mother, to his years with his bungling, ostentatious, materialistic little college of twelve cardinals.

A.A. would go out of business if everyone were sensible and good and unselfish, but it is made up of human clay and it takes a very catholic tolerance to understand its adjectival errors and mistakes.

After you die, A.A. will cling to your substantive spirit and will continue to make the same percentage of irritating (to the non-alcoholic) mistakes. So Christ's Church today will have as one of its marks the presence of sinners and the weak, few and pontiff.

Just as the non-alcoholic must not be scandalized at the human in A.A. and even the sub-human selfishness, so you must not be scandalized at the human in Christ's followers.

The road to truth has never been better charted than Christ charted it. "Dwell in My way and you will know the truth."

I believe that for you that way is lodemarked[16] by the 12 steps; especially for those who can pray by the 7th step; for the more privileged who cannot pray easily, by the 6th step.

I believe there is a priesthood of husband to wife and wife to husband. The Catholic Church teaches that on their wedding day the minister or priest of the sacrament of matrimony is the couple themselves. As for other priestly functions, Lois is the important key to the solution of your worries these days. Give her my love.

Sincerely,
Edward Dowling, S.J.

The first line of Father Ed's letter says as much about his understanding of Alcoholics Anonymous as it does about his understanding of the Catholic Church: "Of course there is a fellow-traveler department, even as A.A. has a fellow-traveler department." From his very first encounter with A.A., Dowling saw the fellowship as a near parallel (and, in a certain way, even an extension) of the Catholic Church's own fellowship. What is more, in his eyes, the symbolism went both ways (as noted in chapter 8). The Church, in light of A.A., was to Father Ed a sort of "Christians Anonymous"—a fellowship united by Christ's teachings and by its members' love and suffering.

It is fascinating to see how Dowling maintained that same line of argumentation as he responded to what he accurately sensed was Bill's concern: how could the Church, being governed by human beings, claim to have authority in all that is holy? Regardless of whether one shares Father Ed's Catholicism, there is, from a rhetorical standpoint alone, something masterly in the way he subtly weaves a continuous parallel between A.A. and the Church:

- A.A. came to save alcoholics; Christ came to save sinners.

- After Bill's death, A.A. would continue to confound non-alcoholics by holding fast to the spirit he imbued in it—which includes welcoming drunks. After Christ's death and resurrection, the Church continued to confound non-Christians by holding fast to the spirit he imbued in it—which includes welcoming sinners.

• Non-alcoholics must not be scandalized at A.A.'s human imperfections; non-Christians must not be scandalized at Christians' human imperfections.

Father Ed knew Bill would appreciate his logic—not least because, in Dowling's likening A.A. to the Church to which he had dedicated his life, he demonstrated the tremendous respect he had for the fellowship and its mission. But Bill was probably unaware of the extent to which the Jesuit's words reflected his deep self-identification with Bill's own journey. Father Ed's Gospel-inspired guidance—"Dwell in My way and you will know the truth"—was the very message by which he himself was delivered from unbelief when he was in the novitiate (see chapter 5).

Dowling's respect for A.A. is likewise evident in his observation that, for Bill, the way of (and to) Christ "is lodemarked by the 12 steps." To Father Ed, the steps were a gift from God, given through Bill for the healing of the world—including Bill himself. They offered the A.A. co-founder a way to direct his heart, his mind, his way of life, and his entire being toward a closer union with God. Father Ed therefore trusted that if Bill continued to work the steps, especially those directed toward purity of heart—the sixth and seventh steps—he would obtain the wisdom he longed for.

In his letter's closing words, writing of the "priesthood of husband to wife and wife to husband," Father Ed seems to be offering Bill a gentle correction. He likely sensed that, once Wilson lost interest in the Catholic Church, his fascination with spiritualism would again take precedence. In reminding Bill that Lois was "the important key to the solution" of his worries, Dowling was effectively telling the A.A. co-founder that the answers to his spiritual questions were not "out there" but right at home. Any efforts he made to perfect his fellowship with Lois would help him perfect his fellowship with God, and his fellowship with others in God.

As Father Ed signed, sealed, and addressed the letter, he hoped Bill would put in the necessary work to overcome his reservations about entering the Catholic Church. But he found himself unable to raise his hopes very high, for he knew his friend too well.

The next letter Father Ed typed was a reply to his journalist friend Gretta Palmer. Herself a convert to Catholicism who had been brought into the faith by Monsignor Sheen, she had written asking Dowling if rumors were true that Bill Wilson was about to follow that same path.

Father Ed kept his letter to Gretta brief. The one to Bill had taken a lot out of him. After thinking for a moment of how best to answer Gretta's question, he settled on a weather term. "Bill Wilson's letter today speaks highly of the Church and of Monsignor Sheen," Dowling wrote, "but between the lines he seems to be in the horse latitude." In other words, Bill's spiritual climate was warm and dry.

Six days after Father Ed mailed his letter to Bill, the A.A. co-founder typed a reply. "Thanks so much for your good letter of September 8," Wilson began. "You always catch me where the hair is short. As though I had standing to confess anyone's sins!"

Bill then admitted that the real obstacle to his accepting the Church's authority was not its claim to holiness but rather its claim to be the source of infallible truth:

> I'm not the least bit scandalized by the sins of the Church or any of the people in it. I don't see how an ex-drunk could be scandalized about anything. The thing which is a little disturbing seems to be the inability of the Church to confess its own sins. Historically, it's difficult to reconcile perfect infallibility at certain moments with very human carrying-on at other times. Did I not think so seriously of joining, I wouldn't even think of raising the question.

Wilson's emphatic assertion that he was seriously considering joining the Catholic Church must have impressed Father Ed. So much for the horse latitude! Yet Bill's words stand in contrast with Lois Wilson's claim, many years after his death, that he never was interested in becoming Catholic. According to Lois's onetime personal secretary Francis Hartigan in his biography *Bill W.*, she "seemed to bristle at the notion that Bill could need to take instruction from anyone"; she claimed "Bill and Sheen were friends, and their discussions were more like debates than conversations."[17]

However, as Hartigan's book notes in several places, Lois could be an unreliable witness about Bill if she feared that the truth might tarnish his reputation. For example, Hartigan wrote, she "consistently denied" that Bill ever received psychological therapy, whereas Bill openly admitted receiving care from two psychologists during the mid-1940s.[18]

After raising the question of infallibility, Bill in his letter went on to explain that he found it "ever so hard to believe that any human beings, no matter who, are able to be infallible about anything." He granted that "one would find enormous security and assurance if one could affirmatively believe that proposition" that God works infallibly through human beings. "But," he added, "the Church asks those who would embrace her to believe it implicitly. It is the affirmative step in this direction I find so difficult."

Moving to earthly concerns, Bill wrote with real feeling that he was sorry Father Ed was unable to visit him when he was in Memphis. "There is no one in the world among all my spiritual contacts I would rather share the hours with. If I ever come to the Faith, I am sure it will be through the demonstration of those in it like you."

In reading those words, and indeed all of Bill's letters to Father Ed about his study of Catholicism, one has the feeling that the A.A. co-founder so admired his Jesuit friend that it pained him to be unable to share Dowling's faith. But could there also have been something more? Could Bill have been testing Father Ed?

Sometimes a child will test his or her parents to see whether they would truly love him no matter what he or she did. If—as many have suspected—Bill saw Father Ed as a substitute for his own father, then it would not be surprising if he tested him in such a way, to reassure himself that Dowling would not reject him as his own father had done.

Although it is impossible to know for certain, some of Bill's later statements about Father Ed are consistent with such an attitude, as we will see.

Dowling, responding to Bill's reservations about infallibility, continued to develop the parallels he had drawn between the Catholic Church and A.A. He wrote to Bill on October 1, 1947,

> You are so right that "it is ever so hard to believe that any human beings are able to be infallible about anything." Infallibility is more than human. It calls for an intervention by a Power greater than ourselves. As I understand it, it does not mean that the teaching body of the Church will talk horse sense but that it is protected from formally teaching moral nonsense.[19]
>
> Even as you in the hospital witnessed a superhuman intervention for the sake of a relatively unimportant quantity of people, so the point you correctly make that human infallibility, as hopeless, would seem to force a merciful and just Father to intervene. Historically, there have been superhuman interventions —yourself, Horace Crystal, The Incarnation.

Father Ed's message could not be clearer. Just as God intervened to send Bill and his friend Horace (an A.A. pioneer) onto the right track when all seemed hopeless—for each of them had a spiritual experience that led them to sobriety—so too, God intervened with the Incarnation to set all humanity on the right track. On this account, it is not merely possible for God to reveal infallible truth to human beings; it is actually necessary for God to do so, if they are to be saved.

As before, Dowling's line of argumentation was ingenious. The Jesuit employed the tools of phenomenology—reasoning his way to Catholic faith on the basis of Bill's own experiences. It was a method inspired by his careful reading of John Henry Newman, who likewise saw the "yes" to Catholic faith as a "yes" to a personal encounter with Jesus Christ speaking truth. For Dowling, as for Newman, it was Christ's own truth-speaking voice that continued through the millennia in the voice of the Church, whose bishops were the successors of the apostles.

Having made his dramatic comparison of Bill's and Horace's personal revelations with God's descent to earth in the Incarnation, Father Ed quickly drew back, as though he feared veering into triumphalism. In his very next sentence, he wrote, "If you and Lois ever believe in Catholicity, it must be despite us Catholics."

But even as Dowling wrote that brief self-effacing comment, he realized he could not stop there. He had to press Bill on his professed inability to affirm that God taught infallibly through the Catholic Church.

"There is a tremendous amount of implicit faith involved in explicit doubt or rejection," Father Ed observed. "Maybe it boils down to a choice of infallibility."

He left the matter there. It was unnecessary to elaborate; Bill understood. The point was simple and devastating: Bill, despite his protestation that he was unable to make a choice, had in fact already made his choice. He gave himself away with his admission that he longed for the "enormous security and assurance" that would come through accepting the Church's infallibility. What, then, was keeping him from trusting the Church's infallible mind, if not his trust in his own "infallible" mind?[20]

But Bill held his ground. Writing to Father Ed on October 14, he said, "I seem congenitally unable to believe that any human beings have the right to claim unqualified authority and infallibility about anything, whether dogma, morals, or politics," he wrote. And, with good humor, he granted Father Ed's criticism: "I suppose my Yankee ancestry is showing up here with its special egotism and infallibility."

Dowling, in his reply, seemed to recognize that his St. Louis Irish stubbornness faced a formidable sparring partner in his Vermont-born friend. "You have my shoulders pinned down on that infallibility matter," he wrote

to Bill on October 24, "but it takes two out of three falls to win. I think I
will back off and try to get my wind."

Even then, Father Ed could not resist including a few sentences de-
fending the doctrine of infallibility. But he admitted it was a difficult teaching to accept.

"The road to truth is probably through the eye of a needle, calling for
deflation unto littleness," Dowling wrote (almost certainly aware that the
idea of ego "deflation" carried great resonance for Bill).[21] "I wonder if both
our steps now and all successful next steps would not be as humiliating as
the acceptances we balk at."

At this point, there is a gap in the record of Dowling and Wilson's correspondence. In the next surviving letter, written by Father Ed on November 26, 1947, the Jesuit picks up on an earlier comment of Bill's.

"As you say, you feel like a Catholic," Father Ed writes. "This I know."
"But," he adds,

> I doubt if you think like a Protestant. If you did, you would be at
> Sunday services at a Protestant church and subscribing to that code
> and creed. Protestant with a capital P is not only negative but also
> positive. I think you may be a protestant, spelled with a small p,
> which is happy, but semi.

Once again, Father Ed had identified with pinpoint accuracy that which
Bill W. was reluctant to admit. Bill's reluctance to follow what he had
called the "sweet and powerful aura of the Church" was not because he believed that Protestant Christianity had a greater claim on truth. It was rather
because, for reasons known only to himself, he consciously chose to remain
in the horse latitude.

If Father Ed was correct in assuming that Bill had interior reasons for re-
sisting entering the Catholic Church—reasons that went beyond his opposition to the Church's claim of infallibility—what might they have been? A
clue may be found in Bill's relationship with another person who played an
important role in his life at this time.

The anonymous authors of the official A.A. history *Pass It On* write
that Bill Wilson saw his therapist, whom they identify as "Frances
Weekes," "once a week on Fridays, and Msgr. Sheen for Catholic instructions on Saturdays."[22] Although a later historian found that the therapist was

actually Frances Gillespy Wickes, who was a prominent disciple of Carl Jung, no one has yet explored how her opinions might have affirmed or influenced Wilson.[23] It is to that question that we will now turn.

Bill first sought therapy in early 1944 after he fell into a severe depression. Initially he met twice a week with psychiatrist Dr. Harry Tiebout, who was one of A.A.'s greatest supporters in the medical field. (It was Tiebout who gave a pre-publication copy of the Big Book to Marty Mann.)

Although Bill told friends that he benefited from his sessions with Dr. Tiebout, at some point in 1945 he switched to seeing Wickes, who, although not a doctor, had studied psychoanalysis under Jung. How Bill met Wickes is unknown; possibly it was through another former student of Jung's, Margarita Von Lüttichau, a non-alcoholic who befriended Wilson in 1945.[24]

It is unsurprising that Bill would have wanted to switch from seeing Tiebout (who was something of a Freudian) to Wickes, for he considered Wickes's mentor Jung to be a co-founder of A.A. In 1931, Jung advised an alcoholic, Rowland H., that his only chance of recovery would be through "a spiritual or religious experience—in short, a genuine conversion."[25] Rowland did have such a conversion through the Oxford Group, and it was through his intervention that Bill's friend Ebby Thacher. likewise encountered the group and found sobriety through a spiritual experience. And it was Ebby, in turn, who sought to help Bill when he was bottoming out, which led to Bill's own spiritual experience and the start of A.A.

Wickes's therapeutic approach would also have appealed to Bill. Whereas Tiebout focused on Wilson's need to control his ravenous inner child, which the psychiatrist disparaged with the Freudian expression "His Majesty the Baby," Wickes viewed Bill's desires in a much more positive light.

In July 1947, two years into his therapy with Wickes, Bill wrote approvingly of the analyst in a letter to Lüttichau:

> Her thesis is that my position in A.A. has become quite inconsistent with my needs as an individual. Highly satisfactory [as it is] to live one's life for others, it cannot be anything but disastrous to live one's life for others as those others think it should be lived. One has, for better or worse, to choose his own life. The extent to which the A.A. movement and individuals in it determine my choices is really astonishing. Things which are primary to me (even for the good of A.A.) are unfulfilled. I'm constantly diverted to secondary or even useless activities by A.A.'s whose demands seem to them primary, but are not really so. So we have

the person of Mr. Anonymous in conflict with Bill Wilson. To me, this is more than an interesting speculation — it's homely good sense.[26]

In encouraging Bill to find his identity apart from that which was imposed upon him from outside, Wickes was faithfully following Jung's understanding of how a person "individuates"—that is, how one discovers and enters into his or her truest individual identity. Jung taught that "one cannot individuate as long as one is playing a role to oneself; the convictions one has about oneself are ... the most subtle obstacle against any true individuation."[27]

Wickes's "homely good sense," as Bill called it, was indeed in many respects what the A.A. co-founder needed at that moment. He was increasingly concerned to bring A.A. to become completely self-governing, so that it would no longer be dependent upon him and Dr. Bob.

However, in other ways Wickes's therapeutic approach was profoundly unhealthy for Bill. A paper that the psychoanalyst presented at a conference during the time Bill was seeing her, "The Creative Process," provides a detailed picture of the beliefs she carried into her treatment of him. She had a special interest in those she called "artists": "I use the term *artist* in its broader sense of the one who apprehends the art of living, one who out of the raw materials of his personal and collective heritage has created a life of form, of beauty."[28]

Under that description, Bill surely would have qualified as an artist to Wickes. And artists, in her mind, were above mortal men. They did not have to obey "the pseudo-conscience ... [that] says, 'Thou shalt not,' to living desires that stir within us ... [, that] demands, not obedience to the inner law of our being, but conformity to superimposed convention."[29]

Moreover, Wickes held that these artists of life had command of "magic": they had contact with "phantoms of the unknown deep"; they could enter into "communion with the Great Spirit above, or the earth forces below"; they were in touch with the Socratic "*daimon* of creativity that lives within each psyche"; they received "images from the unknown depth"; they experienced the "spiritual realm," where they experienced "illuminations" from "transcendental energy."

One can only imagine how Bill would have responded to such language coming from an authority figure who was one step removed from the great psychiatrist whose insights he credited with helping inspire his sobriety. Through Wickes, Wilson would have felt completely affirmed in his efforts to harness the unpredictable power of the spiritual world.

A more detailed image of Wickes's ideal artist comes to us through her novel *Receive the Gale*. Its protagonist, David, is an aspiring writer who passes through a series of lovers and wives while trying to find his path to greatness. As the novel begins we meet him as a teacher who finds romantic excitement in a dalliance with a schoolgirl. But when he then turns his eye to a schoolboy, he is fired. David then marries, has an affair, divorces, and takes a new lover. Last of all, he ditches the new lover in favor of a woman named Helena—which, coincidentally, is one letter away from the name of Helen, the lover Bill Wilson would take after he had completed four years of therapy with Wickes.[30]

With Helena, David is finally able to "receive the gale" of inspiration—and in Wickes's view, that is ultimately all that matters. As the psychoanalyst wrote in "The Creative Process," why should an artist subject himself to the "pseudo-conscience" of the "Thou shalt not," when he can become a god?

> In moments of creation we live as do the gods. If God created man in his own image, did he not make man also a creator, not an imitator? ...Imitation, even the imitation of Christ, becomes a violation of the original design of man and a denial of the real meaning of the one whom we imitate. For Christ became fanatically possessed by the creative idea to which he gave birth; the flaming, incendiary power of love. Christ did not imitate anything. He created life that was new and more abundant.[31]

Although Wickes employed Christian language—even referencing Jesus's words about abundant life (John 10:10)— the Christian might find in her words an echo of the promise of Eden's fabled serpent: "You will be like gods" (Genesis 3:5). She seems to be suggesting that readers might snatch the divine life for themselves instead of receiving it from the hand of their Father in heaven. Her claim that the imitation of Christ violates the "original design of man" likewise poses problems for the Christian: not only does it contradict New Testament passages that urge readers to imitate Jesus as the pattern for the spiritually regenerated human person, it also contradicts Jesus's own repeated exhortation, "Follow me."

And so it was that, during the same period from 1947 to early 1948 when Bill discussed Catholicism with Sheen on Saturday afternoons, he was seeing Wickes on Fridays. Wickes encouraged Bill in his desire to receive secret knowledge from the spirits of the dead—which he did, or tried to do, on Saturday evenings.

The spirits had Bill coming and going. Sheen didn't stand a chance of getting through.

Father Ed was likely unaware that Bill's therapist maintained that only through *not* imitating Christ could Bill discover his divine calling. But he did sense that Bill, despite his admiration for Jesus, struggled to accept the full implications of the Incarnation—that Jesus was both truly God and truly man.

Another Catholic friend of Wilson's likewise noticed that that the A.A. co-founder was hesitating at the threshold of the Catholic Church. Given that Bill had been receiving instruction from Monsignor Sheen throughout most of 1947, Clem L., a newspaper editor and prominent early member of A.A.'s Chicago chapter, had expected that Bill would enter the Church on Easter Vigil, when converts were traditionally received. So, when Easter Vigil 1948 came and went, Clem wrote to Bill asking what was preventing him from making a leap of faith. He pointed out that, given that A.A. was by then well established, Wilson couldn't make the excuse that he feared his becoming Catholic might cause a division in the fellowship.

Bill wrote Clem a lengthy reply on April 8, detailing his reasons for re-sisting conversion to Catholicism. He had already mentioned nearly all of them in his letters to Father Ed. But in responding to Clem's arguments, Wilson felt the need to say something he hadn't yet expressed in writing:

> Your feeling that A.A. is already so strongly built that no action on my part could split us along religious lines makes me wonder.... If the A.A. movement knew me as I really am, I agree no one would care very much what I did. But unfortunately, that is not the case. They believe in me as the symbol of the whole. And A.A. as a whole does not make any endorsements or commitments. There is the rub.[32]

The language Bill used, describing himself as "the symbol of the whole" with regard to A.A., was classic Jungian terminology. Symbols for Jung were vital tools for individuals to employ in their journey to self-dis-covery. Wilson would have picked up such language from Jung's writings as well as from Wickes, who wrote in her book *The Inner World of Man* (which Bill owned):

The harmonious relation of the inner and the outer [self]... is a realization of the connection between the archetypal symbol and the
individual experience. A first step in this realization is an acceptance of one's own unique nature and an attempt to discover oneself as one really is.[33]

Once Bill hit upon the idea (perhaps suggested to him by Wickes) that
he was a "symbol of the whole" of A.A. and thus could not even consider
becoming Catholic, it became fixed in his mind. In 1957, nearly a decade
after his letter to Clem L., he expressed that same sentiment in a letter to his
and Dowling's friend Joe Diggles, using even more emphatic language than
before:

As you probably know, I feel very close to the Church in many,
many ways. There are, however, several propositions about which I
have no affirmative opinion. And some of these are quite vital to
membership. There is also the question of my status in A.A. Theoretically I have the same right to form other associations as any
other A.A. does. But in quite a practical sense I am hogtied by the
A.A. tradition of which I am a symbol. This is very emphatic about
alliances and endorsements for Alcoholics Anonymous. Since I
happen to be a symbol for the whole, this tradition bears down
upon me with very special force.[34]

Given that Bill said Wickes taught him that "one has, for better or
worse, to choose his own life," it is striking to see him argue that he is
"hogtied by the A.A. tradition" of which he is a symbol. He didn't let his
symbolic representation of A.A. stop him from promoting niacin in the
mid-1960s. Perhaps, when corresponding with devout Catholics, he felt
the need to say something that would definitively close off the possibility
of his entering the Church, so that they would no longer press the matter.

That, at least, appears to be the case with Bill's April 8, 1948, letter to
Clem L. After writing that he felt himself to be a "symbol of the whole" of
A.A., he closed his letter with a sort of apologetic for remaining outside the
Church: "I believe that my duty would lie in helping the non-Catholic alco-
holic to discover the grace of God."

From a Catholic perspective, it is difficult to understand how a person
attracted to Catholicism could claim, as Bill did, that only by resisting
conversion could he fulfill his divinely given vocation. A Catholic could

ask: might not Wilson have been better equipped to help suffering non-Catholics if his own non-Catholicism, like his drinking, were a thing of the past? Yet, in some ways, his struggle was similar to that of the French Jewish philosopher Simone Weil (1909–1943), who had a profound mystical attraction to Christian faith but felt her vocation was to remain "waiting for God" on the threshold of the Catholic Church. Like Wilson, and against self-divinizing contemporaries such as Ayn Rand, Weil placed a high value on humility. A passage from her diary in 1942 could practically have come out of one of Bill's letters: "The virtue of humility is incompatible with the sense of belonging to a social group chosen by God, whether a nation or a church."[35]

If there is a constant in Bill's spiritual history after his attainment of sobriety, it is his desire to have again the "wonderful feeling of Presence"[36] that he enjoyed in his life-changing spiritual experience at Towns Hospital. His attraction to the Catholic Church was driven by his fondness for his friend Father Ed, whose presence always brought him that same "touch of the eternal."[37] But ultimately he could not reconcile himself with the Church's claim to divine authority to teach the truth, to judge between truth and falsehood, and to "test the spirits to see whether they belong to God" (1 John 4:1). Instead, for the rest of his life, this man, who convinced innumerable alcoholics to admit their powerlessness before God,[38] attempted to harness the exhilaration and consolation of his Towns Hospital experience by his own power—whether through Ouija boards, LSD, or the burning flush induced by three grams of nicotinic acid.[39] He had indeed made what Father Ed presciently called "a choice of infallibility."

Bill appears to have felt a continued need to assert the rightness of his choice to Father Ed, for he sent the Jesuit a carbon of his April 1948 letter to Clem L. explaining his reasons for not converting. Dowling's gracious reply contains the final words that we see from him concerning Bill's decision to remain outside the Church. After thanking Bill for the letter, Father Ed writes, "I have a feeling that anyone who sincerely tries to apply the Twelve Steps is following in Christ's footsteps with the result which Christ promised when he said, 'Dwell in My way and you will know the truth.'"

That was all Dowling had to say on the matter. No judgment. No arguments. There was no need. He had already presented Bill with arguments for entering the Catholic Church. With Bill now showing himself firm in his resolve to stay where he was, Father Ed chose to find what was good in his actions and affirm them.

How did Bill feel when he read Father Ed's words of affirmation? There is no record of a reply, but it seems from his later writings that Dowling's letter brought him a sense of relief as well as deep gratitude for the Jesuit's spiritual fatherhood. I sense Bill's relief particularly in a pair of statements he made about Father Ed in 1957.

The first of these statements appears in his September 1957 *Grapevine* article "Let's Be Friendly with Our Friends...the Clergymen." Bill caps off a paragraph of effusive praise for Father Ed by writing, "It is characteristic that he has never, in all these years, asked me to join his church."

The second statement appears in Wilson's 1957 letter to Joe Diggles. It is clear from the letter that Joe, a friend of Father Ed's for a quarter-century, had chided Bill for implying Dowling never encouraged him toward Catholicism. A clearly embarrassed Bill replied,

> I'm afraid I put Father Dowling a little bit wrong in that *Grapevine* piece. What I meant to say was that he had never insisted on my joining his church. I am sure he has had his hopes, which he has expressed in his mild way. But he never put pressure on me— that's what I meant to infer.

These two statements together suggest to me that Bill indeed tested Dowling to see whether the Jesuit would still love him if he came to the brink of conversion to Catholicism and then stepped back. And, if that is the case, the statements also leave no doubt that Dowling passed the test.

Preserved at Maryville University Library's Father Dowling Archive is a highly confidential exchange of letters from this period of Father Ed's life. A priest from Texas wrote asking his help with a case of suspected demonic possession, adding that he had heard of Dowling's great success in a similar case. Father Ed responded with a brief note saying that there must be a mistake, as he did not have experience in such matters. He explained that whoever recommended him must have confused him with another St. Louis Jesuit: Father William Bowdern.

The tantalizing exchange hints at the extent to which Father Ed was aware of Father Bowdern's work on the case that would later inspire William Peter Blatty to write *The Exorcist*. Dowling not only lived in the same Jesuit residential community as Father Bowdern but also worked alongside his brother, Father Thomas Bowdern, SJ, at The Queen's Work. It is therefore highly likely that Father Ed heard inside details of that spring 1949 case of the boy known as "Roland Doe."[40] He may even have been consulted on it, as was his good friend and mentor Father Laurence J. Kenny, SJ.

Whatever he may have known about the Roland Doe case, there is no question that, from spring 1949 onward, Dowling stepped up his efforts to educate people—including Bill—on how to resist the devil's temptations. Granted, he was not the only one interested in the topic. The crimes of Hitler and Stalin, and their aftermath, led many public thinkers to reflect upon the devil and on evil in general. But, as might be expected, Father Ed added his own distinctive perspective, especially in a talk he gave that has never before been published.

Although no date appears on the manuscript of "The Devil and the A.A."[41] (which Dowling also referred to as "The Devil You Say"), the talk appears to be from the late 1940s. It may be that Father Ed delivered it at an A.A. meeting in St. Louis on November 24, 1949, when Bill Wilson visited him.[42] There are three factors in favor of that date. First, in the talk, Father Ed jokes that the devil tells the A.A. member that the member is smarter than Bill Wilson. It is the sort of joke he would have made with Wilson in the audience. Second, the talk's content contains many things about spiritual warfare that Father Ed seeks to teach Bill in his letters. Finally, given that the story about "Roland Doe"'s exorcism was leaked to newspapers in August 1949, a talk on the devil's tactics would have been especially topical in November of that year.

In the talk, Father Ed employed his journalistic gifts to great effect. Although he acknowledged his debt to C. S. Lewis, recommending his audience read *Screwtape Letters*, he framed his account of the devil's tricks with a martial-arts metaphor all his own:

> [The Devil]'s the author of the spiritual jiu jitsu method, the stratagem of using a man's strength against himself. Two men are struggling. One is a jiu jitsu expert. When the man pulls, the expert pushes. When the man pushes, the expert pulls. The principle is to help a man lick himself—to help him throw himself off balance so he'll be at the expert's mercy.

One would be hard-pressed to find a better six-sentence encapsulation of St. Ignatius Loyola's Rules for the Discernment of Spirits. But Father Ed was just getting started.

Dowling went on to describe how the devil was "a liar," "a confidence man," and "a great builder-upper of the ego," before bringing in a second metaphor from the athletic world:

> The Devil is tricky. He's a great quarterback. When one play doesn't succeed, he tries another, and another. If he can persuade the alcoholic to drink, he knows that he has the alcoholic by the ears, that the alcoholic's power for good is destroyed.
>
> But he knows that the A.A. [member] is alert for a head-on power play, [namely,] a direct suggestion to drink, so the Devil rarely uses that one.
>
> No. The play starts 'way over here. It goes all around the mulberry bush, upsy-daisy through the window. There's plenty of razzle dazzle—of now you see it and now you don't.
>
> The object is to get us confused, to get us angry, to get us desperate, to get us exhausted, and then when he gets us into one or more of those states, bango! comes the forward pass to the goal line—
>
> "What you need is a little drink."

At that point, Father Ed proceeded to present specific examples of how the devil might insinuate himself upon an A.A. member at each step of the program. For example, he said, once an A.A. member has made it past the First Step, the devil might again try "the jiu jitsu trick":

> "Sure," he says, "go ahead and quit drinking. And while you're at it, let's do a good job, a hundred percent job. If you're going to reform, let's have no halfway measures.
>
> "Why don't you quit smoking, too? Remember more than once you blamed the cigarettes for the hangovers. Why don't you start a diet? Why don't you start saving your dough?... Why don't you spend more time on the job? [...]
>
> "Get strict with yourself. Get strict with your wife. Get strict with your kids. Get strict with everybody."
>
> If you insist on reforming, the Devil will give you a million suggestions on how to do it. He wants you to go to the extremes so that your new way of life will become burdensome beyond toleration, will become ridiculous; will reach a point where you'll say: "Aw, to hell with it," and reach for a drink.

If the A.A. member "doesn't fall for this jiu jitsu trick"; if his sponsor tells him, "take it easy" and "easy does it," then, Father Ed said,

> there's the routine he gives us about the Twelve Steps: "Say, what is this anyway? All you wanted to do was quit drinking. That's what you're in A.A. for. So why all this rigamarole, turning your life over to God, telling some guy what a heel you've been. What does all this have to do with drinking? This stuff sounds like a church—worse still, like a cult. Watch your step."

It is moving to see how Father Ed, although not an alcoholic, demonstrated total identification with the A.A. member. He would do the same in his other addresses to A.A., most famously at the 1955 A.A. International Convention, where he constantly referred to "we" and "us." If there is a constant in Dowling's ministry to A.A. members, it is his continual insistence upon viewing the alcoholic as his other self.[43] Father Ed was effective with alcoholics because he loved every one of them with a compassionate love that expressed itself as perfect empathy. He was not above those to whom he ministered; he was always one with them, and he felt honored to be in their company.

For a particularly affecting example of Father Ed's compassion for the A.A. member, one need look no further than this aside that he made in his "Devil and the A.A." talk when discussing the Fifth Step:

> As one who has been on the receiving end of Step Five on a couple of occasions, let me remark parenthetically to any man here present who has not yet taken the Fifth Step:
> Never have I heard anything from another man that I hadn't done myself, that I wasn't fully capable of doing, and that—if I hadn't done exactly the same thing—I had done things as bad, maybe worse.
> That's the group experience.[44] A second experience—the man to whom the story is told just doesn't remember the details, they fade into the back of his mind. A third experience—the reaction is never one of horror or contempt, but rather of admiration for the man's courage, his honesty, his humility in telling his story.

Upon finishing his account of how the devil tries to steer A.A. members away from the spirit of each of the Twelve Steps, Father Ed offered "some general observations":

[The Devil] doesn't like to see us attend meetings.

"You've got the program down pat," he says. "You know all there is to know about A.A. You probably know more about A.A. than Bill Wilson does—after all, you were a smarter guy to start with. [...]

"Won't hurt you to skip a couple of meetings. Might even do you good. Keep you from going stale. Take it easy. Easy does it."

If we miss meetings, the Devil knows our alcoholic problem is going to fade from its sharp reality. Danger there.

Father Ed then drew upon the spiritual principles that he normally shared with married couples at Cana Conferences:

The Devil knows that a house divided against itself shall not stand. He knows that if he can introduce discord, dissension, conflict into a house, into a group, his principles will supplant the principles of the Twelve Steps.

Maybe he starts with the family. Maybe your wife, your family, don't appreciate you. They don't give you credit for the struggle you've put up, the grand job you've done.

Although he was not an alcoholic, Father Ed may have drawn upon personal experience in imagining how the devil tries to tempt someone who has done a "grand job" in beating addiction. As he later wrote in *Grapevine*, it was around this time that he "arrested [his] own nicotinic addiction with the help of the A.A. Steps."[45]

Father Ed's listeners would have laughed in recognition as he gave further examples of the devil's methods:

He won't try to tell you your wife isn't a good woman. He knows you won't fall for that. You can't forget how she stood by you in your drinking days. But if he can get you a little critical of her. Oh, sure, she's a fine woman—

"But why the hell does she leave the cap off the toothpaste? Can't she serve anything but hamburgers? Why doesn't she dress as snappy as that blonde down at the office? Why is she letting herself get too fat? Why does she rush out and spend my dough faster than I can make it?

"And why doesn't she do something about the kids? Do they have to chew that bubble gum? Do they have to put on that silly

radio program? Do they have to make all this racket? Do they have
to have their friends cluttering up the house when I want a little
peace and quiet?"

Cheers from the Devil, a dry drunk for you. And dry drunks
have a habit of getting wet, awfully wet.

Then, Father Ed went on, the devil might try to turn the recovering alcoholic against his or her A.A. group:

The Devil is quick to suggest there is plenty wrong with our fellow
A.A.'s, with our groups, but he never suggests that there's something wrong with me—that I could quit resting on my big, fat lau-
rels and do something for myself and for the group.

Dowling concluded the talk with a reflection on how "A.A. is just one
paradox after another":

One A.A. paradox is this: We in A.A. are never in danger. We in
A.A. are never safe.

We are never in danger while we practice the principles of the
A.A. program. We are never safe when we deviate from those
principles.

Virtue for the alcoholic lies in the high middle of the road. We
must stay right spang in the middle, [not] veering to the right in
smugness, in overconfidence, in pride; nor to the left in fear, discouragement, or resentful anger.

Often you've heard the A.A. paraphrase: "Eternal vigilance is
the price of sobriety."

The eternal vigilance should be directed, to my mind, against
the Devil. But if some of you reject the idea of the Devil as a
source of temptation, and again I say that in A.A. you are at perfect liberty to do so, let me suggest this:

We must be eternally vigilant, eternally on guard against anything that will take us from the high middle of the road where
virtue stands. Time is no safeguard. Weeks, months, years of sobriety are no assurance. The first move away from A.A. principles
has in it all the potential danger of the first drink.

Some 1900 years ago, a man named Peter sat down and wrote
a letter to the members of some new groups that had formed. And
this is one [thing] he said: "Be sober and watch, because your ad-
versary, the Devil, as a roaring lion, goeth about, seeking whom he

may devour. Whom resist ye, strong in faith" [1 Peter 5:8–9].

Strong in faith. God keep you so.

If Bill Wilson was indeed in the audience, he would surely have been touched to hear the Jesuit say that whoever practiced the principles of the Twelve Steps would be safe from the enemy's clutches. It was yet another affirmation that, in Father Ed's eyes, the Twelve Steps were divinely inspired—and that, as the priest had written to Bill, whoever practiced them sincerely was "following in Christ's footsteps."

13

⮑〜⮕

Bringing Recovery to the Non-Alcoholic

*In moving their therapy from the expensive clinical couch to the
low-cost coffee bar, from the inexperienced professional to the amateur expert, AA has democratized sanity.*
                                — Father Ed, "A.A. Steps for the
                                Underprivileged Non-A.A."[1]

Father Ed's love of language led him to seek out a word to identify what
distinguished Alcoholics Anonymous from other approaches to curing alcoholism. He found that word in *isopathy*, which refers to treating an illness
by applying the substance that causes the illness. At the 1950 Summer
School of Catholic Action, he praised the "democratic drift" in psychiatry
that was breaking the grip of the expensive "monarchic practitioner" in
favor of "isopathic" groups such as A.A.[2] After years of trying to reconcile
his call to ministry with his passion for democracy, he finally found in
isopathy a means of merging the two.

One isopathic group became so important to Father Ed that he brought
his brother Paul and sister Anna into it and even applied its principles in his
own life. That group was Recovery, Inc. (now known as Recovery International), founded by Dr. Abraham Low "to prevent relapses in former mental
patients and to prevent chronicity in nervous patients."[3]

Low was a pioneer in what is now known as cognitive-behavioral therapy. At a time when harsh techniques such as electroshock therapy and
even frontal lobotomies were still in the mainstream of mental-health treatments, his approach was gentle and, in its way, revolutionary. The idea was
that trained lay facilitators who themselves suffered from anxiety disorders
could help fellow members develop healthy habits of thinking and thereby
reduce their need for ongoing professional mental-health care.

Dowling, who had been following Recovery's progress since 1942,
stepped up his support of the group after Low published *Mental Health*

through Will-Training in December 1950, which became for Recovery what the Big Book was for A.A. At about the same time that Low's book arrived in Father Ed's office, a woman from Louisville, Kentucky, came to him for advice. Like so many of Dowling's meetings with suffering individuals, this encounter would lead to an endeavor that would have a positive effect upon many lives.

Cleo D. had suffered two major family hardships over five years. First, her husband Bill, a liquor-store owner, had sunk into alcoholism.[4] She responded by interesting him in Alcoholics Anonymous and hosting meetings at their home. But even as her husband was sobering up, her son was suffering a nervous breakdown after experiencing trauma while serving in the Navy during World War II. By the time she visited Father Ed, her son was an inpatient at the Alexian Brothers hospital in South St. Louis.[5]

News of the success Dr. Low was having with former mental patients in Chicago led Cleo to wonder whether the Recovery program might be appropriate for her son. Her husband knew where she should go to find out. "Take the next flight into St. Louis," he advised, "as Father Dowling will know about Recovery and Dr. Low and whether this has any value."[6]

Father Ed urged Cleo to travel to Chicago and see for herself the good work that Recovery was doing. Once she met Dr. Low and sat in on some Recovery meetings, she was so impressed with the program that she returned to Father Ed to ask his help in starting a St. Louis chapter of the group.

It should be no surprise that Father Ed lent Cleo his full support, giving meeting space at The Queen's Work to the St. Louis chapter of Recovery and spreading the word about the group. But he did more than that. As the chapter rapidly expanded—spawning seven more groups during its first three years—Dowling went to Chicago to receive facilitator training so he could lead meetings. He also encouraged another St. Louis Jesuit, Father John J. Higgins, who had himself recovered from a severe nervous breakdown, to involve himself in the group. Higgins in turn became a leading advocate of Recovery, writing a pamphlet about it for The Queen's Work that sold in excess of 100,000 copies.

The group Cleo and Father Ed started at The Queen's Work was the first chapter in Recovery, Inc.'s history to meet in a public place. Previously, Recovery groups had met only in private homes, as members were too afraid of the stigma associated with mental illness to risk discovery. But Father Ed felt that the human dignity of Recovery members demanded that they not hide themselves in shame.[7]

Although the full impact of Father Ed's work with Recovery can only be guessed, the few stories that have surfaced testify to lives transformed.

St. Louis native Joseph Dunne shared one such story with me in an email, telling how Father Ed helped his mother during 1951 or 1952—the first year of Recovery's activity in St. Louis:

> In addition to his work with alcoholics Father Dowling was also something of a savior to people with mental illness.
>
> When I was a boy, my mother suffered a crippling breakdown resulting in hospitalization for what seemed an extended period. I was perhaps ten or so. Afterward she became involved with a local chapter of Recovery, Inc. which Father Dowling was instrumental in establishing and I think facilitated. She would go weekly to meetings at Queen's Work.
>
> This experience and support she received from Father Dowling was instrumental in restoring her. She was a person of tremendous courage in facing her illness.
>
> I recall meeting Father Dowling once. For some reason, I think [my mother] needed to go by Queen's Work so she took me along. I recall an elevator ride, an office piled with papers, and what seemed a hulk of a man. Previously she'd said he was not well. "He's turning into stone," she said. But in our brief meeting, his slow movement, a handshake, a few words about what a fine lad I was, I found him kindly. Knowing what a pillar he was for my mother I was very impressed. I have always been grateful that he came into her life.
>
> So there's a personal recollection about a man I've always considered a giant.[8]

In 1954, Father Ed spoke before an audience of one thousand in Detroit to share what Recovery, Inc., had come to mean to him.

"In the last four years," Dowling said, "I have had two members of my family belong [to Recovery], and I have had a very fine opportunity not merely to watch the meetings—they occur in my building two floors below me—but I also have telephone conversations with these people."[9]

Father Ed then said something dramatic, something that he could not have said of the A.A. program (at least, not with respect to its intended application to alcoholism): he was not only a facilitator of the Recovery program but also a participant like any other.

"I have used it in my own life, I've used it with others. And I'm speaking especially to people who may be bothered by hardening of the dignity—dignosclerosis, see?"

The audience laughed, as Father Ed expected they would, and he chuckled too. "Dignosclerosis" was a favorite neologism of his.

Father Ed went on, speaking in his typical, disjointed, almost stream-of-consciousness fashion—his thoughts trailing off in mid-sentence, only for him to pick them back up later: "There are a lot...." He chuckled again. "Come on in, the water's fine: menopause, hypertension—a lot of things that we never go to a doctor for. It can help. It can help." His audience knew that by "it," he meant Recovery.

Always aware of how valuable his priestly witness was to the causes that he promoted, Dowling closed with a message to his fellow members of the faithful:

"If the non-Catholic people won't listen for a minute, I want to say something to the Catholics."

The audience laughed. Father Ed went on: "I remember a Catholic one time who was an alcoholic. He was distinguished in a distinguished, alcoholic way...." He paused as scattered chuckles arose. "But," Dowling continued,

> he tells the story in Alcoholics Anonymous now. He said he always wondered if this Alcoholics Anonymous would do anything against his religion, see. It never occurred to him, he says, to bother whether this drinking and knocking lampposts down and ruining his family might hurt his own religion, see.
>
> There is less religion in Recovery than there is in Alcoholics Anonymous. Now, I suppose the majority in this room are Christians. Alcoholics Anonymous does not bring Christ in. You bring Christ in at your own discretion and at your own risk, see. Now Recovery [...] does not bring God in, but Recovery is on the side of the angels.[10]

Father Ed chose his words carefully, especially since Recovery's founder was seated just a few feet away. He was aware that Dr. Low felt uncomfortable when people drew comparisons between Recovery and A.A. The psychiatrist was intent to maintain the program's secular nature, and did not want people to think it involved spirituality or God-talk.

Thankfully for Dowling, he could always find spiritual refreshment among A.A. members." In a pamphlet he wrote about A.A. that was published by The Queen's Work, he praised the "unabashed spiritual conversation" he found in the fellowship's rooms, adding, "I know of very few places incidentally where one can count on getting [such conversation] outside of A.A."[11]

In October 1950, Father Ed spoke before more than nine hundred people gathered to celebrate the tenth anniversary of A.A.'s presence in St.
Louis. As he reflected upon how far the St. Louis fellowship had come, he
thanked God for the opportunity he had been given to aid its members—
"one of the great graces of my life."[12]

A.A. member Chuck C. told a story of speaking at a St. Louis A.A.
banquet—perhaps this very tenth-anniversary event—where Father Ed was
in attendance. Afterwards, Father Ed accepted an invitation from Chuck's
wife to join the couple for coffee. Chuck's account of the conversation that
transpired offers a rare glimpse into what it was like to be in Father Ed's
presence. It gives a hint of how other-directed he was, and especially how
uplifted he was to hear A.A. members' stories.

"We sat down in the booth," Chuck recalled,

and he started plying me with questions, and he never quit. I
would say every fifteen minutes, "Father. You talk. I've been talking all night. You talk. I love to hear you talk." But he'd ask another question, and the last question he asked was, "Chuck, tell me
about the family. What's happened in the family?"

And I said, "No, Father, I won't tell you. Mrs. C.'s here. Let her
tell you." And so, she told him what had happened in our family.
And he sat there with his little mouth perched up, looking out the
window, seemingly forever. That was a great habit of his; his mouth
just looked like a little ol' rosebud, and he'd look off into space.

He finally turned to me, and he said, "You know something,
Chuck?" And I said, "What, Father?" And he said, "Sometimes, I
have to believe that heaven is just a new pair of glasses."[13]

It was Father Ed's gift to see heaven through the lives of people who
were striving to overcome great suffering one step at a time—and to help
them see for themselves the divine grace he saw at work amidst their
struggles.

Dowling's witness had special power because the hand of God was so
clearly active in his own life. After his death, his journalist friend Martin
Duggan marveled at what he had been able to accomplish. "Father Dowling
was impossible," Duggan wrote. "The man suffered from crippling arthritis

so severely that he could barely move. Yet he was always a man in motion, shuffling along on the arm of a friend, and going more places than anyone had a right to believe he could."[14]

Duggan recalled a poignant moment during a European pilgrimage that Father Ed made with Queen's Work colleagues and lay members of the Sodality of Our Lady during the Holy Year of 1950. They had come to the healing spring in Lourdes, France, where, in the years since the shepherdess Bernadette reported visions of the Blessed Virgin in 1858, some two thousand pilgrims had reported receiving miraculous cures.

"At Lourdes," Duggan wrote,

I fully expected to see Father Dowling go into the water and come out cured. If ever there was a man who was perfect material for a miracle, it was Father Dowling. He was as stiff as stone. How wonderful, I thought, if he comes out of the grotto soaked like a sponge.

After an endless time, Father Dowling did come out. He was as stiff as ever. Stiffer, perhaps, having been in that cold water all that time.

We were shocked speechless, all of us, except Father Herbert O'H. Walker, SJ, Father Dowling's lifelong friend and editor at The Queen's Work.

"Well, Puggy," said Father Walker, "I guess you haven't been good."

The preposterous notion that good old Father Dowling hadn't been good made us realize that we didn't deserve to witness a miracle, much as he might have deserved one.

Throughout the 1950s, Father Ed continued to tour actively in support of the Cana Conference movement, leading days of reflection for married couples and mentoring priests in marriage ministry. A major message of his Cana talks was that the laity, within their own distinctive state of life, were called to the same heights of spiritual perfection as priests and members of religious orders. It was a message he had been sharing since his earliest days as a Jesuit—and it was still many years ahead of its time. Not until the Second Vatican Council would the Church proclaim the "universal call to holiness."[15]

In an address that Father Ed gave to Cana couples in Chicago in 1952, the prophetic similarity between his language and the language the Council employed twelve years later in *Lumen Gentium* is striking, if not outright astonishing:

> Every age has its moral heresies; usually they seem to be omissions. I sometimes think there are three suspicious prevalent feelings among people today. *One* is our failure to recognize the importance of one of the sacraments—Confirmation. *Two* is our failure to recognize the sanctity of the state and of politics. The *third* is the one that most applies today on our talk—the failure to recognize that you two and everybody is called to sanctity and to perfection....
>
> We must not confuse the life of the [evangelical] counsels, the life of perfection, with a religious order. The Blessed Mother was a wife and a mother, and yet she lived them. St. Benedict's Rule was written primarily for laymen. The life of the counsels, the life of perfection, is entirely compatible with marriage and parenthood.[16]

When people heard Father Ed speak, they came away with the hope that, no matter how messy their lives might be, God cared about them and was with them, to help them grow and heal.

Even after Bill ceased receiving instruction from Monsignor Sheen, he continued to approach Father Ed with questions about the Catholic faith. In July 1952, he wrote to Dowling excitedly that a spirit who "turned up" during one of his spook sessions claimed to be St. Boniface. "I'd never heard of this gentleman but he checked out pretty well in the Encyclopedia," Bill wrote. "If this one is who he says he is—and of course there is no certain way of knowing—would this be licit contact in your book?"[17]

Bill's words betrayed his hope that maybe, just maybe, he could have it all—both the thrill of conversing with "spooks" and the security of his Jesuit friend's approval.

When Father Ed read Bill's letter, he was not at all convinced that the purported saint was of heavenly origin. But, as so often, he avoided bringing down the hammer of doctrine upon his friend. Instead, he drew upon the wisdom of Shakespeare—punctuated with self-deprecating humor: "I still feel, like Macbeth, that these folks tell us truth in small matters in order to fool us in larger.[18] I suppose that is my lazy orthodoxy."[19]

Despite the Jesuit's attempt to lighten the mood, it is clear from Dowling's letter that he was greatly concerned to see Bill continue his fascination with the spirit world. Immediately after joking about his "lazy orthodoxy," Father Ed recommended that Bill read the Two Standards meditation in the edition of the Spiritual Exercises of St. Ignatius that Dowling had recently sent him. And he added that it was this meditation that led Pope Leo XIII to "assign a prayer at the end of the Mass against the snares of the Devil" (that is, the St. Michael the Archangel prayer).

The edition of the Spiritual Exercises that Dowling had given Bill was a translation by the Anglican Rev. W. H. Longridge that had become a favorite among Jesuits in the English-speaking world. It included not only Ignatius's own words but also an extensive commentary that drew upon leading interpretations of the Exercises. So, when Dowling invited Bill to read the Two Standards meditation, he was asking him to read both the meditation itself and Longridge's observations on it.

In the Two Standards meditation, Ignatius invites the retreatant to visualize two opposing camps (the word "standard" here refers to a battle flag): a camp of the good, led by Jesus Christ, and the enemy camp, led by Lucifer. The retreatant visualizes each captain—the poor, humble, and meek Christ versus the vain, proud, and vicious Lucifer—and imagines what each of them is saying and doing. Through this exercise, the retreatant seeks to gain knowledge of the enemy's deceits, as well as knowledge of the true life offered by Christ and the grace to imitate him. At the end of the exercise, he or she is to pray to be received by Christ under his standard, and so to attain the humility that Jesus wishes his friends to have.

Longridge, commenting on Ignatius's description of how "Christ calls and desires all to come under his standard," delves into the distinctions between the call of Christ and the call of Lucifer. "Our Lord *calls*, because he respects our freedom; but he also *desires*, which indicates his love.... Lucifer in like manner *calls and desires all*, but in order that he may lead them to perdition, and if possible use them also to corrupt others."[20]

In suggesting to Bill that he read Longridge's commentary on the Two Standards, Father Ed was effectively letting the book say to Bill what he would like to say. The book thus served as a kind of buffer: through it, Father Ed could educate Bill on the dangers of occult experimentation without having to sermonize in a manner that might damage their friendship.

Bill obligingly read the meditation and commentary. But in his reply to Dowling, he objected vehemently to the implication that any effort to obtain direct communication with the spirit world, even with a saint, opened up a potential channel for demonic deceit.[21]

Father Ed, had he wished, could have responded that, outside the realm of prayer, the Catholic faithful may not attempt contact with saints because, where revelation is concerned, the Church upholds the primacy of the divine initiative. Only God decides whether and when he or his saints or angels may enlighten a person. By contrast, the devil appeals to people's pride by promising them that, through their own power, they may obtain arcane knowledge through contact with the spirit world. Such knowledge, however, only results in enslaving people to the false god of their own self-will. Thus, the Two Standards emphasizes that humility, which opens a person to the divine initiative, is the only path to truth. That was what Father Ed was trying to impress upon Bill through recommending Longridge's commentary.

But it was never Dowling's style to have the last word, least of all in a discussion about spiritual topics. He preferred always to present the truth, in all its attractiveness, and then leave the door open so that his discussion partner could, when ready, return to him for further dialogue. That was the approach he took with Bill Wilson, and that is why, until Dowling's death, Bill continued to come to him for guidance and informal instruction in Catholic doctrine.

What Father Ed did with Bill, as with countless others whom he helped, was plant seeds, like the sower in the Gospel parable. Not all of them would bear fruit, but he trusted in God that if he were patient, some would. In Bill's case, one seed Father Ed planted that bore fruit in God's time was the Two Standards meditation. Even though it failed to dissuade him from attempting to contact spirits, Ignatius's vivid depiction of the temptations of money, honor, and pride—and the urgency of countering them through cultivating humility—strongly affected Bill. As Robert Fitzgerald has noted, Bill appeared to draw upon it in his 1954 letter to Yale University declining an honorary doctorate; certainly it informed his 1955 *Grapevine* essay "Why Alcoholics Anonymous Is Anonymous." It also appears to have influenced his reflections on humility in *Twelve Steps and Twelve Traditions*, which he was writing at the time that Dowling sent him the Spiritual Exercises.[22]

On April 8, 1953, at 8 p.m. at a Queens, New York, retreat house, Father Ed took the speaker's podium to address an audience of his fellow Catholic priests at the National Clergy Conference on Alcoholism (NCAA).

It was Father Ed who first suggested to alcoholic priest Father Ralph Pfau in 1948 that he bring together other priests who were interested in A.A. The following year, Pfau and three other priests founded the NCCA, an annual meeting bringing together priests with A.A. members, medical professionals, and others involved in the study of alcoholism or outreach to alcoholics. Since then, he had tried each year to book Dowling for the conference, finally succeeding in 1953 after he moved the event from its usual summer date to the week after Easter, when Dowling had fewer commitments.

Father Ed chose for his topic "Alcoholics Anonymous, the Twelve Steps, and Traditional Catholic Asceticism." The theme was in some ways an expansion of his 1947 Queen's Work pamphlet on A.A.,[23] in which he noted parallels between St. Ignatius Loyola's Spiritual Exercises and the Twelve Steps. But by this time, Dowling had additional wisdom to add from the extensive experience he had gained guiding alcoholic priests, who wrote to him for help from as far away as Singapore.

In discussing the Twelve Steps, Father Ed stated his firm belief that the principles were written under divine inspiration. He recalled a conversation that took place during Bill's 1942 visit to The Queen's Work (the priest in question was likely Father John Markoe, SJ):

> Bill told a priest, who asked him how long it took him to write those twelve steps, that it took twenty minutes. If it were twenty weeks, you could suspect improvisation. Twenty minutes sounds reasonable under the theory of divine help.[24]

It was a bold claim for Dowling to make, particularly before an audience of priests. But he meant what he said, and he knew what he was doing. He wanted to impress upon the assembled Catholic clergy that the Twelve Steps were a gift from God.

Father Ed's talk revealed how, during the six years since he had written his Queen's Work pamphlet on A.A., he had continued to puzzle out the parallels between the Twelve Steps and the Spiritual Exercises. In the pamphlet, he had repeated Father John Markoe's observation that certain Steps were akin to the Foundation and First Week of the Exercises. But with the passage of time, he had become increasingly convinced that some hint of the Second, Third, and Fourth Weeks of the Exercises was present in the Twelve Steps as well. He had written to Bill in 1952, "I keep feeling that the Steps blueprint the roadmap of vertical growth of the individual A.A."[25]

Dowling now had the confidence to tell the assembled priests at the conference,

> The Eleventh and Twelfth Steps give a rather limited parallel to the positive asceticism of Christianity. The Eleventh Step bids one by prayer and meditation to study to improve his conscious grasp of God, asking Him for only two things: knowledge of His will and the power to carry it out. Now, that is a true and accurate description of the positive aspects of Christian asceticism as well as of the Second, Third, and Fourth Weeks of the Spiritual Exercises of St. Ignatius.

As he finished reflecting upon the individual Steps, Father Ed offered an insight that he hoped would help those priests in the audience who were alcoholics or who, like him, ministered to alcoholic priests:

> Then, the Twelfth Step. Having had a spiritual experience or awakening as a result of these steps, we carry this message to other alcoholics and practice these principles in all our other affairs. In our apostolic work we should be an instrument in God's hands. The A.A. Steps before this Twelfth Step are to improve my instrumental contact with God. This dependence of work for others on my growth toward Christ-like sanity and sanctity has significance to an alcoholic priest. Often such a one will say, "If I could only get a little work, I feel that I could stay sober." Gradually he finds out that if he approaches sobriety through work, the work isn't going to come and the sobriety may not come either. But, as soon as he says, "Once I become sober, work will come," the hope of success is much greater.

Father Ed then turned to what was for him a particularly rich topic—how his experience of A.A. as a non-alcoholic had changed his own life.

> Alcoholics Anonymous has helped me as a person and as a priest. A.A. has made my optimism greater. My hopelessness starts much later. Like anyone who has watched Alcoholics Anonymous achieve its goals, I have seen dreams walk. I expect them to walk. You and I know that in the depths of humiliation we are in a natural area, and, rightly handled, especially in the inner spirit of that Sixth Step, I think we can almost expect the automatic fulfillment

of God's promise to assist the humble. Where there is good will, there is almost an iron connection between humiliation and humility and God's help.

He described how he had successfully used the principles of A.A. to quit smoking after numerous unsuccessful attempts to break the habit:

Thinking of A.A., I realized that I had seen men in that same boat who couldn't give up drinking. I realized that A.A. does not directly cause a man to quit drinking, but rather it causes him to quit thinking about drinking. Well, it seemed easier to give up thinking about smoking, but I didn't think I could do even that. I thought of A.A. novices saying, "I can't do it for my life. I can't do it all day. I can do it for maybe ten minutes." Inspired by the humble example of A.A. men, I said at that point to myself, "I won't try to quit smoking but I will, with God's help, postpone the thought of smoking for three minutes." That is a humiliating admission for a priest who tells others to give up much harder things.

From A.A. I learned to respect the little suffering of denying self the thought of a smoke and to pool that suffering with the sufferings of Christ, in the spirit of the Sixth Step. At that moment, like a breath of fresh air, came the thought of the widow and her mite and the importance which love can give to unimportant things. With humiliation came humility, and with humility came God's promised help. It is three or four years since I have thought of myself smoking, and I have learned that you can't smoke if you don't think about smoking.

With that in mind, Dowling turned to discuss questions that would likely be on the minds of any priests in his audience who were considering entering A.A. or recommending it to another clergyman: "First, what will be the effect on the Church? Secondly, what will be the effect on the priest?"

To the first question, he answered with characteristic bluntness:

Frankly, I don't think the Church needs saving nearly as much as this man. God's cause is often hurt by people who are trying to save God. There is an apostolic opportunity that you can find in dealing with Alcoholics Anonymous, which has therapeutic value to the individual and which offers great opportunity for the Church.

"God's cause is often hurt by people who are trying to save God." A prophetic observation if ever there was one, given the scandals that would rock the Church fifty years later as many of its representatives, embarrassed by sexual abuse, compounded the evil by covering it up.

As to the second question—that of the effect A.A. might have on the priest—Father Ed built upon a theological term familiar to his listeners—the "indelible mark" imprinted upon a priest's soul through the Sacrament of Orders:

> Priests of A.A. have two indelible marks: once an alcoholic, always an alcoholic; once a priest, always a priest. Two invisible, indelible marks, both of tremendous significance to others. As alcoholics they know insanity from the inside. As members of A.A. they know the techniques and they know the wonders that can come from amateur group psychotherapy based on the human will aided by God's help.

At the end of Father Ed's talk and the ensuing question-and-answer period, an elated Father Pfau thanked him for the "wonderful" and "thought-provoking" insights. If (as is likely) some attendees approached him for private conversation, Father Ed likely did not arrive at the Manhattan Jesuit residence where he was staying until midnight. There would be little time left for him to sleep, for he had an early train—and, before that, a visit from Bill.

Father Ed had invited Bill to attend the clergy conference, but Bill politely demurred. The A.A. co-founder was not ready to face questioning by the conference's members, some of whom were skeptical of the fellowship.[26] But he still wanted very much to see Father Ed. So Dowling suggested that, on the morning after the conference, they meet at Campion House (home to *America* magazine's staff), where he was staying .

The sky was still dark on the morning of April 9 when Bill drove down Riverside Drive toward West 108th Street. But it was worth it to him to arrive early, for he wanted to experience something he had never experienced before. He wanted to watch Father Ed celebrate Mass, and Father Ed had promised him a private one if he arrived early enough.

Bill thought on the way about what he would discuss with Father Ed. He wanted to thank the Jesuit for going out of his way to review and comment upon the manuscript of *Twelve Steps and Twelve Traditions*. At one point, after Bill sent him some chapters, Dowling suffered a retinal stroke that impaired his ability to read. Yet Father Ed didn't let that stop him; he found someone to read him the chapters so he could convey his feedback to Bill in time.

As Bill continued to reflect, he realized he had something on his conscience. In keeping with Step Ten—"Continued to take personal inventory and when we were wrong promptly admitted it"—he knew he needed to tell someone. And if there were one person who would listen with a heart of mercy, he knew it would be Father Ed.

Dowling did not disappoint. Once he was back in St. Louis, he received a grateful letter from Bill, who wrote,

> After Mass, at breakfast, I saw your face beaded with sweat; due, if I may guess, to physical pain. I then thought that I ought not press my own woes and demerits upon you. But with characteristic inconsistency, I turned about and did just that. Forthwith, I received the demonstration so characteristic of you: that however you may dislike the sin (about which you said nothing) you surely make the sinner feel understood and loved as no other mortal in my life can. What a Grace![27]

Bill's comment that "no other mortal" was like Father Ed is revealing. He saw Dowling as more than a mere man. In a letter to Joe Diggles, Bill said of the Jesuit, "I think he is one of the great men of our time—a genuine saint."[28]

What was the "sin" that Bill admitted to Father Ed? More than one historian has speculated that it had something to do with women, whether it be merely temptation or outright infidelity.[29] If that is the case (and it does seem likely), it may help explain a moral issue that Bill struggled to work out in a letter he wrote to Father Ed the following year.

In May 1954, Bill sent Dowling a four-page, single-spaced letter in which he shared some spiritual reflections that he indicated were at least partly sparked by his correspondence with Death Row inmate Caryl Chessman.[30] He had a growing interest in psychology with respect to the characteristics that distinguished the sane personality from the insane one. "The saint, for example, would be a super-normal gent," he wrote.[31]

Bill went on to say that he believed that the emotion of anger fell outside the bounds of both sanity and sanctity:

I'm truly sorry that, in most religions, righteous indignation has a place; its positive value is certainly theoretical, when we look at the way people behave. It leaves every one of us open to the rationalization that we may be as angry as we like provided we can claim to be righteous about it. I can't imagine a real saint being mad at anyone. Nor can I imagine him spending much time hating sin lest he fall into the easy error of hating the sinner.

Given that Bill had earlier written to Father Ed, "however you may dislike the sin [. . . ,] you surely make the sinner feel understood and loved," in his May 1954 letter he once again seems to be testing the Jesuit. It is as though he were saying, "Can you really love me while hating my sin?"

Father Ed took some time in his reply to consider the different points of reflection that Bill had put forth. Some of them he affirmed. But when he came to Bill's claim that a saint could not hate sin for it might lead to hating the sinner, Dowling stated his disagreement straightforwardly and directly: "If sin does to the sinner what I think it does, and if I love the sinner, then I think I should risk the error involved by hating the sin."[32]

In January 1954, The Queen's Work was rocked by the news that Father Daniel A. Lord, SJ, had been diagnosed with terminal lung cancer. Although Lord was no longer in charge, he continued to have an office there and, with his enormous popularity as an author and lecturer, remained the Jesuit most identified with the apostolate.

The impact of Lord's illness on Dowling must have been great. Apart from Bill Wilson, Lord was the person who had the greatest effect upon Dowling's life. As the news of the diagnosis sank in, Dowling sent a letter to Lord at his room at St. John's Hospital in St. Louis, suggesting he write his autobiography.

Lord's reply gives an indication of the depth of affection that ran between the two Jesuits. As was his wont, he used ellipses when he switched trains of thought:

Dear Ed:

Please don't think that I disregarded your kind note about my possible autobiography. You were nice to think that I could do it or that it might be worth doing. I still hold back for a number of obvious reasons. . . . I could not make it complete for I could not be completely honest.... I would probably find myself in mock humility playing myself down, in order to avoid the imputation of conceit and pride ... and among the many, many wonderful people I have known, I have met a modicum of the other sort ... and my omission of them would make it look blankly white ... not to mention the fact that I should try to explain the ultimate collapse of so much of my work....[33]

Having explained why he hesitated to take up Father Ed's suggestion, Father Lord then suggested a solution that had been proposed to him by a nun friend. Instead of writing a linear historical account of his life, he could write a series of personal letters to close friends, each letter recalling events of his past.

"Is that an approach?" Lord asked. "Would you think that answered your suggestions? Should I try that as a somewhat different approach to an autobiography?"

Lord reflected a bit more on how he would go about undertaking such a project, and then asked again, "What do you think?"

"In any case," he added, closing out the letter, "thanks for suggesting that I do the autobiography, and maybe ... who knows ... anyhow, say a prayer. Thanks again."

Dowling surely responded enthusiastically, for Lord did undertake the project, resulting in his inspiring memoir *Played by Ear*.[34]

Just one other piece of correspondence between Lord and Dowling survives from the time between that February 1954 letter and Lord's death the following January. It is a telegram Dowling sent Lord in October 1954 to congratulate him on the opening night of the Marian Year Pageant that he had directed in Toronto. Against all odds, Lord had succeeded in putting on what his associates said was the best musical production he had ever done—all while suffering intensely painful complications from his illness.

Father Ed's telegram read,

CONGRATULATIONS ON FULFILLING COMMITMENT. EVEN [WEARYING] CRAFTSMANSHIP AND NATIONWIDE PRAYERS WERE NOT GREATEST PREPARATION.[35] GREATER WAS SEEMINGLY UNPRODUCTIVE HOURS OF GETHSEMANE PAIN.

WITH CHRIST AS COAUTHOR[,] PREPARATION WAS DRAMA GREAT IN HIS EYES. TONIGHT'S SHOW WOULD BE DEAR TO HIM EVEN IF NO ONE ELSE WERE IN THE AUDIENCE. PLEASE FORGIVE REGRETTED ABSENCE.[36]

When Lord flew back from Toronto the following week, Dowling was at the airport to meet him and escorted him to St. John's Hospital, where Lord would remain until his death.[37]

Father Ed would also be at Lord's side during his final hours on the afternoon of January 15, 1955. At one point, Dowling said, "Father Lord, we are all here, all who love you," and he named those present. Lord responded by lifting his arms as though he were embracing everyone.

A witness reported that when Lord breathed his last, "People, nuns, doctors, and priests all over the hospital knelt in the hallways and a hush came over the hospital. They all whispered that a saint had just died."[38]

On Valentine's Day, 1955, Bill Wilson wrote to Father Ed expressing sorrow at the news of Father Lord's death. He added, "We are looking forward to seeing you at St. Louis—much sooner, if possible!"

The St. Louis reference was to the Alcoholics Anonymous International Convention coming to that city in July, where the fellowship would celebrate its twentieth anniversary. Bill had invited Father Ed to speak there so he might convey to representatives of A.A.'s worldwide membership the "touch of the eternal"[39] that Bill himself always felt in the Jesuit's presence.

Dowling's presence at the convention would also provide Bill with needed moral support, for the event would mark a major personal transition for him. In the final address of the convention, Bill intended to explain what he called the "Third Legacy" of A.A. The first legacy was unity; the second, recovery; and the third was service, in the form of A.A.'s General Service Conference. (The General Service Conference, which was fully established in 1955 after a four-year experimental period, replaced the Alcoholic Foundation as the guiding force of the fellowship's headquarters in New York City.)

Bill would tell the convention attendees of his years-long effort to guide the fellowship toward assuming a properly democratic structure, so that A.A. could be both self-governing and self-sustaining. His talk was intended to prepare them, for, at its end, he would put forth a resolution to place A.A.'s continuing care in the General Service Conference's hands, making the GSC the successor of the fellowship's founders. Once the resolution was carried—and Bill had assurance that it would be—A.A. would officially come of age.

Back when Bill was developing the Third Legacy, during the early 1950s, he had hoped Father Ed would review and comment on his plans for

A.A.'s self-governance. But, to his surprise, Dowling declined to advise him on the topic.

The Jesuit explained in a letter that he saw three dimensions to A.A.—its breadth, meaning its geographical spread and the consolidation of that spread; its length, meaning the application of the Twelve Steps to situations other than alcohol; and its depth, meaning the spiritual and moral implications of the Steps.[40] Unlike the latter two dimensions, A.A.'s breadth was the exclusive province of the fellowship's members.

"Since A.A. came along," Father Ed wrote, "I have nothing to offer to alcoholics except a phone number as far as breadth is concerned. Hence I have not been able to meet your friendly hopes in sharing your interest in the legacy."[41]

Bill's good-humored response is important for what it reveals about Dowling's influence upon his plan for A.A.'s governing structure—a plan that, in its substance, endures to this day:

> I can well understand your reluctance to give an opinion, though as the student of A.A. and of political and social and religious structures that you are, I had hoped you would do so. As a fact you are, my friend, the very one who years ago drew my attention to the extreme importance of social and political structures as these bear on the morality and effectiveness of those who have to live in them. Speaking of Tammany, you very charitably said, "those fellows couldn't be honest if they tried." Right there you set me off on structure. So if the Third Legacy is a bust, you're going to be held accountable anyhow![42]

Father Ed addressed the Alcoholics Anonymous International Convention in St. Louis on its final day, July 3, 1955, a Sunday morning. The date had personal significance for him. Not only was it the feast of St. Thomas the Apostle—the disciple who was given the great gift of touching the wounds of Christ—but it was also the twenty-fourth anniversary of his first visit back to Loyola Academy after his ordination. That was the day when he celebrated Mass for the first time in the familiar chapel where he had worshiped while teaching there. It was there at Loyola, after Mass, where he experienced the joy of having his former students come to his room to discuss their problems with their newly ordained teacher. He wrote to his family at the time, "This is my idea of my paradise."[43]

Now, as Father Ed looked out upon the crowd of five thousand assembled at the Kiel Auditorium, he felt grateful that, by the grace of God, he continued to experience that paradise. He might well have thought of the words of St. Paul: "[A]lthough our outer self is wasting away, our inner self is being renewed day by day" (2 Cor 4:16).

Noting that he had been asked to speak on "God as We Understand Him," Father Ed began by discussing the "we." And, as he always did when addressing members of A.A., he included himself in that. It did not matter to him that some assumed he was an alcoholic himself. (A former coworker recalled that "people would come to The Queen's Work and say, 'Where's the alcoholic priest's office?'")[44]

"We are three things, I think—alcoholics, Alcoholics Anonymous, and agnostic," Dowling said.

> Alcoholic means to me that we have the tremendous drive of fear, which is the beginning of wisdom. We have the tremendous drive of shame, which is the nearest thing to innocence. [...]
>
> Alcoholics Anonymous—not merely alcoholics, but Alcoholics Anonymous. Bill spoke last night of the outside antagonist in A.A., John Barleycorn. But I have always felt there is an inside antagonist who is crueler, and that is the corporate sneer for a phony, and who of us is not a phony? I think that in all groups you have the problem of people of lynx-eyed virtue.
>
> A third qualification is that I think we are all agnostic. [...] A very good priest friend of mine says, "I really think that the first thing we will say when we get to Heaven is, 'My God, it's all true!'" I think all of us are rusty in some phases of our application of beliefs.

Father Ed then moved on to consider the word "understand":

> As we move from an obscure and confused idea of God to a more clear and distinct idea, I think we should realize that our idea of God will always be lacking, always to a degree be unsatisfying. Because to understand and comprehend God is to be equal to God. But our understanding will grow.[45]

"To understand and comprehend God is to be equal to God." Might Father Ed have intended that as a subtle admonishment to Bill Wilson, whose search for satisfaction left him forever attempting, like Prometheus, to seize for himself the divine fire that had once seized him?

Dowling's next point embodied the comfort he brought to those who, like Bill, often struggled to remain on the upward path, feeling bereft of consolation:

> There is a negative approach from agnosticism. This was the approach of Peter the Apostle. "Lord, to whom shall we go?" I doubt if there is anybody in this hall who really ever sought sobriety. I think we were trying to get away from drunkenness. I don't think we should despise the negative. I have a feeling that if I ever find myself in Heaven, it will be from backing away from Hell. At this point, Heaven seems as boring as sobriety does to an alcoholic ten minutes before he quits.

The Jesuit acknowledged that there were those whose spiritual experience was a "sudden, passive insight"—passive, meaning on God's terms and not their own, as with Saul when he was struck to the ground while on the road to Damascus (Acts 9:1–22). But, he added, "there are other types, probably dearer to God since they are commoner, and those are our routine active observations. 'I am sober today.'"

Gradually, Father Ed worked his way to a confession of the personal truth that grounded his profound empathy with A.A. members: "I would like to share with you what I have found to be God's will. I believe the problem which half the people in this room have had in obtaining sobriety I have had in attaining belief and faith."

Then, speaking directly to those who were as he once was, he said, "Where do you start? Well, I believe there's something to be said about starting at the nearest manifestation of God. Where is God nearest to me?"

To answer that question, Father Ed quoted Francis Thompson's poem "In No Strange Land":

> Not where the wheeling systems darken,
> And our benumbed conceiving soars!—
> The drift of pinions, would we hearken,
> Beats at our own clay-shuttered doors.

It was Dowling's way of saying that the angels' feathered wings are no longer merely in the heavens. With the Incarnation, the Spirit of God entered our own earthly vessel—the "clay-shuttered doors" of Jesus's human nature, a nature like ours in all things but sin.

He built upon that point by proposing, as a companion to "A.A.'s Twelve Steps of man toward God," "God's Twelve Steps toward man"—

from the First Step of the Incarnation, down to the Twelfth Step of the sacrament of Communion.

That led Dowling to his final point: "The picture of the A.A.'s quest for God, but especially God's loving chase for the A.A,, was never put more beautifully than in what I think is one of the greatest lyrics and odes in the English language. It was written by a narcotic addict, and alcohol is a narcotic."

The addict in question was the same poet Father Ed had quoted earlier, Francis Thompson, and the poem contained the most consoling words he knew apart from the Gospel. It was "The Hound of Heaven," in which the narrator discovers that the divine Person he fled in fear has pursued him not to inflict harm but to offer love.

Most meaningful for Dowling were the words that the poem's narrator uttered in wonderment:

> Halts by me that footfall:
> Is my gloom, after all,
> Shade of His hand, outstretched caressingly?

Those were the words Father Ed most frequently turned to when he sought to comfort people during their darkest hours. One can only imagine how greatly he relied upon them to illuminate his own Gethsemane.

The former Dowling family home at 8224 Church Road, Baden, St. Louis—Father Ed's birthplace—as it appeared in February 2020. From 1907, when young Eddie's last sibling was born, until Eddie left for St. Mary's College in 1915, seven Dowlings lived there: parents Edward Patrick and Annie, and children Eddie, Anna, James, Paul, and Mary. At that time, the home's reddish-brown bricks were unpainted. Photo by Paul Hohmann; used with permission.

Annie Cullinane Dowling with children (from left) Eddie, James, and Anna, probably at the Dowling farm in Baden, circa March 1905. Photo courtesy of the Father Edward Dowling, SJ, Archive, Maryville University. All Dowling Archive photos are the property of the archive and are used with permission.

Puggy (center of the first row) with St. Mary's baseball teammates, circa May 1918. He was team captain. Photo from The Dial, June 1918.

Edward stands at far left with his fellow Jesuit novices at St. Stanislaus Seminary, Florissant, Missouri, June 7, 1921. Others pictured include his future spiritual director Charles (later Dismas) Clark (second row from top, second from right); his onetime admonition partner Frank Mehigan (second row from bottom, third from left), and his friend Clarence Merkle (bottom row, second from right). Photo licensed from the Jesuit Archives & Research Center. All Jesuit Archives photos are the property of the archive and are used with permission.

Father Ed speaks with an acolyte following his first Solemn Mass at the Church of Our Lady of Mount Carmel in Baden, St. Louis, June 28, 1931. His worn shoes testify to the seriousness with which he lived his Jesuit vow of poverty. Photo courtesy of the Father Edward Dowling, SJ, Archive, Maryville University.

Father Ed pauses for a photo at his desk while clipping an article about his labor-leader friend Philip Murray from the St. Louis Star-Times, June 20, 1941. Behind him to the right is an autographed photo of Heywood Broun. He liked to be surrounded by photos of friends and people he admired. Photo courtesy of the Father Edward Dowling, SJ, Archive, Maryville University.

Father Ed, circa 1935, taking a break between delivering lectures at a session of the Summer School of Catholic Action, location unknown. His SSCA name tag hangs from his cassock, and his worn leather satchel is close at hand. Photo licensed from the Jesuit Archives & Research Center. All Jesuit Archives photos are the property of the archive and are used with permission.

This August 1944 photo of Bill Wilson with Father Ed was likely taken when Dowling was in New York City with the Summer School of Catholic Action. Father Ed had it enlarged and sent it to Lois Wilson, writing at the bottom, "I do wish you were with us." Photo courtesy of the Father Edward Dowling, SJ, Archive, Maryville University.

Father Ed with an unidentified young couple in the Queen's Work chapel, circa 1946. At this time, Dowling was talking about reviving the ancient betrothal ceremony; that may be what is taking place here. Photo courtesy of the Father Edward Dowling, SJ, Archive, Maryville University.

John A. Madison, Jr., great-grandson of Dred Scott, along with his wife Marcy and children Lynne and John, looks on as Father Ed points to Scott's unmarked grave at Calvary Cemetery in St. Louis, February 1957. Photo from the collection of Catholic Cemeteries of the Archdiocese of St. Louis. Used with permission.

Alcoholics Anonymous

an interview with

Edward Dowling, S.J.

by

Frank A. Riley

THE QUEEN'S WORK
3115 South Grand Boulevard
ST. LOUIS 18, MO.

Although Father Ed enjoyed compiling news items for The Queen's Work, he found it difficult to write anything lengthier than the occasional column. This Queen's Work pamphlet on Alcoholics Anonymous, published in 1947, sold more than 100,000 copies and did much to make A.A. known among Catholics.

A Red Cap porter greets Father Ed at St. Louis's Lambert Airport on what would be the last full day of Dowling's life, April 2, 1960. Photo courtesy of the Father Edward Dowling, SJ, Archive, Maryville University.

SPIRITUAL EXERCISES

TO CONQUER ONESELF, REGULATE ONE'S LIFE AND AVOID COMING TO A DETERMINATION THROUGH ANY INORDINATE AFFECTION

ANALYZED AND ADAPTED FOR AN EIGHT DAY RETREAT

PROGRESSIVE PURPOSE		EXERCISE	MECHANICS or EXERCISES	TO REALIZE:	SPIRITUAL FRUIT
PRINCIPLE-FOUNDATION		1. END OF MAN			
		2. END OF CREATURES			
		3. Right Use of Creatures			
		4. INDIFFERENCE			
FIRST WEEK		1. TRIPLE SIN			
		2. PERSONAL SIN			
		3. Purity of Conscience			
		4. REPETITION OF 1 & 2			
		5. HELL			
		6. PRODIGAL SON			
		7. Death and Judgment			
KINGDOM		KINGDOM OF CHRIST			
SECOND WEEK		1. INCARNATION			
		2. NATIVITY			
		3. Devotion to Mary			
		4. HIDDEN LIFE			
		5. CHRIST IN TEMPLE			
		6. TWO STANDARDS			
		7. The Election			
		8. THREE CLASSES of MEN			
		9. CHRIST'S FAREWELL			
		10. THREE MODES			
		11. Zeal for Souls			
THIRD WEEK		1. LAST SUPPER			
		2. AGONY IN GARDEN			
		3. TRIAL—CONDEMNATION			
		4. Suffering			
		CRUCIFIXION			
FOURTH WEEK		1. RESURRECTION			
		2. ASCENSION			
		3. The Sacred Heart			
		4. CONT. FOR LOVE			

Prepared by JOHN P. MARKOE, S.J.

THE QUEEN'S WORK
3742 West Pine Boulevard · ST. LOUIS, MO.

THE QUEEN'S WORK
PRINTED IN U.S.A.

John P. Markoe, SJ's chart representing an eight-day adaptation of the Spiritual Exercises retreat, from a fold-out pamphlet published by The Queen's Work, 1930. This is likely the poster that Bill W. saw on the wall during his 1942 visit to The Queen's Work. Photo licensed from the Jesuit Archives & Research Center.

PART III

A SERVANT UNTIL THE END

14

ACCOMPANYING THE SUFFERING

*The sense of knowing where we are going, how our next months
and years are to be plotted is not only a precious comfort, but it
must sometimes beget a sort of independence from God's hand because so often this information seems to be ladled in teaspoonfuls
rather than bucketsful.*
　　　　　　　　— Father Ed, letter to Bill Wilson, May 27, 1942[1]

At the time that the teenage Ronnie Creighton-Jobe met Father Ed, he had
already known two extraordinary priests. He was a nine-year-old Episcopalian singing in St. Louis's Catholic cathedral's choir when he was introduced to Bishop Fulton J. Sheen, who encouraged him in his desire to become Catholic. And he was twelve when Father Joseph T. Adams, who had
given up a lucrative business career to become a Capuchin Franciscan friar,
convinced his parents to let their child enter the Church.

Finally came the day in 1958 when the Third Order (lay) Franciscan
group to which young Ronnie belonged was having its semi-annual Mass
and brunch—"and who was talking, but this extraordinary Jesuit called Father Edward Dowling."[2] The now-Father Ronald Creighton-Jobe, a member
of the Brompton Oratory in London, remembers that morning clearly, for it
changed his life.

"[Father Ed] was very funny, and eccentric and amusing, and already
obviously in great pain, with all the arthritis," Creighton-Jobe says.

> He had little bits of newspaper and notes in his fingers, and he said,
> "I have five very important points to tell you"—and he said, "Point
> number 1," and then he was terribly funny. "Point number 2," and
> he'd tell that. But all the points were "very important." And "point
> number 3," and then he said, "Oh, point number 4 is not important.
> We'll skip that."

He had a *huge* sense of humor. He was a great communicator, because, basically, he had the heart of a journalist. I thought, "What a wonderful man! Isn't he amusing!"

And so I was introduced [to him] as the youngest Franciscan tertiary. I was about thirteen.

Creighton-Jobe, who lived near The Queen's Work, was in the habit of attending weekday Mass at his neighborhood parish each morning before he left for school. One morning, on his way to Mass, he was delighted to spot Father Ed on the street. When he saw Father Ed again on another morning not long afterwards, he called out to him, "Father, I remember you."

"Well, I remember you too," Father Ed replied. "What are you doing?"

"I'm going to Mass."

"Well, you know," Father Ed said, "we have The Queen's Work." He motioned in his office's direction. "There's a chapel there. Why don't you come to Mass at The Queen's Work?"

And so, Ronnie began to attend Mass at The Queen's Work each weekday morning. Usually the Mass was celebrated by Father William Barnaby Faherty, SJ.[3] By then, Creighton-Jobe says, Dowling's arthritis was so severe that he no longer said his own Mass in the chapel. He celebrated it in his room instead.

Creighton-Jobe believes that Father Ed's private celebration of the Mass was in keeping with his "slightly eremitical" way of life. He hastens to add that Dowling was no hermit. Rather, the Oratorian priest says, Father Ed "understood being slightly outside of one's context. He knew that to be close to God you really had to have the experience of solitude and not necessarily always belonging, because he dealt with people who didn't quite fit or belong."

From the first morning that Ronnie attended morning Mass at The Queen's Work, Father Ed began what would become another weekday tradition for the two: he invited Ronnie to join him for breakfast afterwards. The teen would collect his breakfast from the German bakery next door and then come up to Father Ed's office, where they would eat and talk.

Ronnie was overweight at that time, which was a source of concern to Father Ed, who knew the effects of overeating all too well. As Dowling watched the teen tear into his breakfast, he would say to his sister Anna, who was his secretary, "That boy's going to die before me! I mean, he's eating so many awful rich cakes."

The schoolboy and the aging priest would talk and talk. "And we became huge friends," Creighton-Jobe says.

He was like a father figure to me. It was wonderful. And it brought home what a very lonely life the Jesuits had then, because they were not encouraged to have friendships in [their] communities. The only friend Father Dowling had at The Queen's Work was Father Faherty.

Despite Dowling's near-continuous travels, "he spent a lot of time on his own," Creighton-Jobe notes. "He taught me about the necessity to embrace solitude. He said, 'There's a huge difference between being isolated and being solitary.'"

Not every Jesuit that Ronnie met was able to appreciate such a distinction. He sometimes visited a priest in the St. Louis University community who had a drinking problem and who once said of himself and his fellow Jesuits, "We live very lonely lives."

"Father Dowling would not have said that," Creighton-Jobe says, "because I don't think he conceived his life as lonely." He recognized that even though he might be isolated from certain human consolations, he could never truly be alone, for he always had the companionship of God.

With that in mind, Creighton-Jobe observes,

solitude is something that we all have to embrace—and indeed, it is part of our [Christian] vocation. Isolation is destructive; solitude is positive and liberating. And [Father Ed] had that. In that sense, he was a free spirit. But the marvelous thing was for me to have had this experience, to have found a man who helped me understand that you mustn't flee from solitude.

One morning over breakfast, Ronnie said to Father Ed, "Oh, Father, I think I really want to be a priest."

Father Ed replied, "Well, you're very young yet. Now, what are you thinking of?"

"Well, I don't know," Ronnie said. "I suppose I could be a Franciscan."

Father Ed cocked his head in the familiar way that he did when he was listening and reflecting at the same time. "Well, I suppose," he said.

After a moment's silence, Ronnie asked, "What about the Jesuits?"

"No," Father Ed answered firmly. "You wouldn't fit."

"Why?"

"Because you are too independent."

Ronnie was surprised. "What do you mean?"

Father Ed responded in a reflective tone, "You know, Ronnie, there are people who never quite fit."

"Oh, I might!" Ronnie answered hopefully.

But Father Ed was serious. "You may never do," he said.

"Well, that sounds rather like a curse, Father."

"No," Dowling said with feeling. "That's a blessing from God. It means that you can give more of yourself outside your particular context."

Today, as Creighton-Jobe reflects upon that conversation, he observes that Father Ed "was obviously talking about himself, because he had all these different interests." Dowling, he notes,

> was very keen on proportional representation because he was third-generation Irish and he was old-fashioned Yeatsian Irish; he believed passionately in Irish independence. In that sense, he was a romantic, and there weren't many romantics in the Jesuits.

When Creighton-Jobe brings his mind back to Father Ed's Queen's Work office in the late 1950s, he remembers how the crippled Jesuit would sit there—"he could hardly stand"—and "what he did was, he gave himself to people." Dowling's ministry was not so much to people with problems, he adds, as it was to "people who didn't just quite fit into the pattern."

Another thing that stands out in Creighton-Jobe's memory is how Dowling both was faithful to Catholic doctrine and made that doctrine come alive by applying it in ways that helped people find healing. The Oratorian says he himself experienced such healing through Father Ed's caring counsel at a time when his home life was under great strain:

> [Father Ed] believed, absolutely, all the teachings of the Church, and you get that coming out in his theology of suffering—"Glad Gethsemane"—because he lived with great suffering.
>
> My father was very ill. And [Father Ed] taught me as a child—I mean, I was basically a child—to embrace God's love, and also what it means to hand over the difficulties of one's life to the Lord and to grow.

It was in that same spirit that Father Ed once recommended a book to Ronnie as the teen perused The Queen's Work's in-house library.

"You were received by a Franciscan," Dowling observed, for he knew it was Father Adams who had brought the teen into the Church.

Then, Creighton-Jobe recalls,

He said to me, "You read *The Little Flowers of St. Francis* and you'll get the spirit of joy."

That's I think what he meant by Glad Gethsemane. He had joy, but it was not based upon facile happiness. It was real joy. He was a joyful person and he handed that on. And wasn't I lucky, as a young man, to have it!

The source of Father Ed's joy was obvious. "I wouldn't say that he was a contemplative," Creighton-Jobe says, "but he was a man of prayer. He was absolutely grounded in Our Lord's presence in the Blessed Sacrament."

What especially struck Ronnie was the intentionality with which Father Ed would enter the Queen's Work chapel to sit down and pray. A Jesuit brother who knew Dowling several years earlier, when he would celebrate his morning Mass in the sacristy at St. Louis University's College Church, was similarly impressed. Brother Phil Malone, SJ, later said that, after Mass, Dowling would sit in the chair behind the kneeler and stare at the carved wooden crucifix for a short while, as though he were transfixed.[4]

What was in Father Ed's mind during those morning moments of contemplation? Perhaps he was following his own advice that he used to give people who were suffering: "Look to the crucifix and thank Christ for letting you hang there with him for this hour."[5]

At some point after Ronnie began attending Mass on weekday mornings at The Queen's Work and having breakfast afterwards with Father Ed, the teen fell ill with the flu and had to stay home for several days. One morning while he was sick, the doorbell rang. His Irish nanny went to answer it. She came back to Ronnie's room wearing a surprised expression.

"There's a beggar at the door, quite an old beggar," she said. "He's asking for you."

"I went to the top of the stair," Creighton-Jobe recalls," and there was Father Edward. He had brought me Communion. And he'd walked from the Queen's Work."

That story, perhaps more than any other, brings to life the impression that so many people reported of Father Ed during his final years—that, despite his increasingly calcified joints; his obesity; his heart disease; and his serious breathing difficulties, he was unstoppable. Here is a man who could barely cross a street without assistance; yet he walked six city blocks to minister to his ill friend. And if he caught Ronnie's flu, it could easily put him in the hospital or even kill him.

Another compelling aspect of the story concerns the circumstances of Dowling's visit. It is not much of a stretch to imagine that, in the back of his mind, he was thinking of when his brother James caught the flu forty years earlier, during that horrible pandemic year. He could not be at James's side then, let alone bring him Holy Communion, but he could do those things for Ronnie now.

Why did the Irish nanny mistake Father Ed for a beggar (as did so many others over the years)? Creighton-Jobe says, "He actually looked like a nice old-fashioned Jesuit. However, because he had all this arthritis, he couldn't get himself dressed very well."

Necessity forced Father Ed to come up with creative ways to dress himself. Creighton-Jobe recalls one "wonderful solution" of his: "To put on his socks, he cut out the bottom, the foot, so he could put them on either way."

Father Ed's nephew Paul Murphy Dowling witnessed another approach the Jesuit took to expand his limited range of movement. "I can remember taking a train with him and we were in a Pullman bunk—I had the upper, he had the lower. And in the morning as we pulled into the station, he was trying to get his clothes on, and he had to use his cane to do it."

Yet, Paul told me, although Father Ed "couldn't bend over to get his pants on, there was no self-pity there." He never complained about his arthritis.[6]

"I realize now that his back must have been in pain a lot," Paul added. But when people would express sorrow over his arthritis and back pain, "he used to say, 'You don't die of it, you die with it,' and then he'd change the subject. He didn't want to talk about himself and his own suffering. He wanted to talk about others' problems and others' suffering."[7]

Because of the time elapsed from Father Ed's death in 1960 and my beginning to seek out eyewitnesses to his life in 2020, most of the eyewitnesses I interviewed knew him during their childhood. Their memories complement contemporary reporters' accounts of Father Ed in ways that are enlightening, for children notice things that adults often do not.

Every child eyewitness I interviewed remarked upon Father Ed's clothing—not only that he dressed shabbily, but also that he always wore clerics. Catholic children in St. Louis and Chicago were used to seeing Jesuits, and even during the 1950s Jesuits typically dressed casually when not teaching or ministering in an official capacity. Father Ed, by contrast, was never seen publicly in casual dress. From the time he entered the Society of Jesus, every existing photo of him, including family photos, shows him wearing clerics.

"Matthew," a son of Father Ed's former Loyola Academy student "Carl" (whose story was told in chapter 7) says, "He was always in black—a black suit, clerical collar, and black hat—and I never saw him dressed casually, unlike when other priests visited. He was such a casual man in many ways; that seemed unusual."

Although Father Ed was tradition-minded when it came to Catholic orthodoxy, his nephew Paul provides an additional reason why he dressed the part of a priest. Father Ed once took Paul to a downtown St. Louis bar and grill that he would visit after attending public events. "He used to go there with his Roman collar on," Paul says, "because he always said that if people see a priest in a bar and grill, they figure, 'If he can be here, then he can probably listen to my sins.'"

"He really had no interest in alcohol," Paul adds. "For him, [visiting a bar] was a way of getting people to open up and talk about their problems."

Another eyewitness who knew Father Ed during childhood is Michael E. Fox Sr., whose father, J. Raymond "Ray" Fox, was one of Father Ed's students at Loyola Academy and, as noted earlier, one of the first Cana Conference participants. Dowling used to visit the Fox family during his frequent visits to Chicago. "My father always gave him twenty dollars to buy a new hat, and he never bought it," Michael says. "He gave the money away."

After Michael shared that recollection with me, I found a passage in one of Father Ed's favorite literary works, the English poet John Drinkwater's 1918 play *Abraham Lincoln*, where a visitor to Mary Todd Lincoln describes the future U.S. President as having "his battered hat nigh falling off the back of his head, and stuffed with papers that won't go into his pockets." Mary responds, "I've tried for years to make him buy a new hat." Father Ed, who had an astonishingly good memory for things he had read, quoted Drinkwater's play frequently, including in a letter to Bill Wilson. I have no doubt that on some level, whether consciously or unconsciously, he identified with the humble Lincoln and enjoyed the idea of wearing a battered hat like him.

Also like Drinkwater's Lincoln, Dowling filled his pockets (although not his hat) with papers. In the Dowling Archive, I found a clear plastic envelope containing what appear to be the contents of his pockets at the time of his death. It has scraps of paper of all different kinds, containing names, phone numbers, and various memoranda—and a pocket address book, new and unmarked.

I laughed out loud when I realized how the address book must have gotten in there. Some well-meaning person, probably a woman (but not Dowling's sister/secretary Anna, who knew his habits), said to him, "Father, look at all those scraps of paper! You need an address book to keep track of everything. Here, I have an extra; take mine."

"Thanks, kid!" Father Ed would have replied—and put the book in his pocket. And the next time he needed to write down a phone number, he would have written it on a scrap of paper, completely forgetting he had an address book in his pocket for that purpose.

Mary Louise Adams, the Dowling Archive librarian who, during the early 1980s, compiled information for a (never-realized) biography of Father Ed, wrote that a couple who were in a St. Louis A.A. group that the Jesuit frequented

> wanted to give him a present. So it was decided that he needed a new suit; Anna supplied the proper size, [the wife] pressed it and put tissue paper in the box, and wrapped it beautifully. Father was delighted with the gift and said he would wear it to next week's meeting. The next week he looked as "unneat as ever"![8]

There was another noteworthy aspect of Father Ed's dress, perhaps not of great interest to most adults but intriguing to children. Jayne Lahey Kobliska, daughter of Dowling's friend Ed Lahey, says, "I remember the shoes he wore, because I'd never seen that type before. They had a side buckle that aided in putting them on. He needed it, because he had swollen arches, which stretched the shoes' leather and caused it to wrinkle." Photographs of Father Ed bear out Jayne's recollections perfectly.

The rail vacation on which Father Ed took his nephew Paul, when Paul witnessed his uncle struggle to dress himself with the help of his cane, was part of Dowling's larger effort to be a substitute father for the boy.

Although the nephew's father, Father Ed's brother Paul Vincent Dowling, had managed to marry and have children, his mental-health issues intensified during the 1940s and grew progressively worse. His other child, Mary, told me that Paul Vincent was diagnosed with manic depression, which today is known as bipolar disorder, for which he was hospitalized several times. He also had a heart condition, the result of a bout of rheumatic fever that he had suffered as a child.

At the end of 1945, Paul Vincent Dowling's physical weakness and psychological vulnerability were such that he was no longer able to maintain steady employment. But just because he was home did not mean he was psychologically present as a father for five-year-old Paul Murphy and three-year-old Mary. Father Ed therefore took it upon himself to fill that gap in his niece and nephew's lives, becoming a fatherly presence to them and striving to ensure they had a rich variety of positive childhood experiences.

Paul Vincent Dowling was then living with his wife and children at the house in Baden where he had grown up with Father Ed and their other siblings. On most Sundays, Father Ed would come to dinner. Father Ed's niece Mary recalls, "We always looked forward to seeing him. He was always fun. He brought the whole outside world into us. We were in a very parochial setting in Baden. He opened the world to us."[9]

Those Sunday-night dinners left Father Ed's nephew Paul with happy memories as well. "I can remember at the dinner table [Father Ed] would amuse my sister and me when we were kids by twirling the cane, one finger to another," Paul says. "He was good at it." The cane also came in handy when young Paul was chasing Mary around the dinner table. "[Father Ed] used the cane to block me from getting at my sister."

Just as Father Ed employed his cane to prevent conflict, so too with his words. Mary says, "There was never an unkind word that he said against anybody that I can recall, ever."

Occasionally Alcoholics Anonymous-related topics were discussed at table, for Father Ed sometimes brought friends from A.A. over for dinner. He also would bring others to whom he was ministering. Mary Dowling's high-school classmate Mary Claire McDonnell remembers being at the Dowlings' Baden home one evening in the mid-1950s when a middle-aged female guest was discussing her battle with scruples. "She had eaten a banana and had gone to receive Communion, and she was obsessing about it. [Father Ed] said, 'Well, dear, I wouldn't worry about it. Just try and remember the next time.' And then she stopped; she didn't say anything more about it." The Jesuit's serene and merciful words made a great impression upon Mary Claire at a time when the Church's rules on fasting before Communion were far stricter than today.

Carl's son Matthew was similarly taken with Father Ed's gentle and understanding manner. He says,

> If you had been accused of the worst crime in the world, the first person you would call was Father Dowling, and somehow he would find a way to put you at ease—saying that this will work

out, we will figure out a way, it's not as bad as you think. He was that kind of a person; he always could put you at ease.

Just as Father Ed visited other former students such as Ray Fox, he also visited Carl's home whenever he was in Chicago and had time to spare. Matthew told me,

> When I first saw him, I thought he was rather short, kind of heavy, walked with great effort with a cane—and kind of hunched over, although he was short—and had a shock of white hair. His movements were so labored that I'm sure that it was awfully hard for him to travel.

But, Matthew added,

> About two minutes later, you didn't notice anything. All you noticed was Father Dowling—his face, his words. It was like we had a saint in the room. You just would listen to him, and we'd talk back and forth, but everything was as though you were talking to a saint. He was just full of love, full of understanding.
>
>   There was nothing boring about him. It would be so easy for a kid to be bored with the conversation, but he always kept it at a level where he retained your interest.

Matthew remembered how all the family would gather around Father Ed in the living room. "You would think that kids would get up after a while and let the next kid—we had a lot of kids in the family—let the next kids come in and talk to him, but we would always stay and listen to him." It was "a moment of reverence, but informality. It wasn't like being in church. He was a very informal person and always commanded respect—he didn't *command* it, but you just gave it."

It was a testimony to Father Ed's greatness, Matthew said,

> for a kid to be at rapt attention to an older [person]—and he was a lot younger than he looked, he always looked a lot older—to be at rapt attention with this priest talking about whatever the topic. [His topics were] usually in the area of love and understanding, helping your parents, and things like that. You would listen to him.

Father Ed's sense of humor also made him attractive to children as well as adults. "He could make you laugh," Matthew said. "I always remember being very surprised [by his humor]. We had a very stern pastor, and my impression of priests was that they were kind of stern. He was just the opposite."

In short, Matthew reflected,

He was a wonderful man, and you couldn't dislike him. You would feel like you could tell him any problem you had, and he would be helpful in putting you at ease and even finding some forgiveness along the way. He made you come away thinking that it wasn't as bad or it wouldn't be as bad; he just had that way of settling everything down.

And he'd talk about God, but not preachy—"God's grace" or "God understands." He was a priest first.

Matthew's sense that Father Ed was "full of love [and] full of understanding," was echoed by others I spoke with who encountered him when they were children. They spoke of the warmth of his gaze; there was something in the way he looked at them that made them trust him. He treated them with reverence and he paid attention to them.

Father Ed was also attentive to mothers' needs and to the needs of couples who experienced hardships while trying to conceive. One woman who came to see him at his office was suffering grief over a recent miscarriage. He encouraged her to join a support group of Catholic women he had assembled who had, like her, suffered pregnancy loss.

The pregnancy-loss group was just one among many that Father Ed would start during the final decade of his life as his desire intensified to find new applications of what he termed A.A.'s "isopathic" approach. Another was for women who had seven or more children. He named it after his favorite drink: 7 Up.[10]

Throughout this period, and indeed to the end of his life, Father Ed maintained his fatherly concern for his former students, and especially for their marriages. Nephew Paul Murphy Dowling remembers spending a Sunday with Father Ed at the summer home of one such student, Neil C. Hurley Jr., and his wife. Father Ed celebrated Mass, and then they all had lunch together. Then the Jesuit did something that made a great impression on his nephew.

"After the meal," Paul told me, Father Ed

insisted on helping Neil Hurley's wife with the dishes. He took time then to ask her how things were going—how that marriage was doing and how they were getting along. It must not have been a pleasant way to do counseling, because with his arthritis, standing up and drying dishes was not an unpainful experience. But he did it.[11]

Father Ed's increased outreach to people with problems coincided with his moving from the St. Louis University Jesuit community in 1951 to a community consisting of Jesuit staff of The Queen's Work. For Dowling, his new residence had the advantage of being situated on the sixth floor of the Queen's Work headquarters at 3115 South Grand Boulevard in St. Louis—just one floor above his office, accessible by elevator. (In an unusual design feature, the building's elevator also went to the roof—a nice amenity for when Dowling wished to entertain guests in the open air.)

Some of Father Ed's brother Jesuits—particularly those in the St. Louis University community he had left—were bemused by the unique nature of his ministry as well as that of another local Jesuit who lived separately from their community.

Father Charles "Dismas" Clark, SJ, like Father Ed, had been something of an outlier at the SLU Jesuit residence. He too assisted people with problems—in his case, prisoners and ex-convicts, for which local newspapers dubbed him the "Hoodlum Priest."[12] It is quite likely that he was inspired by Father Ed's early work in prison ministry (and Dowling took the vow name Dismas long before Clark appropriated it). He also seems to have been inspired by Father Ed's friend Dempster MacMurphy, who (also likely through Dowling's inspiration) spread devotion to St. Dismas during the 1930s. When Clark spoke of the saint, he used language nearly identical to that of MacMurphy's articles. In any case, he and Dowling were good friends from their novitiate days, and at some point in the 1950s he became Father Ed's spiritual director.

Although Clark began his outreach to convicts while living in the SLU Jesuit community, by 1953 his Jesuit neighbors could no longer tolerate the stream of troubled young men who came seeking his aid.[13] It was then that Father Daniel A. Lord, SJ, along with Queen's Work community superior Father Frederick L. Zimmerman, SJ, invited Clark to live at The Queen's Work.

Given that both Lord and Zimmerman advocated racial justice—Zimmerman as administrator of African-American parish St. Malachy's—one wonders whether the SLU Jesuits' real issue was not with Clark's having criminal visitors but with his having Black visitors. Whatever it was, the presence of both Clark and Dowling at The Queen's Work led some of their former Jesuit neighbors at SLU to wisecrack about their exotic clientele.

One joke that made the rounds was that if Catholics needed marriage preparation, they should seek out Father Clark or Father Dowling if they were
"whores, convicts, or alcoholics"—otherwise they could seek assistance
from any priest.[14]

The joke was not without foundation. Father Ed's niece Mary Dowling
says Father Ed "would surround himself with people who were drunk or
neurotic."

"You would go to his office and you would never know who you were
going to meet," Mary adds. "You could meet somebody who was very important and influential, and then you could meet somebody else who looked
like they had been dragged in off the street." In either case, she says, Father
Ed took the same level of interest in his visitors.

One day when Father Ed's nephew Paul was visiting him at The
Queen's Work, an alcoholic man came in to see the Jesuit. "My uncle
started playing penny-ante poker with him, just to distract the guy's mind,"
Paul says. "His point to the guy was, 'A minute at a time.' 'I didn't have a
drink this minute.' 'Don't look ahead too far.'"

The advice was Father Ed's personal variation on the "one day at a
time" philosophy of Alcoholics Anonymous. He expanded upon it in a talk
he gave in the late 1940s:

> I think the Alcoholics Anonymous movement has caught one of
> Christ's great teachings—it's an explicit teaching in regard to any
> cross-bearing—and that is to take up one's cross daily. Dr.
> [William] Osler of Johns Hopkins had an adaptation of that, which
> Dale Carnegie is now using in his latest book on worry [*How to
> Stop Worrying and Start Living*], and he calls it the "day-tight
> compartment." That is the self-denial involved in keeping our nose
> out of tomorrow and keeping our thoughts away from yesterday so
> as to concentrate.[15]

Immediately after describing the notion of the day-tight compartment,
Dowling added an idea that he almost certainly adapted from Cardinal
Newman.

"Actually," he said,

> I don't think there is a pain in the world that a person can't stand
> for one second. And that's actually about all that we ever stand, re-
> ally. No one ever heard of two seconds happening in one second.
>
> I think the joy in the Cross isn't total—or it wouldn't be a cross.
> But I have a feeling that the great distinction made in religious

training—I remember [it] in my novitiate, which was typical, I
guess, of a great many [methods of] asceticism training—is a first
distinction between feelings and the will. You have that in the
Agony in the Garden; Christ's feelings were all opposed to going
on, and that never stopped him there....

[Regarding] getting a correct code of suffering: someone has
said, "I admire the man who can take it." I know that our Lord,
when the mother of the sons of Zebedee asked him if those two
boys would have a good place in heaven, Christ simply said to her,
"Can they take it? Can they drink the chalice?"[16] ...

Although there is power in Father Ed's words, his overarching point is
somewhat obscure. I believe that the key to understanding his meaning is to
be found in the part of his reflections that he draws from Newman—along
with the way he takes Newman's idea to a new level.

Newman says in his sermon "Mental Sufferings of Our Lord in His
Passion," he says that during the Crucifixion, Jesus Christ, upon being offered drugged wine, rejected it "because [it] would have stupefied His
mind, and He was bent on bearing the pain in all its bitterness." The wine,
Newman says, would have reduced Christ's perception of pain to that of a
brute animal, which (he claims) feels pain less intensely than a human because it is incapable of reflecting upon its pain. Jesus wished instead to feel
pain as a human being does—with each moment of it compounded and intensified by the memory of the previous moment and the fear of the next.

"It is the intellectual comprehension of pain, as a whole diffused
through successive moments, which gives it its special power and keen-
ness," Newman writes, "and it is the soul only, which a brute [animal] has
not, which is capable of that comprehension."[17]

What Father Ed does is take Newman's basic point and turn it on its
head. Yes, he says, as human beings, we do feel the compounded weight of
successive moments of pain—and that is why we must combat the temptation to add the pain of yesterday and tomorrow to that of today. By God's
grace, we have the power to live in each individual moment of pain. We do
this not by stupefying ourselves to the level of animals, but by directing our
will toward "taking it"—accepting this moment of pain, because it is the
chalice that Jesus is offering us.

Although it may appear at first glance that Dowling's message runs
completely counter to that of Newman, in fact he is taking a different (and,
I would argue, more profound) route to affirm the larger point of New-

man's sermon—namely, that Jesus, in his desire to accomplish the Father's will to save us, consciously chose to immerse his entire self in every moment of pain.

People unfamiliar with such notions of redemptive suffering may think them bizarre. Others, who grew up in households where such teachings were used to shush complaining children—"Offer it up!"—may deem them scandalous, even sado-masochistic, because they attribute some sort of goodness to pain. But Father Ed was no masochist and he was no sadist. He was unafraid to seek help for his own mental and physical sufferings, and he spent his entire ministry helping others overcome every kind of suffering (including injustice). People came to him with their problems because they knew he would do everything in his power to solve them.

Yet Dowling knew that not every problem could be solved. That was why he believed that people needed, in his words, "a correct code of suffering"—so that, when unavoidable suffering came, they could enter into it as fully as the moment demanded, having faith that behind it lay the "joy in the Cross."

Jayne Lahey Kobliska was six in December 1941 when her father, Ed Lahey (he who introduced Dowling to A.A.), moved out east from Chicago with his family to take up his new assignment as the Chicago *Daily News*' Washington correspondent. She told me that Father Ed would visit her family whenever he was in town, which was usually at least twice a year. Her mother, Grace, had a special dish she would make for him: baking-powder biscuits.

"They were biscuits that crumbled easily and had their origins in Irish cuisine—very much like soda bread," Kobliska said. "Father Dowling would just devour them. If there were six on the plate, he would eat four of them. My mother would never think of having a dinner without them if he were there."

It is not surprising that Dowling would devour such biscuits, given that their main ingredients apart from baking powder were the very ones that he later identified as his greatest "craving-creating" triggers: "starch, butter, salt, and sugar." In his final article submission to *Grapevine*, written three months before his death, he described how, after his overeating led to serious health problems, he employed A.A.'s Twelve Steps to combat such cravings:

Alcoholism is, when unchecked, *gluttony* for alcoholic drink. A.A.'s success with this type of gluttony opens new hope for the better-known gluttony, which is killing many people—respectfully autopsied as obesity or overweight.

My 240-pound gluttony gave me two heart attacks. An alcoholic doctor got me down toward 180 when he advised a total A.A. abstinence from starch, butter, salt and sugar. He said these four foods were probably my "alcohol." Abstinence was so much easier than temperance. The "balanced" diet often prescribed was loaded with these four "craving-creating appetizers." I was like a lush tapering off on martinis. Only after the discovery of the A.A. approach to craving-creating intake did I realize that the Jesuit Ignatius's first rule for diet in his Spiritual Exercises was to go easy on craving-creating food and drink.[18]

Dowling never missed an opportunity to let Alcoholics Anonymous members know how grateful he was for the new insight that "the A.A. approach" gave him into the Jesuits' spiritual patrimony. He had done the same in his previous *Grapevine* article, when he wrote,

An A.A. member once told me that he had been skeptical about the A.A. spiritual program until he realized that it was the systematic expression of an old Jesuit prayer he had learned as a boy. The prayer was:

"Take, Lord, and receive all my liberty, my memory, my intellect, and all my will—all that I have and possess. Thou gavest it to me: to Thee, Lord, I return it! All is Thine, dispose of it according to all Thy will. Give me Thy love and grace, for this is enough for me."

I told my AA friend that I was afraid of that prayer. I feared that if I made that offering to God at eight o'clock in the morning I would have taken it back by ten o'clock.

"How do you know you'll be alive by ten o'clock?" he said. "How do you know but that God may give you even greater help after making that offering? That's the way that A.A. has taught me to look at it," he said.

Since then I have not been afraid of that prayer. This A.A. member had given me an understanding of that old Jesuit prayer, which I had not got in my thirty Jesuit years.[19]

Writings such as these show that all the while that A.A. members looked to Father Ed as a spiritual guide, he himself looked to A.A. members for guidance and inspiration. Through the beauty of his humility, he restored to them their sense of dignity.

Given his reputation as a priest who would do his best to help people with any kind of problem, it is to be expected that many who approached Father Ed sought help overcoming sexual temptations that caused them shame.

However—and not surprisingly, given the stigma attached—no one whom Father Ed assisted with sexual problems has left a testimony. Dowling's surviving papers likewise give almost no evidence of how he helped people with such issues. The near-absence of material on the topic leads me to believe that Father Ed's sisters Anna and Mother Mary, who handled his papers after his death, destroyed correspondence that they deemed sensitive. Thankfully, the few items that exist regarding Dowling's assistance to people suffering unwanted sexual temptations provide enough information to envisage how he advised on such matters.

Among the applications of the Twelve Steps that Father Ed envisioned for non-alcoholics, the healing of sexual obsessions, compulsions, and addictions was prominent on the list. In the original manuscript of his *Grapevine* article "Three Dimensions of A.A.," which he submitted on May 11, 1955, Dowling wrote, "I have seen the effectiveness of the A.A. Steps in marriage counseling, in triangular infatuations, in baffling homosexuality, and in the current quest for abstinence from smoking."

What stands out is the reference to "baffling homosexuality," by which Father Ed apparently meant that the Twelve Steps could help people resist gay temptations even though the cause of such temptations was a mystery. Although his implication that gay attraction was something that could (or should) be countered is highly contentious today, it should be noted that Dowling's main interest was not to pass judgment on gay identity. At a time when not only the Catholic Church but also society at large deemed same-sex attraction unacceptable, Father Ed was effectively making several points about it that went against the current of his times.

First, in calling homosexuality "baffling," Dowling was saying that it was not consciously chosen. In that respect, he was ahead of many non-professional observers of the time (and even today). Second, in recommending the Twelve Steps as a means of countering gay temptations, he was promoting an approach significantly more humane than many then-accepted anti-gay "therapies," some of which were positively horrific.

Third, and most importantly, Father Ed was making an important statement simply by mentioning homosexuality alongside marital problems and smoking. At that time, gay relations were illegal in every U.S. state. For a Catholic priest even to raise the issue of gay attraction as though it were something that ordinary people might struggle with was a bold move in 1955. Too bold, in fact, for *Grapevine*; the published version of Father Ed's article deleted all mention of homosexuality.

If Father Ed noticed he had been censored, he did not let it sway him from making homosexuality, and the needs of gays for fellowship with one another, a topic of public discussion. In November 1959, he agreed to write what would be his final *Grapevine* article. Written in December and published in June 1960 (two months after Dowling's death) as "A.A. Steps for the Underprivileged Non-A.A.," the article made several references to the relevance of the A.A. approach for gays. This time, the editors let them stand.

Father Ed used "A.A. Steps for the Underprivileged Non-A.A." to amplify points he had made in his previous *Grapevine* article on the relevance of A.A.'s approach for non-alcoholics—particularly those rejected by polite society:

> "It's like A.A." has been the passport to acceptance among the dignosclerotic (hardening of the dignity) for such stigma-pilloried movements as Narcotics Anonymous, Crime Prevention, Recovery, Inc., Divorcees Anonymous, Divorcees Unanimous, WANA, Adiposics Anonymous, the Mattachine Society, Average People, Nicotinic Nobodies, Daughters of Bilitis, Gamblers Anonymous, Check Writers Anonymous, Security Cloister, Politicians Anonymous and other self-help groups in areas of varying degrees of seriousness and helplessness.[20]

Dowling's list of "stigma-pilloried movements" included not one but two early gay-rights groups: the Mattachine Society, for gay men, and the Daughters of Bilitis, for lesbians. That was his way of acknowledging that gays were marginalized by society and that they deserved the opportunity to find comfort in mutual support. Here, once again, Father Ed was pushing the boundaries of acceptable discourse for an American Catholic priest in the 1950s. Society in general and the Catholic Church in particular did not normally speak about gays as human beings in need of fellowship. To society at large, they were criminals and perverts; to the Church, they were additionally sinners. In either case, they were commonly viewed as caricatures or stereotypes, not as individuals.

When I first read Dowling's references to the Mattachine Society and the Daughters of Bilitis, I wondered whether perhaps Father Ed mistakenly believed that those organizations were for people who were seeking to be healed from homosexual temptations. That seemed especially possible since he wrote in that same article, "I have seen, in one case, the arresting of homosexuality and resultant normal behavior through the help of the A.A. Steps in a non-alcoholic man."

However, upon researching the Dowling Archive, I found evidence that Father Ed was fully aware that the Mattachine Society was a rights organization and not a recovery group, for he possessed an official publication of the group: the 1958 pamphlet *Mattachine Society Today*. And he clearly read it. It bears an "Ex Libris Edward Dowling, SJ" endplate, and inside is a note in Father Ed's handwriting about One, Inc., which he accurately describes as an "outbranch" of the Mattachine Society.

The pamphlet lists the Mattachine Society's "Aims and Principles," which include "to dispel the idea that the sex variant is unique, 'queer,' or unusual, but is instead a human being with the same capacities of feeling, thinking, and accomplishment of any other human being." Although Father Ed may not have agreed with every goal of the Mattachine Society, he would unquestionably have sympathized with their call to be recognized as people. In that light, it is not difficult to imagine how he could view homosexual temptation as a problem for those who had it, while at the same time holding that gays deserved to have their human dignity affirmed.

Another Dowling Archive document, one that has never before appeared in print, gives a more in-depth understanding of how Father Ed perceived and ministered to people who had sexual problems. It is an undated letter that Dowling sent a teenage boy named Billy, probably in the 1950s, after the boy wrote asking advice on behalf of his girlfriend, who was ashamed about her past sexual behavior.

Interestingly, the archive's only copy of the letter has been retyped, with Billy's last name and address omitted. That suggests to me that Father Ed decided to use what he had written to answer questions from other priests on how to counsel people with sexual issues.

Billy had written to Father Ed seeking advice for his eighteen-year-old girlfriend. The young woman was living with shame due to having streaked naked in front of boys twice as a child and having recently gotten into "moral trouble" with a boy—"not extreme but very indiscreet," Billy wrote.

Since she wanted to confess but was too shame-filled to do so, Billy had proposed to her a solution that she was willing to try. He would approach a confessor himself, explain his girlfriend's situation, and then bring the young woman to the priest. But before undertaking this plan, Billy wanted to know whether Father Ed thought it prudent.

Dowling in his reply approved of Billy's approach and added words intended to encourage him and his girlfriend. The letter is a priceless window into the wisdom and mercy Father Ed offered people who approached him seeking help with their most intimate problems. He began,

Dear Bill,

It is a great grace to be one of Christ's Plain Clothes Men.

"Dear Bill"—this small touch was significant in that the young man had signed his name Billy. Normally Dowling called younger people "kid," but here he wished to affirm the young man's maturity in seeking to help his girlfriend.

Dowling's affirmation extends to his calling Bill "one of Christ's Plain Clothes Men." It is a delightful touch from the former newspaper reporter—likening a layman to a plain-clothes police detective. Here again, years before the Second Vatican Council proclaimed that clergy, religious, and laity shared a universal call to holiness, Father Ed was implying that the layperson's service to Christ was in its way as valuable as that of the priest. The "plain-clothes" term is also a beautiful way of expressing the hidden nature of lay ministry—how, in the Council's words, the laity "live in the midst of the world and its concerns" and "are called by God to exercise their apostolate in the world like leaven"(*Apostolicam Actuositatem* §2).

Dowling then wrote,

The girl is probably a mentally capable person with lots of temptations to pride which don't bother her much and she is quite unnecessarily disturbed by sensual temptations. If she had the humility to talk it over with a confessor simply, she would long ago have rooted out the chief source of her worry and fear—the utterly mistaken idea that she is uniquely bad in these matters. Scads of people, men and women, are up against the same difficulty.

In evaluating the young woman as "probably a mentally capable person," Father Ed was affirming the first thing an anxious woman would want to hear: that she is not crazy. Then he identified the source of her exhibitionism—"lots of temptations to pride"—as well as the reason she needed to confess, because her temptations "[didn't] bother her much." In other words, her shame came from her belief that her sensual temptations were the problem, but her real sin was pride, which she had failed to recognize. A confessor could have helped her discover that her pride was even present even in her thinking herself "uniquely bad."

Father Ed then explained the spiritual mechanics behind the young woman's misplaced shame:

> The essential malice of all sin—be it thievery, lust, or anything else—is that we freely, deliberately, calmly CHOSE to do something when it conflicts with the clearly known will of God. That is the thing to be ashamed of. Most of us get worried about the wrong thing—[the] fact that we are caught or get disease or disgrace a family or pull stuff that doesn't look hot in the society column or the Family Bible.
>
> The essential and real badness of all forms of impurity is that we chose our willful desire for satisfaction and thumb our nose at God's wish that we avoid it. That's the shameful thing. Now, instead, we get ashamed at the results of this choice.

From this encapsulation of the theology of sin, Father Ed moved on to consider the specific issue of sexual temptation. This section of his letter (which perhaps is influenced by his fellow Jesuit [and friend of A.A.] John C. Ford, SJ, a prominent moral theologian) is perfectly orthodox—yet with a pastoral sensitivity that presages the thought of Pope Francis:

> Essentially all impurity boils down to illicit bodily satisfaction. Now—and this may be important, *very* important. Not all people are born with the [same] types of temptations. Majority are attracted by opposite sex. Many are not, and are stimulated only by their own sex. Then there are classes of people who are sexually excited only by cruelties. Then there is a class who have fierce temptations—and temptations are not sins; rather they are rare chances for virtue—to be stimulated by exhibitionistic conduct. [...] The further these temptations drift away from other-sex objects, the more difficult they become for confession, until one realizes:
>
> 1. That lots of other people are in [the] same boat and confessors realize it.

2. That the *direction* the temptation leads is almost always out of the penitent's control, and is not the thing to be ashamed of. The yielding to the temptation, not the characteristic of the temptation, is the shameful part.

3. That in practically all cases, the subjective guilt is no more in yielding to an abnormal temptation than there is in yielding to a normal temptation, in the case of a person whose ordinary temptation image is abnormal. I believe that [in] such cases the character of the temptation is not voluntary.

Father Ed's third point is especially remarkable for his time. Even today, there are priests and theologians who claim that because the Catholic Church holds that homosexual acts are "intrinsically disordered,"[21] yielding to a homosexual temptation is more sinful than yielding to a heterosexual one. But Father Ed's assertion to the contrary finds support in Catholic tradition as well as the writings of ecclesiastically approved moral theologians.

Returning to the specific case of the shame-ridden girl, Dowling says,

From what you write, it is impossible to determine to what extent a possible continuance of abnormal temptations may be the basis of your friend's worry. Let us for the sake of argument take it to be a fact, just to make sure of all possibilities. If it were true, it would explain a lot. I have known cases similar—very good and pure people who were tormented by the off-side quality of their temptations, and their modesty and distaste for the temptations prevented them from asking confessors about them, and the result was years of confusion and unnecessary worry. As in the present case, if such be the case, the temptations need not turn to sin or be externalized to cause great anguish. Not infrequently they are the cross of very good and pure people. [. . .]

There is considerable probability—tho I couldn't tell without knowing the situation better—that there have been very few, if any, mortal sins in the past nine years that she worries about. A nervous person, warped by worries, and cloistered by inability to talk things over from getting straight moral notions, often has great difficulty in getting the sufficiently calm reflection which is required for such a serious thing as a mortal sin.

One phrase that stands out in Father Ed's reflections is his repeated assertion that temptations outside the norm are often the cross of "very good and pure people." How comforting such words must have been for Billy's girlfriend as well as others whom Dowling helped overcome feelings of misplaced guilt and shame.

Father Ed's words of affirmation grow even more emphatic as he closes out the letter:

> The carelessness with the other fellow a few years ago should not worry her because worry is not what Christ wants. He prefers the childlike confidence in his forgiving powers.
>
> The girl shows that she WANTS to do the right thing and has all the signs of being on the road out of her worries.
>
> Reading between the lines, I am very much impressed by the goodness of the girl—and I am awfully glad she ran into you—and you into her. Don't be dismayed by anything she tells you. I suspect she has unusually fine stuff and has been entrusted by God with an unusually heavy cross that has her flattened for the present.

Although the absence of other correspondence between Dowling and people with sexual problems is history's loss, his letter to Billy gives as comprehensive an account of Father Ed's counsel on such matters as one could hope to find. He who himself carried an unusually heavy cross had an extraordinary gift for lightening others' burdens. He continued to do his unique brand of non-alcoholic Twelfth-Step work with increasing urgency even as the end of his own "glad Gethsemane" approached.

15

RACING AGAINST TIME

Thank God for the now.
— Father Ed, advising Cana Conference couples[1]

If there is one thing that distinguishes Father Ed's work during the last decade of his life from that which preceded it, it is the intense attention he devoted to promoting racial justice. Since his novitiate, he had sought to help improve the lives of Black people and other people of color, but the Fifties saw him work toward that goal with renewed fervor.

Nephew Paul Dowling told me "one of [Father Ed's] heroes was A. Philip Randolph," who organized the Brotherhood of American Sleeping Car Porters, the first Black-led union to receive an AFL charter. The admiration was mutual. In the Dowling Archive is a 1950 letter of endorsement from Randolph in which the civil-rights pioneer (who would go on to co-direct the March on Washington) wrote, "I have the highest admiration for the great work Rev. Dowling is doing. He and I believe that the right to work is a God-given right of everyone and must be guaranteed by our American democracy."[2]

It would seem that Dowling carried Randolph's endorsement on his person; the letter is well-frayed from having been folded and unfolded many times. He may have taken it out to show to Pullman porters, whom he enjoyed chatting with during his frequent rail journeys, as his nephew Paul shared with me: "He made friends with these guys, because he would talk to them guy-to-guy as they would help him with his bags coming out of Union Station—'What do you think about the Cardinals [baseball team] this year?'" That was Father Ed's way to "break the ice to let them know that this was something more than a commercial transaction, although he was very generous with them in tipping."

Not everyone in Dowling's Irish-American family shared his openness toward Black people. Nephew Paul remembered that an in-law of the same generation as Father Ed "was a racist. He just didn't like Black people, period, and he spent a lot of time talking about this dislike."[3]

When Father Ed found out about the in-law's racism, he "pretty much cut him off from contact," Paul said. The in-law had been trying to ingratiate himself to Dowling "because he was a businessman and he knew Uncle had contacts in business. And Uncle Edward just cut him off because of his racist attitudes."

"Uncle Edward wasn't much for cutting people off," Paul added. "He liked to reach out to people." But Dowling could not bear racism. He was additionally offended when he learned the in-law was boasting of their relationship so that he might gain social advantages in St. Louis society, where Father Ed was highly respected.

Father Ed "was a gentle man, but he wasn't a weak man," Paul told me. "He could be harsh when he thought people were doing something wrong." One occasion when Dowling felt harshness was appropriate was when his racist in-law approached him during the wake for his brother Paul Vincent Dowling on November 12, 1955.

Nephew Paul (the son of the deceased), who was fifteen at the time, remembers the exchange between the in-law and Father Ed, who had become a substitute father to him. "In those days, the wake would begin in the afternoon, then there would be a break for a meal, and it would continue in the evening." After the afternoon part of the wake,

> [the in-law] wanted Father Ed to come to dinner. He said, 'My wife has prepared this beautiful meal for you,' and so on. And my uncle replied harshly, 'I'd rather go to [the fast-food chain restaurant] White Castle.' Not exactly where the elite meet to eat. And he did! We walked up together with [the in-law] following us for a while, until we got some hamburgers.

Given Father Ed's infirmity, even the three-minute walk from the Cullinane Brothers Funeral Home to the nearest White Castle would have been a challenge for him. But he wanted to make a statement, as well as to model good behavior for his nephew—and he did.

A major concern of Father Ed's with respect to racial justice was the problem of residential segregation, for which St. Louis was especially notorious. Early in his priesthood, he actively campaigned for fair housing, which led the St. Louis Housing Association to elect him as its first president in 1937. However, the bureaucratic work of planning housing projects did not suit him, and he was relieved to lose his office in 1939, when the association's rules were changed to restrict its membership to taxpayers.

Once Dowling was no longer involved in the housing association, he could continue speaking his mind on civil-rights issues minus the burden of being seen as a representative of the government. He proved to be no less outspoken on racism than he was about other issues where democracy was at stake. In an August 1940 talk at the Summer School of Catholic Action, he assailed the hypocrisy of a Southern politician who spoke out against Hitler's racism while ignoring lynchings in his own state.

"Senator [Claude] Pepper," Dowling said, "was obviously sincere and bore an almost martyrlike attitude, but how can anyone get indignant about the estoppal of democracy who comes from Florida, where American citizens are found hanging by the neck from trees because they dared to vote?"[4]

Father Ed also worked to encourage people in business to improve opportunities for Black people. Nephew Paul told me that one of the ways he did this was through his friendship with Catholic layman Joseph H. Vatterott, who, with his brother Charles, operated a major real-estate development company in suburban St. Louis.

"My uncle persuaded Mr. Vatterott to offer some of his homes to Black people who were trying to get out of the city and get into better housing," Paul said. "That took some persuasion," he added, "because Vatterott probably lost business because of that. But Uncle persuaded him that it was the moral thing to do, because these people were striving upward and they would appreciate a home in the suburbs."

The events Paul described likely took place in the early 1950s, when the Vatterott brothers built the De Porres subdivision in the suburban St. Louis township of Breckenridge Hills. Although both Joseph and Charles (with whom Dowling was also friends) had long sought to improve opportunities for Black people, and had founded a foundation for that purpose,[5] Father Ed's encouragement strengthened them to persist amid community opposition.[6]

It was not in Father Ed's nature to celebrate his own good works. As with his assistance to alcoholics and other people with problems, he likely did many more things to promote racial justice than have been recorded. Certainly A. Philip Randolph's enthusiastic endorsement of him suggests as much. Father Ed also supported civil-rights organizations such as the Urban League and the American Civil Liberties Union, whose co-founder Roger Nash Baldwin called him "one of my ardent admirations." Baldwin, a Unitarian, wrote of Dowling to a mutual friend, "If the Catholic Church can keep such as he in its fold, with all his apparent heresies, most anybody could join and stick."[7]

However, there was one instance when Father Ed did seek publicity for a racial-justice effort that he undertook—and it would become a defining moment of his public witness.

Father Ed was reading *Ebony* magazine in April 1954 when a poignant image captured his attention. It was a photograph of two Black women in winter coats standing amid the bare trees at a cemetery. Between them was a little girl, no more than three years old, also dressed for cold weather, touching a mittened hand to a large standing wreath placed atop an unmarked grave.

The cemetery was familiar to Dowling; it was Calvary Cemetery, which adjoined his home neighborhood of Baden. His brother James, mother, grandparents, and other deceased relatives were buried there, their graves encircling a tall monument of the Virgin Mary that was purchased by the family.

But the Black girl and women in the *Ebony* photo, Father Ed realized with sadness, had no such monument to memorialize their late relative— and that was a tragic injustice. For the unmarked grave belonged to Dred Scott, the slave whose courageous bid for freedom was shamefully denied by the Supreme Court. The March 1857 decision, which is regarded as the worst ruling of the court's history, helped precipitate the Civil War.

Two and a half years after Father Ed saw the photo of Scott's descendants in *Ebony*, the memory of it continued to weigh upon him. But by that point, he and his sister Anna, who was also his secretary, were in a position to do something about the unmarked grave. They had co-founded the Old Baden Society, a group dedicated to promoting the history of the Baden neighborhood. Together with Anna, Father Ed began to form a plan to bring the unmarked grave to the attention of the Old Baden Society members and to the wider public, so that they might raise funds for a marker.

However, as soon as Father Ed and Anna began to explore the possibility of marking Scott's grave, a challenge arose. Calvary Cemetery informed them that the grave was owned by the descendants of Taylor Blow, a son of Scott's former owner.

Blow had supported Scott in his bid for freedom. After the Supreme Court ruled against Scott, he was able to gain ownership of the enslaved man and freed him in May 1857. But sadly Scott had little time to enjoy his freedom, for he contracted tuberculosis and died in 1858. Nine years later, when the cemetery where Scott was interred shut down, Blow arranged for Scott's remains to be transferred to Calvary. Nearly a century later, the grave remained the property of the Blow family—and no marker could be placed upon it without their approval.

So Father Ed reached out to one of Taylor's grandsons, Thomas Richeson Blow, by telephone in early September of 1956. Thomas was open to the idea of marking the grave but had no interest in paying for it. On September 5, he sent Dowling a letter of understanding based on their phone conversation, which required the Jesuit to agree to three conditions: "Father Dowling holds himself responsible for all expense, in the sense that the Blow descendants will not be put to any expense"; "that a sketch with measurements of the marker be sent to Thomas R. Blow," and "that the marker be up and in place sometime within the year 1957."

Father Ed, having agreed to Blow's conditions, then worked with Anna to organize a meeting of the Old Baden Society at a private home on November 17, 1956. Anna led a discussion on Dred Scott for an audience of sixty, about half of whom were Black, including honored guests John A. Madison, Jr.—Scott's great-grandson—and his wife.

By the meeting's end, the society's members had agreed to sponsor a drive to fund a marker on Scott's grave, which they hoped to have in place by March 6, 1957, the centennial of the Dred Scott decision. That gave Dowling the angle he needed to place an item on the Associated Press newswire announcing the drive.

But once the story of the drive began to make headlines, a new complication arose. Thomas Blow's cousin, Mrs. Charles C. (Marie Louise) Harrison Jr.—a wealthy Pennsylvania society matron—asserted her right as a granddaughter of Taylor Blow to approve the marker. When Father Ed in December 1956 sent her his own ideas for it, which had met with approval from Scott's great-grandson and his wife, she wrote in reply,

> I do not see how the lettering for the Dred Scott marker can be decided upon until we have a design and know the size.
>
> Personally, I lean towards the smallest and most modest marker possible and I surely would not have the quotation from the Supreme Court.
>
> I belong to those who think that many and large monuments destroy the peace and beauty of our churchyards and cemeteries.
>
> May I ask you to wait and do nothing about the marker until I send you a design as a suggestion?

Dowling's heart must have been heavy upon reading Harrison's letter, but he replied accepting her wishes without complaint. He also saw a benefit in Harrison's proposed delay. "To dramatize the need for a marker," he wrote, "I would be inclined to let the centennial of the Supreme Court decision in the spring occur with the grave unmarked. This may attract more attention."

While he waited to hear back from Harrison, Father Ed continued to think of ways to commemorate Scott. He wrote to a local alderman to suggest that in honor of the centennial of the Dred Scott decision, a small city park abutting Calvary Cemetery, William F. Busche Park, be renamed Dred Scott Park—"and another city landmark be named for Mr. Busse [*sic*]."[8] There is no record of a reply, but, as of this writing, the park is still named for Busche.[9]

Dowling also wrote dozens of letters to local and national media outlets urging them to cover the centennial of the Dred Scott decision.[10] Nearly every one of those who bothered to respond said they were not interested. A *Look* magazine editor wrote that the magazine had recently published a story about 1955 lynching victim Emmett Till and thus needed to let some time elapse before publishing another article on racial justice.

Through his contacts at his former employer the *Globe-Democrat*, Dowling did manage to place a feature story in the newspaper about the fund-raising drive, which ran on February 10, 1957. With typical diplomacy, he told the reporter that the Old Baden Society desired to erect a humble marker—omitting that the size limitation was in fact imposed by Harrison: "We have in mind putting up only a simple monument with what money we can raise, costing maybe only $75 or $100. Then if someone someday wants to put up a better monument, it will at least be known where Dred Scott lies."

When Harrison finally wrote back to Father Ed on February 17, 1957, she told him she had decided to finance the marker herself. To her credit, she sought Dowling's advice for what the inscription would say. She had by this time developed sincere admiration for him. Although she was a Christian who believed in charity, she moved in a blue-blood world and had little firsthand knowledge of Black people, let alone their needs for racial justice.[11] It was Dowling who brought her to realize that she could do a good Christian work by honoring Scott's legacy.

For the day of the centennial of the Dred Scott decision, March 6, 1957, Father Ed and Anna organized two commemorative events. In the morning, a wreath-laying was held at Scott's grave. Several of Scott's descendants took part, together with faculty and students from St. Louis University School of Law. That event was followed by an afternoon ceremony at St. Louis's Old Courthouse, where Scott and his wife Harriet had sued for their freedom. A Baptist minister chosen by the Madison family gave an invocation; Dowling had invited him at the family's request. Scott's great-grandson John A. Madison Jr. gave a brief talk, and Thomas Blow read Harrison's letter expressing her intention to mark the grave.

The final item on the agenda at the Old Courthouse event would have the greatest significance for posterity. Father Ed led a brainstorming session to solicit the opinions of the Madison family and other Black people present on what the inscription on Scott's marker should say.

Father Ed had thought it appropriate that the marker include a quotation from the Dred Scott decision, due to its historical significance. However, the Madisons and other Black participants were opposed to this. Dowling took their wishes into account when he gave Harrison his recommendation for the marker's text.

Especially in light of the many injustices that were done to Scott, one may be rightfully appalled that white people who were unrelated to him had the final say on the text of his gravestone. Nonetheless, Father Ed deserves credit for his repeated and intentional outreach to Scott's descendants and other Black people with an interest in Scott's legacy. It is solely due to his concern for their wishes that they had any input at all regarding how Scott would be memorialized. He did his best to be an ally to Scott's descendants and an ambassador on their behalf to Blow's descendants amid what he must have sensed was a fundamentally unjust situation.

It is difficult to convey how busy Father Ed was during the last five years of his life, and even more difficult to describe the great fortitude he displayed amid serious illness. Many of his friends said after his death that they had thought him indestructible, for nothing seemed to slow him down. He persisted in his ministry through multiple hospitalizations, three heart attacks, and two retinal strokes.[12]

At The Queen's Work, Father Ed continued to minister by phone and in person to a constant stream of people seeking his help with all manner of problems. Eyewitnesses later told researcher James A. Egan, SJ, that Dowling took care to combine his practical assistance with prayer:

> One secretary remembers almost a continuous string of telephone conversations and a practice that was new to her of praying with people over the phone and often giving them his blessing as his "sign off."

One young Jesuit recalls consulting him about his brother-in-law's drinking problem. Before he knew it he was ordered down on his knees to pray while Father Dowling began making the phone calls to the distant city to set up what today would be called a "family intervention."[13]

Dowling also kept up his ministry to engaged and married couples—which sometimes gave him the opportunity to relive a favorite childhood pastime, as his friend Dolores Tygard wrote after his death:

An attractive engaged couple we know went to him for instructions. The girl said, wonderingly, "He is so terrific with us...and yet a character. Sometimes, after instructions, we take him for a hamburger and a ride. He asks us to take him down to the yards, to listen to the trains and to watch them being uncoupled." She added, with wide eyes, "Father Dowling loves trains!"[14]

Tygard added, "I don't know how he kept track of all of us. His lights burned late, late at night, and streams of people came at all hours—happy people, troubled people."

Many people remembered the cigar box with Father Ed's handwritten legend "ST. DIMAS RICH BOX" that he had attached waist-high to the door-frame of his office. (He used the Spanish spelling for his patron saint's name, for the English spelling looked too much like "dismal.") "It was always filled with folding money," Tygard said. "Some of his callers needed it, and dipped into it. Others felt they could help, and they dropped something into it. There were no records. No names."[15]

Frequently the effects of Dowling's activity caught up with him. On June 11, 1957, he was in Hendersonville, North Carolina, to speak at the Summer School of Catholic Action when he had a nosebleed caused by hypertension. At first it was feared he had suffered a heart attack, as he had endured one less than a year earlier, also while on the road with the SSCA.

After a brief hospitalization in North Carolina, Father Ed was well enough to travel home to St. Louis. As soon as he arrived, he checked himself into St. John's Mercy, his hospital of choice when in town, where he remained for about a month. A sense of relief comes through in a letter he wrote on June 17 to Jack I.: "My illness was a rather acute attack of high blood pressure (no heart attack though) which already is clearing up nicely and I feel well. Rest and diet are prescribed for the present."

Although he accepted the hospital's restrictions on his diet, Father Ed was less scrupulous in observing his prescribed rest. He was at St. John's so frequently that he came to know everyone there. The cleaning ladies would come in to chat, as well as the Mercy nuns who administered the hospital, and the nurses on the various shifts. Niece Mary Dowling told me that he also continued to receive outside visitors at the hospital just as at The Queen's Work: "It seemed like there were lots of people there in and out. He would show you his latest meal plans. He was of course fascinated with everything. They were always putting him on diets."

Other eyewitnesses said the same, according to Dowling Archive librarian Mary Louise Adams: "One told me that he came so often that the hospital room became his office with the phone ringing, his secretary (Anna his sister) [there] to take dictation so that his correspondence was current, and a constant stream of visitors."[16]

There was also the time, Adams wrote, when Father Ed was sent to be X-rayed and the nurses thought they would do him a favor by hurrying in to straighten his cluttered room—

> putting all the piles of letters on his bed in neat order, gathering all the little slips of paper he used for jotting down things to be remembered from his phone conversations, and tidying up generally.
>
> He returned and growled, "There's order in my disorder! I knew where everything was, and now I have to start all over again!" Five minutes later, the room was in total Dowlingesque order.

One of Father Ed's visitors during his June 1957 hospital stay was someone who flew in from Cleveland to see him: Bill Wilson. It was typical of Bill to stop in St. Louis during his midwestern trips so he could receive advice and encouragement from his spiritual sponsor.

Dowling had recently corresponded with Bill in response to the A.A. co-founder's request that he comment upon the manuscript for *Alcoholics Anonymous Comes of Age*, which was compiled to commemorate the 1955 A.A. International Convention. He offered Wilson a few suggestions for minor changes and many words of encouragement:

> I thought I knew A.A. substantially. The fill-ins I gained from reading the book are terrific. The writing, and I think especially your own (with its juxtaposition between the sublime and the skid-row vocables) is clear, economically effective....

All you have to do is remember the deep raw ego-satisfaction you have had from your association with A.A. to know how happy your references to me make me. They bring dividends of so many acquaintances and friendships. I am deeply grateful to you.[17]

As Bill made his way to The Queen's Work on the morning of June 17, he looked forward to being able to thank Father Ed in person for his help reviewing the manuscript. But once he arrived, he received the disconcerting news that his friend was in the hospital. Anna Dowling assured him that Father Ed still wanted to see him, so he hastened to St. John's.

Exactly what Bill and Father Ed discussed on that visit is unknown, but the encounter affected Bill deeply. Upon returning to Stepping Stones, he wrote to Father Ed on June 25, "The inspiration and grace that I received through you has always stood by me and I know this latest visit can but greatly increase the store of good things that you have given me."

Father Ed was impressed with Bill's spiritual progress. Privately, he and Sister Ignatia—the revered hospital nun who guided thousands of alcoholics into A.A.—were united in prayer that Bill might yet find his way into the Catholic Church.[18] He wrote to Sister Ignatia about Bill's visit, "I feel as you do about Bill's evolution. He seemed 'closer' this time than ever."[19]

Despite all Father Ed did to ensure that Dred Scott's grave site was memorialized, he was unable to be present when the gravestone was dedicated on September 17, 1957, the ninety-ninth anniversary of Scott's death. On that day, he was in Rome as the official delegate of the National Catholic Welfare Conference's Family Life Bureau to the conference of the International Union of Family Organizations. But the Scott ceremony remained in his thoughts, and he wrote to his sister during his trip that he intended to celebrate Mass that day in the Roman catacombs for Scott and his commemorators. He told her he chose the location for its "symbolic" value. Scott was a martyr in his way as were the Christians in ancient Rome.

Father Ed's European visit also afforded him the opportunity to spend several days in his ancestral homeland of Ireland, stopping there both on his way to Rome and on his way back. He had visited Ireland before, but this time his trip included a new kind of travel experience, courtesy of his former Loyola Academy student Neil C. Hurley, Jr., a wealthy business executive: a flight on a private Beechcraft plane so he could see the sights from above.[20]

Although Father Ed had a longstanding fear of flying, he employed the techniques he had learned through Recovery, Inc., and found to his delight that he was able to weather the small-plane flight without anxiety. Hurley arranged for the plane to fly over places that were significant to Dowling's family history, including the Croppy Hole in Carlow where the Maher brothers were buried along with others slain in the 1798 rebellion (see chapter 1). In a letter to his sister Anna, Dowling called the flight "one of the great events of my life."

The rest of Dowling's time in Ireland, between visiting friends, family members, and members of A.A., was taken up with research on three areas of interest. First, he wanted to study proportional representation. To that end, he sought and received an audience with Taoiseach (Prime Minister) Éamon de Valera, who granted him a full hour of his time. Second, he wished to investigate the authenticity of the "Black Diaries" that the British had used to undermine support for Irish nationalist Roger Casement prior to his execution in 1916. To that end, he met with several researchers, including poet Alfred Noyes.

Finally, since his Cana work had led him to become interested in preventing divorce, Dowling wished to meet noted matchmaker Biddie Brewster. That meeting left him so encouraged that he resolved that, upon his return to the United States, he would find a way to get the Catholic Church involved in matchmaking.

However, before he could do any matchmaking back home, Father Ed would have to recover his strength after an exhausting month of overseas travel. The cumulative effects of the trip began to hit him as soon as he arrived in New York on the *Queen Mary* ocean liner on October 16. By the time he arrived back in his office five days later, he sensed that he was going to need to scale back his public appearances for a while.

There was a letter on Dowling's desk from a priest in Illinois requesting a Cana Conference. He flipped it over and typed a reply on the other side in which he recommended a different priest, explaining, "Because of a heart condition, I do not think I am yet ready for a complete afternoon's conference."

In his exhaustion, Father Ed mailed his letter without signing it. A day later, he was in the hospital.

What happened next is something of a mystery. The desk calendar of Dowling's sister Anna appears to indicate that Father Ed came back from the hospital after two days—"Home sick," it says on October 24. A few items are listed on the calendar over the next four days, but it's not clear whether they belong to Father Ed's schedule or Anna's own. On October

30, Anna scrawled "Canceled" over the entire day's events, perhaps because Father Ed was too tired or ill to go out.

But the following day, Father Ed boarded a train to Washington, DC—a trip of about twenty-two hours—and it's not clear why. There is no record of him having any business there at the time.

Granted, not every engagement of Dowling's was written on his or Anna's calendars. He might have been called to a meeting at the National Catholic Welfare Conference, whose headquarters were in Washington, or he might have had an A.A. speaking engagement to fulfill, or he might simply have wanted to make a research trip.

However, given what happened next, I like to think that something—or Someone—told Father Ed that he had to visit Ed Lahey.

Whenever Bill Wilson spoke of his first encounter with Father Ed, he always emphasized its providential timing—how Dowling dropped in unexpectedly when his spirit was sinking, and brought him the hope he needed to persist in his mission.

King M., an A.A. member who knew Dowling, heard similar stories after the Jesuit's death as he conducted research in hope of authoring a biography. In a letter to Bill Wilson, he wrote,

> Some people I've talked to have said they heard from Father Dowling when they needed his help most. In fact, one A.A. member said when something went wrong in his life, Father Dowling either called him on the phone or unexpectedly dropped in on him.[21]

Bill wrote back affirming what others had told King of Father Ed: "His unexpected calls upon people in need have been legion—and I have often been a beneficiary."[22]

What follows is the story of one of those unexpected calls, as told to me by Ed Lahey's daughter, Jayne Lahey Kobliska.

"On October 30, 1957, I was in a very bad auto accident in Italy, a few miles outside Terracina," Jayne said. She was twenty-two at the time and had been driving through the country with two friends, both of whom were left in critical condition. "The accident was extremely serious. I have a lifelong disability as a result—I walk with a limp and have some paralysis in the leg."

"My father was in Washington at the time," Jayne continued,

but my mother and sister happened to be traveling in Europe, so they immediately came to me in a town south of Rome where I remained for four months in the hospital. So my mother had to send a telegram to alert my father to what was happening, and also deal as best she could with bank transfers to pay hospital bills.

The telegram went out on November 1, a Friday. That morning at about eleven a.m., before the wire arrived, Dowling rang Lahey from the National Press Club (his unofficial center of operations when in Washington) to say he was in town and suggest they meet for dinner. "Since my mother was away, my father suggested they meet at a restaurant downtown," Jayne said.

"Then the telegram arrived. When my father called Father Dowling to let him know about it, Father Dowling immediately said, 'Forget about dinner, I'm coming out right away.'"

It was a chance for Father Ed once again to be present for Lahey, just as he had been nearly eighteen years earlier, when the accomplished newspaperman hit bottom. And, in a way, it was a chance for Dowling to repay a debt that he knew he could never repay—his debt of gratitude to the alcoholic who had first introduced him to A.A.

But although the reporter had remained dry since becoming one of the fellowship's earliest Chicago members, Ed Lahey in 1957 did not have the same ardor for Alcoholics Anonymous that he had in 1940. He admitted as much in a 1951 *Grapevine* article where he wrote that he had lost his enthusiasm for participation in the fellowship: "After all these years of sobriety, during which I have received blessings beyond measure, I find myself a 'marginal' member of Alcoholics Anonymous. That means I rarely attend meetings, and even more rarely perform Twelfth-Step work."[23]

Describing himself as "spiritually dried-up," Lahey added (somewhat ominously),

> I suspect there are a good many old-timers in A.A. like myself, who feel that they have somehow missed the boat, that they have come to accept the blessings of sobriety as the normal course of events, and are prone to forget that they, like the newest and shakiest member of the group, are suspended above personal disaster by the slender margin of the first drink.

Six years after writing those words, as Lahey sat alone in his Washington apartment, chain-smoking while staring out the bay windows wondering whether his daughter would survive, that margin seemed more slender than ever. He later wrote to Jayne that it was the first time since he became sober that he wanted to take a drink.

Accessing Lahey's apartment was never an easy task for Dowling, and it must have been even more difficult given that he had been in the hospital just a few days earlier. But as he began the painful trek up the marble steps to Lahey's second-floor apartment, with his black-leather traveling bag in his left hand and his cane in his right, all he could think about was being present for his friend. He stopped briefly upon the landing to catch his breath before finally approaching Lahey's door.

Upon entering, Father Ed dropped his bag next to the wing chair and settled into it as Lahey sat down on the adjacent couch, a bundle of nerves. Dowling used that chair whenever he visited the Laheys; it enabled him to sit at a comfortable angle, as he had to lean to one side in order to extend his stiff left leg.

Father Ed must have sensed that if he could keep his friend from drinking that night, the most difficult part of the battle to maintain his sobriety would be won. And so this recently hospitalized priest, who had not slept in a decent bed since leaving St. Louis a day and a half earlier—this priest sat up and talked with Lahey, comforting him, all night long.

Although Jayne no longer has the letter her father wrote about that night, she remembers one thing he shared about Father Ed's words of consolation: Dowling quoted the same poem by Francis Thompson that he had used at the close of his address at the 1955 A.A. International Convention, "The Hound of Heaven." Without question, Father Ed would have laid particular emphasis upon his favorite lines of it, which he often quoted in his funeral preaching:

> [']All which I took from thee I did but take,
> Not for thy harms,
> But just that thou might'st seek it in My arms.
> All which thy child's mistake
> Fancies as lost, I have stored for thee at home:
> Rise, clasp My hand, and come!'
> Halts by me that footfall:
> Is my gloom, after all,
> Shade of His hand, outstretched caressingly?

"He really kept my father from starting to drink again," Jayne told me.

Lahey, for his part, never forgot how Dowling was there for him in his hour of need. After Father Ed died, the reporter paid tribute to him in an obituary:

A Census enumerator this week might have reported that Father Dowling, in a material sense, was so poor that he could put his socks on at either end.[24]

But the people whose lives have been straightened out by Father Dowling during moments of personal crisis could make an inventory of spiritual bequests by the St. Louis priest that would stagger the mind of the clerk of the probate court.[25]

Once Father Ed returned from visiting Lahey in Washington, he began once again to mull over a project that had been on his mind for some years. His visit to Irish matchmaker Biddie Brewster had reignited his desire to start a matchmaking firm.

Dowling reached out to Dolores Tygard, who worked actively in support of local Catholic charities, and asked her to meet him at the Walgreens drugstore next door to The Queen's Work. ("He loved their chocolate sodas," Tygard said.) After lunch, he presented her with his idea for the marriage bureau and proposed that she run it.[26]

"It would be called Introduction, Inc.," Tygard recalled, "and would serve to introduce nice young boys, alone and lonely in the city, to nice young girls. We would keep a card index. It would be a free, refined, high-class dating bureau."

Tygard quickly grasped that Dowling's vision was unworkable. She argued with him all through the chocolate sodas. As they walked back out onto Grand Avenue, she turned to him and pleaded, "Father, so help me, you'll have trouble and lawsuits galore. It just isn't practical!"

Father Ed looked at Tygard for a long moment. Finally, he exclaimed, "*Practical!* Dear Lord, it wasn't 'practical' for my mother to make her [society] debut. But she did. And she met my father. If she hadn't, I wouldn't be here."

"With this," Tygard recalled, "he turned on his heel and left me standing there—shook!"

Father Ed had no hard feelings towards Tygard; they remained warm friends. But he had too many prospective projects on his mind to waste time arguing over one that could not be realized. And he knew his time was running out.

16

༄

SPONSOR AND PROTECTOR

Father Dowling was, I believe, a very prudent man, but he would take a chance, often on very lowly people, when necessity demanded.... Father Dowling once told me, "In a wild barroom fight, you sometimes have to start swinging with anything you can lay your hands on."

— Sam Lambert[1]

There are two kinds of people in this world: those who, upon sensing that age or poor health is catching up with them, choose to slow down, and those who, under the same circumstances, choose to speed up.

Father Ed was not one to slow down. As 1958 arrived, he did attempt to cut down on certain commitments to groups—but it was only so he could add many more. His intent was to focus his energies upon the ever-growing "psychosomatic smorgasbord"[2] of support groups that were meeting under his guidance at The Queen's Work. Even then, he had a hard time saying no. He wrote on January 6 to the head of St. Louis's Public Questions Club, a lively debating society, meaning to resign his membership so he could clear his schedule for other things. "I am getting old and the jobs seem to mount. I am impressed by [Walter] Pater's dictum that 'all art is the removal of rubbish.'" But by the end of the letter, it was clear that his resolve was already flagging. "Maybe my resignation could be turned into a leave of absence," he wrote.

Dowling continued to seek out ways to spread the gospel of Alcoholics Anonymous to his fellow clergy and to others in the Catholic world. In April 1958, Bill Wilson wrote to thank him for his review of *Alcoholics Anonymous Comes of Age* that appeared in the February issue of the Jesuit magazine *Social Order*.

Although there was little in the review that he had not said before, Father Ed added a few new turns of phrase that, taken together, showed how

279

his appreciation of the fellowship continued to grow. He wrote that the essays in *Alcoholics Anonymous Comes of Age* were

> gripping recitals of the evolution from one man's hopeless alcoholic insanity to the international movement which, in a neurotic and pagan world, is a benign gulf stream whose trade winds whisper hope to millions, alcoholics as well as non-alcoholics.

Writing of the fellowship's spirituality, Father Ed used a theological framework that he knew the journal's Catholic audience would appreciate. "The clue to the religious dynamic of A.A.," he said,

> is that outside of penitentiaries and mental hospitals, its members have the greatest corporate capital of humiliations in the world. The masters of the spiritual life say that in humiliations, where they do not lead to despair and suicide, we have the shortest cut to humility. And the New Testament assures us that while God takes a stand against the proud, he "assists the humble." This salvaging of one of the most potentially wasteful human experiences is great human drama.

Dowling's references to humiliations as the "shortest cut to humility" and to the scripture verse about God assisting the humble (James 4:6) are familiar from his previous comments on A.A. But his nod to the "corporate capital of humiliations" present in "penitentiaries and mental hospitals" is a new addition to his writings on the topic. It reflects the degree to which he admired and even envied the alcoholics and prisoners and mental patients he worked with (save for their sins), for they understood their total dependence upon the grace of God. He saw not only every alcoholic but also every mental patient and every prisoner as his other self. His vow name was Dismas, after all.

In a particular way, Father Ed saw Bill as another self, but there was a notable difference—one that went beyond his fatherly role as Wilson's spiritual sponsor.

I would put the difference this way: although both men had played baseball in their youth, Bill was a pitcher, whereas Father Ed was a catcher. Both in baseball and in life, their roles were complementary and mutually supportive.

Someone with deep philosophical knowledge of baseball could write at length about the pitcher-catcher relationship as embodied in Bill and Father Ed. I am not that person, but I do see something relevant to them in a 1941 *Atlantic* article by legendary Major League Baseball catcher and coach Moe Berg, "Pitchers and Catchers." In the article—which Dowling, with his love for both baseball and news magazines, almost certainly read and enjoyed—Berg writes,

> The catcher squatting behind the hitter undoubtedly has the coign of vantage in the ball park; all the action takes place before him. ...The catcher has to be able to cock his arm from any position, throw fast and accurately to the bases, field bunts like an infielder, and catch foul flies like an outfielder. He must be adept at catching a ball from any angle, and almost simultaneously tagging a runner at home plate. The catcher is the Cerberus of baseball.[3]

What a dramatic image—likening the role of the catcher to that of Cerberus, the three-headed dog of Greek mythology who blocks the living from entering the underworld!

It might seem strange to compare Father Ed, who loved "The Hound of Heaven," to the mythological Hound of Hades. But as Wilson's spiritual sponsor, Dowling in his final years sought to guard the A.A. founder from losing himself in the underworld of his psychic explorations—particularly his interest in the experimental (and then-legal) drug LSD.

Bill became interested in LSD in 1956 when he learned that psychiatrists were having some success in using it with alcoholics who had previously been resistant to recovery. It was believed that the psychedelic drug enabled them to overcome their ego-resistance to confronting their alcoholism and perhaps even to have a genuine spiritual experience.

Under the guidance of a psychiatrist, Bill began to engage in his own experiments with LSD. A.A. historian Ernest Kurtz wrote that throughout these experiments, which took place at various intervals over a period of several years, Wilson's primary intention was to find a way to "remove the mental or psychological and physical obstacles that impeded some persons from openness to the spiritual."[4]

At some point in 1957 or 1958, Father Ed joined Bill to witness an LSD experiment in New York City in which the drug was administered to a researcher from Duke University as part of a study of extra-sensory perception. Afterwards, Bill enthused in a letter to the Rev. Sam Shoemaker, "The result [for the researcher] was a most magnificent, positive spiritual experience. Father Dowling declared himself utterly convinced of its va-lidity, and volunteered to take LSD himself."[5]

Bill's account of Father Ed's impression of the experiment appears to be more wishful thinking than reality, as it is not supported by any of the existing correspondence between him and Dowling. Rather, as will be seen, Father Ed raised concerns to Bill over the prudence of engaging in such ex-periments.[6] (It does seem that, in Wilson's excitement over the drug's possi-bilities, he gave exaggerated accounts of the opinions of people close to him. He claimed in a letter that Lois tried LSD once and had a "most pleas-ing and beneficial experience," whereas Lois herself later said she "could not tell any difference.")[7]

The first mention of LSD in Bill's letters to Father Ed comes in a letter of December 29, 1958, which, judging by its tone, appears to have been written some months after Dowling witnessed an experiment.

"On the psychic front, the LSD business goes on apace," Wilson writes, adding,

> This material should be of some value for those who already have the faith, as a further reassurance of heaven itself. As for those who have no faith, it could act very much as my original experi-ence at Towns did. It might bring the gift of faith. However, I don't believe that it has any miraculous property of transforming spiritu-ally and emotionally sick people into healthy ones overnight. ...But unless the theologians and psychiatrists wish to make an issue of it, I do not see how the material can seriously upset their own thinking or methods. After all, it is only a temporary ego-reducer.

For Wilson even to suggest that the LSD experience could have the same effect upon users as his Towns Hospital experience—the dramatic moment that A.A. members called "Bill's Hot Flash"—indicates he had high hopes for the drug's effectiveness. But what really seemed to excite him was its possibilities in the psychic world, where he believed it could improve clairvoyance and precognition. He added in the same letter that he had reached out to the Parapsychological Foundation, whose funder—"an immensely rich woman"—would likely be interested in LSD. "Though I haven't pressed these matters much, new people and possibilities keep walking in on me," he wrote. "Where they may lead, I can have little idea."

All in all, there is an obsessive tone to Bill's letter, reminiscent of the single-minded attitude that the authors of the official A.A. history *Pass It On* say

Bill often took during the early days: "When he was working out a new aspect of the Fellowship, . . . he would become nothing less than monomaniacal, talking (some described it as monologuing) endlessly about the project. It was not only uppermost in his mind, it was the only thing on his mind."

Father Ed was worried by Bill's curiosity about LSD's paranormal possibilities as well as the increased attention he was devoting to investigating the drug. But he decided to refrain from expressing his concerns until he could discuss them with Bill one-on-one. Admonishing by phone was not the style of this clerical Cerberus.

Although Father Ed's heart problems forced him to pare down his speaking schedule during the late 1950s, he continued to give Cana Conference talks as much as he was able. In fact, if a full account were given of his work with engaged and married couples, it would show that he devoted at least as much time to marriage ministry as he did to his ministry to alcoholics and other people with problems.

So it must be said that Father Ed's Cana talks (some of which have been preserved in recordings and manuscripts) are underrepresented here in comparison with his talks on recovery, and that is for two reasons. First, they do not lend themselves well to being quoted. Father Ed had an almost stream-of-consciousness manner of speaking. For example, when addressing Cana couples, Father Ed would often deliver an extended riff on how the conditions of modern urban life conspired to keep husband and wife apart save for the times when they were most likely to be annoyed at each other—namely, before and after the husband's workday. It began,

> A city never allows a couple to be alone when they are nice people—say around ten in the morning. You are nice now, but you are not alone. And a city forces them to be together when they are not fit to be with anybody. That's before coffee in the morning and after industry has said [to the husband], "This fellow is no good."
>
> I live in a community of very, very saintly men, but just to keep the murder rate down, we are forbidden to talk to each other until we have had some coffee in us.[8]

Father Ed continues with more observations along those lines. His thoughts are witty, psychologically incisive, and no doubt helpful to married couples. But they cannot be condensed without losing their immediacy and charm. It would take a separate book, judiciously edited (perhaps with added commentary from theologians), to capture adequately the unique and at times prophetic insights of Dowling's Cana talks.[9]

The second reason Father Ed's Cana talks are underrepresented here is because he framed much of his advice in examples drawn from the culture of his time. Thus he spoke of the needs, wants, and foibles of working husbands and stay-at-home wives. It was not at all wrong for him to make such assumptions; he knew his audience and met them in their concrete circumstances. However, the person reading Dowling's Cana talks might assume that he intended his references to stereotypical sex roles to be not only descriptive but also prescriptive. In fact, nothing could be farther from the truth.

The Irish-American culture in which Father Ed was raised was a culture in which it was widely accepted that women could be strong, intelligent, and politically active—as were his own mother and sisters. From the start of his ministry until his final months, Dowling encouraged women to pursue their dreams. Many of those he mentored went on to enter male-dominated fields, including journalism, politics, and law.

There was Patricia Prendergast, the twenty-four-year-old Queen's Work secretary who, after learning about politics from Father Ed, in 1936 decided to run for the Missouri state legislature on a proportional-representation platform. Although she lost, she made a respectable showing against veteran politicians, placing fourth in a field of seven. And there was the *Star-Times* newspaper staffer Mary Clynes, who dropped by in 1945 to see Father Ed after she had been offered a job at the Democratic National Committee's Washington headquarters. Clynes was then in her mid-forties—a difficult time of life for anyone to change jobs and cities, but especially for a single woman of her era.

"I asked his advice about making the change," Clynes recalled.

> He said, without hesitation, "How can you miss? You have the chance of a lifetime to sit in a ringside seat at the political scene. When do you leave?"
>
> Actually, I had many misgivings, but after our little talk, I felt reassured and made my choice, and not for a minute have I regretted him as a counselor, guide, and most of all a good friend.[10]

Not every woman who approached Father Ed was capable of making a prudent major life decision so quickly. There were some whom he accompanied over a period of weeks, months, or years, giving them spiritual guidance and practical advice as they confronted deeply rooted mental-health issues or addictions.

Mary Kathryn Barmann was twenty-one when she was introduced to Father Ed in the spring of 1950 by his sister Mother Mary Dowling, RSCJ, who was then the librarian at Maryville College. An extremely bright young woman, Mary Kathryn had graduated from Maryville College in just three years, after which she had entered the novitiate of the Religious of the Sacred Heart. But her independent spirit rebelled against the regimentation of novitiate life, and she was kicked out—sending her into an emotional tailspin.

In a letter to her parents after Father Ed's death, Mary Kathryn wrote, "Father Dowling, I believe, and so did he, saved my mental and psychological life." She explained,

> I was on the verge of a nervous or mental or both breakdown when I came out of the Sacred Heart novitiate. He literally nursed me back to health over a period of about six or seven years. Those were years during which I offered him, his family, and his friends practically every insult and display of ingratitude imaginable. He never ceased to love me and he never ceased to help me. I knew I could count on him ALWAYS, UNDER ANY CIRCUMSTANCES.[11]

Although Father Ed always had a heart for people who were suffering, Mary Kathryn's plight affected him in a special way because he remembered the difficulties his brother Paul had adjusting after he left the Jesuit novitiate. A letter he composed in 1958 to Catherine Rockwood, who likewise had to leave the Sacred Heart novitiate in Kenwood, New York, gives an idea of the consolation that Mary Kathryn would have received from him. Father Ed wrote, "The experience [of departing the novitiate] can be a most precious one.... You will always have the vocation to become Christlike. The step away from Kenwood is in your case a step closer to Christ."

In 1959, Bill Wilson—perhaps sensing that Father Ed's time was growing short—renewed his conversation with his spiritual sponsor about Christian faith. A decade had passed since his discussions with Monsignor Sheen, and over that time he had come to understand better why he resisted identifying as a Christian despite his admiration for Jesus's teachings. He explained to Mel B. in a 1956 letter that the greatest obstacle to Christian faith for him was the accepted Christian teaching on the Incarnation itself:

Christ is, of course, the leading figure to me. Yet I have never been able to receive complete assurance that He was one hundred percent God. I seem to be just as comfortable with the figure of ninety-nine percent. I know that from a conservative Christian point of view this is a terrific heresy. But it must be remembered that I had no childhood conditioning in religion at all....

I guess I'm still a shopper at the theological pie-counter, still wondering in many respects what it's all about.[12]

To my knowledge, there is no evidence that, in his relationship to Christianity, Bill ever became anything more than a "shopper at the theological pie-counter." But throughout his dialogue with Dowling on matters of faith, Father Ed surely appreciated his great openness to the workings of grace.

In May 1959, Father Ed wrote to Bill with the dates when he would be in New York City with the Summer School of Catholic Action, in the hope that Bill and Lois might be available then to see him. He included a copy of the appreciative letter he had sent to Wilson's friend Tom Powers in gratitude for the copy Tom sent of his book *First Questions on the Life of the Spirit*.

Bill replied on June 2 saying he likewise hoped to see Father Ed in New York, and that he had not yet read Powers's book. "But a peek at it leaves me a little puzzled," he added, for Powers's approach when expressing his own philosophy was different from that which he took when discussing A.A.

"Tom is on the side of 'perfection or bust,'" Wilson explained, and said that he and Powers had disagreements on that issue.

Bill did not go into the historical nature of A.A.'s controversies regarding whether perfection should be held up as the fellowship's explicit goal. He didn't have to. Father Ed knew that one of the major issues that led to A.A.'s break from the Oxford Group was the Oxford Group's emphasis on the "Four Absolutes"—absolute honesty, absolute purity, absolute unselfishness, and absolute love. Alcoholics Anonymous, by making its only requirement for membership a desire to stop drinking,[13] gave members the reassurance they needed that sobriety was in their grasp. That reassurance, Bill realized, would be threatened if alcoholics were faced with an absolute moral code.

Ernest Kurtz observed that the fellowship's "explicit rejection of any claim even to an aim that was absolute became more significant to Alcoholics Anonymous than anything it derived more positively from the Oxford Group."[14] That is why, according to Wilson in a 1955 talk, Father Ed once said, "Bill, it isn't what you people put into A.A. that makes it so good—it's what you left out."[15]

In Bill's June 2, 1959, letter, after describing his differences with Powers, the A.A. co-founder manifested his conscience to Father Ed in a manner that showed how deep his trust in his spiritual sponsor had grown:

> I expect too, that I'm too complacent, theologically speaking. The immense array of views which are around—views which so often cut off communication between good people—are interesting, but not too important speculations. At least, so it seems. In some ways I feel very close to conservative Christianity. In other respects—important ones to Christians—no particular convictions seem to come. Maybe down deep I don't want to be convinced—I just don't know.

Twelve years earlier, Bill had bristled at Dowling's suggestion that his resistance to Catholicism amounted to a choice of whose infallibility to accept—the Church's or his own. Now, in 1959, he was willing to admit to Dowling and to himself what he had been unable to admit before: that perhaps there was indeed an element of willfulness in his reluctance to embrace Christian faith.

When Father Ed replied to Bill on June 16, he made a comparison that he knew his friend would readily understand—likening Wilson's resistance to membership in Christ to an alcoholic's resistance to membership in A.A.

> Your feeling of closeness to conservative Christianity without particular conviction of course interests me. From my bigoted perspective it sometimes looks like an alcoholic feels very close to conservative A.A. (who doesn't today?) but lacks particular conviction about it—not wanting to be convinced. Christianity Anonymous could be as appalling as Alcoholics Anonymous.

It was a familiar (if not outright predictable) rhetorical move for Father Ed to make—he had made it many times before in correspondence with Wilson on the topic. But Bill took it seriously and wrote a sensitive response on June 22.

> When you suggest that I may believe what I want to believe rather than what I ought to believe, there probably isn't much doubt that you are right. Which I suppose is to say that egotism, pride of

opinion, conditioning and the like, all have a very large hand in determining what we want to believe versus what we ought to believe.

Once again, even more so than in his previous letter, the A.A. cofounder showed a willingness to discuss the movements of his heart with humility and without the defensiveness he had shown in earlier times.

Bill went on to explain that he genuinely had difficulty weighing the truth claims of different spiritual approaches: "While it may well be suspected that this is an alibi for failing to completely adopt the Catholic point of view, it still seems like a good question to which I consciously do not know the answer." Although he admitted it was "certainly uncomfortable to be unsure about many matters of high importance," he felt "the only worse fate would be to become cocksure and then turn out to be dead wrong."

Father Ed replied on June 29, 1959, offering thoughts that showed he was touched by Bill's honesty, his seriousness, and his openness to truth. He explained that the type of certainty associated with faith was not the type of absolute certainty required by mathematics or even the type of relative certainty required by physical science. Rather, it was a type of relative certainty known as moral certainty, which is the kind of certainty we have when we trust in a person whom we know intimately. "For example," Father Ed wrote, "you are morally, not absolutely, certain that if you visited me you would not be assaulted or robbed. This is the kind of certainty that faith brings."

Although Father Ed did not make explicit reference to John Henry Newman in his letter, the distinctions he outlined regarding faith and certainty showed his deep familiarity with Newman's writings. This is significant because it helps explain an aside that Dowling made in his 1955 address at the A.A. International Convention in which he criticized the fellowship's decision to change the wording of the Twelfth Step.

A.A.'s original Twelfth Step read, "Having had a spiritual experience as the result of these Steps, we tried to carry this message to alcoholics, and to practice these principles in all our affairs." However, the term "spiritual experience" caused controversy within the movement. As Bill later observed, it "gave many readers the impression that these personality changes, or religious experiences, must be in the nature of sudden and spectacular upheavals."[16] So, by the time the Big Book went into its second printing in March 1941, the Twelfth Step had been changed to begin, "Having had a spiritual awakening."

It was that alteration of the Twelfth Step that led Dowling to say in his 1955 convention speech, "I still weep that the elders of the movement have dropped the word 'experience' for 'awakening.'"[17] But although he let his objection be known, he did not explain why he objected. That is why his words to Bill, writing of the type of certainty required for faith, are important. They show that Dowling, like Newman, held that we cannot develop faith on our own volition. Faith requires an encounter with a person—or a Person—who inspires us to faith. Thus, faith always comes first through an experience, although in its aftermath the experience's effects may further unfold in the manner of an awakening.

In his June 29 letter to Bill, after describing the type of certainty that faith brings, Dowling went on to respond to Bill's fear that he might become "cocksure" only to find out he was wrong:

> Absolute cocksureness is not the mark of the faith of the Christian. "Lord, I believe, help Thou my unbelief" [Mark 9:24]. "Lord, to whom shall we turn" [John 6:68]? "Blessed are they who have not seen and have believed" [John 20:29].
>
> The best road to truth is suggested by Christ. "Dwell in My way and you will know the truth." This does not involve doing much different than you are doing. But it means that we should do those things better, more unselfishly. Because I believe that you are doing this—stumblingly, as Christ Himself did[18]—you possess much of that promised truth and are possessed by it.

This letter was the last from Father Ed to Bill in which the Jesuit offered explicit guidance in following the "road to truth." As usual, he was careful to include himself in his preaching; he did not say, "*you* should do those things better, more unselfishly" but rather, "*we* should do those things better, more unselfishly." And he ended on a note that reflected his overwhelming belief that grace was working in Bill's life. As long as Bill sought to dwell in Jesus's way, not even his occasional stumbles could prevent him from imitating Christ more closely with every step.

The records of Father Ed's final months give the impression that he felt he could not die until he had started a support group for every conceivable problem. Among those groups, there are two that especially exemplify the ways in which Dowling extended himself to reach people on the margins of the Catholic Church and society at large: Divorcees Unanimous and Drug Addicts Anonymous.

Father Ed's involvement with Divorcees Unanimous began after Mary Jane Coffey, a Catholic mother who was recently divorced from her alcoholic husband, approached Father Ed with a seemingly insoluble problem.[19]

Her bishop in the Diocese of Belleville, having learned of her divorce from the legal-notices section of a local newspaper, chose to use his prerogative to have her excommunicated. (This was a special prerogative that the U.S. bishops had sought in the nineteenth century so as to discourage divorce. It remained available to bishops until Pope Paul VI eliminated it in 1977.)

Mary Jane's son Michael told me that his mother was pained at being separated from the sacraments and life of the Church that she loved. "She had other Catholic friends who had been through divorce and were [likewise] branded active sinners. They were still trying to love the Church and stay in it." One of those friends was Angela "Kiki" Desloge Meslans, who was descended from one of St. Louis's founding families.

In 1957, Mary Jane, Kiki, and other divorced Catholic women began to meet with Father Ed so that he might help them find legitimate ways to remain active in the Church. Over the next year, he guided them to form a support group, Divorcees Unanimous, which they hoped would become national. Calling their individual chapter Stella Maris, they drew up a formal constitution on January 11, 1959, then the Feast of the Holy Family.

Divorcees Unanimous published a brochure later in 1959 that said their name "[had] its humorous side—whoever heard of a group of women being unanimous—and its serious side, for should we not be of one (*unus*) mind (*animus*) with Christ and his Church." They took the chapter name Stella Maris from a Latin title for Mary meaning Star of the Sea—"in our case, the stormy Sea of Matrimony."

Despite the women's having been excommunicated, Dowling found ways to give the Stella Maris group spiritual accompaniment, including leading an annual retreat for them. "He saw a whole subset of people who were being harmed by the Church," Michael Coffey told me. "He thought it was his job to keep them in the Church but keep them safe."

The founding member of Drug Addicts Anonymous was Donald Mitchell, a thirty-one-year-old African-American who had played for a baseball team that was affiliated with the Harlem Globetrotters. He had been addicted to heroin for more than a decade until he managed to quit the habit in 1957, with the help of friends and his pastor, Father Fred Zimmerman, SJ, of Old St. Malachy's.

Zimmerman, who was also the superior of the Jesuit residence at The Queen's Work, recommended that Mitchell work with Father Ed to find a way to stay drug-free through helping other addicts. Dowling's involvement was key not only for his spiritual accompaniment but also because of his friendships with local officials. At that time, federal narcotic laws made it a crime merely to be a narcotics addict, even if one was not found in possession of drugs. Father Ed worked with Mitchell to secure endorsements of a number of officials as well as the circuit attorney so that the group could advertise itself publicly without fear of prosecution.

On the afternoon of Sunday, October 4, 1959, Drug Addicts Anonymous held its first meeting at The Queen's Work, with Father Ed as spiritual director. That same day, a news item promoting the meeting, and mentioning Mitchell's and Dowling's involvement, ran in the *St. Louis Post-Dispatch*—no doubt placed by Father Ed through a phone call to an editor friend.[20]

The news item must have caused readers to look twice. It was a time when Black people were still being arrested for attempting to dine in whites-only St. Louis cafeterias—and here was a Catholic ministry in the heart of the city hosting a group of drug addicts under a Black man's leadership. But Father Ed had no fear, and, with his and Zimmerman's support, neither did Mitchell. After Dowling's death, Mitchell continued his outreach to addicts, eventually founding a drug-treatment facility that served the local community until the 1990s.

On November 14, 1959, Father Ed flew to New York City, for Bill had invited him to speak at a dinner marking a milestone in the A.A. co-founder's life: the celebration of his twenty-fifth sobriety anniversary. Dowling's expenses—including an oxygen tank to use on the flights—as well as the expenses of his traveling companion, cousin James Cullinane, were covered by several A.A. members as an anniversary gift to Wilson.

From Bill's perspective, the most memorable part of Father Ed's visit was not the anniversary dinner on November 16, as special as it was. It was rather his experience at Father Ed's Mass the next morning at St. Patrick's Cathedral.

The reason the Mass so deeply affected Bill likely has to do with a discussion that he and Father Ed had been having during the weeks prior to Dowling's visit. The two friends had been in conversation about a theological topic that they had never discussed before. It began when—probably during Father Ed's August 1959 visit to New York for the Summer School of Catholic Action—Dowling mentioned to Bill the Catholic teaching on baptism of desire.

The teaching allows for the possibility of salvation for people who desire what baptism brings—union with God, forgiveness of sins, and the life of grace—but have not received actual baptism. Given Father Ed's devotion to St. Dismas, he almost certainly cited the Good Thief as the classic example of a person who was saved by baptism of desire. Dismas never had the opportunity to be baptized—yet he was the only individual to whom Jesus promised heaven.

Bill was intrigued by the teaching, so Father Ed followed up by sending him a note on October 12, 1959, along with a one-page typed excerpt from a pamphlet explaining the teaching. In his note, Dowling observed that the teaching on baptism of desire was a "Christian theory" and not merely a Catholic one, "because this doctrine prevailed long before the Reformation." The pamphlet excerpt that he enclosed said in part, "If men have the necessary good dispositions and yet cannot receive the actual rite of baptism, they may be considered implicitly to desire baptism and may be saved through this desire."[21]

If Bill genuinely believed that, due to his symbolic importance as co-founder of A.A., he could not in good conscience identify himself publicly as a member of a Christian community, this teaching would have been an enormous comfort to him. And, indeed, his response to Dowling seemed to indicate as much. He wrote on October 26, 1959, saying, "thanks very much indeed" for the information. "This I have read with intense interest and very considerable satisfaction. I had never known that such a thing could be possible."

Bill's "intense interest" and "very considerable satisfaction" upon reading about baptism of desire helps to explain his emotion on that November 17, 1959, morning when he accompanied Father Ed through heavy rain into St. Patrick's Cathedral. At Dowling's invitation, he remained and accompanied Father Ed in prayer as he celebrated Mass at one of the side altars. Afterwards, Bill said of that Mass, "I have never felt closer to Christ."[22] That day would be the last time the two friends were together in the flesh.

After Father Ed returned home, Bill sent a flurry of thank-you letters to A.A. members who had subsidized Dowling's trip to New York. He wrote to one member, "As you know, Father Ed is one of the best friends that I shall ever have—he is a veritable saint and a spiritual example that I and thousands of others will treasure always. He came here at great risk to his health."[23] To another member, Bill said of Dowling, "His personal demonstration of Christian grace is the most superb thing that has come my way."[24]

Father Ed's time with Bill in New York City in November 1959 provided him the opportunity to have a conversation that he had been waiting to have with him. After Bill had some time to reflect upon it, the A.A. co-founder wrote to Father Ed on November 23, "Please be sure that I am very glad that you set out your apprehension about the LSD business." Wilson added that he had already disbanded the group that Dowling had witnessed engaging in an experiment, as other members had lost interest.

However, even as he insisted he did not have "the slightest disposition to rush back into these experiences, or to push them upon anybody else," Bill longed to show Dowling that he had some grounds for believing LSD might help alcoholics. To that end, he enclosed a transcript of his comments during his first LSD experiment, on September 20, 1958—the one time he had an experience on the drug that reminded him of the transformative one he had at Towns Hospital. "It is hard for me to believe this episode to have been either phony or malign," Bill wrote.

Father Ed replied on December 14, 1959, beginning with an explanation for his delay in responding: he had spent nine days in the hospital. "Conservative doctor said I over-extended [myself]."

Dowling then moved on to discuss the transcript Bill had sent. Here he was in classic Cerberus mode—affirming what was positive in Wilson's LSD experience, while seeking to protect him from the dangers of fascinating but ultimately futile "snares":

> So much of the good, the true, and the beautiful in the September 20, 1958, transcript. That fact, plus your psycho-sensitivity, plus loss of will control at a stage, plus the proved value of psychic experiment, PLUS the Devil's shrewd malignancy ("Thane of Cawdor / Thane of Glamis..."), plus my Jesuit theory makes me cautious in these matters—possibly more cautious than prudent.

The "Thane of Cawdor" quote came from Shakespeare's *Macbeth*. As Father Ed had in the past, when his Cerberus role led him to warn Bill against trying to commune with the dead, here too he turned to the *Macbeth* witches' predictions as an example of "the Devil's shrewd malignancy." His message was that Wilson's natural gift of "psycho-sensitivity" (as well as his desire for occult knowledge) made him vulnerable to temptations to pride—which could be particularly dangerous under the influence of a drug that caused "loss of will control."

Father Ed then quoted St. Ignatius of Loyola's Rules for the Discernment of Spirits:

> It is the mark of the evil spirit to assume the appearance of the angel of light. He begins by suggesting thoughts suited to a devout

soul but ends by suggesting his own,... little by little drawing the soul into his snares and evil designs.

Ignatius's meaning, Dowling wrote, was that "with centuries of time at his disposal the Devil (like a broker) is a percentage player. He will settle for a lesser good—fearing that the greater good might turn out to be another Assisi."

What stands out in Father Ed's letter is the way he expresses himself honestly and at the same time with great delicacy. Just as he had waited until he could speak one-on-one with Bill before expressing his concerns about the LSD experiments, so too, in this letter, he took care to avoid damaging the most precious friendship of his life.

Having said what he had set out to say, Father Ed closed out the letter in his usual mode of encouragement:

> Letting me share your and Lois's 25th milestone was a peak in the high plateau of my A.A.-hood. Please tell Lois I am so grateful to her for having my nephew Paul to lunch with you. It will be something for him to tell his grandchildren.
>
> You and Lois will be in my Christmas prayers. For the New Year I borrow Thompson's wish that there be no darkness for you but "the shade of His hand outstretched caressingly."[25]

Finally, as if to underline that he was not disturbed by Bill's mystical capabilities but rather by the way he sought to exercise them under LSD's influence, Father Ed wrote that he was enclosing a book about the Catholic mystic Susanna Mary Beardsworth: "Because of her psychosensitivity, I thought you might find some of the pages of interest."[26]

After sending the letter to Bill, Father Ed completed what would be his final article for *Grapevine*, "A.A. Steps for the Underprivileged Non-A.A." He sent it to Wilson on December 28 with an apologetic note saying "it rakes over some old obvious matter." Fortunately, Bill's assessment of the article was far higher than Dowling's own; *Grapevine* associate editor Helen Wynn responded on December 30 assuring the Jesuit that Bill "glowed as he was reading it."

17

⮌⁓⮎

GOING HOME

Yesterday was once a reality. But it is no longer so. Tomorrow will or may become a reality. But it is not reality yet. Only today is reality. Only by attention to today can the mind be saved from absorption into the unreality of yesterday and tomorrow, and free to focus on reality.

— Father Ed, "Psychological Cloister"
(unpublished article, 1959)

What God has turned up, let no man turn down.
— Father Ed, advice to a friend[1]

Father Ed began 1960 full of excitement about the new groups he was forming—especially one for high-school and college students who were old enough to become politically engaged but too young to vote (given that the voting age was still twenty-one). The primary goal of the Future Voters Caucus was to introduce students to political participation. But it also "fulfilled [Dowling's] ideal of providing meeting opportunities free of heavy social pressure or of impetus to get married in any great hurry," as a reporter put it.[2]

Although his health was hardly able to take giving lengthy lectures, there were certain invitations that Father Ed found difficult to resist. One of them was from Mona Barzizza, the daughter of one of the first Cana couples, who was now married and living with her husband, Frank, in Memphis. Dowling gladly accepted an invitation to give a Cana Conference at the Barzizzas' parish on January 10, for the couple were like family to him. Two Sundays later, he fulfilled another invitation he could not refuse: giving a Cana Conference at Mount Carmel in Baden, the very parish where he had once served Father Phelan's Mass.

His Memphis Cana Conference was such a success that Mona wrote to him afterwards saying, "My friends refer to all their arguments as 'B.C'— Before Cana." Would he return to give another conference in April, she asked? This second conference would be for Maryville College alumni living in Memphis and would benefit the college.

As with the previous Memphis invitation, given Dowling's affection for the Barzizzas—as well as his fondness for Maryville, where his sister, Mother Mary, was the librarian—he could hardly say no. Father Ed responded agreeing to make a return visit to Memphis during the first week of April.

During what would prove to be the final weeks of his life, Dowling continued to seek ways to expand the "psychic smorgasbord" of self-help groups meeting at The Queen's Work. More and more, he sought to find ways to apply to these groups the ideals of A.A.'s Twelfth Step—"to carry this message" to others in need of it, "and to practice these principles in all our affairs." The answer he seems to have devised was to form groups with the idea in mind that, as soon as they gained momentum, they would generate and mentor new and more specialized groups.

For example, the previous year, Father Ed had founded Security Cloister, which he called "a mutual-counseling group for prevention of nervousness." It gave him an opportunity to apply techniques he had learned from Recovery, Inc., in a religious context, along with principles from the Spiritual Exercises, Catholic psychiatrist Frank R. Barta, and, of course, Alcoholics Anonymous. Once Security Cloister began to meet and thrive, Father Ed then recommended to the group's members that they sponsor and mentor a new group for people who suffered from scruples.

The scruples group met for the first time on Friday, February 19, 1960, at 8 p.m., at The Queen's Work. Father Ed led a round-table discussion and suggested the group call itself the Montserrat Circle, in recognition of the Spanish pilgrimage site where Ignatius of Loyola overcame his own struggle with scruples.

However, on February 24, Father Ed was back at St. John's Hospital for the third time in eighteen months, suffering extreme shortness of breath. The doctors found he had suffered a heart attack. Yet, once again, nothing seemed to stop him. On the 26th, Anna sent a letter on his behalf to Fred W. of the Emporia, Kansas, chapter of A.A., tentatively accepting a speaking invitation for May 6 on Father Ed's behalf. "He feels that he will be in good shape," she wrote.

Once Father Ed's condition stabilized, visitors began to make their way to his hospital room, although he had fewer guests than during past stays— perhaps due to the unusually harsh winter weather. Among those who did come were a couple who were making a road trip down Route 66 on their honeymoon: Michael Fox, the son of Father Ed's former Loyola Academy student J. Raymond Fox, and his bride Mary Ellen.

Sixty years later, the couple could still recall the visit. "We arrived in St. Louis in the middle of a big snowstorm," Mary Ellen told me.[3]

We stopped at the hospital, and I just remember Father Dowling being a big, handsome Irish guy. He had a beautiful head of white hair. He was very friendly and very open. As I recall, he was interested in finding out how our marriage was going and offered a bit of advice.

One of those pieces of advice, Michael recalls, was to remember that marriage, like a see-saw, required that the spouses be ready to give in when necessary to meet the needs of the other. "He had a cane and he was saying that marriage was like a teeter-totter"—that is, a see-saw—"and he used the cane [to illustrate]—keeping it level or raising it on one side or the other." (Kathryn Spearing, who, with her fiancé, received similar advice from Father Ed, told me he put it this way: "Think about a see-saw: the one at the bottom is in control.")[4] Michael also remembers Dowling's admonition to be careful not to say things that one might regret. "He said that bad words were always bad and couldn't be taken back."

Anna Dowling visited Father Ed frequently during his hospital stay to help with his correspondence. In early March, Father Ed dictated to Anna a letter to his friend Ben S. Allen of the Associated Press, offering suggestions for Allen's research into the veracity of the alleged Black Diaries of Roger Casement. Allen and his wife Victoria wrote to Anna on March 9 thanking her for passing on Father Ed's letter to them, adding, "We are hopeful that [Father Ed] will slow down a bit, but also realize that this is not easy for his restless and dynamic spirit and brain."

Around March 10, Dowling dictated a letter to Mary Kathryn Barmann giving an enthusiastic account of the progress of Future Voters Caucus: "They do not want to play house at politics but want to work on student government, public-opinion polls, initiative petitions, and similar ways in which they can take part in politics." He added with approval that the group included non-Catholic members; it was also trying to interest Black students in joining. And he was already envisioning the new groups it might generate: "Scholarship Anonymous or Education Anonymous or Education Unconscious, [and] Mutual Tutoring seem possible by-products of this group, as well as strengthening of family political strength, as well as an opportunity for cheap, relaxed co-ed association."

Father Ed also kept up with the newspapers while in the hospital. On March 13, after reading the *St. Louis Post-Dispatch*'s full-page story about his friend Rabbi Ferdinand M. Isserman's celebrating his thirtieth anniversary in the rabbinate, he called the rabbi to congratulate him and offer prayers. Dowling remembered how, during the mid-1930s, Rabbi Isserman was among the first non-Catholic religious leaders to collaborate with him on social-justice projects.

On March 21, Father Ed was discharged from St. John's after nearly a month in the hospital. He returned immediately to The Queen's Work, where he soon was met by Rhea Felknor, a former newspaperman in his late thirties who was an enthusiastic convert to Catholicism. Father Ed had promised him an interview for *The Voice of St. Jude* about the new "three-dimensional approach" that he was planning for the Cana movement.[5]

In Felknor's writeup of the interview, composed after Dowling's death, the journalist wrote, "One could notice a change in the man. The extravagant 'Dowlingisms' for which he was famous were reduced and made more exact as the unseasonably severe winter melted away and a belated spring came. As April approached, the priest checked a second and third draft of the copy, deleting references he felt were unkind to anyone."

During the interview at The Queen's Work, Father Ed said to Felknor with a smile, "I've gone through life like that famous Pickwickian horse—north by northeast. It isn't traditional, but it does give one a remarkable perspective."

There is something sweet in how Father Ed, at the end of his life, likened himself to the sideways-traveling horse in *Pickwick Papers*, given that he received detention as a high-school student for reading the Dickens novel in study hall.

Felknor wrote that Dowling "expressed great anxiety over the way married couples have accepted marriage as an equal contract—a 'comradeship'—where neither gives in to the other for fear of being dominated." Such an idea, Father Ed said, was drawn from Sigmund Freud's materialistic understanding of the human person, which reduced husband and wife to their appetites, ignoring their spiritual needs.

"Whenever Freud saw any deviation from a static equality—horizontal—it was the one of Maggie bossing Jiggs, or the reverse," Dowling explained (using for his example the names of characters from the comic strip

"Bringing Up Father"). "The followers of Freud have made dominance and submission to be abnormal and perverse. Chesterton's idea—and St. Paul's and Chaucer's—that marriage was a 'splendid see-saw' seems to have escaped them completely."

Father Ed then turned to discuss the scriptural admonition, "Be subject to one another out of reverence for Christ. Wives, be subject to your husbands, as to the Lord" (Eph 5:21–22). In Dowling's understanding, the verses did not endorse an unequal power relationship but rather a mutual give-and-take: "St. Paul, just after saying that all Christians must submit one to another, tells the wife to start the see-saw and get the old man off the ground."[6]

It had been Father Ed's hope that the Cana Conference would help couples navigate the challenges they faced in relating to each other and to society at large, which he noted often failed to support married couples. Yet, he sighed to Felknor, "Cana had hardening of the arteries at birth. It was meant to be a dialogue between couples. It started as a *monologue* aimed at them, and it stayed that way."

To bring more depth to Cana, Father Ed said, "We need to make a more probing analysis of marriage itself. If only we understood the evangelical counsels better!" It was time, he said, that the Church investigate how those counsels of poverty, chastity, and obedience, as practiced in religious orders, might be adapted to married life. And in this, without knowing it, he was once again giving a prophetic witness to the universal call to holiness that the Second Vatican Council would proclaim in *Lumen Gentium*.[7]

During the final week of March 1960, Anna Dowling assisted Father Ed as he made travel arrangements to attend the A.A. International Convention in Long Beach, California, in July, which would celebrate the fellowship's twenty-fifth anniversary. He was scheduled to take part in a presentation on "God as We Understand Him," just as he had at A.A.'s 1955 convention in St. Louis.

A letter Father Ed wrote on March 25 to his friend Sister Ignatia Gavin, C.S.A., reveals why the Jesuit thought it especially important for him to accept such conference invitations even though traveling was a trial for him.

"I must strongly urge you to attend the Long Beach convention of A.A., if your Superior gives you clearance,"[8] Dowling wrote to Ignatia. "Non-Catholic America, with Devil's help, is frightened of and irritated at Catholicity. America will be reached morally rather than mentally, by works rather than words."

Although Father Ed's assessment of "non-Catholic America" might seem severe, he was writing at a time when anti-Catholic polemic was rising in response to Senator John F. Kennedy's campaign for the Democratic presidential nomination.

Dowling's next words offer great insight into how closely A.A.'s spirituality and Catholic faith had become united in his mind:

> The two best approaches to Catholicity for the non-Catholic heart that I know of are marriage and alcoholism. They admire our marriages. And you know how A.A. has been a theoretical and personal introduction to Catholicity for so many.

That last sentence is remarkable. The late A.A. historian Glenn Chesnut, who was the first to reproduce it, thought it meant that Father Ed saw his and Sister Ignatia's work as that of covert missionaries seeking to lead A.A. members into the Catholic Church.[9] But given Father Ed's correspondence with Bill W. and, indeed, the witness of his entire life, I believe that Chesnut fundamentally misread Dowling's intention—for Dowling did not speak of A.A. as an introduction to *Catholicism* but rather to *Catholicity*.

Whereas Catholicism is a religion, Catholicity is a more general perspective on God, the world, and one's own place in it. Although I would not go so far as to say that Father Ed held to Karl Rahner, SJ's understanding of "anonymous Christianity" (which holds that a person could be Christian without knowing it), he did believe that anyone who followed the Twelve Steps was on the path of grace. For that reason, I strongly suspect that he would say that these words of Christ apply to such people: "No one who does a mighty work in my name will be able soon after to speak evil of me. For he that is not against us is for us" (Mark 9:39–40). In other words, a person who followed the Catholicity of the Twelve Steps could not be "frightened and irritated at Catholicity."

In his letter to Sister Ignatia, Dowling went on to assure the nun that he would keep her health and her intention in his daily Mass. His last words before his signature were, "I have been here [at The Queen's Work] for about a week and feel quite well."

Father Ed also downplayed his health woes in a March 30 letter to Mary Kathryn Barmann, who had moved to Venezuela to teach. "3½ weeks in St. John's," he wrote. "Took off 14 pounds. Feel fine."

At the end of the letter, Dowling wrote that upon returning from Memphis on the evening of April 3, he would begin his annual weeklong retreat—emerging from it on Palm Sunday. With words that honored the spiritual value of her struggle with anxiety, he asked Mary Kathryn to remember him in her prayers during his retreat: "Intention in your interior sufferings, please."

On Friday, April 1, the day before Father Ed was to leave for Memphis, Ronnie Creighton-Jobe stopped by The Queen's Work for morning Mass and stayed for breakfast with Dowling. When Father Ed mentioned he was preparing to fly out of town to give a Cana Conference, Creighton-Jobe was distressed.

"Oh, Father Edward, don't!" the teenager exclaimed. "You're just out of hospital. You're not well."

Dowling replied with what Creighton-Jobe aptly told me was "one of his great lines."

"I'm a perfectly well sick man," the Jesuit quipped (which, as Creighton-Jobe observed to me, "was very typical of him"). But when he saw the youth's worried expression, he realized he had to say something more.

"Ronnie," Dowling said gently, "it's just another curtain call."

We now arrive at Saturday, April 2, 1960—Father Ed's last day on earth. And if there is one constant to his activities on that day, it is this: from start to finish, he was surrounded by love. Every person he had contact with that day was special to him in some way, and he was special to them. But, more than that, he had contact with every *group* of people he loved. He interacted with members of his family; with members of A.A.; with participants in Recovery, Inc., and the Cana Conference; and with some of his dearest friends.

Thanks to three photographs taken by Pat Cavin, it is possible to reconstruct Dowling's afternoon from the point when he arrived at St. Louis's Lambert Airport for his 2:45 p.m. flight to Memphis. Cavin, a Catholic woman in her mid-thirties, was indebted to Father Ed for helping her overcome extreme scrupulosity.[10]

The first of Pat's photos shows Father Ed approaching the airport entrance with his black-leather overnight bag in his left hand and his wooden cane in his right hand. His black coat and clerics hang loosely on him, reflecting his recent weight loss. An African-American Red Cap porter who has come out to meet Father Ed is pointing to his cane; we can almost hear the porter asking if Dowling would like a wheelchair.

In the second photo, the porter, bearing a warm and kindly expression, is preparing to wheel Father Ed into the airport. Dowling had always felt close to porters; after all, it was his friend A. Philip Randolph who had unionized them. If he had felt any recurrence of his old fear of flying when he arrived at the airport, the assistance of this caring Red Cap would have helped him feel at ease.

The third and final photo shows Father Ed inside the airport, seated at a table in a coffee shop. Pat has asked him to take off his glasses, without which he can hardly see; he gazes off to his left with a pensive expression. He does not look unhappy. But he does look tired.

Bill G. of the newly established Memphis chapter of Recovery, Inc., was at the airport with his wife Ola, an A.A. member, to meet Father Ed when he arrived. The couple quickly helped him out of his long black coat; the temperature was quite a bit warmer than when he left home. Dowling was glad to spend some time with Bill and Ola before they brought him to Frank and Mona Barzizza's home, for he was eager to be brought up to date on the local Recovery and A.A. groups.

When Father Ed arrived at the Barzizzas' home—a modern, ranch-style red-brick house—Bill G. had to assist him as he hobbled up four difficult steps to make it to the front door. A delighted Frank Barzizza greeted him there and helped him over the threshold. Several Cana couples crowded the living room; Frank and Mona had invited them all to dinner. Children were there too, including the Barzizza's two toddlers, Lise and John.

Mona had studied theater in New York before choosing marriage and motherhood over an acting career. Her sister Mary Spearing as well as her sister-in-law Kathryn Spearing described her to me as a bright, charismatic Catholic woman who, with her husband, was greatly fond of Father Ed.

"She was the kind of person that loved interesting evenings," Kathryn told me, "and she just couldn't wait to share that friendship of Father Dowling with all of her friends. She just loved him so and respected him so, and felt that he would bring so much into their lives by being there and meeting with them."

After Father Ed greeted everyone present, he took a moment to use the Barzizzas' phone. Before he left St. Louis, he had corresponded with a Memphis A.A. friend, Paul H., who had wanted to join him for dinner with other local A.A. members.

Paul H. later recalled in a letter, "[Father Ed] phoned me that it had gotten a trifle crowded and could I come out after dinner. I told him to let it ride, Sunday would do.... But he sounded so disappointed that I said I'd be glad to come—and for that will I ever be eternally grateful."[11]

When Paul arrived at the Barzizza home, he brought with him a female member of A.A. who had been sober for three years. "[Father Ed] was very glad to show us off," Paul wrote. "Those in the Fellowship were always his 'pets,' so to speak—you could tell that by the way his eyes lit up when we came in the room."

The A.A. members' personal witness was particularly valuable to Father Ed that evening, because, Paul wrote,

> The others belonged to the Cana Conferences ... and he wanted to emphasize how A.A.'s faced their problems and spoke directly about their problems and about "God directly and not as if the word were immodest like 'legs' in the Victorian age." The quotes are direct.

At ten-thirty or so, the gathering began to wind down. "We left [Father Ed] saying we'd see him on Sunday," Paul wrote, "but, as you know, he had a higher engagement. One look at him and I knew he wouldn't be with us long; he left as he would have liked—among friends he loved and who loved him, and with A.A. the night before."

Once Father Ed had said good night to Frank and Mona, at 11 p.m., he used their phone again. This time, he called his sister-in-law Beatrice, widow of his brother Paul Vincent Dowling, asking her to do an errand for him the next day. Then he asked her to put his niece Mary on the line.

What could be so important for Father Ed to want to speak to Mary— then a high-school senior—at that late hour, after a long day of travel and socializing? At that time, Beatrice was planning to take both her children— Mary and Paul—on a pilgrimage to Europe with their pastor, Monsignor Martin Hellriegel. However, it seems that Mary, who was known for having a rebellious spirit, had not yet committed to be part of the trip—or at least, Father Ed feared she might back out of it.

"He was encouraging me to get a lot out of the trip," Mary told me. "I don't remember saying that I wasn't going to go, but there must have been some reason that he felt he should say that. Maybe Anna [Dowling] had suspected that I might be having second thoughts."

Mary's recollection is the last personal account we have from Father Ed's final night. However, it is possible to make an educated guess about what Dowling's last waking moments were like—for he was, after all, a priest, and would have prayed the Divine Office before going to bed.

Father Ed, having been with friends all afternoon and evening, likely would have said the Vespers prayers that he had missed earlier, as well as the Compline prayers. The next day was Passion Sunday, which was what the Sunday before Palm Sunday was called at that time, and the readings were oriented toward entering into the spirit of Jesus's Passion.

Given the depth of Dowling's self-identification with Jesus's sufferings, he would have read the reading from Hebrews with great emotion:

> But Christ, being come an high priest of the good things to come, by a greater and more perfect tabernacle not made with hand, that is, not of this creation: Neither by the blood of goats, or of calves, but by his own blood, entered once into the holies, having obtained eternal redemption.[12]

It was the custom at that time for Catholic churches to cover all crucifixes and holy statues with violet veils from Passion Sunday until the beginning of the Easter Vigil. The removal of the deathlike veils from the images made for a beautiful symbol of the Resurrection.

So I like to think that, after completing his prayers, as he struggled painfully to adjust the sheet and blankets over himself, this priest—who was known for saying he was "turning to stone"—thought of how statues in Catholic churches were being veiled that very night. And perhaps too he thought of how, one day (probably sooner rather than later), his own body would lie under a veil. And on another future day, in God's time, that veil would be lifted just as the veils over the statues were lifted on Easter Sunday. And he would rise with Christ.

Father Ed had intended to sleep late on Sunday morning and celebrate Mass around nine a.m. in the Siena College chapel.[13] But Frank and Mona were up early that day—they had two toddlers, after all. At six-thirty, they heard Dowling moan slightly, but not enough to indicate that he was sick. It was not until eight o'clock, when Frank entered Father Ed's room because he had not responded to their calling out to him, that they discovered he had died—in his sleep, the doctor would conclude.

That night, Frank and Mona, along with their pastor, brought Father Ed's body back to St. Louis on the Illinois Central. Not even death could keep him from his beloved trains.

Ronnie Creighton-Jobe came up to The Queen's Work as usual on Monday morning, April 4, intending to attend Mass and have breakfast with Father Ed afterwards. One of the staff members stopped before he entered the chapel and broke the news to him.

"It really was like the loss of a father or a grandfather," Creighton-Jobe told me.

"I went in the chapel there," he continued,

and then I thought, "Here I am, in front of the Blessed Sacrament. This is exactly where he would have wanted me to be." Because, you see, he taught me—well, not only he, but [his sister] Mother Mary Dowling too—living in the presence of God.

There is no record of how Bill Wilson learned of Father Ed's death, but almost certainly it was through a phone call from Anna Dowling. Father Ed's nephew Paul remembers being with his family and a few other mourners at the funeral parlor on the afternoon of April 5 when a taxi pulled up to the curb and Bill stepped out.

"He came through the door, put his suitcase just inside the door, and walked over to Uncle's casket without taking note of the family," Paul told me.

"In fact," Paul added,

he walked past Anna Dowling, whom he knew. He stood at the casket, put his hands on Uncle's, and stayed there several minutes just looking at Uncle. Then he returned to us and specifically to Anna Dowling.

It was a very moving thing. I had never seen anybody do that. I think it was for the sake of reuniting for the last time with his old friend.

Those two men, Bill W. and Uncle, had a deep friendship.

Father Ed's former Loyola Academy student Neil C. Hurley, Jr., also was present at the funeral parlor. Two days later, he wrote to Anna,

I couldn't help but be struck by the tremendous number of people who knelt before the casket for identically the same reasons that I did. So many of them told me that it was because of him that their lives were manageable and beautiful, and all of them felt that they alone were the "some special person" in Father's life. It was incredible to hear the number of people he had spoken to the day before or within the past week, which shows how close he kept in touch with all those who needed his assistance and understanding.[14]

The funeral, on April 6, was at St. Louis University's St. Francis Xavier College Church, the stunning Gothic Revival church where Father Ed had so often celebrated Mass in the sacristy. But intra-Jesuit politics almost prevented the service from being held there, for the College Church's pastor refused to host Father Ed's funeral. He suggested that it be held instead at the tiny chapel within the office building where The Queen's Work was located.[15]

Although the reasons for the pastor's refusal are unknown, they can be guessed. In the hierarchy of Jesuit elites, Father Ed was the lowest of the low. He was not on the staff of *America* magazine, neither was he a university professor or a pastor. He wasn't even a high-school teacher (not since he was a scholastic, anyway). All he did was counsel people with problems—including drunks, drug addicts, and the mentally ill. And what a sight it would be if they all tramped their ill-shod feet into the College Church!

At any rate, when the Society of Jesus's provincial superior, Father James McQuade, SJ, learned of the refusal, he was appalled. McQuade personally intervened to order that Father Ed's funeral Mass be held at the College Church.

Dolores Tygard—the friend whom Father Ed had tried to talk into starting a matchmaking bureau—later wrote that Dowling's friends "jammed" the cavernous church:

> I have never seen a funeral like it. Police blowing whistles, trying to keep order. Limousines bearing city officials. Cars of ancient origin. There were Negroes and whites, Catholics who followed the Mass and non-Catholics who sat in reverent silence, many minks and lovely spring hats... and in my pew, a representative little old lady, shabbily dressed, rattling a paper bag which I thought contained her lunch. She cried all through the Mass.[16]

Afterwards, when the funeral cortege headed from the College Church to the Jesuit cemetery at Florissant,[17] "the cars stretched for miles," Father Ed's niece Mary Dowling told me. She and her brother Paul were with Anna in the first car. "Whenever there was a turn, I would look back and it went on forever."

However, one of the family members who was closest to Father Ed— and the most like him in personality—was absent from the funeral and burial. His sister Mother Mary Dowling, was not permitted to attend, for she was a cloistered Religious of the Sacred Heart. The most that her superior could permit was that she be transported on that day from the convent where she lived at Maryville College in South St. Louis to City House, her order's midtown St. Louis convent.

"She was allowed to stand at the window as the cortege went past," Father Ronald Creighton-Jobe told me. "And she waved goodbye from there."

At Florissant, Father Leo C. Brown, SJ, who had worked extensively in the social-justice arena, leaned over to Father Fred Zimmerman, SJ and remarked, "So this is the man they would not bury from the College Church?"

"The cemetery and the grounds were packed with cars and people who came from all over the country," Zimmerman later wrote. "Mr. Wilson was there to give Puggy Dowling a sendoff that was rarely seen at Florissant."

Following the burial, Bill Wilson joined a large number of Father Ed's friends and family members who crowded into Anna Dowling's small house in Baden. Father Ed's niece Mary told me that the depth of his grief was visible on his face: "Bill was terribly sad."

Yet, even as the A.A. co-founder suffered, he found a way to reach out to others, as he had done so many times before in the face of anguish. I do not know exactly when he conducted this outreach, whether it was before or after the funeral. But I do know from a letter he wrote to Anna on April 12, 1960, that before Bill left town, he made a special trip to Maryville College to express his condolences to Mother Mary Dowling.

Father Ed's sisters Anna and Mother Mary were comforted during the weeks after his death by scores of letters that poured in from people whose lives he had touched. One such letter, from Vincent P. Dole, a former Loyola Academy student of Father Ed's, would take on special significance in years to come. Dole, who was then a scientist at New York City's Rockefeller University wrote of Dowling, "He was a great man. I don't know anyone who has contributed more of himself to his fellow mortals."[18]

During the weeks and months after Father Ed's death, his memory remained on Dole's mind. He thought about how Dowling at Loyola Academy had taught him about "ethical conduct, not as an abstract thesis, but as a practical obligation toward others, and as a service that brings its own reward."[19] And he began for the first time to contemplate what, if anything, he might do to help the drug addicts he passed by every day on his way to work.

The idea came to Dole that he could use his scientific gifts to study the pharmacology of heroin addiction. This eventually led him, with the addiction expert Dr. Marie Nyswander (who became his wife) to develop methadone treatment for heroin addicts—revolutionizing the science of addiction management.

Dole also became, at Bill Wilson's invitation, a Class A (nonalcoholic) trustee of Alcoholics Anonymous. When he delivered the 1991 Distinguished Science Lecture at the Annual Meeting of the American Society of Addiction Medicine, he spoke of Father Ed along with Wilson and Nyswander as three people who "cared for people who suffered and especially those with the double jeopardy of being sick and being rejected."

Bill Wilson, for his part, never forgot what his spiritual sponsor did for him. Through the late 1960s, he continued to exchange letters with Anna and Mother Mary. His grief, over time, softened into undiluted gratitude.

"Ed was the greatest human soul that I'm sure I shall ever know," Bill wrote to Anna in June 1960.[20] In another letter, he said, "Since Ed's passing, I frequently see his face and feel his presence. His wonderful counsel and influence will be with me for life—and, I trust, for life everlasting."[21]

ACKNOWLEDGMENTS AND POSTSCRIPT

Date your letters. It will make your biographer's work so much easier.
— Father Ed[1]

Acknowledgments. I have been blessed to know many priests who share Father Ed's generosity of spirit—priests who are, in Pope Francis's words, "shepherds with the smell of the sheep." But there was one who made such an impact on my life and personal vocation that I cannot imagine this book existing without his influence.

Father Francis Canavan, SJ, was a professor emeritus of political science at Fordham University and had just turned eighty-nine when I met him at a fundraising dinner in October 2006. I was excited to meet him because I had read a book of his essays and was inspired by the way he wrote about living out one's faith in the world. When I told him about my upcoming book *The Thrill of the Chaste*, he expressed interest and I promised to send him a copy.

The Thrill of the Chaste was marketed as a "how-to" for single adults seeking to build happy lives and healthy relationships without engaging in premarital sex. But when I sent it to Father Canavan, he saw something in it that no one else saw—not even myself. In his thank-you note, he wrote that I was making a contribution to the literature of recovery.

Father Canavan knew something about recovery. For more than twenty years, he had been a spiritual director to a local chapter of the Calix Society (calixsociety.org), a fellowship of Catholics maintaining their sobriety through their Catholic faith and a twelve-step recovery program such as Alcoholics Anonymous. During that time, he had published two books of talks, *The Light of Faith* and *By the Grace of God*, in which he spoke in the spirit of A.A., as one alcoholic sharing with another.

I was mentored by Father Canavan during what proved to be the final years of his life (he died in February 2009). It was because I wanted to be like him that I began to study Jesuit spirituality, beginning with memorizing St. Ignatius of Loyola's *Suscipe* prayer ("Take, Lord, and receive...") and praying it every morning. His belief that I had a gift for writing about recovery inspired me to write books in which I opened up about my journey of healing from childhood sexual abuse.[2] And his faith in me gave me the courage to persist in my doctoral studies.

For the rest of my life, Father Canavan's spirit will be in every good thing I do. I trust it is in this book—especially because he, like Father Ed, had a great pastoral love for people in recovery.

I also want to thank a reader of my Dawn Patrol blog (dawneden. blogspot.com) who, in 2007, sent me a care package of vintage pamphlets that someone had deposited in the nave of her parish church. Through those pamphlets, I discovered Father Daniel A. Lord, SJ, and became a devoted reader and collector of his works. When I later learned of Father Ed, my appreciation of Father Lord led me to be more interested in him than I might have been otherwise, since he was Lord's friend and colleague. To my shame, I cannot recall the name of the reader who sent me the pamphlets, but she is in my prayers with gratitude.

Mark Judge, whose online article first brought Father Ed to my attention, also has my gratitude, as does everyone who has ever shared with me their experience of recovery in twelve-step groups, especially Colin O. and Don L. They impressed upon me that "it works if you work it." Thanks too to David C., who took me to an open A.A. meeting at my request in 2015 and who connected me with Dowling's friend Father Ronald Creighton-Jobe, CO.

In January 2011, while I was visiting St. Louis, local photographer/historian Mark Scott Abeln took me to see Father Lord's and Father Ed's names on the memorial monument in the Jesuit section of Calvary Cemetery, where both priests are buried. As we drove away, we saw a vertical rainbow appear in the sky, which added a numinous feeling to the experience.

Abeln also took me to visit Father William Barnaby Faherty, SJ, who had worked closely with Father Lord and Father Ed at The Queen's Work. Father Faherty was ninety-six and very weak. But when I mentioned Father Lord, his eyes lit up and he exclaimed that the Jesuit was "a wonder of the world." He said the same words when I mentioned Father Ed. But then he added something more, relating a story that made a deep impression upon me.

With emotion, Father Faherty told me that Father Ed spent the last night of his life with representatives of the three groups of people who were most important to him in his ministry: members of A.A., the Cana Conference, and Recovery, Inc. He went to bed happy and he died happy.

Seven months later, Father Faherty died. I am forever grateful to Abeln for giving me the opportunity to meet him.

During that same 2011 trip, I visited the Midwest Jesuit Archive (now the Jesuit Archives & Research Center) for the first time and met its director, David Miros. Since I was not yet a professional researcher, I was not permitted to access Father Ed's personal papers. But Dr. Miros gave me a tour of the archive and scanned some articles about Father Ed for me, which furthered my interest in Dowling. Nearly ten years later, when I returned to the archive to research *Father Ed*, he and reference archivist Ann Knake opened the files to me completely and complied with all my many requests. Many thanks to them both!

From that visit onward, whenever I did research in St. Louis, the Benedictines at St. Louis Abbey provided generous hospitality. Sometimes they even offered me a *hemina* of wine as prescribed in St. Benedict's Rule—though, as I entered more deeply into my research, I found myself abstaining in solidarity with A.A. members.

Gary Jansen is the friend I mentioned in the introduction who asked me what was the book I most wanted to write. He read my original proposal for *Father Ed* and was wholeheartedly supportive. This book would not exist without his encouragement. When, for reasons beyond his control, he was unable to place it with a publisher himself, he urged me to find a home for it elsewhere. Thank you, Gary; you have been a wonderful instrument of providence in my life.

Words cannot describe how grateful I am to Robert Ellsberg of Orbis Books. It has been a joy to work with him. I am honored to have him as my editor and friend.

In February 2020, when I arrived to do research at the Father Edward Dowling, SJ, Archive at Maryville University Library in St. Louis, archivist Emma Prince gave me valuable assistance. But no sooner did I return home to Washington, DC, than the pandemic hit and Emma's position was cut.

The loss of Emma's assistance threatened my research, as I had intended to make a return visit to the archive. For some months, I tried to find another staff member to assist me. But in the wake of the health emergency, outside researchers were (understandably) low on the library's list of priorities.

Help finally arose in the form of library staff member Kyle Jenkins. When he learned of my situation, he proceeded to do everything in his power to assist me. Not only did he grant me access to the archive, he also scanned hundreds of documents for me. He is my hero.

Thank you to Father Ed's niece and nephew, Mary and Paul Dowling, for reading and commenting on every chapter of this book, for your interviews, and most of all for enabling me to be confident that I was doing justice to your uncle's memory. Thanks also to Jayne Lahey Kobliska, who likewise reviewed chapters, and to everyone else who granted interviews or otherwise provided information on Father Ed.

Many others deserve thanks for the help they gave this project or just for being supportive friends. I hesitate to list them because, having researched

Father Ed for more than a decade, I am sure to forget to mention many worthy names. But it is worth recording those I can recall. In alphabetical order: Carl B. of the A.A. Area 38 Archive; Father John Beal; Patrick T. Carroll; Michael Coffey; Sally Corbett-Turco and all the staff and volunteers at Stepping Stones; Matt DeWitt; Katherine DiGiulio; William Doino Jr.; Father Timothy Geiger, OFM Conv.; Matt Ghio; E.O. Gibson; Monsignor Edmund Griesedieck; Father William Gurnee; Paul Hohmann; Bill Inglot; Lynne Jackson/DredScottLives.org; Susan Lietzke; Madonna House; Ian McCabe; Kevin O'Brien; Carolyn Osiek, RSCJ; James Owen; Father Sean Raftis; Phil Fox Rose; Father Michael Smith, SJ; John Samuel Tieman; Luba Timchinna; Bill Vatterott/Vatterott Foundation; and the staff and volunteers of the Alcoholics Anonymous G.S.O. Archives.

Postscript: **Saint Puggy?** If you have read this far, perhaps you believe, as I do, that Father Edward Dowling, SJ, was a man of such prophetic wisdom, heroic virtue, and personal holiness that he deserves to be named a saint of the Church.

The sainthood process is perhaps the only truly democratic process in the Church. No person becomes a saint unless there are members of the Catholic faithful in that person's home diocese who are devoted to his or her memory. In the Church's language, such devotion is known as a local cult. It will take the form of private devotion to the person and "the spontaneous spreading of his reputation of holiness or martyrdom and of intercessory power."[3]

Thus, if it is God's will that Father Ed be named a saint, his cause for sainthood will begin with people in the Archdiocese of St. Louis spreading the word about him and privately asking his prayers. Although people outside St. Louis may aid Father Ed's cause for sainthood, St. Louisans will have to complement their efforts if the cause is to progress.

Readers interested in promoting Father Ed's cause should write to the archbishop of St. Louis and copy the provincial superior of the Midwest Province of the Society of Jesus.[4] In their letter or email, they should share how they have been affected by Father Ed's life and witness, and describe the form that their devotion to him takes.

If an organized effort to promote Father Ed as a candidate for sainthood were to arise, and if it were to gain official sanction from the St. Louis Archdiocese or the Jesuits, I would place my personal research at its disposal. Those organizing such an effort may reach me through the email address listed in the "Contact" section of my blog (dawneden.blogspot.com) or through Orbis Books.

APPENDIX

The Twelve Steps

1. We admitted we were powerless over alcohol—that our lives had become unmanageable.

2. Came to believe that a Power greater than ourselves could restore us to sanity.

3. Made a decision to turn our will and our lives over to the care of God as we understood Him.

4. Made a searching and fearless moral inventory of ourselves.

5. Admitted to God, to ourselves, and to another human being the exact nature of our wrongs.

6. Were entirely ready to have God remove all these defects of character.

7. Humbly asked Him to remove our shortcomings.

8. Made a list of all persons we had harmed, and became willing to make amends to them all.

9. Made direct amends to such people wherever possible, except when to do so would injure them or others.

10. Continued to take personal inventory and when we were wrong promptly admitted it.

11. Sought through prayer and meditation to improve our conscious contact with God as we understood Him, praying only for knowledge of His will for us and the power to carry that out.

12. Having had a spiritual awakening as the result of these Steps, we tried to carry this message to alcoholics, and to practice these principles in all our affairs.

The TwelveTraditions (Short Form)

1. Our common welfare should come first; personal recovery depends upon A.A. unity.

2. For our group purpose there is but one ultimate authority—a loving God as He may express Himself in our group conscience. Our leaders are but trusted servants; they do not govern.

3. The only requirement for A.A. membership is a desire to stop drinking.

4. Each group should be autonomous except in matters affecting other groups or A.A. as a whole.

5. Each group has but one primary purpose—to carry its message to the alcoholic who still suffers.

6. An A.A. group ought never endorse, finance, or lend the A.A. name to any related facility or outside enterprise, lest problems of money, property, and prestige divert us from our primary purpose.

7. Every A.A. group ought to be fully self-supporting, declining outside contributions.

8. Alcoholics Anonymous should remain forever non-professional, but our service centers may employ special workers.

9. A.A., as such, ought never be organized; but we may create service boards or committees directly responsible to those they serve.

10. Alcoholics Anonymous has no opinion on outside issues; hence the A.A. name ought never be drawn into public controversy.

11. Our public relations policy is based on attraction rather than promotion; we need always maintain personal anonymity at the level of press, radio, and films.

12. Anonymity is the spiritual foundation of all our traditions, ever reminding us to place principles before personalities.

NOTES

Introduction

1. Athanasius, *On the Incarnation*, 7.43, translation mine.

2. Edward Dowling, SJ, "Editor of Modern Schoolman," *Modern Schoolman* 1, no. 2 (February 1925): 9.

3. Dowling, "Editor of Modern Schoolman."

4. "A Scheme to Salvage Lost Ideas," *Scientific American* 130, no. 5 (May 1924), 330.

5. E. J. Dowling, SJ, "Salvage the Dum-Dum Thought!", *Modern Schoolman* 1, no. 1, 13–14. Given that Dowling's middle name was Patrick, the middle initial "J." in his byline either is a typo or reflects his using a different middle name at the time (perhaps in tribute to his late brother James). In any case, there is no doubt that the author of the article is the same Father Ed of A.A. fame, as he was the only Edward Dowling doing philosophy studies for the Society of Jesus's St. Louis province at the time.

6. "A Scheme to Salvage Lost Ideas."

7. "Thirteenth, Greatest of Centuries" is an actual quote from Dowling in "Salvage the Dum-Dum Thought!" Even beyond the "rubbish" line, he used so much sarcasm in the piece that a misreading was all but inevitable.

8. Dowling, "Editor of Modern Schoolman."

9. Dowling, "Editor of Modern Schoolman."

10. The essay was Mark Gauvreau Judge's "Twelve Steps to Man," Catholic Education Resource Center, catholiceducation.org.

11. Robert Fitzgerald, SJ, *The Soul of Sponsorship* (Center City, MN: Hazelden, 1995), Kindle loc. 122.

12. Bill Wilson, "Alcoholics Anonymous," in *The Blue Book*, Proceedings of the National Clergy Conference on Alcoholism, vol. 12 (1960), 182.

13. See the "Carl and Susie" story in chapter 7.

14. Dorothy Day, "Peter the Materialist," *The Catholic Worker* (September 1945), 6.

15. See John 1:9.

Chapter 1: Beginnings in Baden

1. At the time Dowling wrote this letter, he was completing his first year of the Jesuit novitiate. Anna was trying to decide whether to go to college and what she might study. Unless otherwise noted, all correspondence cited is from the Father Edward Dowling, SJ, Archive, Maryville University, St. Louis, MO.

2. Written to Anna as she was completing her first semester of college. The unabridged passage refers to "a Galileo, a Casement, a Light Brigade, a Joe Falk, a McSwiney [*sic*]." Dowling wrote those words just a few weeks after Terence MacSwiney, Lord Mayor of Cork, died a prisoner of the British, after more than two months on hunger strike. MacSwiney was revered by St. Louis's Irish community, and the local archdiocese ordered that bells be tolled in his memory for five minutes on All Souls Day, October 31, 1920. I have been unable to find out who Joe Falk was.

3. "To Hell or to Connacht" was the threat popularly believed to have been made by English military commander Oliver Cromwell against Catholic Irish during the Cromwellian war of 1649 to 1653. Catholics who escaped Cromwell's executions were forced to resettle in the provinces of Connacht or Clare, where the land was inferior to that of other parts of Ireland.

My account of the senior Edward Patrick Dowling and his tale-spinning comes from a 1961 essay that Father Ed's niece Mary Dowling wrote about her grandfather, "The Storyteller." It is in the archive of the Society of the Sacred Heart in St. Louis among the papers of Father Ed's sister, also named Mary Dowling, who was a religious sister of that congregation. All the quotations from the senior Edward Patrick Dowling that follow are from this essay.

Ffarrell Dowling's story is mentioned in Rhea Felknor's article "Glad Gethsemane: The Story of Father Ed Dowling, SJ," *Voice of St. Jude* (June 1960): 14–19, at 15. According to a letter of Edward Dowling, SJ, Ffarrell's last name was actually spelled Dooleing or Dowleing. Edward Dowling, letter to Collins Healy, October 31, 1956.

4. Felknor, "Glad Gethsemane," 15.

5. Felknor, "Glad Gethsemane," 15.

6. Mary Louise Adams, "Father Dowling Remembered," *Dowling Journal* 1 (Fall 1985), 3–11, at 3; accessed at the Jesuit Archives & Research Center, St. Louis, MO.

Adams (d. 2008) knew Father Ed during his life as a Jesuit. Some years after his death, she came to manage the Dowling Archive at Maryville University. During that time, in the 1970s and the 1980s, she collected stories about Dowling's life from people who knew him, some of which she published in the lone issue of the *Dowling Journal* and some of which survive in unpublished notes in the archive.

7. Fitzgerald, *The Soul of Sponsorship*, 13. Fitzgerald attributes this anecdote to Mary Louise Adams in an interview given to Jim Egan, SJ, who was collecting information on Dowling for an intended biography.

8. Unless otherwise noted, details of the life of Father Ed's grandfather Edward Dowling are taken from William Hyde and Howard L. Conard, eds., *Encyclopedia of the History of St. Louis*, vol. 1 (New York: Southern History Co., 1899), 593–94.

9. Paul Dowling (nephew of Father Ed), email to author, January 18, 2021.

10. Edward Dowling, SJ, letter to John G. Scott, September 8, 1958, 1.

11. The 1854 date for Grandfather Edward Dowling's arrival in St. Louis is from his entry in Hyde and Conard, *Encyclopedia of the History of St. Louis*; however, an obituary of his son Edward Patrick Dowling (Father Ed's father) dates the senior Dowling's arrival to 1851. See "Edward P. Dowling Dies at 84; Retired Merchant," *St. Louis Post-Dispatch*, March 27, 1956, 26. Information concerning Thomas Donnelly comes from Regina Donlon, *German and Irish Immigrants in the Midwestern United States, 1850–1900* (Cham, Switzerland: Palgrave Macmillan, 2018), 111. Donlon cites Hyde and Conard, *Encyclopedia of the History of St. Louis*, vol. 1, 590.

12. Hyde and Conard, eds., *Encyclopedia of the History of St. Louis*, vol. 1, 594.

13. Hyde and Conard, eds., *Encyclopedia of the History of St. Louis*, vol. 1, 594.

14. This story comes from local historian William Barnaby Faherty, SJ, who does not give a source. See William Barnaby Faherty, *The St. Louis Irish: An Unmatched Celtic Community* (St. Louis: Missouri Historical Society Press, 2001), 93. Faherty refers to the pastor as Father Peter Wigger, but other sources show that it was Peter's brother Herman; see Mary Constance Smith, *Our Pastors in Calvary: Biographical Sketches of Parish Priests in St. Louis 1854–1924* (St. Louis: Blackwell Wielandy, 1924), 59.

15. Faherty, *St. Louis Irish*, 93. Father Ed's nephew Paul Dowling confirmed to me that Edward Dowling did object to Wigger's prayers for Prussia and was a key figure in persuading Kenrick to establish Our Lady of Mount Carmel. Paul Dowling, email to author, January 18, 2021.

Regarding Mount Carmel's location: although the church's original location's mailing address was 8333 Halls Ferry Road, where its rectory looked out over an expansive front lawn, the building was actually situated at 8308 Church Road. For comparison, Holy Cross was about 350 yards away at 8115 Church Road. Between the two churches, and slightly closer to Mount Carmel, lived the Dowlings at 8224 Church Road. See Sanborn Map Co., "St. Louis, Missouri, 1908 October, sheet 108, Volume Eleven," online at Digital Library, University of Missouri, dl.mospace.umsystem.edu/mu/islandora/object/ mu%3A145117.

16. The land managed by Father Ed's father included some businesses, which perhaps explains why the Jesuit modestly said his father ran a corner grocery store. This information comes from a note in the Dowling Archive, handwritten in the early 1980s by the archive's then-librarian Mary Louise Adams on the manuscript of an article she wrote on Father Ed's childhood, "A Boyhood in Baden."

17. "Crowned Kings of Kerry Patch," *St. Louis Post-Dispatch*, March 22, 1896, 35.

18. "Death of James Cullinane," *St. Louis Post-Dispatch*, December 16, 1891, 6. In using his power to help others less fortunate, Cullinane resembled Frank Skeffington,

the hero of Edwin O'Connor's 1956 novel *The Last Hurrah*, which would become a favorite of Father Ed's.

19. Adams, "Father Dowling Remembered," 3. One of Father Ed's favorite sports memories was watching two of his Cullinane cousins take part in the Christian Brothers College High School team's soccer game against Illinois University.

20. Adams, "Boyhood in Baden."

21. Adams, "Father Dowling Remembered," 4.

22. Adams, "Boyhood in Baden."

23. Dowling's paper, "My Literary Autobiography," which appears to have been written during the 1921–22 school year, is in the Dowling Archive at Maryville University and is the source for all my references to Father Ed's early literary interests, unless otherwise noted.

24. Sam Lambert, "Father Edward Dowling: A Modern Saint?" *Jesuit Bulletin* (October 1970), 13.

25. Bill W., *My First Forty Years* (Center City, MN: Hazelden, 2000), Kindle ed., loc. 257.

26. Edward Dowling, SJ, "Some Notes Taken from a Cana Conference Conducted by the Rev. Edward Dowling, SJ, November 28, 1952" (photocopied notes distributed by Cana Conference of Chicago), 12.

27. Adams, "Excerpts from Letters Home," 8.

28. Dickson Terry, "Friend of People with Problems," *St. Louis Post-Dispatch*, April 17, 1960, 1H.

29. Dowling, "My Literary Autobiography."

30. Library of Congress, "Murder of Stanford White and the First 'Trial of the Century,'" online at guides.loc.gov/chronicling-america-stanford-white-murder. Since Eddie and his family enjoyed researching their family tree—years later, he would be thrilled to learn that actor Eddie Dowling was a cousin—his interest in the Thaw case likely intensified when the judge was named for the second trial: a New Yorker named Victor James Dowling.

31. William Barnaby Faherty, SJ, *Dream by the River: Two Centuries of St. Louis Catholicism* (St. Louis: Archdiocese of St. Louis, 1997), 94.

32. Dowling, "My Literary Autobiography," 2.

33. Humphrey J. Desmond, "Our Press 50 Years Ago," *The Tablet* (Brooklyn, NY), July 5, 1930, 4.

34. D. S. Phelan, *Western Watchman*, May 18, 1893, quoted in Faherty, *Dream by the River*, 94.

35. "Dancing Tango Is Doing God's Work, Priest Declares," *St. Louis Post-Dispatch*, January 3, 1914, 1.

36. "Kaiser Don't Like Tango," *Marysville Evening Democrat*, 5.

37. Concerning Verdun, see "Puts Ban on Tango," *Montpelier Morning Journal*,

December 30, 1913, 4; concerning Nashville, see "No Absolution for Tango, Says Bishop," *Washington Times*, August 5, 1913, 4.

38. "Pope Denounces the 'New Paganism,'" *The New York Times*, January 16, 1914.

39. "Dancing Tango Is Doing God's Work, Priest Declares," *St. Louis Post-Dispatch*, January 3, 1914, 1.

40. Dowling, "My Literary Autobiography," 2–3.

41. Edward Dowling, SJ, from the LP record *Voice of Father Dowling: Selections from an Early Cana Conference* (The Mary Shop [private pressing], 1962). Dowling gave this talk in about 1947.

Chapter 2: A Distant Call

1. At the time of Edward's letter, Mary had recently entered the novitiate of the Religious of the Sacred Heart.

2. Edward Dowling, SJ, letter to Mary Dowling, February 20–April 9, 1922, 3. Edward began the letter on February 20 and wrote at intervals until he completed it on April 9.

3. For general information on this period in the life of St. Louis University and St. Louis Academy, see Gilbert J. Garraghan, *The Jesuits of the Middle United States*, vol. 3 (New York: America Press, 1938), 435–46.

4. Dowling, "My Literary Autobiography," 3. The course was taught by Urban H. Killacky, SJ.

5. Terry, "Friend of People with Problems."

6. Edward Dowling, SJ, to Mary Dowling, February 20–April 9, 1922, 3–4.

7. Terry, "Friend of People with Problems."

8. St. Louis University, *Archive 1916* (yearbook), 140–41, online at digital collections.slu.edu. This 1916 university yearbook included a special tribute to the 1914 high-school team. The Undergrads' lone defeat was in their much-anticipated final game of the season, against the visiting Western Military Academy team.

9. "Undergrads Ball Team Hustling for O'Brien," *St. Louis Globe-Democrat*, March 30, 1915, 11.

10. Father Aloysius McCormick, SJ, quoted in "Assumption Day at Nazareth Convent," *Concordia Empire* (Concordia, KS), August 19, 1915, 3.

11. Edward Dowling, SJ, to Mary Dowling, February 20–April 9, 1922, 4. I have guessed at Dowling's words; his letter relates only McCormick's side of the conversation.

12. Edward Dowling, SJ, to Mary Dowling, February 20–April 9, 1922, 4.

13. The résumé that Father Ed used for publicity purposes during his years at The Queen's Work listed his years of summer factory work as 1913–1916. However,

his Jesuit personnel record lists the dates of his work as a "factory hand" as 1912–1918. It seems that the best way to reconcile the two ranges of dates is to assume either that the Jesuit personnel record is inaccurate or that Dowling worked only occasionally at the factory in 1912 (when he would have been only thirteen) and during 1917–1918.

Additionally, according to a note in the Dowling Archive by archivist Mary Louise Adams, Edward Dowling wrote his brother Paul in a letter dated October 27, 1925, that he worked not only at Star Bucket Pump but also at a factory that made screws. I have not located the original letter.

14. See Megan Cotner et al., National Register of Historic Places Registration Form, "Star Bucket Pump Company Building," 2012, 8–12, online at https://mostateparks.com/sites/mostateparks/files/Star%20Bucket%20Pump%20Co.%20Bldg.pdf.

15. Paul Murphy Dowling is the son of Paul Vincent Dowling, who was Father Ed's youngest brother, and a great-nephew of the other Paul Dowling mentioned above—Paul M. Dowling, who was Father Ed's uncle and a co-owner of Star Bucket Pump.

16. Paul Murphy Dowling, email to author, January 27, 2021.

17. Paul Murphy Dowling, January 27, 2021.

18. Paul Murphy Dowling, January 27, 2021.

19. Edward Dowling, SJ, address to Alcoholics Anonymous 1955 International Convention, in *Pass It On: A Brief History of A.A.* (New York: A.A. World Services, 1985 [originally published 1957], 258.

20. Garraghan, *Jesuits of the Middle United States*, vol. 3, 449–50.

21. John L. McKenzie, *Did I Say That?* (Chicago: Thomas More Press, 1973), 212.

22. William R. Bernard, "Memoirs of an Alumnus," St. Mary's Priory, online at stmarys-p.prod.fsspx.org/en/memoirs-alumnus. Although Bernard attended St. Mary's College from 1927 to 1931, his recollections comport with contemporary newspaper accounts from Dowling's time that tell of major-league teams playing at the college. His story appears on the website of the Society of St. Pius X, which now owns the former site of St. Mary's College.

23. Puggy's love of sleeping late and eating candy are evident in the diary he kept during his time at St. Mary's.

Chapter 3: Problems on the Prairie

1. Dowling, "Diary at St. Mary's," September 9, 1915. In the diary entry, Puggy indicates that he was impressed to learn that Woods was still alive. I am presuming that Dowling's father was the source of the tales Puggy had heard, since the elder Dowling was a St. Mary's alumnus and enjoyed telling stories about days gone by.

2. B. M. Kirke, "'Pat' Woods Dead," *St. Mary's Star* (St. Mary's, KS), December 14, 1916, 5.

3. Thomas J. Brennan, "Pat Woods Is 110," *St. Mary's Star* (St. Mary's, KS), September 30, 1915, 4.

4. See, for example, Dowling's 1943 essay "How to Enjoy Being Miserable," in which he describes how self-identification with Jesus's mental sufferings in Gethsemane enables "the closest approach to God." The essay is reprinted in Fitzgerald, *The Soul of Sponsorship*, 128–30 (which mistakenly dates it to 1954, when it was republished).

5. Edward Dowling, letter to Bill Wilson, July 24, 1952, and Edward Dowling, letter to Bill Wilson, December 14, 1959.

6. Dowling, "My Literary Autobiography," 4.

7. See John L. McKenzie's memories of St. Mary's study hall in John L. McKenzie, *Did I Say That?* (Chicago: Thomas More Press, 1973), 213. McKenzie began his studies at St. Mary's in 1924, six years after Dowling left the school. Given that St. Mary's was known for maintaining its traditions, it is unlikely that the conditions he describes were significantly different in Dowling's time.

8. "Mr. Walsh"—John Walsh, SJ, one of two prefects of the Senior Division— targeted Puggy at least twice for unofficial punishments. Puggy wrote that on October 1, Walsh "suggested" his schoolmates put him "over the rail"—some sort of embarrassment that was likely painful. (In his diary, he used "suggested" in a wry fashion when he meant to say "urged.") On October 4, Walsh egged boys to "roughhouse" Puggy. His urgings do not appear to have been in a spirit of fun; the boys relished the times when he was away from his post. Dowling, "Diary at St. Mary's," October 1, 1915, and October 4, 1915.

9. John J. Egan, "Remarks of Msgr. John J. Egan: Msgr. Ignatius McDermott Receives the First Rev. Dowling Award," March 12, 1988, 8, Jesuit Archive & Research Center.

10. "St. Mary's College Notes," *The Catholic Tribune* (St. Joseph, MO), April 15, 1916, 5.

11. Charles DeMotte, "Baseball and Freemasonry in American Culture," in *The Cooperstown Symposium on Baseball and American Culture, 2001*, ed. William Simon (Jefferson, NC: McFarland & Co., 2002), 289. DeMotte notes that the White Sox had close ties with St. Mary's; team owner Charles Comiskey was a graduate of the school.

12. After Dowling's death, Ray Schmandt told a reporter that Dowling declined an offer of a White Sox tryout. I am assuming that the offer took place after this game, as it is the only occasion I have found on which Dowling had contact with anyone associated with the team. However, the offer could have come at a different time. See Dickson Terry, "Friend of People with Problems."

13. W. M. B., "St. Mary's College Notes," *St. Mary's Star* (St. Mary's, KS), June 8, 1916, 4.

14. Ross Klingensmith, "Lawrence Francis O'Toole," *The Dial* (St. Mary's College), 430.

15. W. M. B., "St. Mary's College Notes," *St. Mary's Star*, June 8, 1916.

16. "St. Mary's College Notes," *St. Mary's Star*, June 8, 1916.

17. "Lawrence Francis O'Toole," 430.

18. "St. Mary's College Notes," *St. Mary's Star*, June 8, 1916.

19. St. Mary's Senior Yard Prefect Diary, June 1, 1916.

20. "Lawrence Francis O'Toole," 430.

21. See Dowling's letter to Tony Harig in chapter 4.

22. This information comes from the vocation story that Edward, as a Jesuit scholastic, related in his letter to his sister Mary. Edward Dowling, SJ, to Mary Dowling, February 20–April 9, 1922, 4. Edward wrote that his father wrote to him "at end of 4th High at St. Mary's." He didn't specify the career his father recommended, but Star Bucket Pump and the family's real-estate business are the most obvious possibilities.

23. Edward Dowling, SJ, to Mary Dowling, February 20–April 9, 1922, 4.

24. Gloria Lasker, "St. Louis University Presents 'A Tribute to Achievement': Rev. Edward Dowling, SJ," unpublished radio script, 2. Maryville Archive. The program, which aired November 19, 1950, on WEW, dramatized events from Dowling's life. Dowling approved the script, which appears to be drawn from answers he gave to questions about his personal history.

25. Edward Dowling, SJ, to Mary Dowling, February 20–April 9, 1922, 4.

26. Edward Dowling, SJ, to Mary Dowling, February 20–April 9, 1922, 4–5.

27. "Diary of the Prefect of Studies, 1904–1921," unpublished MS at Jesuit Archives & Research Center, 88.

28. "Diary of the Prefect of Studies," 88.

29. "Diary of the Prefect of Studies," 88.

30. Edward Dowling, SJ, to Mary Dowling, February 20–April 9, 1922, 5–6.

31. See Martha Gruening and W. E. B. Du Bois, "The Massacre of East St. Louis," *The Crisis*, September 1917, 219–38.

32. See Gruening and Du Bois, "The Massacre of East St. Louis," and Tim O'Neil, "Race Hatred, Workforce Tensions Explode in East St. Louis in 1917," *St. Louis Post-Dispatch*, July 2, 2020, on stltoday.com.

33. Dowling, "Diary at St. Mary's," December 13, 1915.

34. Dowling, "Diary at St. Mary's," section on "The Holidays" (i.e., Christmas break, 1915).

35. Father Ed's nephew Paul Dowling told me of a time when he saw his uncle pointedly refuse a lunch invitation from a racist male in-law who was trying to ingratiate himself with the priest (see chapter 15). Similarly, his niece Mary Dowling recalled to me that, at some point during the 1950s, when she heard her aunt (an in-law of Father Ed's) make racist remarks, she thought about how appalled Father Ed would have been if he had been present. Paul Dowling, interview with author, April 30, 2020; Mary Dowling, telephone conversation with author, September 22, 2021.

36. "Segregation to Be Fought in Courts; Won by 34,000," *St. Louis Post-Dispatch*, March 1, 1916, 1.

37. A photograph of the pledge appears in Jeffrey H. Smith, *From Corps to CORE: The Life of John P. Markoe: Soldier, Priest, and Pioneer Activist*, Midwest Jesuit Historical Series, vol. 1 (Florissant, MO: St. Stanislaus Historical Museum, 1977), 59. John Markoe, SJ, would eventually become an important link in the chain of connections that would bring Dowling into friendship with Bill W. (see chapter 9).

38. Edward Dowling, SJ, to Mary Dowling, February 20–April 9, 1922, 5.

39. The 1916 directory for the Society of Jesus's Missouri Province lists Dowd as the *Dial*'s faculty advisor. Edmund J. Fortman mentions his Reds fandom in *Lineage: A Biographical History of the Chicago Province* (Chicago: Loyola University Press, 1987), 166.

40. Edward Dowling, SJ, to William Dowd, SJ, January 20, 1959. By then, Dowd had become a world-renowned biblical scholar. He composed the translation of the book of Daniel that appeared in the original 1970 edition of the *New American Bible*.

41. Edward Dowling, SJ, to Mary Dowling, February 20–April 9, 1922, 5.

Chapter 4: The Reluctant Soldier

1. Mary had just entered the Religious of the Sacred Heart at the time Edward gave her that advice.

2. Bernard M. Kirke, "St. Mary's College Notes," *St. Mary's Star*, December 20, 1917, 5.

3. Edward Dowling, SJ, to Mary Dowling, RSCJ, June 1, 1921, excerpted in Mary Louise Adams, "Excerpts from Letters Home by Edward Dowling, SJ," unpublished MS, 6.

4. "St. Mary's College Notes," *St. Mary's Star*, March 14, 1918, 3.

5. Leo H. Mullany, SJ, *The Dream of the Soldier Saint* (Chicago: Loyola University Press, 1915), 8.

6. Daniel A. Lord, SJ, *Played by Ear* (Chicago: Loyola University Press, 1956), 266.

7. Dowling, "My Literary Autobiography," 4–5.

8. Lasker, "St. Louis University Presents 'A Tribute to Achievement,'" 2.

9. Lasker, "St. Louis University Presents 'A Tribute to Achievement,'" 2, and Dowling, "My Literary Autobiography," 5.

10. "Globe-Democrats Defeat Republic Ball Nine, 8 to 5," *St. Louis Globe-Democrat*, July 30, 1918, 7.

11. Lasker, "St. Louis University Presents 'A Tribute to Achievement,'" 2.

12. Adams, "Excerpts from Letters Home," 2. "Flo" was almost certainly Florence Hulling, who was then in her mid-twenties and a waitress at Childs. In decades to come, as owner of Miss Hulling's Cafeteria, she would become one of the most successful independent restaurateurs in the country. See Harley Hammerman, "Lost Tables: Miss Hulling's," losttables.com/hullings/hullings.htm.

13. Edward Dowling, SJ, to Mary Dowling, February 20–April 9, 1922, 6.

14. Daniel A. Lord, SJ, *Played by Ear* (Chicago: Loyola University Press, 1956), 175.

15. D. S. McKinsey et al., "The 1918 Influenza in Missouri: Centennial Remembrance of the Crisis," *Missouri Medicine* 115, no. 4 (2018), ncbi.nlm.nih.gov/pmc/articles/PMC6140242/.

16. "All Class Room Work Suspended at Washington U.," *St. Louis Star*, October 9, 1918, 1.

17. D. S. McKinsey et al., "The 1918 Influenza in Missouri."

18. "Four Records Are Shattered in Swim Races at Fairground," *St. Louis Globe-Democrat*, August 17, 1918, 4. This appears to be the only extant newspaper record of James Dowling from his lifetime. Although it could conceivably refer to another person of the same name, the age bracket for the competition—eleven to fifteen—makes it likely that it refers to Edward's brother, who was six weeks shy of fifteen at the time.

19. "St. Mary's College Notes," *St. Mary's Star*, October 17, 1918, 1.

20. St. Mary's Senior Yard Prefect Diary, October 13, 1918.

21. Per St. Mary's Senior Yard Prefect Diary, October 21, 1918, reporting on James's death, which says James had been ill for a week.

22. St. Mary's Senior Yard Prefect Diary, October 17, 1918.

23. St. Mary's Senior Yard Prefect Diary, October 21, 1918.

24. John F. O'Connor, "The Jesuits in the Kaw Valley" (unpublished MS, 1925), 672.

25. St. Mary's Senior Yard Prefect Diary, October 21, 1918.

26. St. Mary's Prefect of Studies Diary, October 21, 1918, Jesuit Archive & Research Center.

27. Vincent A. Burns, letter to Edward Dowling, October 21, 1918. Burns and Dowling remained close friends for the rest of Dowling's life.

28. Anna preserved the laminated fragments in an envelope among Father Ed's files; a notation that she typed on the outside of the envelope is dated 1959.

29. "James J. Dowling Dead," *St. Mary's Star*, October 31, 1918, 1.

30. Adams, "Father Dowling Remembered," 3–4.

31. Dowling, "Diary at St. Mary's," 17.

32. "Closing Order in Effect to Curb Influenza," *St. Louis Star*, October 8, 1918, Night Edition, 1.

33. St. Mary's Senior Yard Prefect Diary, October 14, 1918.

34. O'Connor, "The Jesuits in the Kaw Valley," 671–72.

35. Puggy's existential wrestling is evident in his letter to Anthony Harig, which is quoted later in this chapter.

36. St. Mary's Prefect of Studies Diary, October 21, 1918, Jesuit Archives & Research Center.

37. Edward Dowling, SJ, to Mary Dowling, RSCJ, January 21–February 7, 1931 (the letter was begun January 21 and completed February 7).

38. Edward Dowling, SJ, from his quotation for the book jacket of *Alcoholics Anonymous* (New York: Works Publishing, 1946). The quotation first appeared on the tenth printing of the book's first edition.

39. Lasker, "St. Louis University Presents 'A Tribute to Achievement': Rev. Edward Dowling, SJ," 3.

40. Lord, *Played by Ear*, 175. Unless noted otherwise, the remaining SATC references are likewise from *Played by Ear*, 175–78.

41. Adams, "Excerpts from Letters Home by Edward Dowling, SJ," 3.

42. Edward Dowling, SJ, to Mary Dowling, February 20–April 9, 1922, 8.

43. Edward Dowling, SJ, to Mary Dowling, February 20–April 9, 1922, 7–8.

44. Edward Dowling, SJ, to Mary Dowling, February 20–April 9, 1922, 7.

45. Edward Dowling, SJ, to Mary Dowling, February 20–April 9, 1922, 8–9.

46. "Printers Defeat Editorial Team with Score 13–6," *St. Louis Globe-Democrat*, August 8, 1919, 11.

47. The letter on the St. Louis University President's stationery, dated September 3, 1919, is in the Dowling Archive. I am assuming that the letter, which refers to Dowling's examination by four Jesuit priests, was given to Dowling immediately after the examination took place, so that he could deliver it to Archbishop Glennon. However, the examination could have been done at some point prior to the letter's composition.

48. Edward Dowling, SJ, to Mary Dowling, February 20–April 9, 1922, 8.

49. *Jebbie*, which Puggy shortens to *Jeb*, is popular slang for *Jesuit*.

50. Only three months earlier, John Alcock and Arthur Brown had made the first transatlantic flight.

51. Edward Dowling to Anthony J. Harig, ca. September 18, 1919, 2–3. Although the letter is undated, it is possible to date it to about September 18, 1919, because Dowling says he is responding to Harig's letter of "the 16th" and he mentions the Cincinnati Reds' National League pennant win under manager Pat Moran, which took place on September 16, 1919.

52. Edward Dowling, SJ, to Mary Dowling, February 20–April 9, 1922, 9.

53. Edward Dowling, SJ, to Mary Dowling, February 20–April 9, 1922, 9–10. Puggy seems a little confused about the timeline. If he stayed at Kinealy's house two

nights before he entered the novitiate, as he says in his letter, then he would have entered the novitiate one day after breakfast, not two days.

Merkle did not last in the Jesuits beyond the novitiate. He became a doctor, married, and fathered three sons.

54. Terry, "Friend of People with Problems."

55. Edward Dowling, SJ, to Mary Dowling, February 20–April 9, 1922, 10.

56. Terry, "Friend of People with Problems." The article quotes Touhill as saying that Dowling's only luggage was the trousers, but it seems likely that he would have brought the letter as well.

Chapter 5: Darkness and Light

1. Dowling, "My Literary Autobiography," 5. "Canonical impediments" refers to things that might disqualify a man for the priesthood according to canon law. The passage shows Dowling's sense of humor as well as his honesty. Instead of portraying the novitiate as it is normally portrayed—a time when the novice hopes to confirm a call to his religious and (usually) priestly vocation—he suggests he spent it trying to *avoid* his vocation. As with all good wit, his lighthearted gibe at himself points to a deeper truth.

2. Edward Dowling, SJ, to Mary Dowling, RSCJ, May 7, 1930, 1. He is referring to a 1553 letter of Ignatius of Loyola that is the definitive document on how obedience is to be observed in the Society of Jesus.

3. Edward Dowling, SJ, quoted in James A. Egan, SJ, letter to Ernest Kurtz, July 7, 1985, 11. I have not been able to locate the original text of the talk from which this quote was taken, which Fitzgerald in *The Soul of Sponsorship* says was delivered April 18, 1944.

James A. Egan, SJ (1935–2008), interviewed people who knew Dowling and did research in the Dowling Archive during the mid-1980s, apparently in hope of publishing a book or articles. Although he did not succeed in publishing on Dowling's life, he shared some of the fruits of his research in his letter to Kurtz and in an unpublished 1986 manuscript, "Worthy to Be Remembered," that is at the Jesuit Archives and Research Center.

4. Bill W., "Alcoholics Anonymous—Beginnings and Growth," in Bill W., *Three Talks to Medical Societies by Bill W., Co-Founder of Alcoholics Anonymous* (New York: A.A. World Services, 2013 [reprint edition]), 11.

5. James A. Egan, SJ, was, to my knowledge, the first to have this insight concerning the source of Dowling's empathy with A.A. members. Egan to Kurtz, July 7, 1985, 11.

6. In a 1943 article, Dowling speaks of how "God's suffering and mine" are bridged by the "union of suffering" that St. Paul describes in Colossians 1:24 when he speaks of rejoicing in filling up the sufferings of Christ. See Edward Dowling, SJ, "How to Enjoy Being Miserable," *The Queen's Work* (December 1943), reprinted

with slight emendations (as it appeared in a 1954 republication) in Fitzgerald, *The Soul of Sponsorship*, 128–30.

7. Fitzgerald, *The Soul of Sponsorship*, 14.

8. New arrivals at Florissant went through a brief period of postulancy—usually one week—before receiving the cassock.

9. *Catholic Telegraph* (Cincinnati, OH), October 2, 1919, 1. It was not unheard-of for the Society of Jesus to send out press releases boasting of men giving up enviable careers to enter the Jesuit novitiate. After John Markoe entered Florissant on February 18, 1917, the Society sent out a similar announcement describing him as a "West Point football star."

One of the indications that Dowling had nothing to do with this item, besides its being highly unlikely that the Jesuits would have let him know they considered him a person of importance, is that he never used the suffix *Jr.*

10. Edward Dowling, SJ, letter to Mary Dowling, RSCJ, undated; a later hand dates it "Summer 1930."

11. Most of the information presented here on the Florissant novitiate is from an unsigned article written by Edward Dowling, SJ, himself: "The Training of a Jesuit," *The Jesuit Bulletin* 1, no. 1 (March 1922): 1–4. (In a letter to his sister Mary [December 2, 1931] he states that he wrote the article.) Other information is garnered from Daniel A. Lord, SJ's recollections in *Played by Ear* of his experiences there from 1909 to 1911 (exactly ten years before Dowling's novitiate); Joseph T. McGloin, SJ's account of his experiences there from 1936 to 1938 in *I'll Die Laughing!* (Milwaukee: Bruce Publishing Co., 1955); and John J. O'Malley, SJ's study of the Missouri Province's other novitiate (in Milford, Ohio), "How We Were: Life in a Jesuit Novitiate, 1946–1948," *Studies in the Spirituality of Jesuits* 51, no. 2 (Spring 2019), 1–46. (There were few significant changes in the customs of Midwest Jesuit novitiates during the first half of the twentieth century.) Information on the Rules (such as modesty of the eyes and the ban on touching) is from August Coemans, SJ, *Commentary on the Rules of the Society of Jesus*, tr. Matthew Germing, SJ (St. Louis: Missouri Province Educational Institute, 1948). It is McGloin who mentions that only Latin conversation was permitted outside of recreation (*I'll Die Laughing!*, 27).

12. McGloin, *I'll Die Laughing!*, 27.

13. When Dowling looked back on his novitiate, he was grateful for having had the opportunity to practice patience with the few "socially gauche and difficult characters" he encountered. Edward Dowling, SJ, to Mary Dowling, RSCJ, August 13, 1930, 2.

14. McGloin, *I'll Die Laughing!*, 26.

15. Lord, *Played by Ear*, 134.

16. "The Training of a Jesuit," 3.

17. "The Training of a Jesuit," 3.

18. The play on the word "society" is clearly intentional; it implies that the novice wishes to become closer to Christ by following a divine call to vow himself to God through the Society of Jesus.

19. "The Training of a Jesuit," 2. Although it is common today for practitioners of Ignatian spirituality to use terms borrowed from the psychological field, Dowling's snappy, journalistic précis of the aims of the novitiate's methods—self-examination, self-mastery, and self-realization—is progressive for its time. It indicates his budding interest in psychology, which would cause problems for him in the Society (see chapter 6).

20. "The Training of a Jesuit," 3.

21. Edward Dowling, SJ, to Mary Dowling, February 20–April 9, 1922, 10.

22. O'Malley, "How We Were," 27. The novices who knelt were chosen on a rotating basis.

23. O'Malley, "How We Were," 26. Admonition partners were likewise chosen on a rotating basis.

24. Father Daniel A. Lord, SJ, wrote of Florissant's Jesuit brothers, "I have not praise sufficient to their virtues and obscurely heroic lives." Lord, *Played by Ear*, 122.

25. I have added the word "don't," as the context suggests Thirolf intended it.

26. The remainder of this last sentence is illegible due to the frayed condition of the note.

27. Dowling to Harig, 3. See chapter 4 for a fuller quotation of this letter.

28. Edward Dowling, talk to Alcoholics Anonymous group (location unknown), April 18, 1944. Quoted in Egan to Kurtz, July 7, 1985, 11, Dowling Archive.

29. Edward Dowling, SJ, to Mary Dowling, February 20–April 9, 1922, 15.

30. "The Training of a Jesuit," 2.

31. This quote comes from Elizabeth Mulligan's biography of Dowling's fellow novice Dismas Clark, SJ; it is not from Clark himself but an anonymous source who is identified as a contemporary of Clark's in the novitiate. Elizabeth Mulligan, *Hoodlum's Priest* (St. Louis: Sunrise Publishing, 1979), 19.

32. "The Training of a Jesuit," 2.

33. Edward Dowling, SJ, letter to Anna Dowling, July 4, 1920, 2.

34. Dowling is using *versatile* here in its less common meaning of "variable" or "fluctuating."

35. It is intriguing that Dowling lists "physical weakness" among his characteristics at a time prior to the onset of his debilitating arthritis, when he was continuing to engage in athletic activities such as baseball and soccer. According to James A. Egan, SJ, Dowling was remembered as the best soccer player of his novitiate class. So his reference to physical weakness likely refers not to lack of ability but rather to vulnerability to temptations such as overeating and oversleeping, as well as his desire for cigarettes, which were prohibited in the novitiate. Egan's comment is in Egan to Kurtz, July 7, 1985.

36. Edward Dowling, SJ, handwritten note in pencil, undated; a later hand added the date "1919."

37. The *Suscipe* of St. Ignatius Loyola, as quoted by Edward Dowling in "Depth of A.A." (later reprinted under Dowling's original title "Three Dimensions of A.A."),

Grapevine (July 1955). Unless otherwise note, all *Grapevine* quotes are taken from the online versions at aagrapevine.org.

38. Dowling, "Depth of A.A." In the *Grapevine* article, Dowling writes that he remained afraid of that prayer until an A.A. member taught him how to properly pray it (see chapter 14).

39. Edward Dowling, SJ, to Mary Dowling, February 20–April 9, 1922, 15–17, with paragraph break added. This section was written on March 20. The tenderness that Dowling shows for his sister in this letter is touching, as is the great respect he shows for her intelligence. She was fifteen at the time.

40. This information comes from James A. Egan's letter to Ernest Kurtz. Although Egan names the friend who visited as "Michael," it was almost certainly Henry Kinealy, whose newspaper byline was Mike Henry (see chapter 4).

42. For the context of Dowling's "If you can name it" comment to Wilson, see chapter 9.

43. "We Agnostics" is the title of chapter 4 of *Alcoholics Anonymous*, popularly known as the Big Book, which is the basic text for A.A.

44. Edward Dowling, SJ, in *Alcoholics Anonymous Comes of Age*, 255–56.

45. Edward Dowling, SJ, to Mary Dowling, February 20–April 9, 1922.

46. Jesuit lay brothers do their tertianship after having completed their studies and several years of work.

47. Edward Dowling, SJ, to Anna Dowling, October 1, 1920, excerpted in Adams, "Excerpts from Letters Home by Edward Dowling, S.J.," 4.

48. Ignatius Loyola, Spiritual Exercises no. 100, Louis J. Puhl, SJ, translation. I have amended Puhl's translation from "*Following of Christ*" to "*Imitation of Christ*"; both titles refer to the same book. Puhl's translation is online at spex.ignatianspirituality.com/SpiritualExercises/Puhl.

49. Thomas à Kempis, *Imitation of Christ*, Everyman's Library edition (New York: E.P. Dutton, & Co., 1910), 2. An indication of how Dowling reacted to these words of the *Imitation* can be found in a pair of sermons he delivered circa 1935. In each of them, he draws heavily upon the *Imitation* as he warns against the "intellectual fetishism" that marred the Catholic educational programs of his time. The manuscripts of these sermons, "John 8:12" and "Learn of Me, Because I Am Meek and Humble of Heart," are in the Maryville Archive.

50. Edward Dowling, SJ, to Anna Dowling, June 19, 1921, 2.

51. Edward Dowling, SJ, to Anna Dowling, June 19, 1921, 4.

52. Edward Dowling, SJ, to Anna Dowling, June 19, 1921, 2–3.

53. Kempis, *Imitation of Christ*, 219. In the Everyman's Library edition that Dowling likely used in his first reading of the *Imitation*, those words appear in part 3, chapter 61, which is titled "That We Ought to Deny Ourselves and Follow Christ by the Cross."

54. Edward Dowling, talk to Alcoholics Anonymous group, April 18, 1944.

55. Dowling, "Learn of Me, Because I Am Meek and Humble of Heart," 1. I have made minor corrections to Dowling's punctuation and grammar.

56. Dowling, "Learn of Me, Because I Am Meek and Humble of Heart," 1.

57. Dowling, "Learn of Me, Because I Am Meek and Humble of Heart," 2.

58. Edward Dowling, SJ, letter to Mary Jane [last name unknown], December 23, 1959. After writing those words, Dowling added a couple of pieces of advice tailored to the woman's particular situation as an alcoholic:

"The Alcoholics Anonymous twelve steps is an experimental proof of the truth that you were taught as a child.

"Don't despise small gains."

The last sentence may be Dowling's paraphrase of Zechariah 4:10: "For who hath despised the day of small things? for they shall rejoice...." (KJV).

59. Edward Dowling, SJ, to Annie Cullinane Dowling, July 6, 1921, excerpted in Adams, "Excerpts from Letters Home," 10.

60. Edward Dowling, SJ, to Annie Cullinane Dowling, July 6, 1921, in Adams, "Excerpts from Letters Home," 10.

61. Edward Dowling, SJ, *Excerpts from Talks by Father Dowling*, side B. This record was a 7-inch vinyl extended-play disc issued by Maryville College in about 1961. The particular radio discussion from which this quote was taken was likely one of his "Cana Conversations" for WEW in 1946.

62. Edward Dowling, SJ, to Annie Cullinane Dowling, July 6, 1921, in Adams, "Excerpts from Letters Home," 10.

63. In this sentence, Edward, who is clearly writing quickly, uses the abbreviation "F."; I am guessing from the context that he means "Faith."

64. The study of the Constitutions of the Society of Jesus is a key part of the modern Jesuit novitiate, but that was not the case in Dowling's time. Dowling was exposed only to the Rules of the Summary, which summarized the Constitutions, and the Common Rules, which dealt with everyday life. Both were read to novices from the reading pulpit in the refectory (dining room) at the beginning of every month. O'Malley, "How We Were," 22–23.

65. In making the League of Nations comparison, Dowling appears to be have in mind how France acted out of its own self-interest during a drawn-out dispute with England over where the boundaries of Upper Silesia should be drawn. Thus he is saying that the Society of Jesus, in claiming that the will of the Jesuit superior should be taken as the will of God, gives license to superiors who might abuse their power.

It is interesting that Dowling is up-to-date on the League of Nations controversy, as novices were denied access to newspapers. Perhaps summaries of the news were read to the novices, or perhaps his friends and relatives kept him informed. In any case, the political analogy is typical of Dowling, who saw politics simply as interpersonal relations writ large ("the art of politeness on a big scale," as he would later put it).

66. Luke 10:16.

67. See chapter 9.

68. John Henry Newman, *Meditations and Devotions of the Late Cardinal Newman: New Impression* (New York: Longmans, Green, & Co., 1916), 301. I have Americanized the spelling.

69. Edward Dowling, SJ, to Mary Dowling, RSCJ, December 2, 1931, 3.

70. After writing those words, Dowling adds, "And I have hardly ever recovered the use of my reason—thank God for that." Edward Dowling, SJ, to Mary Dowling, RSCJ, December 2, 1931, 3–4.

71. Ignatius of Loyola writes in the Spiritual Exercises (no. 146) that the exercitant should develop "a desire for insults and contempt, for from these springs humility."

72. After that sentence, Edward (with an eye to the vocation that Mary was discerning) scrawled into the margin, "Now do you see why nuns prefer bleak convents to their own fine homes?"

73. Edward Dowling, SJ, to Mary Dowling, February 20–April 9, 1922, 13–14.

Chapter 6: Becoming a Teacher

1. McGloin, *I'll Die Laughing!*, 43.

2. This information comes from a comment inserted by former Dowling Archive librarian Mary Louise Adams in a document she assembled that collected posthumous tributes to Father Ed. She wrote that Father Ed "would celebrate the anniversary date of his arthritis," which I assume means that he would remember the anniversary in his celebration of Mass. Adams had access to Dowling's card file of important dates, which has since gone missing. Mary Louise Adams, "Father Dowling, S.J., Remembered," 4.

3. Gloria Lasker, "St. Louis University Presents a Tribute to Achievement: Rev. Edward Dowling, SJ," undated final version of script for program that aired November 19, 1950; Edward Dowling, SJ, letter to Gloria Lasker, October 24, 1950. Father Dowling saw a draft of the script; his letter makes suggestions for revisions that are included in the final version of the script.

4. Lasker, "St. Louis University Presents a Tribute to Achievement," 5.

5. Edward Dowling, SJ, to Mildred Cavanaugh Diggles, 1933, quoted in Egan to Kurtz, 4.

6. During the years since Dowling's death, ankylosing spondylitis has come to be linked to a genetic mutation. However, not everyone who has the mutation will develop the disease. Some scientists believe that, in those with the mutation who do develop ankylosing spondylitis, the disease's onset is triggered by an intestinal bacterial infection.

Sadly, if the science is correct, it is highly possible that Puggy experienced an intestinal infection at Florissant that hastened his development of arthritis, as there is evidence that the seminary's water supply was highly vulnerable to bacterial contamination. Father Daniel A. Lord, SJ, who entered the novitiate ten years prior to Dowling, wrote in his autobiography, "The water supply came from our slanted roofs into vast underground cisterns; and once, during drought days, each of us young fellows was restricted to a daily washbasin of water from which all his ablutions from dawn to dawn must be taken." Lord also recounted an incident from when he was in the juniorate in which nineteen men developed an intestinal infection caused by bacteria—namely, typhoid fever—after drinking from a nearby spring that, unbeknownst to them, had been contaminated by river water due to a recent flood.

On bacterial infections and ankylosing spondylitis, see James T. Rosenbaum and Mark Asquith, "The microbiome and HLA-B27-associated acute anterior uveitis," *Nature Reviews Rheumatology* 14 (2018), nature.com/articles/s41584-018-0097-2. The Daniel A. Lord anecdotes are from *Played by Ear*, 124–25 (see also 137) and 364–65.

7. In an Easter Sunday 1926 letter to his family ("Dear Folks"), Puggy writes hopefully, "My back is better than it has been in several years and, tho I can't take liberties with it yet, still after the summer's heat I expect to be in the finest kind of shape." Three years later, he mentions in a letter to his sister Mary that he is seeing an osteopath twice a week.

8. Perhaps the Society of Jesus began to invest more heavily in Dowling's medical care in hope of strengthening him for the new responsibilities he would have upon his ordination later that year.

9. Adams, "Excerpts from Letters Home," 14. The undated letter was sent from St. Mary's College while Dowling was doing graduate studies there during 1931 through 1933.

10. Edward Dowling, SJ, to Mary Dowling, February 20–April 9, 1922, 13.

11. Edward Dowling, SJ, to Mary Dowling, February 20–April 9, 1922, 11.

12. Second Vatican Council, *Lumen Gentium* 40, online at vatican.va/archive/hist_councils/ii_vatican_council/documents/vat-ii_const_19641121_lumen-gentium_ en.html.

13. Edward Dowling, SJ, to Mary Dowling, February 20–April 9, 1922, 11.

14. Edward Dowling, SJ, to Mary Dowling, February 20–April 9, 1922, 12.

15. William Markoe, SJ, cited in Paul John Schadewald, "Remapping Race, Religion, and Community: William Markoe and the Legacy of Catholic Interracialism in St. Louis, 1900–1945," PhD diss. (Indiana University, 2003), 26.

16. John A. Wright Sr., citing an unidentified historian, in *St. Louis: Disappearing Black Communities* (Charleston, SC: Arcadia Publishing, 2004), electronic edition accessed via Google Books.

17. Garraghan, *Jesuits of the Middle United States*, vol. 3, 564; "Catholic News Items," *Catholic Tribune*, St. Joseph, MO, January 28, 1922, 6.

18. Edward Dowling, SJ, to Francis X. McMenamy, SJ, May 19, 1926.

19. "Roosevelt Bluffing on Court Issue, Father Lord Says," *St. Louis Globe-Democrat*, February 24, 1937, 5; "Irish Method of Polls Urged by Fr. Dowling," *Washington Post*, August 17, 1939, 11.

20. See chapter 15.

21. Edward Dowling, SJ, to Mary Dowling, February 20–April 9, 1922, 12.

22. Juniorate beadle's diary, October 7, 1922.

23. The Bertillon Bureau was responsible for cataloging physical information about criminal suspects.

24. The original St. Louis Police Department copy of Puggy's fingerprints is in the Dowling Archive files without any explanation of how the fingerprints came to be taken. I have assembled this account based on the fact that the date of the fingerprints coincides exactly with the date of the news story on his cousin John M. Shea. Dowling's niece Mary Dowling and his nephew Paul M. Dowling, the children of his brother Paul, have confirmed to me that this account conforms with what they recall about their uncle's personality.

25. *Okeh* was an early version of OK.

26. Edward Dowling, SJ, to Paul Vincent Dowling, June 8, 1921, 2.

27. Edward Dowling, SJ, to Mary Dowling, RSCJ, May 7, 1930.

28. Austin O'Malley to Edward Dowling, SJ; letter is undated, but Dowling wrote on it that it was sent around September 3, 1925.

29. James Joseph Walsh to Edward Dowling, SJ, September 15, 1925.

30. Edward Dowling, SJ, to Catherine Rockwood, January 8, 1958.

31. Edward Dowling, SJ, to Michael O'Connor, SJ, May 20, 1924.

32. Alcoholics Anonymous Step Twelve, "The Twelve Steps" (see appendix).

33. Edward Dowling, SJ, to James I. Shannon, SJ, January 5, 1925, 2.

34. Edward Dowling, "A.A. Steps for the Under-Privileged Non-A.A.," *Grapevine* (June 1960).

35. Edward Dowling, SJ, "A Psychological Study of the Spiritual Exercises of Saint Ignatius," 48.

36. On Catholic objections to Freud during the early 20th century, see Paula M. Kane, "Confessional and Couch: E. Boyd Barrett, Priest-Psychoanalyst," in Kyle B. Roberts and Stephen R. Schloesser, eds., *Crossings and Dwellings: Restored Jesuits, Women Religious, American Experience, 1814–2014* (Boston, MA: Brill, 2017), 409–453.

37. Dowling's mention of "Scholasticism"—that is, the Aristotelian approach to philosophy and theology of which St. Thomas Aquinas is the most eminent representative—reflects more upon his desire to win his provincial's favor than upon his actual interests. Although he respected Aquinas's intellectual authority, in his private correspondence and in the *Modern Schoolman* editorial that got him into hot water (see introduction), he tended to bristle against the limitations of the Thomist intellectual framework as it was taught in his day. In this, as in many other ways, he presaged the more open attitude of the Second Vatican Council, which—although maintaining Aquinas's pride of place—encouraged that Thomas be read in light of the biblical and patristic sources that inspired him. See Second Vatican Council, *Optatam Totius*, 16,

online at www.vatican.va/archive/hist_councils/ii_vatican_council/documents/vat-ii_
decree_19651028_optatam-totius_en.html.

38. At the time of Dowling's letter, the Sodality of Our Lady, a Jesuit apostolate,
had come under the leadership of Daniel A. Lord, SJ, who was busily revitalizing its
monthly magazine *The Queen's Work*. Among Lord's colleagues there was Puggy's
beloved St. Mary's professor Leo Mullany, SJ. It is no wonder that Puggy wanted to
work at the sodality, given that two of the Jesuits he most admired were on staff.

39. Edward Dowling, SJ, to Francis X. McMenamy, SJ, May 19, 1926, 1.

40. Dowling, "Some Notes Taken from a Cana Conference Conducted by the
Rev. Edward Dowling, SJ," 11.

41. Edward Dowling, SJ, to Anna Dowling, January 29, 1927.

42. These recollections from Joe Cahill and those that follow are presented as
they were told to James A. Egan, SJ, in 1984. Egan to Kurtz, July 7, 1985, 9–10.

43. Although Cahill assured Egan that he remembered Dowling's exact words, as
they made such a great impression upon him, it is likely that Dowling said "Jesuit"
rather than "priest." That would make more sense, given that he said, "And here I
am," since he was not yet ordained.

44. Tom Diggles, letter to Anna Dowling, May 11, 1960.

45. Today the word "sensuality" has the immediate connotation of "lust," but
that was not necessarily the case in Dowling's time. Although it is possible that
Dowling's occasional references in his notes to problems with "sensuality" or "bodily weakness" might refer to sexual attractions, the terms he uses are so general that
it is not possible to make such a conclusion with certainty. It is more likely that he is
referring to problems that he explicitly cites elsewhere as areas of personal concern,
such as his difficulty remaining awake during prayer and his attachments to cigarettes and coffee.

46. Edward Dowling, SJ, letter to Mary Dowling, undated, circa early June 1929,
emphasis in original.

47. As Robert Fitzgerald, SJ, notes, the priest "caught Dowling well but missed
his wild imagination" (*The Soul of Sponsorship*, 15).

48. Fitzgerald writes that this document, which is in the Dowling Archive at
Maryville, was written by a "Father Moran," who he says was Dowling's superior
during his three years at Loyola (*The Soul of Sponsorship*, 15). However, contemporary catalogs of the Chicago Province of the Society of Jesus indicate that there was
no Father Moran serving at Loyola at that time, neither was there a priest by such a
name in the St. Louis Province.

49. Edward Dowling, SJ, to Mary Dowling, RSCJ, July 5, 1929.

50. Edward Dowling, SJ, address at Recovery, Inc., informational event at Central
Methodist Church, Detroit, Michigan, June 4, 1954. This quote is taken from a transcript published under the (misleadingly dated) title, "Dr. Low in Detroit, September
20, 1954, Part 2," recoveringtreasure.blogspot.com/2010/11/dr-low-in-detroit-september-
20-1954_12.html. The blogger, "treasure2," appears to have been the now-deceased

Treasure Ann Sachnoff, daughter of Treasure Rice, who was the Michigan director of Recovery, Inc.

51. Although today the term *ejaculation* bears only a sexual meaning, through the first half of the twentieth century it was used to describe a short exclamation, particularly within the context of prayers. Such prayers were called "pious ejaculations."

52. It was typical of Puggy to coin neologisms by verbing nouns or nouning verbs, as with "unselving." This letter is undated but is likely from the end of July 1929.

53. At this time, when Dowling wrote of "the problem of minority representation," he particularly had St. Louis's Catholics in mind, as their political representation was small in comparison with their population. With that said, as Dowling would write later, he did also envision proportional representation as benefiting other politically underrepresented groups, particularly Black people and women.

54. Edward Dowling, SJ, "Dear Folks" letter to family, July 19, 1925.

55. Edward Dowling, SJ, to Elsie Parker, March 16, 1930.

56. Edward Dowling to Joe Touhill, March 20, 1930.

57. It should be noted that in early 1931, although Father Coughlin was already being criticized by some as a demagogue, he had not yet gained a reputation as an anti-Semite. In any case, Father Ed's admiration of Coughlin did not last long; by 1935, he was publicly criticizing the radio priest (see chapter 7).

Vincent Burns, a schoolmate of Dowling's from St. Mary's College who remained in touch with him throughout his life, told his nephew Paul M. Dowling about a time in the 1930s when Coughlin's name came up in conversation with Father Ed. When Burns's wife asked Father Ed what he thought of Father Coughlin, Father Ed deferred by turning the question over to Vincent, who was nothing if not outspoken. He responded by saying Father Coughlin was "a God-damned son of a bitch." Then Father Ed turned to Mrs. Burns and said, "Your husband gives a good summary of my attitude." Paul M. Dowling, email to author, January 5, 2022.

58. This "widely traveled" young man may have been Ed Kelly, whom Dowling mentions in one of his letters as a former member of the Loyola community who stayed in touch with him. Prior to Kelly's beginning his studies at Loyola University in 1926 at the age of eighteen, he and a friend had hitchhiked across the United States. During his summers while in college, he went seafaring, visiting Europe and India. See "Edward Kelly: Loyola's Globe-Trotter," libapps.luc.edu/digitalexhibits/s/edward-kelly-loyola-s-globe-trotter/page/home.

59. Edward Dowling, SJ, to Mary Dowling, RSCJ, October 14, 1930.

60. Edward Dowling, SJ, to Mary Dowling, RSCJ, undated, circa February 1931.

61. Edward Dowling, SJ, to Mary Dowling, RSCJ, circa March 1931, 2 (first page missing).

62. Edward Dowling, SJ, letter addressed to "Dear Folks and Mary," July 8, 1931, 1.

63. Edward Dowling, SJ, letter addressed to "Dear Folks and Mary," July 8, 1931, 2.

Chapter 7: A Heart for Democracy

1. At the time that Dowling delivered this speech, Nazi Germany was severely persecuting Jews but had not yet instituted its program of mass murder.

2. Ignatius of Loyola, "Ignatius on Obedience," online at jesuitportal.bc.edu.

3. Edward Dowling, SJ, to Mary Dowling, RSCJ, July 5, 1929.

4. In 1931, the Society of Jesus closed the high-school and college divisions of St. Mary's College and converted it into an extension of St. Louis University's graduate school of theology, for Jesuits only.

5. Edward Dowling, SJ, to Aloysius Kemper, SJ, March 2, 1932, 5.

6. Dowling to Kemper, March 2, 1932, 5.

7. Dowling to Kemper, March 2, 1932, 5. Father Ed seems to have thought the question concerned a written note or treatise on angels. In fact, the examiner was referring to a practice, common in theological manuals of the time, in which teachings were categorized according to the level of certainty with which they could be held. These levels of certainty were called "theological notes," and seminarians were expected to be familiar with them.

Thus, the examiner wanted Father Ed to identify the level of certainty that the Church assigned to the teaching on whether angels had bodies. Given that Dowling responded as though he were ignorant of theological notes, it is understandable that the examiner would conclude that he was unsuited for academia.

8. Over the course of Father Ed's illness, many doctors offered him what proved to be false hope.

9. Samuel H. Horine, SJ, to Edward Dowling, SJ, February 29, 1932.

10. Between the lines, Father Horine's letter appears to reflect a generation gap between older and younger Jesuits concerning Father Ed's social-justice work. Earlier in the letter, the provincial admits that Father Ed's fellow students do not see anything wrong with his extracurricular concerns. It is only the "elders" who are concerned.

11. Horine to Dowling, February 29, 1932.

12. Dowling to Kemper, March 2, 1932, 3.

13. Dowling to Kemper, March 2, 1932, 5.

14. Dowling to Kemper, March 2, 1932, 6.

15. Dowling to Kemper, March 2, 1932, 6.

16. Edward Dowling, SJ, to Samuel H. Horine, SJ, March 9, 1932, 2.

17. Dowling to Horine, March 9, 1932, 2.

18. Not all sodalities were (or are) youth groups, but the Sodality of Our Lady in the United States was geared toward a youth membership. Father Lord's predecessor, Father Edward Garesché, gave the apostolate and its flagship magazine the name The Queen's Work because he sought to do the work of Mary, the Queen of Heaven.

19. The pageant as an art form underwent a revival during the early 20th century.

In Father Lord's words, it was "supposed to be, as is no other piece of dramatic work, a community enterprise" that brought together "an entire section of a country in the presentation of some thought or feeling that belongs especially to that section. It is really the dramatization of the spirit of the people done by the people themselves." Daniel A. Lord, SJ, "After Two Years," *Catholic Opinion* 42, no. 2 (February 1937): 24, quoted in Roy Brooks-Delphin, "Jamaica Triumphant (1937): Daniel Lord, Pageantry, and the Foundations of Jamaican National Theater," in Roberts and Schloesser, eds., *Crossings and Dwellings*, 459.

20. Edward Dowling, SJ, to Mary Dowling, RSCJ, February 23, 1930. I have corrected "expected" to "expect," as it is clear from the context that Father Ed meant to write in the present tense.

21. Thomas F. Gavin, SJ, *Champion of Youth: Daniel A. Lord, SJ* (Boston: Daughters of St. Paul, 1977), 100.

22. Edward Dowling, SJ, to Anna Dowling, June 19, 1921.

23. Sam Lambert, letter to Father Linus J. Thro, SJ, November 10, 1962, 2. Lambert sent a similar letter to the archbishop of St. Louis, Cardinal Joseph Ritter.

24. Later doctors would change Father Ed's diagnosis to ankylosing spondylitis. However, the description that Krida gives of the general progress of Father Ed's disease is correct.

25. Arthur Krida, MD, to Edward Dowling, SJ, October 9, 1933.

26. Tim O'Neil, "Look Back: The Day Smoke Choked St. Louis—Nov. 28, 1939," *St. Louis Post-Dispatch*, November 21, 2020, stltoday.com. Not until 1940, when elected officials voted to require the use of cleaner-burning coal, did St. Louis's air begin to improve.

27. William B. Faherty, SJ, "A Half-Century with The Queen's Work," *Woodstock Letters* 92:2, 105.

28. Faherty, "A Half-Century with The Queen's Work," 109.

29. Edward Dowling, SJ, quoted in Gavin, *Champion of Youth*, 100.

30. This anecdote comes via a note in the Dowling Archive written by then-archivist Mary Louise Adams, who was told the story by Kinealy. The note is dated October 15, 1984.

31. Overdurff's ailment was in fact far more serious than Dowling's, as he likely suffered from fibrodysplasia ossificans progressiva, an extremely rare disease that changes damaged fibrous tissue into bone.

32. Henry W. Shoemaker, "This Morning's Comment," *Altoona Tribune* (Altoona, PA), October 2, 1934, 4.

33. By "liturgy" in this context, Day means the Liturgical Movement of which the SSCA was an important part. This movement presaged the developments of the Second Vatican Council in encouraging the faithful to understand the meaning of the liturgy and to participate actively in the Mass. It also emphasized that the Mass was, spiritually speaking, the vital center from which all social-justice activity should flow.

34. Day appears to be mistaken in thinking her SSCA talk was her first, as she had given a public lecture a couple of weeks prior at the Catholic Summer Center in Stamford, New York.

35. Dorothy Day, "Peter the Materialist," *The Catholic Worker*, September 1945, 6.

36. Mary C. Darrah, *Sister Ignatia: Angel of Alcoholics Anonymous*, 2nd ed. (Center City, MN: Hazelden, 2001), 243.

37. McGloin, *I'll Die Laughing!*, 128.

38. Edward Dowling, SJ, "Alcoholics Anonymous, the Twelve Steps, and Catholic Asceticism," in *The Blue Book, Volume V: Containing the Proceedings of the Fifth National Clergy Conference on Alcoholism*, ed. Ralph Pfau (privately published, 1953), 162.

39. Edward Dowling, SJ, "Is Democracy Doomed?," mimeographed text, 1–2. Lecture delivered at St. Louis University Auditorium, St. Louis, MO, November 4, 1935. Dowling Archive.

40. Dowling's reference to Huey Long as though he were still alive is odd, given that Long had been assassinated two months earlier. Perhaps he wrote the speech well in advance, since it was being mimeographed for distribution, or perhaps he was referring more generally to populist politicians who took after Long.

41. *Pelf*, an archaic slang term for money, is related to the term *pilfer*; it has a connotation of ill-gotten gains.

42. Edward Dowling, SJ, "Votes the Bosses Fear," mimeographed text, 1. Lecture delivered at St. Louis University Auditorium, November 18, 1935. Dowling Archive.

43. See Jeremiah 6:14 and 8:11.

44. Dowling, "Votes the Bosses Fear," 1.

45. Dowling, "Votes the Bosses Fear," 1.

46. Dowling, "Votes the Bosses Fear," 4.

47. Dowling, "Votes the Bosses Fear," 4.

48. Dowling's position is familiar today as that of a "consistent life ethic," but he was speaking nearly forty years before that concept gained currency.

49. Dowling, "Votes the Bosses Fear," 9.

50. Edward Dowling, SJ, "Travel Report" (January 7–16, 1936). Jesuit Archives & Research Center. The luncheon was on January 12, 1936.

51. Edward Dowling, SJ, letter to Sidney Zagri, February 13, 1958.

52. Dowling, "Is Democracy Doomed?", 4.

53. "Jesuits Riddle Red Flag of Communism," *Rochester Catholic Courier* (Rochester, NY), December 10, 1936, 6 and 9.

54. Reed Hynds, "Dictatorship Inevitable in U.S., Father Lord Says in Debate," *St. Louis Star-Times*, October 19, 1936, 7.

55. Names have been changed at the request of the couple's descendants.

56. Msgr. John J. Egan, remarks at the Way Back Inn Dinner, Union League Club, Chicago, March 12, 1988, 4. Jesuit Archives & Research Center.

57. That is, a daily visit to a church to pray before the tabernacle containing the Blessed Sacrament.

58. Westbrook Pegler, letter to Edward Dowling, SJ, June 27, 1950.

59. Today a preferred expression is "human fraternity." In his syndicated column, Broun in 1933 called the notion of the brotherhood of man "a rugged and compelling call for the only mood by which the world may be cured of its mortal illness." Heywood Broun, "It Seems to Me," *Oklahoma News*, October 14, 1933, 4.

60. Dale Kramer, *Heywood Broun: A Biographical Portrait* (New York: Current Books, 1949), 290.

61. John L. Lewis and Franklin P. Adams, eds., *Heywood Broun as He Seemed to Us* (New York: Random House, 1940), 46, and "Priest to Lecture on Heywood Broun," *St. Louis Globe-Democrat*, February 18, 1940, 11D.

62. Heywood Broun, "A Blow to Dictators," *Charlotte News* (Charlotte, NC), March 6, 1939, 4.

63. Kramer, *Heywood Broun*, 294.

64. Louis M. Lyons, "Edwin A. Lahey: January 11, 1902–July 17, 1969," *Nieman Reports* 23, no. 3 (July 1969): 5.

65. Heywood Broun, "Most Harvard Professors Given Passing Grades by Newspapermen-Students Who Win Nieman Fellowships," *The Morning Post* (Camden, NJ), May 15, 1939, 2.

66. Lahey's daughter Jayne Lahey Kobliska told me that her father was serious about his Catholic faith and shared it openly with interested colleagues. Telephone conversation with Jayne Lahey Kobliska, February 5, 2022.

67. "Fr. Dowling Lauds Heywood Broun," *St. Louis Globe-Democrat*, February 20, 1940, 5.

68. *Washington Post*, "U.S. 'Elective Monarchy,' Says Cleric," August 16, 1939, 6.

69. Mother Mary Angela, SND, to Peter A. Brooks, SJ, August 29, 1939.

70. Mary Angela to Brooks, August 29, 1939.

71. Edward Dowling, SJ, to Peter A. Brooks, SJ, September 10, 1939.

72. Dowling to Brooks, September 10, 1939.

73. "Party Government Is Legalized Treason Says U.S. Jesuit," *The Universe* (London), December 22, 1939.

74. "Party Government Is Legalized Treason Says U.S. Jesuit." The news item included several quotes that disturbed the provincial, including Father Ed's calling party government "legalized treason." But, judging by Dowling's letter, it seems that it was his criticism of the "hoodlum parties of Europe" that caused the most concern.

75. Edward Dowling, SJ, letter to Peter A. Brooks, SJ, January 18, 1940.

76. That is, the "tactful omission" committed by the wicked in Matthew 25:41–46; they failed to see Christ in the poor and suffering.

Chapter 8: Finding Fellowship

1. Frank A. Riley, *Alcoholics Anonymous: An Interview with Edward Dowling, S.J.* (St. Louis: The Queen's Work, 1947), 1. Although the pamphlet is officially credited to Riley as the editor/interviewer, Anna Dowling believed that the dedication was written by her brother. Anna Dowling, letter to William K. McGroarty, SJ, June 20, 1974.

2. Edward Dowling, SJ, "Travel Report," November 27–29, 1939. Jesuit Archives & Research Center. Although it is unlikely that the treatment would have succeeded, it would have at least had the benefit of keeping Father Ed away from St. Louis at a time when the city's air quality was at its worst.

3. Daniel A. Lord, SJ, to Edward Dowling, SJ, undated carbon of letter written on or about December 1, 1939. Ellipses and emphasis in original.

4. "Unkindness Caused Broun's Death, Claim," *Cincinnati Catholic Telegraph Register* (Cincinnati, OH), February 8, 1940, 2.

5. Nearly everyone else called him Ed. I am calling him Eddie to distinguish more easily between him and Father Ed.

Although Lahey went on to join Alcoholics Anonymous, I am using his full name here because he has already been widely identified as an A.A. member. Moreover, his only surviving child, Jayne Lahey Kobliska, has given me permission to identify him. Lahey's anonymity was first broken when his obituary in the *New York Times* on July 17, 1969, mentioned his A.A. membership. Five days later, a member of the House of Representatives read the obituary into the *Congressional Record*.

6. I have attempted to reconstruct this phone conversation and the subsequent one from the ample circumstantial evidence that indicates Lahey contacted Father Ed by phone to arrange a retreat. In addition to the notations Father Ed made on his calendar indicating that Lahey would be visiting from January 16 though January 18, the letters noted below from Sister Mary Alice Rowan and Grace Lahey both refer to Edwin's plans to make a retreat under Dowling's direction. It is fair to assume that Father Ed would have struggled to discern how best to assist his friend, as he had yet to discover Alcoholics Anonymous, and he had little experience ministering to problem drinkers.

7. The month's mind is an Irish tradition in which a requiem Mass is celebrated for a person a month after his or her death.

8. Louis M. Lyons, "Edwin A. Lahey: January 11, 1902–July 17, 1969," *Nieman Reports* 23, no. 3 (July 1969), 5.

9. This prayer is preserved at the Dowling Archive along with other items Father Ed kept in his desk drawer.

10. Father Ed was fond of quoting those words of Dempster MacMurphy. John J. Egan, "Remarks of Msgr. John J. Egan: Msgr. Ignatius McDermott Receives the First Rev. Dowling Award," 7–8.

11. This conversation too is reconstructed. The existing letters from Sister Mary

Alice to Father Ed, quoted below, indicate that they had befriended one another over a shared concern for Lahey.

12. Interview with Jayne Lahey Kobliska, January 17, 2022. Several contemporary news accounts reinforce Kobliska's recollections.

13. Because of the need for confidentiality in the Lahey matter, Sister Mary Alice is likely referring to her friends in heaven—the saints.

14. I am assuming Lahey wrote to Dowling to cancel the retreat, as he likely would have been too embarrassed to phone him. Moreover, the later letter from Lahey to Dowling that does exist, below, indicates they had prior correspondence while he was in Hot Springs.

15. Until 1950, first-class mail between cities such as Chicago and St. Louis (and even between those cities and New York) typically took only one day to arrive. Mail was delivered twice a day; in business districts, there could even be a third daily delivery. "Sign of the times: Postal Service cuts in 1950 caused some hubbub," *Chicago Tribune*, February 8, 2013, www.chicagotribune.com/news/ct-xpm-2013-02-08-ct-talk-mail-delivery-flashback-0208-20130208-story.html.

16. In the article, Dowling calls her "Sister Mary Joan," perhaps in acknowledgment of her having the wisdom, strength, and fortitude of St. Joan of Arc.

17. Edward Dowling, SJ, "Alcoholics Anonymous," *The Queen's Work* (March 1944), 30–31.

18. Dowling, "Alcoholics Anonymous," *The Queen's Work*, 30.

19. As noted, the names and identifying details are anonymized in the article. Dowling writes, "A month later, visiting Jim in his hometown . . . ," etc. Dowling, "Alcoholics Anonymous, *The Queen's Work*, 30.

20. Dowling would not have stopped in Chicago on his way back from New York, as he would have had to return to St. Louis quickly to attend the March 1 funeral of his uncle Paul M. Dowling.

21. Dowling, "Alcoholics Anonymous," *The Queen's Work*, 30.

22. See, for example, Robin Gomes, "Pope to priests: Be "shepherds with 'the smell of the sheep,'" *Vatican News*, June 7, 2021, vaticannews.va/en/pope/news/2021-06/pope-francis-priests-students-church-louis-french.html.

23. The term comes from St. Paul's description of the faithful as the "body of Christ" in 1 Corinthians 12:12–27 and elsewhere.

24. Dowling, address to Alcoholics Anonymous 1955 International Convention, in *Alcoholics Anonymous Comes of Age*, chapter 5, Kindle ed., loc. 4102.

25. Fitzgerald, *The Soul of Sponsorship*, 29.

26. Edward Dowling, SJ, to Bill Wilson, December 27, 1957.

27. Fitzgerald, *The Soul of Sponsorship*, 102.

28. Fitzgerald, *The Soul of Sponsorship*, 102. Paul K. added that the quoted words were Dowling's own. The conversation took place on the last night of Dowling's life; he died in his sleep early the following morning.

Chapter 9: Befriending Bill

1. Edward Dowling, SJ, letter to Russell G., February 19, 1954.

2. Bill W., letter to Russell G., October 6, 1964. Bill was writing to thank Russell for sending him the letter from Father Ed quoted above.

3. Father Ed wrote to A.A. member Russell G. (February 19, 1954) that he bought the Big Book at the first Chicago meeting he attended. It is my assumption that he read it on his train ride to Chicago to New York City and his ride back to St. Louis.

4. Father John Markoe, SJ, at that time was assigned as a confessor and spiritual director at the St. Joseph's Hill Infirmary, about thirty-five miles southwest of St. Louis, and was receiving treatment there for his alcoholism. Dowling alludes to Markoe in a 1953 talk to clergy when he says, "A priest alcoholic, who has written with discernment on the Spiritual Exercises, first pointed out to me the similarity between them and the Twelve Steps of Alcoholics Anonymous" (Edward Dowling, SJ, "Alcoholics Anonymous, the Twelve Steps, and Traditional Catholic Asceticism," *The Blue Book*, vol. 5, 157). Markoe's writings on the Exercises, and the nature of the similarity that Father Ed saw between the Exercises and the Twelve Steps, will be discussed in chapter 10.

5. This is my reading of how Father Ed likely would have felt. It would have been natural for him to feel a certain identification with his uncle's physical sufferings. And he too would die at sixty-one. Interestingly, in recent years, researchers have discovered that a genetic mutation links ankylosing spondylitis and Parkinson's disease.

6. "Dr. Bob's sobriety date is usually given as 10 June 1935, which has become known in A.A. as 'Founders' Day,' despite recent evidence that Dr. Smith took his last drink on 17 June 1935." Ernest Kurtz and William White, "Alcoholics Anonymous," in *Alcohol and Temperance in Modern History*, ed. Jack Blocker et al. (Santa Barbara, CA: ABC-CLIO, 2003), 27. Accessed online at williamwhitepapers.com/pr/2003%20Alchololics%20Anonymous.pdf.

7. An early chronology assembled in the mid or late 1940s by a member of A.A.'s St. Louis chapter and reviewed by Father Ed states that he visited both Dr. Bob and Bill Wilson in April 1940. However, Father Ed could not have met Bill at that early date; if he had, then the tone of his correspondence with the New York office between May and July 1940 would have reflected the men's familiarity. The chronology is in the A.A. folder at the Dowling Archive.

Making matters more confusing is Father Ed's letter of February 19, 1954, to Russell G. in which, after mentioning his first visit to the Chicago A.A. meeting, he writes, "Providence seemed to arrange a trip shortly after there, which enabled me to visit Bill and Doc Smith." Whereas there is independent verification (through Henrietta Seiberling's recollections) of Father Ed's first visit to Dr. Bob in the spring of 1940, and there is independent verification (through Bill W.'s many recollections) of his first visit to Bill in November 1940, there is simply no verification of this claim from Dowling that he visited both Dr. Bob and Bill on the same trip. Unless new evidence arises, the answer appears to be that Dowling's memory, over the years, compressed two separate visits into a single excursion.

Seiberling's recollections are in an audio recording of a 1971 phone call with her son John, online at www.youtube.com/watch?v=MVfa8OuEKFs. John Seiberling published them in his article "Origins of Alcoholics Anonymous," *The Almacan* 13, no. 5 (May 1983): 8–9, 12.

8. Dowling, "Alcoholics Anonymous," *The Queen's Work* (March 1944), 30.

9. Seiberling, "Origins of Alcoholics Anonymous," 9.

10. Mary C. Darrah, *Sister Ignatia: Angel of Alcoholics Anonymous*, 2nd ed. (Center City, MN: Hazelden, 2001), 28. Darrah mistakenly identifies Cincinnati as the city where Dowling first encountered A.A.

11. Edward Dowling, SJ, letter to Bill Wilson, May 27, 1942, quoted in Fitzgerald, *The Soul of Sponsorship*, 28.

12. Terence, quoted by Pope Francis, "Address of His Holiness Pope Francis to the Faithful of the Diocese of Rome," September 18, 2021, www.vatican.va. As Francis notes in his homily, the maxim was also a favorite of St. Paul VI.

13. "Democracy's Bars Discussed," *St. Louis Daily Globe-Democrat*, June 25, 1940, 16. Father Ed had been using some variation of this statement in his talks since he first began lecturing on democracy. But it was not until he said it with this particular phrasing in his 1940 SSCA lectures that it gained national exposure.

14. Father Ed's desk calendar lists two different dates for the retreat, October 13 and October 17. I am assuming the correct one is the 17th, as the entry on that date is written in pen, whereas the October 13 entry is written in pencil.

15. Dowling, "Alcoholics Anonymous," *The Queen's Work* (March 1944), 31.

16. In later years, Bill would be grateful that A.A. was forced by necessity to become self-supporting. See "Tradition Seven" in *Twelve Steps and Twelve Traditions* (New York: A.A. World Services, 2019 [originally published in 1953]), 160ff.

17. *Pass It On* (New York: A.A. World Services, 1984), Kindle ed., loc. 3141.

18. *Pass It On*, Kindle ed., loc. 3004.

19. Bill Wilson to Fitz M., October 30, 1940, General Service Office archive, quoted in Jay D. Moore, *Alcoholics Anonymous and the Rockefeller Connection* (Durham, NC: Lulu, 2015), 245.

20. *Pass It On*, Kindle ed., loc. 2376. Ernest Kurtz identifies the recipient as McGhee B. (Ernest Kurtz, *Not-God: A History of Alcoholics Anonymous* [Center City, MN: Hazelden, 1991], 322).

21. Bill W., "Anarchy Melts," *Grapevine*, July 1946, emphasis in original.

22. *Pass It On*, Kindle ed., loc. 3430.

23. Thomsen, *Bill W.*, 274–75.

24. Bill W., talk at Cathedral of the Spirit, Dallas, Texas, 1951, online at recovery speakers.com/bill-w-cathedral-of-the-spirit-talk-in-dallas-tx-in-1951.

25. Ernest Kurtz, *Not-God*, 97.

26. Bill W., spoken introduction to Father Ed's speech at Alcoholics Anonymous International Convention in St. Louis, July 3, 1955. This recording is widely available online, including at www.youtube.com/watch?v=P5a42q2Yh1k.

27. Bill W., spoken introduction to Father Ed's speech at Alcoholics Anonymous International Convention in St. Louis, July 3, 1955..

28. Bill W., talk at Le Moyne College, April 1954, 10. Dowling Archive.

29. See Acts 9:10–19.

30. *Pass It On*, Kindle ed., loc. 3453.

31. The time of the train's arrival is marked on Father Ed's November 1940 desk calendar. Dowling Archive.

32. *Pass It On*, Kindle ed., loc. 3418; Lois Wilson, *Lois Remembers* (New York: Al-Anon Family Group Headquarters, 1994), 131

33. *Pass It On*, Kindle ed., loc. 3418.

34. Bill W., "Alcoholics Anonymous," *The Blue Book*, Vol. 12: The Proceedings of the Twelfth National Clergy Conference on Alcoholism (privately published, 1960), 181.

35. Jack Alexander's first recorded visit to the New York A.A. meeting rooms was November 12, 1940, according to Stepping Stones archivist James T. (email to author, October 6, 2021).

36. Jack Alexander, "Jack Alexander of Saturday Evening Post Fame Thought A.A.s Were Pulling His Leg," *Grapevine* (May 1945).

37. Father Ralph Pfau, introduction to Dowling, "Alcoholics Anonymous, the Twelve Steps, and Traditional Catholic Asceticism," *Blue Book* (1953), 153. Pfau says he was told this by Bill Wilson.

38. Bill W., "Alcoholics Anonymous," *Blue Book* (1960), 181. Bill gave this talk on April 21, 1960; Dowling's funeral was April 6.

39. Bill W., "Alcoholics Anonymous," *The Blue Book*, 181.

40. Bill W., talk at Le Moyne College, 10.

41. Bill W., "When A.A. Came of Age," in *Alcoholics Anonymous Comes of Age*, Kindle ed., loc. 634.

42. Kurtz also interviewed Joseph F. MacFarlane, SJ, who succeeded Dowling at The Queen's Work; he provided general information on Dowling's manner.

43. Kurtz, *Not-God*, 97.

44. Bill W., "When A.A. Came of Age," loc. 637.

45. Bill W., quoted in Ernest Kurtz, Message 6252, January 19, 2010, "AA History Lovers" message board, archived at silkworth.net/wp-content/uploads/2020/07/2010Messages_6185_7089.txt.

46. Ernest Kurtz, Message 6252, January 19, 2010, "AA History Lovers" message board.

47. Edward Dowling, SJ, letter to Russell G., February 19, 1954. This quotation appears in fuller context in the epigraph of this chapter.

48. "Having had a spiritual awakening as the result of these Steps, we tried to carry this message to alcoholics, and to practice these principles in all our affairs." "The Twelve Steps," aa.org/the-twelve-steps. (As noted below, at the time that Father Ed met Bill, the word "experience" was used in the Twelfth Step rather than "awakening.")

49. Kurtz, *Not-God*, 98. I have taken the liberty of turning Kurtz's paraphrase of Bill's question into a direct quote.

50. Thomas à Kempis, *The Imitation of Christ*, trans. Robert Jeffery (New York: Penguin, 2013), 180.

51. Kempis, *Imitation of Christ*, 181.

52. Kurtz, *Not-God*, 98–99.

53. Augustine, *The Confessions of Saint Augustine*, trans. John K. Ryan (Doubleday: New York, 1988), 1.

54. Thomsen, *Bill W.*, 277–78.

55. Newman, *Meditations and Devotions*, 400. The meditation is quoted in full in chapter 5.

56. Thomsen, *Bill W.*, 278.

57. Thomsen, *Bill W.*, 282.

58. Bill W., "Alcoholics Anonymous," *The Blue Book*, 181–82.

59. Anna Dowling, writing to William K. McGroarty, SJ (June 20, 1974), mentions this comment of her brother's but does not say when the letter in question was written or to whom it was written.

60. Riley, *Alcoholics Anonymous: An Interview with Edward Dowling, S.J.*, 1.

61. Although Alexander did not mention Lahey by name in his *Saturday Evening Post* article, it is clear he had Chicago in mind when he wrote of finding that, at an "influential" newspaper, "the city editor, the assistant city editor, and a nationally known reporter were A.A.'s, and strong in the confidence of their publisher." Jack Alexander, "Alcoholics Anonymous," *The Saturday Evening Post* (March 1941): 10.

62. Jack Alexander, "Jack Alexander of Saturday Evening Post Fame Thought A.A.s Were Pulling His Leg."

63. *The Jack Alexander Article About A.A.* (New York: A.A. World Services, 2017), 5.

Chapter 10: Exercises in Obedience

1. Father Ed to Bill Wilson, February 18, 1942, quoted in Fitzgerald, *The Soul of Sponsorship*, 26.

2. "'Alcoholics Anonymous' Aids 'Those Who Ought to Quit,'" *St. Louis Post-Dispatch*, December 26, 1940, 6A.

3. Edward Dowling, SJ, to Luke H., Clem L., and Ed Lahey, January 14, 1941.

4. I have cleaned up Father Ed's grammar. The original sentence, after the word "minimize," says, "the recognition of the new members of the necessity of the spiritual."

5. Father Ed to Luke H., Clem L., and Ed Lahey.

6. It seems that Fulton Oursler was the first to call nonalcoholics "underprivileged" in comparison to those who had the benefit of A.A.'s fellowship. See Fulton Oursler, "Charming Is the Word for Alcoholics," *Grapevine* (July 1944), accessed online at www.aagrapevine.org/magazine/1944/jul/charming-word-alcoholics.

7. John A. Keogh to Edward Dowling, SJ, April 4, 1941, quoted in Egan to Kurtz, 13. Egan does not mention what precipitated Keogh's letter to Dowling. Since Father Ed was not yet nationally known for supporting A.A., I am assuming Dowling made the first contact. The original Keogh-Dowling letters are likely in the Dowling Archive, but I have been unable to locate them.

8. Pius XII, Radio Message to Participants in the National Catechetical Congress of the United States, October 26, 1946, online at vatican.va. Pope Francis quoted Pius's words in his homily of January 31, 2020.

9. Edward Dowling, SJ, to John A. Keogh, April 12, 1941, quoted in Egan to Kurtz, 13.

10. Edward Dowling, SJ, to Frank Riley, November 3, 1958.

11. Edward Dowling, SJ, letter to Bill Wilson, circa November 1945, 2. (Only the second page of the letter is at the Dowling Archive, and it does not show the date.)

12. "America First Group to Form Chapter Here," *St. Louis Star-Times*, March 4, 1941, 19.

13. Bill Kauffman, "Editor's Introduction," in Ruth Sarles, *A Story of America First* (Praeger: Westport, CT, 2003), xxiii.

14. "Lindbergh and His St. Louis Audience," *St. Louis Post-Dispatch*, May 11, 1941, 75.

15. "Sen. Nye to Speak at America First Rally," *Neighborhood News* (St. Louis, MO), July 31, 1941,1.

16. "Nye Assails Movie Makers as Propagandists for War," *St. Louis Post-Dispatch*, August 2, 1941, 3.

17. "Everybody's Column," *St. Louis Star-Times*, October 14, 1941, 12.

18. *Indiana Gazette* (Indiana, PA), August 8, 1941, 17.

19. Edward Dowling, SJ, "Father Dowling's Talk on KDKA," August 9, 1941, 5.

20. The quotation at the end of the invocation is slightly amended from John Henry Newman's sermon "Wisdom and Innocence." As noted earlier, Dowling was fond of quoting Newman, to whom his grandmother believed she was related.

21. The source for this date is Father Ed's October 1941 desk calendar.

22. Bill W., "Alcoholics Anonymous," *The Blue Book* (1960), 182.

23. Bill W., "Alcoholics Anonymous," *The Blue Book* (1960), 182–83.

24. Bill W., "Alcoholics Anonymous," *The Blue Book* (1960), 183.

25. Dowling identified this Jesuit as Father John Markoe in a letter to his provincial superior (Edward Dowling, SJ, to Peter Brooks, SJ, February 18, 1942).

26. Riley, *Alcoholics Anonymous: An Interview with Edward Dowling, S.J.*, 12–13. Father Ed thus indicated that Markoe did not connect the entire thirty-day Exercises with the Twelve Steps—only the Foundation and the First Week. In his 1953 address to the Fifth National Clergy Conference on Alcoholism, Dowling would present some general parallels between each week of the Exercises and the Steps.

27. Ignatius of Loyola, Spiritual Exercises, no. 23.

28. That is, the resolve to attain the true end goal of human existence—salvation.

29. For the full list of A.A.'s Twelve Steps as well as its Twelve Traditions, see appendix.

30. Bill W., "Alcoholics Anonymous," *The Blue Book*, 183.

31. Although I have not found a record that gives the exact length of Father Ed's visit to Bill and Lois, the visit made such an impression upon everyone involved—with Dowling and Wilson recalling it fondly in correspondence years later—that it likely lasted more than one day. Dowling's desk calendar indicates he returned home January 5 and had no other commitments until that time.

32. Bill Wilson to Edward Dowling, SJ, January 14, 1954.

33. Father Ed's calendar has him in Kansas City on that date but does not say what business he had there. He later wrote to his provincial superior that he had visited an A.A. chapter in that city. Edward Dowling, SJ, to Peter Brooks, SJ, February 18, 1942.

34. Bill W., "This Matter of Fear," *Grapevine* (January 1962).

35. Bill W., "The Three Legacies of Alcoholics Anonymous," in *Alcoholics Anonymous Comes of Age*, 194.

36. Alcoholics Anonymous, "The Twelve Steps." The Twelfth Step is to Alcoholics Anonymous what Jesus's commission to "make disciples of all nations" is to Christians (see Matthew 28:16–20). A.A.'s philosophy is grounded in the belief that members' own sobriety depends upon helping others heal. To monetize Twelfth-Step work would make A.A. akin to multi-level marketing or even a pyramid scheme.

37. Bill W., "The Three Legacies of Alcoholics Anonymous," in *Alcoholics Anonymous Comes of Age*, 195.

38. Alcoholics Anonymous, "The Twelve Traditions—Long Form," online at aa.org/the-twelve-traditions.

39. See chapter 2 for a fuller version of this quotation, which includes Dowling's response to the objection to "Churchianity."

40. I am extrapolating about James's personality based on scattered references to him in Father Ed's letters and the letter that Vincent Burns wrote about him (see chapter 4).

41. St. Ignatius of Loyola gives certain cautions to Jesuits in cases where they wish to make their personal preference known to a superior who is to decide a course of action for them. "If you want to proceed in this matter without suspicion of self-love or attachment to your own judgment," the saint writes, "you must maintain, before and after making this representation, not only an indifference towards actually undertaking or relinquishing the matter in question, but one such that you are even more pleased with, and consider as better, whatever the superior may ordain." Ignatius of Loyola, "Ignatius on Obedience."

42. "Crossback" and "mackerel-snapper" were contemporary epithets directed against Catholics. The latter slur mocked Catholics' Friday abstinence from meat.

43. Edward Dowling, SJ, to Bill Wilson, February 18, 1942, in Fitzgerald, *The Soul of Sponsorship*, 25.

44. Peter Brooks, SJ, to Edward Dowling, SJ, March 11, 1942. Jesuit Archives.

45. Dowling to Brooks, March 14, 1942.

46. Dowling to Brooks, March 14, 1942.

47. Dowling to Brooks, March 14, 1942.

48. Dowling to Brooks, March 14, 1942.

49. See Arthur Devine, "State or Way (Purgative, Illuminative, Unitive)," *The Catholic Encyclopedia*, vol. 14 (New York: Robert Appleton Co., 1912), online at newadvent.org/cathen/14254a.htm.

50. Devine, "State or Way."

51. Dowling to Brooks, March 14, 1942.

52. Dowling to Brooks, March 14, 1942.

53. In assuming how Father Ed would have reacted, I have in mind how, more than once, he compared the inspiration he received through his ministry to A.A. with that which he received upon his ordination, e.g., Anna Dowling's recollection to William K. McGroarty, SJ (letter of June 20, 1974) and Chuck C.'s recollection in *A New Pair of Glasses* (Irvine, CA: New-Look, 1984).

    Chuck C. writes that Father Ed once said to him, "Chuck, your cross was alcoholism, my cross was lack of faith. I went through all my studies and was ordained and didn't believe a damn thing.... I came to believe by watching what happens to you people in Alcoholics Anonymous" (*A New Pair of Glasses*, 44–45). I don't believe Chuck C.'s recollection is strictly accurate, given that Father Ed spoke and wrote about having had a spiritual experience upon making his first vows (see chapter 5). However, Chuck's account of Father Ed bears enough similarity to Anna's that it can reasonably be concluded that Dowling, through his encounter with A.A., experienced dramatic growth both in his faith and in his sense of his priestly identity.

Chapter 11: Steps in a New Direction

1. This quote from an unnamed source appears in D. C. Dunne, "Two Out of Many," *Today* (May 1954): 4. Many people observed that Father Ed found his greatest joy in accompanying people who had problems.

2. This anecdote and the following impressions of Father Ed at The Queen's Work, unless otherwise noted, are from my telephone interview with Rosemary Hendron Macken, March 21, 2020.

3. In the decades before the Mediterranean diet became popular, pure virgin olive oil was expensive and difficult to find in the midwestern United States.

4. The fashion statement is the product of my imagination, but Father Ed was indeed sought out by women from elite St. Louis families, including Angela (Kiki) Desloge, Clara Busch Orthwein, and Orthwein's friend Claire Dickey. Although Jesuits generally were viewed with high respect in St. Louis's high society, Dowling seems to have been particularly popular with such women—perhaps because he was uniquely sympathetic to those who were affected by divorce. Desloge became a founding member of a support group Dowling started for divorced women (see chapter 16).

5. Sam Lambert, "Father Ed Dowling: A Modern Saint?", *Jesuit Bulletin* (October 1970), 13.

6. Although Dowling's boyhood nickname was Eddie (before the nickname Puggy took hold), I have not seen evidence that anyone called him Father Eddie, apart from this article. He was most often referred to as Father Dowling. His fellow Jesuits called him Ed or Puggy, and to Bill W. he was always Father Ed.

7. This is an odd detail, as Father Ed never had yellow hair. His hair was brown until it turned prematurely white during his thirties. Perhaps the reporter visited as the afternoon sun shone through his office windows.

8. United Press (Emilie Basel), "Busy Life Led by Priest; Says Progress Never Stops," *Republican and Herald* (Pottsville, PA), February 20, 1943, 3. I have reversed the order of the last two paragraphs quoted.

9. Bill Wilson to Edward Dowling, SJ, March 10, 1943.

10. Wilson to Dowling, March 10, 1943.

11. The dinner, hosted by Alcoholics Anonymous Group One and Wilson Club Group Two, was held June 14, 1943, at the Congress Hotel in St. Louis. A copy of the program is in the Eastern Area of Missouri Alcoholics Anonymous Archive.

12. Joe Diggles has been recognized as an important figure in A.A. history for his support of the first Black A.A. group in Chicago; see Glenn C., *Heroes of Early Black A.A.* (South Bend, IN: Hindsfoot Foundation, 2017), 24. His anonymity was also broken by his godson, writer Patrick Carroll, who is (by affinity) his only surviving descendant. See Patrick Carroll, "Notes of a Footnote 2—Anne and Joe," June 24, 2011, www.patrickcarroll.co.uk/notes-of-a-footnote-2-anne-joe/.

13. By "the book," Father Ed means the Big Book. Diggles had sent Dowling a document he had compiled of quotations from the Big Book. (Apparently the appellation "Big Book" hadn't yet taken hold; Father Ed in the same letter refers to it as the "red book.")

14. Edward Dowling, SJ, letter to Joe Diggles, October 13, 1943, 1.

15. At the time, Vermont was known for being a poor state.

16. Dowling to Diggles, October 13, 1943, 1.

17. Dowling to Diggles, October 13, 1943, 1.

18. Dowling to Diggles, October 13, 1943, 2.

19. Dowling to Diggles, October 13, 1943, 2.

20. As noted in chapter 3, in 1917 Austin Bork, John Markoe, and his brother William Markoe—all Jesuit scholastics at the time—together signed a pledge to "give and dedicate [their] whole lives…for the work of the salvation of the Negroes in the United States." All three followed through on the pledge, becoming pioneers of interracial ministry. Bork died in 1952, drowning while saving the life of one of his Black parishioners who had panicked during a group swim in a stream. See Smith, *From Corps to CORE*, and "Jesuit Priest Drowns Saving Life of Negro Teacher," *St. Louis Globe-Democrat*, July 28, 1952, 1.

21. Edward Dowling, SJ, "In This Corner," *The Queen's Work* (January 1943), 12.

22. Father Ed was enraged both by the commissioner's hypocrisy and by his preventing the CIO from advocating for racial justice. At the time, as a member-at-large of the Newspaper Guild, Dowling was the only priest member of the CIO.

23. Edward Dowling, SJ, to Daniel A. Lord, SJ, December 8, 1943. Jesuit Archives.

24. Edward Dowling, SJ, to Father W. H. Condon, CSC, May 9, 1946.

25. Edward Dowling, SJ, to Daniel A. Lord, SJ, December 7, 1943. Jesuit Archives.

26. After Father Ed died, his sisters Anna (who was his secretary) and Sister Mary oversaw the transfer of his papers to the Dowling Archive at what was then Maryville College (today Maryville University), where Sister Mary was the librarian. Given that correspondence with alcoholics and other people with personal problems makes up only a very small percentage of the correspondence in the Dowling Archive, I suspect that Anna or Sister Mary destroyed documents whose existence might compromise the writers' confidentiality. If that is in fact the case, then it might explain why no letters between Garland and Father Ed exist.

27. Dolores Tygard, "Purely Personal," *To & Fro at St. Joe* (April 1960), 5. The publication was a photocopied newsletter published by St. Joseph Hospital Auxiliary, Kirkwood, Missouri.

28. Bill Wilson to Edward Dowling, SJ, March 16, 1944. Bill is making a winking reference to Father Ed's *Queen's Work* column "Curbstone Caucus."

29. Edward Dowling, SJ, to Bill Wilson, April 18, 1944.

30. An open meeting of Alcoholics Anonymous is one that is open to nonalcoholics.

31. "Jesuit Priest Tells of A.A. Adjustments," *Morning News* (Wilmington, DE), August 29, 1949, 11.

32. It was typical of Father Ed to invite people to do something spiritually advantageous by making a playful dare.

33. Dowling, "Alcoholics Anonymous," *The Queen's Work* (March 1944), 30.

34. Ernest Kurtz writes in *Not-God* that he tried unsuccessfully to locate Dowling's pamphlet on A.A. after Father John Ford, SJ, told him it traced the parallels between the Spiritual Exercises and the Twelve Steps. Kurtz, *Not-God*, 343, n41.

35. Father Ed is here encapsulating a saying from G.K. Chesterton in *What's Wrong with the World*: "The Christian ideal has not been tried and found wanting. It has been found difficult; and left untried."

36. Dowling, "Alcoholics Anonymous," 26–28.

37. Second Vatican Council, *Unitatis Redintegratio*, 4.

38. Dowling used the expression in his address to the Alcoholics Anonymous International Convention in 1955; see *Alcoholics Anonymous Comes of Age*, 258.

39. Margery Frisbie, *An Alley in Chicago: The Life and Legacy of Monsignor John Egan*, "Commemorative Edition" (Franklin, WI: Sheed & Ward, 2002), 81.

40. Delaney brought the idea of "family renewal" day retreats for married couples to the United States after witnessing them during a 1937 visit to France. Frisbie, *An Alley in Chicago*, 50–51.

41. Frisbie, *An Alley in Chicago*, 51.

42. Edward Dowling, SJ, to Mary Louise O'Shaughnessy, October 30, 1944.

43. Telephone interview with Michael Fox, April 17, 2020.

44. Edward Dowling, SJ, "Cana Conferences, *The Catholic Mind* 43:90 (June 1945), 340. The article originally appeared in the March 1945 issue of *The Jesuit Bulletin*.

45. See Second Vatican Council, *Lumen Gentium*, 37.

46. "Bilbo's Critics Told to Take Action in Own Communities," *Chicago Sun*, August 28, 1945, 7.

47. Edward Dowling, SJ, to Grace Perkins Oursler, November 25, 1949, 1.

48. Although there is no record of why he declined to relieve Dowling of his publicity duties, I would not judge Lord harshly on that account. In the dozens of letters that exist between him and Dowling, Lord never once places upon Father Ed the type of deadline pressures that a supervisor would be expected to place upon a publicist. On the other hand, there are numerous letters in which Lord urges Father Ed to take time off to make a retreat, see a doctor, or otherwise take care of himself. All the existing evidence shows that Lord gave Father Ed as much liberty to pursue his passions as he reasonably could.

49. Edward Dowling, SJ, memo (no addressee is listed), June 4, 1946, 2.

50. "Cana Conference Movement," *The National Catholic Almanac* (Paterson, NJ: St. Anthony's Guild, 1949), 411.

51. Edward Dowling, SJ, "Some Notes Taken from a Cana Conference Conducted by the Rev. Edward Dowling, S.J., The Queen's Work, St. Louis, Missouri," mimeograph distributed by Cana Conference of Chicago, dated November 28, 1952. (It is not clear whether the date is that of the talk or that of the publication.) I have made slight corrections to the transcript's grammar.

52. Although this quote is from his final interview in March 1960, Father Ed also wrote in a memo to Father Lord on November 12, 1944—four weeks after the first public Cana Conference—that Cana was "based on Alcoholic Annon [*sic*] experience of Hub-Wife together." Jesuit Archives.

53. Felknor, "Glad Gethsemane," 17–18.

54. It was Grace and her husband, Fulton Oursler (who, as editor of *Liberty* magazine, gave A.A. some of its earliest publicity), who introduced Heywood Broun to Monsignor Fulton J. Sheen. In 1947, the couple did the same for Bill Wilson (see chapter 12).

55. Edward Dowling, SJ, to Grace Perkins Oursler, November 25, 1949, 1.

56. Mrs. Leo (Pat) Butler to Edward Dowling, SJ, November 18, 1946.

57. Bud [no last name given] to Father John O'Sullivan, November 17, 1946.

58. Lewis M. Terman, *Psychological Factors in Marital Happiness* (New York, NY: McGraw-Hill, 1938), 379.

59. Edward Dowling, SJ, *Voice of Father Dowling* LP, side A.

60. This anecdote was related to me by St. Louis writer John Samuel Tieman, who heard it from Father Ed's Queen's Work colleague Father William Barnaby Faherty, SJ, while interviewing him on August 3, 1992.

61. The program was first broadcast April 7, 1946, on St. Louis University radio station WEW and continued at least through 1950.

62. A transcript of this talk, which Father Ed delivered on April 26, 1947, at the Hotel Tallcorn, is in the Dowling Archive.

63. Marty Mann is widely considered to be the first woman who received lasting sobriety through Alcoholics Anonymous.

64. Father Ed's points regarding the Second Step derive from lessons he learned in his own journey of faith (see chapter 5)—first, that the *via negativa* (that is, the negative path, or the process of elimination) is a legitimate way to find God, and second, that Jesus says to each of us, "Dwell in my way and you will know the truth."

65. Edward Dowling, SJ, to Paul F. Smith, SJ, March 19, 1946.

66. Dorothy Willmann oversaw relations with women's sodalities at the Sodality of Our Lady, the parent organization of The Queen's Work.

67. Edward Dowling, SJ, to Mary Ellen Kelly, March 15, 1946.

68. Interview with Rosemary Hendron Macken, March 21, 2020.

Chapter 12: Speaking of the Devil

1. Father Ed's endorsement first appeared on the back cover of the ninth printing of the Big Book's first edition.

2. Bill Wilson to Edward Dowling, SJ, May 20, 1946.

3. *Alcoholics Anonymous*, 1st ed. (New York: Works Publishing, 1939), 20.

4. Dowling, "Alcoholics Anonymous, the Twelve Steps, and Traditional Catholic Asceticism," 170. This comment is from the question-and-answer session after Dowling's talk.

5. *Pass It On*, Kindle ed., loc. 3976.

6. *Pass It On*, Kindle ed., loc. 3942.

7. Hartigan, *Bill W.*, 176.

8. Bill Wilson to Edward Dowling, SJ, September 18, 1945.

9. Edward Dowling, SJ, to Mrs. Isaac Dee (Kathleen McBride) Kelley, February 25, 1945.

10. Plato, *Apology*, Jowett translation.

11. This message permeates Plato's *Phaedo*.

12. In 1933, while Father Ed was completing his theology studies, he wrote to his friend Joe Diggles's mother Mildred, who had recently suffered a heart attack, "The situation in which you find yourself—suffering and limitation of effort—... has a return richer even than the expensive investment of pain it calls for." Jim Egan, SJ, quotes this letter in his letter to Ernest Kurtz, already noted, but I have not been able to find the original.

13. Bill W., "The Next Frontier—Emotional Sobriety," *Grapevine* (January 1958).

14. *Pass It On*, Kindle ed., loc. 4015.

15. Bill Wilson to Edward Dowling, SJ, September 3, 1947. Emphasis and capitalization in original.

16. This word is either an error or an intentional invention of Dowling's, combining *lodestar* and *landmark*.

17. Hartigan, *Bill W.*, 174.

18. Hartigan, *Bill W.*, 166.

19. Dowling is here defining what is also known as indefectibility—the infallibility of the Church as a whole, which is related to papal infallibility but distinct from it. As a theologian who has taught ecclesiology at Catholic seminaries, I cannot help but marvel at how Father Ed in a single sentence sums up a concept that others have taken dense books to describe.

20. Dowling's advice to Bill is reminiscent of a sermon he composed in the early 1930s in which he warned against "[looking] to see if the information offered by Christ is congenial to our own 'infallible' intellect" and whether "his moral program

is congenial to our own 'canonized' habits" before we will believe. When we do so, "we are left with a rich scum of confidence in the adequacy of our own 'infallible' intellect, a self-centering which is practically a moral impediment to faith." Edward Dowling, SJ, "John 8:12" sermon (unpublished), 2.

21. Bill W. often used the expression "deflation at depth" to describe his mental state just prior to his spiritual experience at Towns Hospital. See, for example, *Alcoholics Anonymous Comes of Age*, 64 (which, although written after the correspondence described above, contains material that had long been part of his speeches).

22. *Pass It On*, Kindle ed., loc. 4826.

23. The A.A. historian who corrected the record on Wickes's name was Matthew J. Raphael in *Bill W. and Mr. Wilson: The Legend and Life of A.A.'s Cofounder* (Amherst, MA: University of Massachusetts Press, 2000), 142.

24. Von Lüttichau in turn probably contacted Bill after learning of him from her former boss, Dr. Esther L. Richards of the Phipps Clinic at Baltimore's Johns Hopkins Hospital, who endorsed the Big Book's first edition. During the summer of 1945, she gave him a copy of Jung's *Modern Man in Search of a Soul*. On Von Lüttichau and Wilson, see Ian McCabe, Christine Boyd, and Pádraig Carroll, "Margarita Von Lüttichau: Intermediary between Jung and Bill Wilson," *Journal of Analytical Psychology* 65, no. 4 (2020): 685–706. See also chapter 1 of Ian McCabe, *Carl Jung and Alcoholics Anonymous* (New York: Routledge, 2018).

25. Kurtz, *Not-God*, 9.

26. Bill Wilson to Margarita Von Lüttichau, July 14, 1947, quoted in Raphael, *Bill W. and Mr. Wilson*, 142.

27. Carl G. Jung, *Visions: Notes of the Seminar Given in 1930–1934*, vol. 1 (Princeton, NJ: Princeton University Press, 1997), 821.

28. Frances G. Wickes, "The Creative Process," *Spring: A Journal of Archetype and Culture* (1948): 42. Wickes read this paper before a meeting of the Analytic Psychology Club of New York on March 21, 1947.

29. Wickes, "The Creative Process," 32.

30. See Hartigan, *Bill W.*, 190ff.

31. Wickes, "The Creative Process," 45.

32. Bill Wilson to Clem L., April 8, 1948, quoted in *Pass It On*, Kindle ed., loc. 4072.

33. Frances G. Wickes, *The Inner World of Man* (New York: Henry Holt, 1948 [originally published 1938]), 127.

34. Bill Wilson to Joe Diggles, October 8, 1957.

35. Simone Weil, *Love in the Void: Where God Finds Us* (Walden, NY: Plough, 2018), xix.

36. *Alcoholics Anonymous Comes of Age*, 63.

37. *Alcoholics Anonymous Comes of Age*, 38.

38. See Steps One and Two of "The Twelve Steps."

39. Chapter 24 of *Pass It On* describes Wilson's interest in nicotinic acid, better known as niacin or vitamin B3.

40. The boy who went through the exorcism ritual was also known by the pseudonym Robbie Manheim. In December 2021, *The Guardian* (UK) and other news sources reported that his real name was Ronald Edwin Hunkeler.

41. "The Devil and the A.A." is the title Dowling typed at the top of his manuscript of the talk. Within the talk, however, he gives its title as "The Devil You Say."

In A.A. jargon, a member of the fellowship is often "an A.A." So "The Devil and the A.A." really means "The Devil and the A.A. Member."

42. Dowling mentions Bill's visit in a November 25, 1949, letter to Grace Perkins Oursler.

43. In this, Dowling was like Clarence J. Enzler's depiction of Christ in his 1957 inspirational work *My Other Self*. Enzler likely knew Dowling, as he was a member of the Archdiocese of Washington's Cana Conference committee.

44. By "group experience" in this context, Father Ed appears to refer to the general experience that A.A. group members have reported.

45. Edward Dowling, SJ, "A.A. Steps for the Underprivileged Non-A.A.," *Grapevine* (June 1960).

Chapter 13: Bringing Recovery to the Non-Alcoholic

1. "A.A. Steps for the Underprivileged Non-A.A." was Father Ed's final submission to *Grapevine*. He wrote it in December 1959 and it was published the following June.

2. "Democratic Drift in Psychiatry Called Hopeful Trend," *St. Louis Globe-Democrat*, June 13, 1950, 4.

3. Abraham A. Low, *Mental Health through Will-Training*, 15th ed. (Boston: Christopher Publishing, 1967), inside-cover flap.

4. Jack Alexander, "They 'Doctor' One Another," *Saturday Evening Post* (December 6, 1952): 186. I am omitting Cleo's last name because, as mentioned below, her husband was in A.A.

5. Alexian Brothers Hospital is best known today as the site of the exorcism of "Roland Doe."

6. Cleo D., letter to Edward Dowling, SJ, March 15, 1960.

7. Neil and Margaret Rau, *My Dear Ones* (Chicago: Recovery, Inc., 1971), 239.

8. Joseph Dunne, email to author, June 11, 2020.

9. Dowling, address at Recovery, Inc., informational event, June 4, 1954.

10. Dowling, address at Recovery, Inc., informational event, June 4, 1954.

11. Riley, *Alcoholics Anonymous: An Interview with Edward Dowling, S.J.*, 3.

12. "900 at Dinner Here Marking Founding of 'AA' 10 Years Ago," *St. Louis Globe-Democrat*, October 20, 1950, 3.

13. Chuck C., *A New Pair of Glasses*, 46–47.

14. Martin L. Duggan, *Catholic Messenger* (Davenport, IA), April 14, 1960.

15. See Second Vatican Council, *Lumen Gentium* 5.

16. Dowling, "Some Notes Taken from a Cana Conference," emphasis in original. Compare with the following passages from *Lumen Gentium* 40–41:

> All the faithful of Christ of whatever rank or status, are called to the fullness of the Christian life and to the perfection of charity.... The classes and duties of life are many, but holiness is one.... Furthermore, married couples and Christian parents should follow their own proper path (to holiness) by faithful love. They should sustain one another in grace throughout the entire length of their lives. They should imbue their offspring, lovingly welcomed as God's gift, with Christian doctrine and the evangelical virtues.

17. Bill Wilson to Edward Dowling, SJ, July 17, 1952.

18. The reference is to *Macbeth*, Act 1, Scene 3. When Macbeth suggests that, since the witches' prediction that he would be Thane of Cawdor came true, their other predictions will come true as well, Banquo disagrees: "Oftentimes, to win us to our harm, / The instruments of darkness tell us truths, / Win us with honest trifles, to betray's / In deepest consequence."

19. Edward Dowling, SJ, to Bill Wilson, July 24, 1953.

20. W. H. Longridge, *The Spiritual Exercises of St. Ignatius of Loyola* (London: A.R. Mowbray, 1950), 101, emphasis in original.

21. See Bill's August 8, 1952, letter to Father Ed, quoted in Fitzgerald, *The Soul of Sponsorship*, 61.

22. Fitzgerald, *The Soul of Sponsorship*, 61, 86. "Why Alcoholics Anonymous Is Anonymous" also appears as an appendix to *Alcoholics Anonymous Comes of Age*.

23. That is, the already-noted *Alcoholics Anonymous: An Interview with Edward Dowling, S.J.*

24. This quote and the following ones from the clergy conference are taken from Dowling, "Alcoholics Anonymous, the Twelve Steps, and Catholic Asceticism," *The Blue Book, Volume 5*, 152–76.

25. Dowling to Wilson, July 24, 1952.

26. Bill Wilson to Edward Dowling, SJ, February 19, 1953, quoted in Fitzgerald, *The Soul of Sponsorship*, 67.

27. Bill Wilson to Edward Dowling, SJ, April 20, 1953.

28. Bill Wilson to Joe Diggles, September 2, 1958, quoted in Fitzgerald, *The Soul of Sponsorship*, 92.

29. See Raphael, *Bill W. and Mr. Wilson*, 131.

30. Caryl Chessman (1921–1960) was a former gang leader convicted in 1948 for a crime spree that included robberies, kidnapping, and rape. He was sentenced to death for the kidnapping under a California law that had been enacted during the outcry after the 1932 kidnapping and murder of Charles Lindbergh's young son. While in prison, Chessman became an author and memoirist, his efforts lending strength to campaigns to end the death penalty.

31. Bill Wilson to Edward Dowling, SJ, May 25, 1954.

32. Edward Dowling, SJ, to Bill Wilson, June 7, 1954.

33. Daniel A. Lord, SJ, to Edward Dowling, SJ, February 21, 1954, Jesuit Archives & Research Center.

34. Daniel A. Lord, SJ, *Played by Ear* (Chicago: Loyola University Press, 1956).

35. I have put "wearying" as a possible correction for Dowling's "wearing." The reference to nationwide prayers probably refers to the prayers that were being said for Father Lord by members of the Sodality of Our Lady and by others who had learned of his illness.

36. Edward Dowling, SJ, manuscript of telegram to Daniel A. Lord, SJ, October 7, 1954. Jesuit Archives & Research Center.

37. Joseph T. McGloin, SJ, *Backstage Missionary: Father Dan Lord, SJ* (New York: Pageant Press, 1958), 132.

38. Mrs. Edward Porter, quoted in Gavin, *Champion of Youth*, 202.

39. *Alcoholics Anonymous Comes of Age*, 38.

40. In advance of the 1955 convention, Father Ed adapted these reflections into a July 1955 article for *Grapevine*, "Three Dimensions of A.A."

41. Edward Dowling, SJ, to Bill Wilson, May 7, 1951.

42. Bill Wilson to Edward Dowling, SJ, May 14, 1951.

43. Edward Dowling, SJ, letter addressed to "Dear Folks and Mary," July 8, 1931, 2.

44. Interview with Rosemary Hendron Macken, March 21, 2020.

45. All quotations from Father Ed's talk at the convention are taken from *A.A. Comes of Age*, 254–61. I am using the published version of the address, which is edited from the original. Father Ed personally approved the edits.

Chapter 14: Accompanying the Suffering

1. This quotation, which I have transcribed from the original, may look strange to readers who know it only from *The Soul of Sponsorship*. Robert Fitzgerald, SJ, mistranscribed "it must sometimes beget a sort of independence from God's hand" as "it must sometimes beget dependence on God's hand," which actually reverses Dowl-

ing's meaning. Dowling is telling Bill that, as much as he might long to have the comfort of knowing what lies ahead, there is grace in his uncertainty about the future, for it makes him recognize his dependence upon God's providence.

2. All quotations from Father Ronald Creighton-Jobe are from my telephone interview with him on February 5, 2020.

3. It was my great blessing to meet Father Faherty in January 2011, seven months before his death. We were introduced by St. Louis photographer Mark Scott Abeln, who had collaborated with Faherty on *Catholic St. Louis: A Pictorial History* (St. Louis: Reedy Press, 2009). Faherty was physically weak at that time and his words were few. However, when I brought up Father Ed's name, his eyes lit up and he said with feeling that Dowling was "a wonder of the world."

4. Egan to Kurtz, 19.

5. "Father Dowling, S.J., Remembered," 4. Mary Louise Adams, who compiled this manuscript of posthumous tributes to Father Ed, wrote in it that a Cenacle nun (whom she did not name) remembered that advice from Dowling.

6. In Father Ed's existing correspondence, there are occasional references to other health problems, such as heart issues, obesity, and (in one letter to Bill Wilson) depression triggered by blood-pressure medication. But, outside of letters to doctors or descriptions of his hospital treatments, Father Ed never mentioned his arthritis except in response to concerns expressed by the person to whom he is writing—and even then, he never, ever admitted that it caused him pain. On the contrary, he consistently claimed his arthritis was painless. But everyone I have spoken with who was close to him has told me that, however much Father Ed tried to hide his pain, it was evident that he suffered a great deal.

7. Telephone interview with Paul Dowling, April 30, 2020.

8. Adams, "Father Dowling, S.J., Remembered," 12.

9. Telephone interview with Mary Dowling, April 23, 2020.

10. Robert Fitzgerald in *The Soul of Sponsorship* mentions that Father Ed encouraged a mother of a large family to join the 7 Up support group but doesn't say whether Father Ed actually started it. However, it is likely that he did conceive and name the group, especially given that, according to his niece Mary Dowling, 7 Up was his favorite drink.

11. Telephone interview with Paul Dowling, April 30, 2020.

12. "The Hoodlum Priest" became the title of an excellent 1961 film in which Father Clark was played by Don Murray.

13. The date is an approximation. My source, Elizabeth Mulligan's Dismas Clark, SJ, biography *Hoodlum's Priest*, is vague about the date Clark joined The Queen's Work Jesuit community but says that Father Lord was living there at the time. Since Lord was in the hospital for much of 1954 until his death in January 1955, and since Clark was not an original member of The Queen's Work residential community when it was established in August 1951, the year 1953 sounds about right for Clark's move.

14. Telephone interview with John Samuel Tieman, November 4, 2021. Tieman heard this story from Dowling's friend Father William Barnaby Faherty, SJ.

15. This quotation and the one that follows are from Edward Dowling, SJ, *Excerpts from Talks by Father Dowling*, side B.

16. See Matthew 20:20–23.

17. John Henry Newman, "Mental Sufferings of Our Lord in His Passion," in *Discourses Addressed to Mixed Congregations* (London: Longmans, Green, 1906), 328.

18. Edward Dowling, SJ, "A.A. Steps for the Underprivileged Non-A.A.," *Grapevine* (June 1960), emphasis in original.

19. Dowling, "Three Dimensions of A.A."

20. Dowling, "A.A. Steps for the Underprivileged Non-A.A."

21. *Catechism of the Catholic Church* §2357. This means that unlike heterosexual genital acts, which can lead to the good of children, homosexual genital acts are in and of themselves unable to lead to a good end.

Chapter 15: Racing against Time

1. Esther M. Venter, letter to Anna Dowling, April 10, 1960, emphasis in original.

2. A. Philip Randolph, letter addressed "To Whom It May Concern," June 12, 1950.

3. I have omitted the in-law's name at the request of another Dowling family member.

4. "Real Democracy for U.S. Is Still to Come, Says Priest," *Chicago Daily News*, August 27, 1940, 6.

5. The Vatterott Foundation (vatterottfoundation.org), founded in 1948, continues to assist members of underprivileged St. Louis communities and the nonprofits that serve them.

6. The authoritative study on Charles Vatterott's civil-rights involvement is Cornelia Frances Sexauer's "Catholic Capitalism: Charles Vatterott, Civil Rights, and Suburbanization in St. Louis and the Nation, 1919–1971" (PhD diss., University of Cincinnati, 2003).

7. This quote and the previously cited one were transcribed onto an index card that is in the Dowling Archive, which cites Roger Nash Baldwin, letter to Mrs. E. M. Grossman, March 14, 1952.

8. Edward Dowling, SJ, letter to A.J. Cervantes, February 7, 1957.

9. It would be another half-century before St. Louis leaders finally agreed to rename a location in Scott's honor. In May 2007, the block of Fourth Street east of the Old Courthouse was renamed Dred Scott Way. A statue of Dred and Harriet Scott

stands there today. Both the renaming and the statue came about through the efforts of the Dred Scott Heritage Foundation (dredscottlives.org), which was founded by Scott's great-great-granddaughter Lynne Jackson.

10. Father Ed also wrote to Catholic media, offering the news angle that some of Scott's relatives said he had been a Catholic. Among those who told him of Scott's Catholicism were Mrs. John A. (Grace Cross) Madison, widow of Scott's grandson, and Mrs. Harry (Ann Blow Johnson) Hubbell, daughter of Anna Wahrendorff Blow and granddaughter of Taylor Blow, who freed Scott.

11. I am gathering this from the tone of Harrison's letters and particularly from the way she relied upon Dowling to be the point of contact between her and Scott's descendants.

12. There are several references in Father Ed's correspondence to his suffering a retinal stroke in the mid-1950s. In addition, in a letter to Bill Wilson on May 8, 1958, he mentions having had "a couple of strokes... a couple of years ago." I am assuming that both strokes were retinal, as I have not found evidence of Dowling's suffering any other type of stroke.

13. Egan, "Worthy to Be Remembered," 5.

14. Tygard, "Purely Personal," 6.

15. Tygard, "Purely Personal," 6.

16. This quote and the following one are from an undated note by Mary Louise Adams in a box marked "Dowling Library" in the Dowling Archive.

17. Edward Dowling, SJ, to Bill Wilson, February 15, 1955.

18. This is my conjecture based on the quotation that follows, which implies that Sister Ignatia and Father Ed had a shared interest in Bill's becoming "closer" to Catholicism.

To be clear, I do not at all believe that Father Ed was ever worried that Bill might fail to attain heaven. Dowling believed in the Catholic teaching, which existed even before Vatican II, that non-Catholics who sincerely sought truth could be saved. He had enormous confidence that God's grace was operative in Bill's life and would continue to guide him on the upward path, regardless of whether he ever entered the Catholic Church. (On pre-conciliar teaching on salvation of non-Catholics, see "Letter from the Holy Office Concerning Fr. Leonard Feeney," August 8, 1949, online at catholicculture.org. I do not endorse all of the original editorial material on catholicculture.org, but it has a helpful repository of historical documents.)

19. Edward Dowling, SJ, to Sister Ignatia Mary Gavin, OSA, August 9, 1957, quoted in Glenn F. Chesnut, *Father Ed Dowling: Bill Wilson's Sponsor* (manuscript version, May 1, 2015), 452–453. Chesnut made an early version of this book available as a free PDF online before publishing it on Kindle through iUniverse in July 2015. Although nearly all the information in it that directly relates to Dowling is reprinted from other sources, Chesnut did gain access to transcripts of two letters from Dowling to Ignatia, which he reproduces in their entirety.

20. The account given here of Dowling's Ireland trip is taken from correspondence and papers in the Dowling Archive, especially "Why Father Dowling Went to Ireland," a typed manuscript of an article written by Maryville College student Carol Wheeler in early 1958.

21. King M., letter to Bill Wilson, July 5, 1966.

22. Bill Wilson, letter to King M., September 2, 1966.

23. "Early Member," *Grapevine* (September 1951). Although the author is not identified, the description of him as "a newspaperman who moved to Washington, DC, a year after he joined the fellowship" in Chicago, as well as the essay's writing style (including its multiple references to Father Ed), point most definitely to Lahey.

The mention of Twelfth-Step work refers to personal outreach to alcoholics who are still suffering, which A.A. members believe is essential to maintaining their own sobriety.

24. This was literally true. See Father Ronald Creighton-Jobe's comments in chapter 14.

25. Edwin A. Lahey, "Father Dowling Dies, Jesuit Aided Thousands," *Chicago Daily News*, April 4, 1960, 5.

26. This story is drawn from Tygard, "Purely Personal," 6.

Chapter 16: Sponsor and Protector

1. Lambert to Thro, 2. As noted, Lambert was on staff at the *St. Louis Post-Dispatch*.

2. Edward Dowling, SJ, letter to Cana Conference of Chicago, quoted in *The Cana Newsletter* (April–May 1960), 1.

3. Moe Berg, "Pitchers and Catchers," *The Atlantic* (September 1941), theatlantic.com.

4. Kurtz, *Not-God*, 137.

5. *Pass It On*, Kindle loc. 5361.

6. Many people have reported that Father Ed was actually part of Bill's group that experimented with LSD. That claim is certainly wrong; it comes from a misreading of Bill's letters. Nowhere does Bill say that Father Ed took LSD, only that he "volunteered" to do so, and that is in itself questionable. In a letter from Bill to Father Ed on November 23, 1959, he refers to "the group which you saw in operation," which likewise shows that Dowling saw the experiment but did not actually take part. Moreover, when Father Ed warns Wilson about LSD, in a letter written some months after he witnessed the experiment, he writes about LSD as an outsider to the drug's experience, not as one who has taken it himself.

7. *Pass It On*, Kindle loc. 5366.

8. Edward Dowling, SJ, transcript of Cana Conference delivered at Our Lady of the Presentation Catholic Church, St. John's Station, St. Louis County, MO, March 5, 1950.

9. Needless to say, I hope someone assembles such a book—ideally one who, unlike me, has firsthand knowledge of married life.

10. Adams, "Father Dowling, S.J., Remembered," 17–18.

11. Mary Kathryn Barmann, letter to "Mother and Daddy," April 10, 1960. A copy of this letter is in the Dowling Archive.

12. Mel B., *My Search for Bill W.* (Center City, MN: Hazelden, 2000), Kindle ed., locs. 321, 339.

13. See Appendix, "The Twelve Traditions," Third Tradition.

14. Kurtz, *Not-God*, 51.

15. Bill W., "Carrying the Message in 'Fifty-five," *Grapevine* (July 1980).

16. *Alcoholics Anonymous*, 4th ed. (New York: A.A. World Services, 2001), 567.

17. *Alcoholics Anonymous Comes of Age*, 256.

18. As Robert Fitzgerald, SJ, has noted, Father Ed is referring to the three falls that Jesus is believed to have suffered on his way to Calvary, as depicted in the third, seventh, and ninth Stations of the Cross.

19. Information concerning Divorcees Unanimous comes from the "Divorce–Stella Maris" file at the Dowling Archive (Stella Maris being the name of the local chapter of the group) and my telephone interview with Michael Coffey (Mary Jane Coffey's son), November 24, 2021.

20. "Group to Aid Drug Addicts," *St. Louis Post-Dispatch*, October 4, 1959, 18.

21. The excerpt is from P.E. Hallett, *Why Are We Baptised?* (London: Catholic Truth Society, 1941).

22. Egan, "Worthy to Be Remembered," 18. Egan does not provide a source for the details he provides about Bill's attendance at Dowling's Mass or his comment afterwards, and I have not managed to locate an outside source for them. However, he conducted extensive research in the Dowling Archive, and I have found his other writings to be well supported by the existing documentation, so I am confident of the veracity of his information.

23. Bill Wilson to Frank C., December 9, 1959.

24. Bill Wilson to Albert K., December 9, 1959.

25. Here again Dowling quotes his favorite line from Francis Thompson's "The Hound of Heaven," which encapsulated his theology of suffering.

26. Father Ed noted that the book itself, *Susanna Mary Beardsworth, the White Dove of Peace*, by Pascal P. Parente, was "poorly written" and "difficult to read."

Chapter 17: Going Home

1. Quoted by Ed Willmann, letter to Anna Dowling, April 14, 1960.

2. Felknor, "Glad Gethsemane," 19.

3. All quotations from Michael and Mary Ellen Fox are from my telephone interview with them, April 17, 2020.

4. Kathryn Spearing, telephone interview, April 5, 2022.

5. This and other quotations of Dowling to Felknor are from Felknor, "Glad Gethsemane."

6. If I have devoted an inordinate amount of space to various accounts of Dowling's see-saw analogy, it is because it was so important to his understanding of marriage. Every person I interviewed who remembered Father Ed's Cana Conferences remembered his employing it.

7. See chapter 5 of *Lumen Gentium*, especially no. 39.

8. Edward Dowling, SJ, to Sister Mary Ignatia Gavin, CSA, March 25, 1958, in Chesnut, *Father Ed Dowling*, 458–459.

9. See Chesnut, *Father Ed Dowling*, 457.

10. Interview with Mary Dowling, May 5, 2022.

11. All quotations from Paul H. are from his letter to Lyb S., April 4, 1960. Dowling Archive.

12. The translation is the Douay-Rheims version that would have been in Father Ed's copy of the Divine Office.

13. The information in this paragraph is taken from a letter of Anna Dowling to Cleo Dieruf, April 15, 1960.

14. Neil C. Hurley Jr., letter to Anna Dowling, April 7, 1960. I have transcribed this from a version of the letter that was retyped by Dowling Archive librarian Mary Louise Adams, as I have not located the original.

15. This information is drawn from a letter from Father Fred Zimmerman, SJ, to Father Jim Egan, SJ, July 16, 1986, quoted in Fitzgerald, *The Soul of Sponsorship*, 103. Zimmerman was the superior of the Jesuit residence at The Queen's Work.

16. Tygard, "Purely Personal," 5.

17. In 2003, the burials in the Jesuit cemetery at St. Stanislaus Seminary at Florissant were transferred to Calvary Cemetery in St. Louis.

18. Adams, "Father Dowling, S.J., Remembered," 23.

19. Unless otherwise noted, quotations from Vincent P. Dole are from Vincent P. Dole, "Addiction as a Public Health Problem," *Alcoholism: Clinical and Experimental Research* 15, no. 5 (October 1991), as it appears on methadone-research. blogspot.com.

20. Bill Wilson to Anna Dowling, June 16, 1960.

21. Bill Wilson to Anna Dowling, quoted in Adams, "Father Dowling Remembered," 22. Adams does not provide a date for the letter.

Acknowledgments

1. Letter to his sister, Mary Dowling, RCSJ, October 14, 1930.

2. *My Peace I Give You* and *Remembering God's Mercy*, published under the pen name Dawn Eden.

3. See Congregation for the Causes of Saints, *Sanctorum Mater*, Art. 117 §2, online at vatican.va.

4. Contact information for the archbishop of St. Louis may be found online at archstl.org. The Jesuit provincial's contact information may be found at jesuitsmidwest.org.

INDEX

365